SilverStripe

static $db = array(

static $has_one = array(

static $has_many = array(

static $many-many = array(

static $belongs_many_many = array(

SilverStripe

The Complete Guide to CMS Development

Ingo Schommer and Steven Broschart

Translated by

Dr Julian Seidenberg and Ingo Schommer

A John Wiley and Sons, Ltd., Publication

Galileo Computing is an imprint of Galileo Press,
Bonn (Germany), Boston (USA).
German Edition first published 2008 by Galileo Press.

This edition first published 2009

Registered office
John Wiley & Sons Ltd, The Atrium, Southern Gate, Chichester, West Sussex, PO19 8SQ, United Kingdom

For details of our global editorial offices, for customer services and for information about how to apply for permission to reuse the copyright material in this book please see our website at www.wiley.com.

ISBN 978-0-470-68183-1

A catalogue record for this book is available from the British Library.

Typeset in 10/12 Optima by Laserwords Private Limited, Chennai, India
Printed in USA

"I feel SilverStripe is a great example of a well-constructed open source project."

Chris DiBona, Open Source Programs Manager, Google Inc.

Publisher's Acknowledgements

Some of the people who helped bring this book to market include the following:

Editorial and Production

VP Consumer and Technology Publishing Director: Michelle Leete

Associate Director - Book Content Management: Martin Tribe

Associate Publisher: Chris Webb

Executive Commissioning Editor: Birgit Gruber

Assistant Editor: Colleen Goldring

Content Editor: Claire Spinks

Publishing Assistant: Ellie Scott

Copy Editor: Andrew Finch

Composition: Laserwords Private Ltd

Marketing

Senior Marketing Manager: Louise Breinholt

Marketing Executive: Kate Batchelor

Contents

About the Authors

Steven Broschart has been active for 6 years as an advisor and developer at one of Germany's leading online marketing agencies, cyberpromote GmbH. Aside from developing PHP and Ruby on Rails business applications and coordinating key accounts for SEO, he advises his clients on selecting appropriate open source software. Steven is a regular author in relevant industry publications.

Ingo Schommer freelanced as a PHP and Flash developer for several years prior to joining SilverStripe in 2006 as a senior developer. At SilverStripe, Ingo analyses and builds modern web applications, making sure that they work well in a browser and not just on paper. He has a key role architecting and implementing core functionality in the SilverStripe platform, and facilitates involvement of the open-source community.

About the Translator

Julian Seidenberg has a background in developing web applications using PHP and Java and has worked in a variety of software engineering roles. He is also a developer at SilverStripe and holds a PhD in Semantic Web technology from the University of Manchester.

Foreword

Sigurd Magnusson

Co-founder and Chief Marketing Officer, SilverStripe Ltd

Thanks for buying the book! After countless long days and nights, it's a real joy to see it come to fruition.

In 2000, the dream of the *SilverStripe* project began: to make a fantastic software platform to build and manage websites. Our company *SilverStripe Ltd*, which had its fair share of geeks, was in the business of building websites for customers. We found the tools out there didn't suit us, and certainly didn't suit our customers. Tools were either too technical, which suited us fine but confused our clients, or were simple enough for our non-technical customers, but insulted us with poorly constructed HTML and limited us from building sophisticated website features. So, we committed to make a system that let professional, experienced web developers build innovative websites which can then be passed, in confidence, to non-technical people to manage.

Several years passed, and by 2006 we had a few hundred customers. We had always sought to make the product global, but because we were the only one developing SilverStripe, adoption was limited to our home country, New Zealand. We were working hard on an entirely rewritten version of SilverStripe, v2.0, and agreed that if we were to make it successful, it had to be released as free software, with a loyal community of developers around it.

In late 2008, we celebrated two years of being open source. It was inspiring to see how quickly we'd moved forward. We had surpassed 100,000 downloads, been invited into the *Google Summer of Code*, had a growing community with external contributors, and our software was powering some impressive websites. For example, a SilverStripe-powered website, `http://demconvention.com/`, served millions of visitors in a 100 hour span as Barack Obama accepted his nomination as the presidential candidate for the United States Democratic Party.

However, writing the software is only half the battle: you also need documentation that teaches the world on how to take advantage of it. If there was one thing I wanted to improve, it was our documentation. So I'm very humbled by the months of work that Ingo and Steven have put into writing a book while holding down their 9 to 5 jobs. Their effort provided the German text that has now been translated into the English edition you're holding. It was very rewarding to see the book come out initially in Germany, because it showed just how international SilverStripe had become, and that a country renown for high quality engineering had given the thumbs up to SilverStripe! With this book now in English, we shift SilverStripe into a new gear, which is very exciting.

The concept of SilverStripe relies on us building up a community of developers, and so we hope that over time you will join us by emailing feedback, submitting code, and fixing bugs. We also hope to see your websites uploaded to the community showcase at `http://silverstripe.org/showcase/`!

In the years since we started SilverStripe, the concept of elegant, web-standard HTML and CSS has shifted from obscurity to being the norm. The idea of writing PHP in an elegant maintainable fashion, complete with object-oriented code, unit tests, and following the MVC pattern is still new to lots of people, but growing in popularity. However, having read the book, we hope that you can appreciate the other evolution of the web we've been anticipating for years: that the combination of a framework, a CMS product, and extension modules can together save developers a huge amount of development time by offering what they need out-of-the-box, while offering a huge potential for extension and innovation.

Welcome to the SilverStripe community!

Preface

Steven Broschart

Co-author of this book, and early member of the SilverStripe open source community.

It wasn't too long ago when a fellow developer at work asked me to look at his screen. He had stumbled across some new technology, and asked: 'Hey, have you heard about this?' All too often such questions are answered with a 'Yeah. Completely useless!', but sometimes the answer is 'No'. It's in those times that a feeling of anxiety creeps in – did I miss a potentially groundbreaking development on the Internet? In this case I decided to defer my answer, and stopped what I was doing to investigate further.

It's a good thing to keep in mind that in our current working environment every person is basically a human content-filter who must grapple with the daily excess of digital information. New products and ideas confront us so often, they don't get the attention they deserve. Hence, a presentation of a 'cool new thing' has only a few seconds of your attention in which to grab your interest, as every marketing guy will tell you.

As you might have guessed, my colleague was showing me SilverStripe for the first time, and he succeeded in quickly gathering my interest. The fact that you're reading this book probably means that you're starting with a certain eagerness towards this 'new thing', too.

For several years now, I've been a consultant and developer in an online marketing agency that specializes in search engine optimization and usability. This means that I've developed a number of internal systems and a fair share of websites. A major internal focus was ensuring a quick and flexible development process. In this context we trialled a bunch of content management systems – scoring them against our set of requirements. Having reviewed several systems so far, I couldn't wait to see what SilverStripe had in store. It seemed to be sufficiently different from the 'big players' to capture our interest. The ease with which usually complex tasks were solved in SilverStripe was promising and exciting. We liked what we saw and our agency began adopting SilverStripe in a big way. Since then, our experience has supported our positive first impression.

During the last couple of years, certain programming concepts have become very popular in the website and web-application development space. In particular, people have become far more interested in rapid development, technical elegance, robustness, and building increasingly interactive websites. Although these concepts aren't necessarily new, most web developers have a fairly informal development methodology – especially those writing in PHP. Writing code in a well-structured way was not common place. One event that influenced this trend was a framework called *Ruby on Rails* (`http://www.rubyonrails.com/`), which was increasing in popularity. This raised the game for everyone: The carefully structured architecture, methodology, and principles of that framework rubbed off and became best practices, which the whole web industry began to discuss, embrace, and challenge.

SilverStripe is written in PHP and has an architecture very much modeled on these contemporary best practices. SilverStripe combines the advantages of a CMS application with a powerful framework 'under the hood'. Time-intensive programming sessions for conceptually simple features should be a thing of the past, which shouldn't only delight the programmer, but also the manager who has to justify budgets and timeframes. After all, time and money are some of the primary factors determining the success of a project. After reading through the first tutorials it became clear to me that in this case these weren't just empty marketing phrases. Because care was put into its architecture, this product was able to give me a glance at advanced functionality without knowing its inner workings. Its shallow learning curve dwarfed many other competitors in the same space.

Anyway, back to the story. Apart from playing around with new shiny web toys, I'm a freelance author in Germany on subjects from search engine optimization to usability to web technologies. Driven by my first SilverStripe experiences, in 2008 I published an article on SilverStripe in a popular German industry magazine called *PHP Magazin* (see announcement at `http://silverstripe.com/silverstripe-main-feature-of-german-php-magazin/`).

While writing this article, I made contact with the company behind the software to check a few facts – the aptly named web development shop *SilverStripe Ltd*, based in Wellington, New Zealand. In particular I reached out to Ingo Schommer, a senior developer at the company. Ingo is a fellow German, who became attracted to SilverStripe after battling other open source CMS products – software too often plagued by complex configuration and the feeling of spending more time disabling features than actually implementing stuff. Emigrating from Germany to New Zealand in order to change this situation might seem like a desperate measure, but it worked out well.

The magazine article was so well received that it supported the idea of writing the book you're now reading. There was no print material to show interested developers a straightforward learning path to implement their own solutions in SilverStripe. The magazine article demonstrated demand, and so I asked Ingo to be a co-author, and sought a German publisher, *Galileo Computing*. Both promptly agreed to produce the book.

Writing the German book took several months of intense collaboration across continents (from Wellington to Munich and back), by which time the CMS had become increasing popular in the German market – which geographically couldn't be much further from New Zealand! The German book was released in early 2009, and sold sufficiently quickly that it had to be restocked on *Amazon.de* days after the book launched.

Of course, there's a larger audience of English readers for a SilverStripe book, and plans by SilverStripe Ltd to have an English book predated me even learning about their software. Translating the German book provided a sensible way to finally achieve this goal, and what you're reading now is the work of several SilverStripe Ltd staff members adapting the work into English.

Now please follow us on a quick tour through SilverStripe, and we'll show you what's behind the buzz. We hope that you have as much fun reading this book as we had writing it. All right, that was quite a stereotypical way to finish the preface of a technical book, but anyway: Enjoy!

So, to answer my colleague: Thanks for your discovery, Robert. No, didn't know this system!

Acknowledgments

Although the names of the authors are prominently placed on the cover of a book, the reality is that such an exhaustive guide couldn't happen without further support. Special thanks go towards our original publisher in Germany, Galileo Computing, especially to our editor Stephan Matteschecck who supported us throughout what happened to be the first book publication for the two of us. And consequently, a big thank you to Wiley Publishing for picking up this work and agreeing to make it available to a much larger English-speaking community, particularly to Martin Tribe and Colleen Goldring, our editors at Wiley, for their patience and giving us a chance to polish content rather than translate word-for-word. 'Dankeschön' to Sigurd Magnusson, who helped us navigate the unfamiliar waters of book publications and spent long nights reviewing content – the book got a lot more 'digestible' with your input! Thanks to Andy Finch for copy-editing our 'Germenglish', and to Sibylle Schwarz for keeping us focused. We'd like to thank SilverStripe Ltd, who 'lent' us considerable resources for the translation effort. Massive thanks to Julian Seidenberg for unexpectedly spending his first weeks as a developer with SilverStripe Ltd. translating the book rather than writing code. Kudos to our 'beta'-readers Andy Adiwidjaja, Claudia Liersch, Joon Choi, Tobias Hoderlein, Sam Minnée; without your comments and ideas the book would've been only half as good. And 'last but not least' thanks go to our families and friends, who lost us to text processing and late night Skype meetings for several months – you're the best!

Target Audience

This book mainly targets PHP developers who're looking for new solutions to quickly build websites, big and small. Because SilverStripe uses some techniques and paradigms that aren't necessarily widespread knowledge to PHP developers, we make some suggestions here for recommended further reading.

If you're not a developer but are evaluating SilverStripe as a platform, you should still find many parts of this book useful. The book doesn't delve deep into code until Chapter 5, 'Development', and even then, there are plenty of explanations, screenshots, and summaries that will give less technical people meaningful insight into SilverStripe.

Of course we also address the actual users of the system, the content authors who manage websites with this tool. If this is you, Chapter 4, 'First Steps', is the one to focus on, because this is where we provide a summary of the CMS content editing interface.

For the more technical chapters of the book, we assume that you have some experience with PHP and that you're comfortable with object-oriented programming. Perhaps you're already familiar with Java, in which case you should feel right at home with the object-oriented capabilities of PHP. If you feel a bit lost with terms such as *objects, classes, interfaces,* or *inheritance,* we'd like to recommend a book covering these basics: *PHP 5 For Dummies* by Janet Valade (published by Wiley; ISBN: 978-0-7645-4166-7). The official PHP website at `http://php.net/` can of course also be used as a primer.

SilverStripe is based on PHP version 5, released in 2004. Because it uses the full capabilities of this version, much of its architecture is impossible to achieve in the outdated PHP4. We'll describe some of these capabilities as we go along, but developers who are used to PHP4 might need to brush up their knowledge about the object-oriented coding to take advantage of this book.

Because this book is aimed at developers, we also assume a basic familiarity with standard web technologies such as HTML, JavaScript, and CSS. We don't ask you to write anything advanced with them in this book – although once you've finished the book, having strong skills in those languages will enable you to make great SilverStripe websites!

Book Structure

This book begins with a mostly non-technical review that describes the underlying principles, technologies, and architecture, as well as the installation of SilverStripe. After everything is set up both conceptually and on your own webserver environment, we dive into code with an example website and application. Building this example project will span multiple chapters and provide a coherent learning path. The later chapters become more independent of this example and can be worked through in isolation if you wish – they relate to topics such as internationalization, security, and performance. The book ends with a set of code recipes that demonstrate useful techniques, and a summary of the most useful extension modules.

Book website: Updates and source code

We've tried our best to provide a perfect book without any mistakes. If that's not the case every now and then, you can find errata and corrections as well as up-to-date information on a website dedicated to the book: `www.wiley.com/go/silverstripe`.

The website is also where you can download the source code mentioned throughout the book.

Terminology: CMS, frontend and backend

- *Content Management System (CMS)*: Although we sometimes refer to the entire software as 'the CMS', in the book this term normally refers to the graphical user interface that the software provides to manage your website content.
- *Backend*: The generic name for an authenticated interface, with the CMS being one prime example.
- *Frontend*: The public-facing website.

Versions, Cutting Edge, and Bleeding Edge

What might sound like the title of a horror film on first reading is actually a way to describe the status of a technology project. If you hear the term *Cutting Edge* in relation to new features in software, you're dealing with fairly new developments, which most likely aren't yet contained in a stable release. *Bleeding Edge* is even further ahead of this, meaning that features and implementations are subject to change, and probably need some further testing – you can metaphorically cut yourself if you're not careful.

We raise this topic because toward the end of the book, you come into contact with some of the fresher and younger features of SilverStripe. Due to the software's modular architecture, it's easy to update individual components later as such features mature.

In our code examples we're referring to SilverStripe 2.3.3, which was released mid-2009. If you're using a newer version to follow our examples, please make sure to read the update notes at `http://doc.silverstripe.com/doku.php?id=upgrading`. If you need more details, please have a look at the changelog at `http://open.silverstripe.com/wiki/ChangeLog/`.

Coding Conventions

Code shown is this book is typically standard PHP, which follows the official SilverStripe coding conventions that you can read online at `http://doc.silverstripe.com/doku.php?id=coding-conventions`. It should therefore need no further explanation. Something we do want to point out is how we treat updating files you've already worked on – we generally show the new code without repeating the whole listing. The existing (but not shown) code is noted by an inline comment. Leave your current code as is, and write around it:

```
// ... PHP/JavaScript Omission
/* ... */ CSS Omission
<!-- ... --> SilverStripe Template Omission
```

But enough introduction, let's get on with the tour!

1

Introduction

At it's heart, the role of a content management system (CMS) is to make it easier to publish content to websites and intranets. It may be used to allow the owner of a one-person company to update his or her website without needing a website developer or learning HTML skills. Or, in a multinational company, it might allow a skilled web team across various cities to manage a complex assortment of updates to products, services, promotions, and news in multiple languages. Either way, it automates various tasks, and makes building a website more efficient and reliable.

Countless products are available based on such a promise, however, all of varying sophistication, histories, programming languages, and geographical dominance. The decision-makers and developers involved in selecting a CMS work in fast-paced environments and are creatures of habit: They have personal favorites to solve the challenges their job provides. Why go through the trouble of trying a new CMS?

1.1 Why SilverStripe?

One thing up front: SilverStripe is not the answer to all problems that you might face throughout the development of a website or web application. No software is ever a silver bullet for *every* situation. You must determine selection criteria based on your needs, skills, budgets, and timeframes, and select the most relevant tool based on those criteria. That said, SilverStripe is *intended* to be both used out-of-the-box and for major customization. This makes it particularly interesting when building websites – because everyone seems to relish having a unique set of needs in terms of design, information architecture, content, features, integration with other systems, business policies, and so on.

The following pages list some major benefits of SilverStripe, and describe how it stands out in a crowded CMS market. We acknowledge that the information here is concise, but this will help you refer back to an overview even when you're familiar with SilverStripe. We try to keep things brief here; the rest of the book will substantiate the claims made, as you begin to build stuff using the software.

1.1.1 An Application and a Framework

SilverStripe is really two products in one: The *SilverStripe CMS* and the *Sapphire Framework*. There are plenty of CMS applications and quite a few programming frameworks in the marketplace; however, SilverStripe is very rare in that it *tightly* weaves the two concepts together.

You will need to read the whole book to understand entirely the value of this unity, but the value is much greater than the sum of its parts. In other words, the CMS has plenty of good things about it, as does *Sapphire*. However, with them joined so closely, their collective value is multiplied. The closeness of the two concepts is possible because *Sapphire* and the CMS were created in tandem, by the same people.

1.1.2 CMS for Content Authors and Framework for Developers

One fundamental reason for SilverStripe being divided into two sections is to honor the needs of two quite separate types of people who use the software. The CMS backend is designed to allow non-technical users to update web pages, images, links, moderate blog comments, and so on. This is the area where content authors do their content management, and anything technical is strictly kept out of sight for the sake of good usability.

The framework is used to build the underlying website, and isn't for content authors. You 'use' the framework by actually writing HTML, CSS, JavaScript, and object-oriented PHP code. The framework enables beginning PHP programmers to achieve quite powerful things, by following recipes and tutorials as shown in this book and elsewhere. However, the framework is targeted at savvy PHP programmers. For them, *Sapphire* allows much more creative freedom in building complex websites quickly and robustly.

Many other CMS products don't have such a separation. In other words, in many systems the CMS user interface is shared by content authors and developers, which typically makes the interface too complicated for it's primary users: the content authors. In some systems, developers perform their work mainly through a graphical configuration interface, which is usually more limiting than raw programming. A graphical interface to accommodate sophisticated needs for developers would require a bewildering set of options, which would add complexity and bloat the software, when the idea in question is likely to be far more efficiently expressed as a few lines of code.

So, this separation in SilverStripe means that the CMS backend can be designed for non-technical users, and the framework can confidently concentrate on being suitable to technically-minded web developers (see Figure 1.1 for an overview of the SilverStripe system).

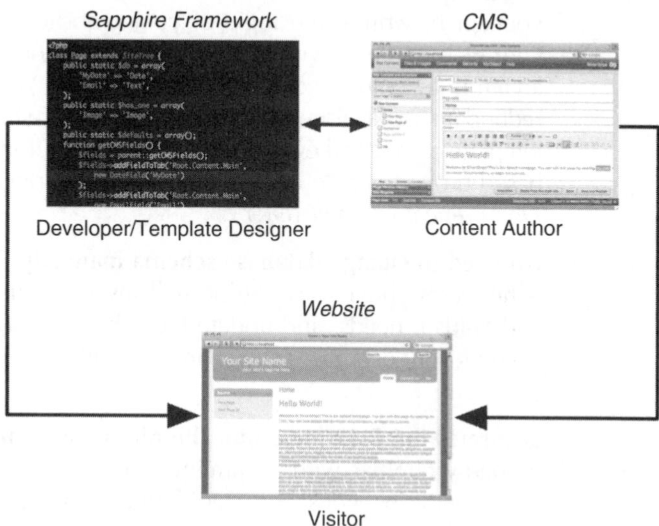

Figure 1.1 SilverStripe system overview.

1.1.3 Clear Separation of Concerns

As we begin to suggest above, a core principle in SilverStripe is the *separation of concerns*. In this introduction, we use that term loosely to mean organizing the software into all sorts of logical divisions. You will be familiar with how HTML and CSS separate the concerns of markup and presentation, and that JavaScript is used to allow for the concern of behavior and interaction on a web page. This structure provides many benefits such as enabling reuse: change a single style in a CSS file, and so long as you've stuck to best practices in your HTML, styles throughout the whole website will update, saving time and maintaining consistency.

SilverStripe follows this principle: Update an isolated area of the system that deals with a particular function, and it produces logical, robust, and application-wide changes. Without this architectural principle, changing a feature of your website means changing a few lines of code here, a few lines of code there, and finding that each step of the way upsets unrelated parts of your website. This domino effect suddenly turns a small change into a major coding and testing fiasco. SilverStripe's architecture therefore helps to keep code changes proportionate to the effort needed to implement them. However, like the HTML, CSS, and JavaScript example, this reward is only given to those who carefully architect their SilverStripe application to its best practices.

Let's highlight a few examples relating to this principle:

- ***Avoid repitition with the Sapphire framework.*** *Sapphire* supports the concept of writing the logic of your website *once*. For instance, if your website deals with selling T-shirts, you define that a T-shirt has an attribute 'color' in one place in your code. You don't have to write redundant code elsewhere to explain that T-shirts have colors; the template, CMS, and even the database will automatically be updated based on your single declaration. This principle is commonly called *Don't repeat yourself* (*DRY*).
- **No need to change database schema manually.** This important point is hinted at above: SilverStripe will inspect your code for the tables and fields it needs, and update the schema accordingly. This makes keeping your database schema in sync with your PHP code a beautiful thing.
- **Separates the PHP logic into the Model and the Controller.** You're probably familiar with separating PHP logic from HTML templates, but SilverStripe goes one step further. This is a very integral part of *Sapphire*, so let's pause for a moment to investigate this in the following box.

Model View Controller as a central concept

The *Model View Controller* (MVC) concept is one of many *design patterns* that have been identified as good programming architecture. A design pattern is essentially a structured way to document the solution to a specific problem in computer science, a term made popular by the 'Gang of Four' in their book *Design Patterns: Elements of Reusable Object-Oriented Software* (Erich Gamma, Richard Helm, Ralph Johnson, and John Vlissides, published by Addison-Wesley). The three parts, *Model, View*, and *Controller*, describe the main roles of any application built with SilverStripe:

- The *Model* is responsible for maintaining the state in the application. It's basically data: Some of it might be transient and only live within a web request, whereas other data might be permanently stored in a database. You can think of the *Model* as essentially the database schema you have for a website. We elaborate on this simplistic definition in later chapters.

- A *View* displays data that's collected from the *Model*, usually through a template on a website or application frontend. One *Model* might have many *Views*: The list of forum users on your website might have a 'public view' and a 'backend management interface view'. In both of these views, the used *Model* logic would be the same: The separation into different roles avoids code duplication and clarifies responsibilities.
- The *Controller* manages the layer in between the *Model* and *View*, and passes data between them. It's the 'glue' of an application. It might take a new forum submission from a *View*, and tell the model to store it in the database. Although the actual input form is rendered in the *View*, the *Controller* is responsible for processing it. The *Controller*, for instance, would ensure that the submitter *can* post to this forum, and might send out emails to moderators or people subscribed to the forum. To clarify, the *Model* should not be responsible for such logic, and instead just store the data once the *Controller* has figured out what needs storing and how. Using the example here, separating the *Model* and *Controller* shows how you can have different form processing logic (multiple *Controllers*) making reuse of the *Model*.

All three roles work closely together. It's just important to understand what goes where on a conceptual and practical level. If that sounds a bit too abstract for you at the moment, don't despair. MVC is a central concept in SilverStripe, and we've dedicated an in-depth explanation to it in Chapter 3, Section 3.2, 'MVC – Model View Controller'.

- **Object Relational Mapper.** The PHP code throughout SilverStripe is heavily object-oriented rather than procedural code, and this architecture extends to how you access the database. This maintains a unified approach to processing data both in and out of your database: you deal with *objects* rather than flipping constantly between arrays, methods, objects, SQL syntax, and so on. This lessens the lines of code used to create, remove, update, and delete data in your database, and improves readability. It also marries the database schema more closely to your PHP code, thereby lessening the risk that these are out of sync. The concept is explained in Chapter 3, Section 3.3, 'ORM – Object Relational Mapping' in more depth.
- **A very flexible data-model.** Because of the ORM and the MVC patterns, SilverStripe is able to consume quite complex data structures.

You might have all sorts of different 'types' of pages, each with different fields. Then you might add products, members, product reviews, coupon codes, and all sorts of other objects to your website. All of this data needs to be stored in your database, managed in the CMS, and presented on your public website. SilverStripe allows you to have a complex entity model, full of relationships, while ensuring the structure and data granularity is elegant.

- **HTML, CSS, and JavaScript.** Being the *lingua franca* of the web, SilverStripe respects that competent website developers need to have control over and separate their website into these three languages. In other words: SilverStripe doesn't make you add CSS into your HTML. Nor does it prevent you from intelligently using JavaScript to *progressively enhance* your website with extra functionality. It stays out of your hair – as a developer, you can craft these files and incorporate them into your project in an elegant fashion. This provides for fantastic flexibility in your markup, therefore providing freedom in visual design.

- **Simple template language.** The 'View' mentioned in the MVC explanation above means that SilverStripe templates don't contain logic. More than simply insisting pedantically that the *Controller* instead should contain this logic – it means that the templates deliberately resemble standard HTML syntax and that they can be created and edited by people without PHP skills. This lets you unleash your zealous HTML- and CSS-skilled designer on SilverStripe templates. Compared to other templating languages, SilverStripe's seems overly simplistic. But you might come to appreciate the benefit of this in the same way you appreciate extracting your CSS out of your HTML: When you need to change something you have only one place to look, making changes easy and encouraging consistency.

- **Class inheritance as a means of customization.** This is really a topic for a later chapter in the book. But it's important, and so we whet your appetite with a preview. If you have the concept of a 'Product' in your application, how do you customize that to make *some* 'Products' a 'Book', which might require an *Author* field? Extensions like this are fundamental to any CMS software package. SilverStripe uses the natural capabilities of an object-oriented language to *extend* Products into Books. This is nothing special in any object-oriented language, and all MVC frameworks do this, but it's rare for a CMS to get out of your way and just let you use these natural features of object-oriented code.

- **Clean file system structure.** SilverStripe's file and folder structure is neatly organized in several ways. The core application lives in a couple of top-level folders. All your project-specific changes go into your own top-level folders, providing convenient separation from the core package. Files containing code are named specifically based on the PHP classes they define. This means a lot of files, but also makes the role of each file specific and deliberate. Template files follow similar naming conventions, which makes SilverStripe websites portable: You can just move files and folders from one installation to another and be confident about what functionality in the application you're shifting.

- **Modules, themes, and widgets.** The core functionality of SilverStripe can be extended by modules (for example 'forum' functionality), themes (changing the visual appearance of your website), and widgets (small features you can add to a page). We will build all of these types throughout this book. Extensions allow the core to be kept compact and succinct, so you don't have a product with features you don't need. Although the ability to have fully-featured modules isn't a surprise for a CMS, having them tightly integrated at a framework level is a unique characteristic.
- **Automated tests.** SilverStripe provides a neat structure for testing any custom code you write. This means that you can test that your application works, automatically (we talk about this a bit more in Chapter 9, 'Testing'). Automated tests allow you to make a code-level change to your website and test that you've not broken other features in your website. This reduces the *friction* of making changes to your application. In turn, this translates to being more able to continuously update your application, which is very appropriate in the world of 'continuous beta', and supports an *Agile development* methodology (see the following box). By the way, SilverStripe uses automated tests to ensure the consistency of its core functionality as well.

Agile development

This term stands for a software development methodology that fosters a process of frequent inspection and adaption after an initial planning phase. It's in contrast to a more rigid methodology, commonly known as *Waterfall*, where you devise a detailed specification upfront and proceed to build to that specification, generally with fixed budgets and timeframes.

The agile approach embraces the idea that it's impossible to predict exactly what you want ahead of seeing your software take shape. Speaking metaphorically, it's very difficult to foresee the impact of a picture in your living room based on the floor plan. Perhaps the lighting is totally different from what the window placement suggests?

Instead of resisting *change requests,* an agile approach involves constant communication, demonstrations, and changes, as well as re-prioritizing what should be worked on. Agile maintains this notion throughout the process: Your software should be working and 'deliverable' most of the time, as opposed to just being launched at the 'eleventh hour'.

A major benefit of an agile approach is that you're more likely to finish with a *useful* set of features – the features implemented are the most important ones. Done well, agile also serves to maintain project schedules and budgets.

Agile is a way of thinking that involves everyone in a project: It impacts project managers and stakeholders just as much as developers – and it requires discipline from each of them. Agile works best with software that can quickly prototype features and that can support change easily.

More information on agile methodologies is available at `http://agilemanifesto.org/` and `http://agilealliance.org`.

1.1.4 Interoperability and Open Standards

SilverStripe makes substantial use of open and common technologies as first-class citizens. The choice of PHP, MySQL, HTML, CSS, and JavaScript for example is very deliberate: They score well in terms of being well understood by the web industry, are open rather than in the control of a private company, and therefore are likely to be supported for a long time into the future. Here are some specific examples of SilverStripe's treatment of interoperability and open standards:

- **Embracing browser compatibility.** SilverStripe does a lot of work to ensure that your website and administration system hums along in different web browsers. We've already covered the main factor here: SilverStripe gives you full control of HTML and CSS in your templates. It's an indictment on other CMS products that we even have to mention this: But yes, content authors using the SilverStripe backend can use a Mac, Windows, or Linux computer for their work because it performs well in Internet Explorer, Firefox, Safari, and Chrome. With all these browsers competing for supremacy, your website and CMS backend need to be cross-browser compatible now if they're to have any hope of being cross-browser in the future. The core developers of SilverStripe also have a watchful eye on HTML 5, which is quickly gaining traction after a long period of stagnation in the HTML standard.
- **JavaScript and progressive enhancement.** Ideally a website should work with JavaScript disabled, thereby ensuring accessible

functionality and content for both users and search engines. This paradigm has two approaches: *graceful degradation* and *progressive enhancement.* SilverStripe supports these for your frontend templates, both by giving you full control over the templates as explained earlier, and by ensuring that automatically generated markup complies with the principles of progressive enhancement. Although the CMS backend does require JavaScript to function, it shies away from excessive Javascript-generated HTML, making debugging easier, allowing the backend user interface HTML to be edited as template files, and encouraging robust customizations.

- **Database Abstraction.** SilverStripe currently only supports MySQL in a stable release, but the underlying architecture allows for other database drivers. Because of this, SilverStripe has been shown to work on other databases such as PostgreSQL or the Microsoft SQL server. Note that both are currently in an alpha state.

- **Server-side interoperability.** SilverStripe requires a PHP webserver but not much else. It supports running on the two most popular webservers, *Apache* and *Microsoft IIS.* Being able to install SilverStripe onto Windows, Mac, and Linux servers means that you can trial or deploy it on an architecture that you're familiar with or that will better support integration into your IT environment.

- **Accessibility.** Having control over HTML, CSS, and JavaScript means that it's easy to write the markup that validates against *Web Content Accessibility Guidelines* (WCAG) as published by the W3C (see `http://www.w3.org/TR/WCAG20/`), and therefore can be processed easily by screen readers. This is a necessity for government sector work, and in case the standard commercial justification is instead important to you: Good markup positively influences your search engine rank!

- **Unicode.** Not everybody has only 26 letters in their alphabet. New Zealanders typically need the *Macron* so that they can spell 'Māori'. Europeans have various diacritics. The Chinese have tens of thousands of *Han* characters. The *Unicode* standard enables SilverStripe templates and the content entered into the CMS to be in multiple languages and alphabets.

- **Supporting the 'web of data' and it's APIs.** There's an inexorable trend away from websites only providing their content and features in a human-readable format. If your website catalogs a hundred books, or adds a dozen fresh news articles every day, this content shouldn't just be accessible in a gleefully designed HTML and CSS webpage. The information should also be available to download as a CSV document. Or an RSS feed. Or better yet, a full *Web Services API,* allowing the content to be machine-readable in a robust and versatile fashion. This lets other websites and tools take information from its authoritative source – your website – and promote it elsewhere. However, you're unlikely to bother with such a feature on your website if it adds time or complexity to your project. Fortunately, as Chapter 6, Section 6.10, 'Web services using RESTfulServer' explains, SilverStripe gives you robust and feature-rich APIs with very little code.

1.1.5 Conventions

As you might have begun to determine already, SilverStripe makes a lot of use of conventions. There are also documented PHP coding standards, conventions for HTML and CSS, and naming conventions for functions, methods, and filenames. As a result, you have a well-considered structure to follow for your projects – this allows teams of people to work on SilverStripe projects, and helps you share your work with others in the overall developer community.

Related to this is the principle of *convention over configuration*, which has two major benefits: Efficiency and robustness to the developer and user-friendliness to content authors, as illustrated by these examples:

- The base package 'just works' out-of-the-box. It provides a helpful installer, and immediately can be used to add pages and run a website. A default theme means that it's feasible to write *no* code and have this as a public website – it would just look a little bland. Extension modules such as the blog and forum adhere to this 'works out-of-the-box' principle, too, which makes getting started with SilverStripe quicker.
- Options are only visible in the user interface where they're commonly used. Functions with less frequent usage exist on the sidelines without cluttering up the interface, and rarely used functions are either possible through extension modules or may be excluded altogether. Those rare features might still be useful to you, and are basically waiting for a developer to write them using one of the many extension points in the framework. Although this may make you consider using an older, more 'feature rich' alternative to SilverStripe, do be careful: In general there's a major switch toward using more lightweight tools that are user-friendly. A good CMS is one that doesn't have a ton of functionality you never use.
- The same is true at the code level, in the *Sapphire* framework. The core package focuses on providing commonly needed features easily. Generally, if functionality is missing, it provides easy means for adding, replacing, or changing behavior – by writing code. This is in contrast to having a multitude of built-in options that serve to complicate and bloat the software. This focus is rare in CMS packages.

1.1.6 CMS Interface

So far we've discussed principles and architecture. They're important to mention because they might not be as readily apparent as the functionality that's visible within the CMS backend functions provided by the SilverStripe backend is to try it out. The best way to understand the functions provided by SilverStripe is to try it out, for instance the official public demo at http://demo.silverstripe.com/ or the screencast at http://silverstripe.org/assets/video/cms.html.

Chapter 4 serves to explain the CMS interface in detail, so we'll just mention some interesting features here.

In comparison to other CMSs, the backend is quite clean and uncluttered, and supports intuitive usage without specialized knowledge. Long training sessions should be a thing of the past with SilverStripe for the average computer user who is familiar with using *Microsoft Word* or similar text processing solutions.

Behind the scenes, SilverStripe was an early adopter of highly interactive interfaces built around *JavaScript* and *AJAX*, which means certain areas of the interface can dynamically adapt to user actions without reloading the entire application. AJAX powers key tasks such as opening and saving pages, inserting images and links, and most strikingly, using drag&drop to organize your sitemap. The use of AJAX makes performing these standard tasks much quicker than the traditional approach of having to reload the entire webpage. Other interesting features include the following:

- A site-tree interface instantly provides users with the idea of the organization of the website's pages, and how to edit and update pages.
- Each page has a private 'draft' view, which you can work on until you're happy to publish it live. Each page version is saved, allowing you to revert to and compare older versions of pages.
- There's support for websites having multiple languages and subsites.
- The user interface used by content authors is translated into many different languages, which makes it more accessible to non-English markets.
- There's powerful and automatic image manipulation. If you insert a 10 megapixel image onto your homepage, SilverStripe automatically reduces it to a filesize appropriate for the web.
- The URLs are friendly URLs, of the format *http://yoursite.com/pagename/*.

- You can use a WYSIWYG editor to update content, sidestepping the need for content authors to learn HTML.
- There's a graphical user interface to manage files and other documents, as well as security permissions.
- Some extension modules provide rich additional functionality to the CMS. For instance, the *Userforms module* lets non-technical people create forms for their website. The *Workflow* module provides the ability for larger groups of people to work on a website, ensuring that content goes through an approval process before being published.
- It's highly customizable. Developers can substantially alter the user interface so that content authors have the ability to manage their unique website. This is much more than being able to add a custom field – you can create entirely new data management interfaces, making the CMS backend capable of managing all sorts of data.

1.1.7 Commercial Open Source Software – Best of Both Worlds?

SilverStripe is open source software, which means that you benefit from access to the source code, and of course that it's free to use. It also serves to build a global community of developers who take interest in the software, sharing best practices, code, documentation, roadmap ideas, and so on.

The source code is managed and predominantly produced by a privately held company, SilverStripe Ltd. This in contrast to a community ownership model that often typifies open source. Despite SilverStripe being produced by a company, which would often suggest there being a 'commercial' and a 'free community' version, the SilverStripe company instead focuses on making a single (free) version great.

Having a company behind an open source project typically allows the best of both worlds: On the one hand it provides access to code, a good price, and minimizes lock-in to a vendor. On the other hand, it also provides assurance that there is a number you can call if you want to pay for professional services, such as resolving an issue or commissioning a feature. You can visit http://silverstripe.com/ for more detail on the professional services that SilverStripe and its partner companies offer, or keep an eye on the community forums on http://silverstripe.org/ for freelancers.

However, the devil is in the detail: Open source has become a coveted term and there's variation in just how 'open' different 'open source content management systems' are. Some companies profess to provide open source software, but fail to honor some key principles beyond just providing access to the source code. In SilverStripe's case, the company does the right thing and provides a number of attributes necessary for the open source litmus test:

- Source code is available in a public versioning repository. All past and upcoming versions of the software are available, with all changes between them shown in a convenient manner. Every change on every line of code can be tracked to a person, a moment in time, and a release.
- The project accepts (and encourages!) contributions in the form of code back to the project. Although nobody outside of the company has *commit* rights to the core package at the moment, contributed patches are regularly added to the core, and many members in the community have commit rights to extensions. So far, the company's control appears to have done a good job prioritizing sound architecture and usability.
- Core developers regularly appear publicly on support forums and use a development mailing list to advise of the roadmap, and actively encourage discussion and input by the wider developer community. A healthy sign of this is that some features rise in the priority list of the core team after community discussion. Multiple language support is an example of an often requested feature that was implemented by SilverStripe based on community feedback.
- The bug tracker and feature request system are all publicly visible and open to the public to use at http://open.silverstripe.com/. A public roadmap and a real-time list of changes to the product are also found here.
- SilverStripe is distributed under the commonly used *BSD* license, which is a *permissive* license approved by the *Open Source Initiative* (http://opensource.org/). SilverStripe refrained from crafting their own open-source license, which means that your legal team will have an easier job reviewing the license details (assuming they know about open source!).

BSD license

BSD is short for *Berkeley Software Distribution,* which is a liberal license model originally developed by the American university of the same name. The BSD license allows copying, modifying, and distributing of software without having to grant access to the altered source code, and is by definition a 'permissive' license. The only requirement is that the original (fairly short) license note has to stay in place. The complete license can be found at http://opensource.org/licenses/bsd-license.php.

In practice, this means that service providers can develop specific extensions for paying customers without obligations to license this work as open source. The created intellectual property stays with the service provider.

SilverStripe is one of very few CMSs that take this liberal approach of BSD licensing. Most open source alternatives use a variant of the *GNU Public License* (GPL), which enforces greater responsibility around contributing your changes back into the core product.

1.1.8 What You Don't Get

Another way to define something is by what it *doesn't* have:

- There's no graphical user interface to manage templates, website logic, alter your database schema, provide a 'control panel', and so forth. These are all managed by editing code at the framework level, offering more flexibility to developers.
- The template files and PHP files are stored on the file system. This means that the responsibility of maintaining a history of old versions of these files, allowing collaboration by multiple people editing these files, and pushing files from 'development' to 'production' is up for you to manage. There's plenty of powerful tools to provide this facility (e.g., *Subversion* and *Rsync*) but SilverStripe doesn't do it for you.
- SilverStripe is not a *document management system,* a term that normally refers to a more heavy-weight product capable of managing many thousands of documents for perhaps just as many staff, and robustly ensuring versioning, integrity, and security of the files. Any document management system worth its salt will have APIs to provide integration with SilverStripe, allowing for instance the uploading of files into the CMS from your document store. SilverStripe does have a powerful 'Files and Images' system that lets website content authors manage thousands of publicly accessible images and documents on your website, and it's well suited to *that* purpose.
- You don't get a Microsoft application with SilverStripe, but if want to want to leverage knowledge or investment in a Microsoft environment, take advantage of SilverStripe being able to run on IIS and talk to SQL Server databases. Use APIs if you need integrate with third party applications such as *Sharepoint.*
- There's no inline editing. Some content management systems allow you to browse the website, find a section of content you want to edit, click it, and edit it right then and there – 'inline'. SilverStripe

has chosen to put more effort into making a 'backend' CMS interface polished and user-friendly. You'll see in this book that forms can be added to the 'frontend', which update pages and content in the CMS, but these are focused on providing specific functions, such as letting members update their profile. However, you *can* have a link shown on webpages that loads the CMS backend for the current page.

- There's not gazillions of modules, themes, widgets, translations, and developers able to give you free support 'yesterday'. If you want something modern you need to be prepared to have less of these amenities. Bear in mind that you don't need so much pre-built code because it should be easy to write it yourself.

- We don't supply an application that runs on the x386 PC you have earmarked for the local museum. SilverStripe is built in an environment where dual-core machines are the lowest-end computers available. That's not to say SilverStripe shouldn't concentrate on client-side performance in the browser, but it makes pragmatic choices. On server-side performance, you can expect several page views to be dynamically generated per second; hundreds if you use static caching.

1.2 History

After giving you a high level overview of what SilverStripe has in store technically, we'd like to give you a little insight into where it comes from. Welcome to our little SilverStripe history lesson!

The website development company SilverStripe Ltd was founded in 2000 in the beautiful capital of New Zealand, Wellington. The three founders Tim Copeland, Sam Minnée, and Sigurd Magnusson originally developed and marketed a closed-source PHP4-based CMS to local small and medium-sized business customers.

In 2005, the business decided to rebuild this CMS from scratch in PHP5, using the experience gathered throughout five years of commercial CMS development. This rewrite was largely motivated by the need to support larger customers with more complex website requirements. The rewrite came with a twist, too: This time it would be open sourced. SilverStripe hoped to foster goodwill and a wider adoption by this move, assuming it would make SilverStripe a better and more mature product in the long run. If they could pull it off and create a thriving community around the newcomer, the feedback and ideas generated would mean welcome improvements to the overall system.

The software was rewritten substantially in 2006, with beta downloads available late that year, and v2.0.0 stable released in February 2007. Just months after the stable release, the project was accepted into the *Google*

Summer of Code, followed shortly later that year by being accepted into the *Google Highly Open Participation Contest* (see later box 'Google's open source initiatives').

These two programs brought SilverStripe to the attention of web developers around the world, and led to many new features being contributed to the software. In 2008, the software won 'Most Promising CMS' at the *PacktPub Open Source CMS awards,* having been a finalist the year before. The software also featured at the annual *MySQL Conference* in California, won at the *New Zealand Open Source Awards,* and was used to power http://demconvention.com/, a high traffic official website in the recent and very visible US Presidential Elections.

In 2009, the software was chosen as one of ten packages bundled with *Microsoft Web Platform Installer,* an automated way to install PHP applications on Microsoft's IIS webserver. The Microsoft installer now accounts for nearly half of SilverStripe's downloads each month. Since launch, the SilverStripe project team have maintained at least one major and a couple of minor releases each year.

On the commercial side, the SilverStripe company has more than tripled its company size since going open source, currently employing over 30 staff. To help grow the company, in 2007 the founders appointed a new CEO, Brian Calhoun, who had spent considerable time working in the Silicon Valley software industry.

All employed developers can dedicate a certain percentage of their work time to open source development. Many new features also find their beginnings in commercial work for specific clients with enough foresight to allow open source usage of their commissioned work. Much of the company's work has come from international clients who became aware of the open source product without any significant marketing effort on behalf of SilverStripe, by virtue of the community spreading the word.

Google's Open Source Initiatives

Through the *Google Summer of Code* (GSOC) and *Google Highly Open Participation* (GHOP) *Contest* programs, the search giant shows generous support for open source software. Both programs encourage students to contribute to established open source projects.

The *Summer of Code* is a reference to the *Summer of Love* that took place in San Francisco, 1967 – and implies similarly youthful and revolutionary energies. The annual event began in 2005, and provides hundreds of paid internships to university students. The students work for about three months over the northern hemisphere summer, and are mentored by members of an open source project to contribute a specific feature or effort to that project. More information is available at http://code.google.com/soc/.

The *Google Highly Open Participation Contest* connects high-school students with open source projects in a similar fashion, but with paid tasks that take only hours, not months, to complete. Further information is at http://code.google.com/ghop/.

The support from Google not only boosted SilverStripe development, but also led to a good chunk of attention from the global open source community, as well as potential clients. SilverStripe is now recognized beyond the southern hemisphere, and finds a lot of adopters in Europe as well as North America.

1.3 Future

SilverStripe is a fairly young CMS. The price you pay for any modern system is that the documentation, features, and support may be more raw than in an older system – but then, an older system clearly has its share of disadvantages too. It is therefore comforting that the project cares a lot about embracing and furthering website development best practices, and that the core developers and the company show regular commitment to growing both the community and the software.

In most cases, the active developer community is able to respond quickly to any questions. Overall, the development velocity is quite high, and this is the main factor that made this underdog a great CMS. It doesn't look as if development is slowing down any time soon; SilverStripe is seeing increased contributions from the community in the form of themes, modules, and new core developers.

The community is definitely at the heart and pulse of the web, which means that new requirements and technologies are embraced very quickly. This is also the reason for sparse long-term roadmap planning – the next SilverStripe version is always dependent on community contributions and appropriate responses to new requirements. Before writing this book, we decided not to include a comprehensive and detailed SilverStripe API reference for this very reason. The young product is moving a lot quicker than the dead trees that compose these pages. If you're looking for a complete reference, the web guarantees you up-to-date information: http://api.silverstripe.com/.

Looking at download figures, the trend is pointing upwards. In late 2008, two years after the first betas, 100,000 downloads were reached. Less than a year later, downloads hit 200,000. A good indicator is also the adoption rate among third party developers: Numerous commercial service providers have included SilverStripe in their service portfolio. SilverStripe is currently transforming from the 'secret weapon' for early adopters to a broadly used application.

1.4 Conclusion

SilverStripe is a user-friendly and versatile CMS, and gets real strength through its MVC underpinnings and developer-friendly framework.

It's not yet at a point where it can compete feature-by-feature, extension-by-extension with some of the more established systems in the market, but it doesn't really have to: The underlying architecture compensates for many missing bullet points because it's comparatively easy to extend and customize the out-of-the-box experience. SilverStripe's focus on using open standards and common technology not only helps to make extending the software easier, but also helps to future-proof projects you make with it.

The BSD license is particularly interesting for commercial service providers who are interested in developing extensions for their clients, both open and closed source. The ability for technical support to come from commercial and community sources makes it suitable for both small and large budget projects.

SilverStripe is able to score well in terms of cost-effective development: Websites and web applications are easy to get started, and importantly, can be quickly customized in an agile fashion. This agility can be a significant competitive advantage.

2
Installation

After our first flight through the SilverStripe world in Chapter 1, it's time for you to form your own impression of the system. Surely you're eager to log in to the SilverStripe backend for the first time, right?

In this chapter we guide you through the installation, and describe how you can deploy SilverStripe on your local Windows, Linux, or Mac OS X system, as well as deploying to a remote web-hosting server. After that's done and dusted, we introduce some essential tools that simplify your work with databases and editing code. At the end of the chapter you should be ready for takeoff, and prepared to follow along with the upcoming examples and tutorials. Put on your flying goggles, we're starting!

2.1 System Requirements

As you probably know by now, SilverStripe is based on PHP5, and is theoretically executable on any webserver supporting this language. SilverStripe is recommended for the most popular choices, notably Apache, Lighttpd, and Microsoft IIS. SilverStripe produces 'friendly URLs' right out of the box, and therefore needs some form of URL rewriting – in Apache this is handled through the *mod_rewrite* module. If you feel so inclined, SilverStripe works without URL rewriting as well. In terms of the PHP version, PHP 5.2 (released 2006) or newer is recommended. Earlier versions of PHP5 are not actively tested by the SilverStripe team.

SilverStripe is still quite picky about the database flavor: Currently only MySQL is fully supported, with PostgreSQL and Microsoft SQL Server support being prepared for release. The developers recommend MySQL 4.1 or newer.

The extensive framework takes its toll on PHP memory requirements: Each PHP process should be granted at least 48 MB of memory, particularly for running the CMS interface and displaying larger site structures. This is more than cheap web hosting packages are willing to grant, hence SilverStripe is best deployed to medium-sized web hosting or ideally a dedicated server. If you're unsure about your memory settings, please ask your provider for the *memory_limit* setting in your *php.ini* configuration.

SilverStripe makes use of *GDLib*, a free graphics library for generating and manipulating images, mainly to generate thumbnails and resized images on the fly. *GDLib* is usually packaged with the default PHP installation.

For uncomplicated data exchange and use of web services, the free library *cURL* is recommended – a bit less common in standard PHP installation, but still fairly standard.

The CMS doesn't make assumptions on the operating system you're running under, as long as the web server stack works as described above. Productive deployments of SilverStripe are common under Unix/Linux, Windows, as well as OS X.

More up-to-date information about official system requirements is available on http://doc.silverstripe.com/doku.php?id=server-requirements.

2.2 Preparation

Deployments with the system requirements mentioned above are so common and popular that ready-made packages exist for different operating systems, consisting of Apache, MySQL, and PHP. For Windows we introduce the *WAMP* package, for Mac OS X we have a look at *MAMP*, and your favorite Unix/Linux flavor usually comes with a comfortable package manager to install all dependencies.

For all the nerds and control freaks: Of course, you can install the components separately from the respective project pages, or even compile all requirements from scratch to have full reign over your environment. For the sake of simplicity and getting something running painlessly, we stick with *WAMP* and *MAMP* for this chapter, or assume a ready-made webhosting environment.

In this section, we download all components necessary for the installation preformed afterwards in Section 2.3 'Installation'.

2.2.1 Webserver as a Package

We recommend the *WAMP* and *MAMP* packages for installing the webserver requirements, although these are by no means the only full packages out there providing this functionality:

- Windows – *WAMP* (**W**indows: **A**pache/**M**ySQL/**P**HP): http://www.en.wampserver.com/download.php
- Mac OS X – *MAMP* (**M**acintosh: **A**pache/**M**ySQL/**P**HP): http://www.mamp.info/en/download.html

Keep in mind: These packages are usually configured for development environments, both in terms of performance and security considerations. We advise against using these packages on a public webserver, which would require a stricter set of configuration and tools.

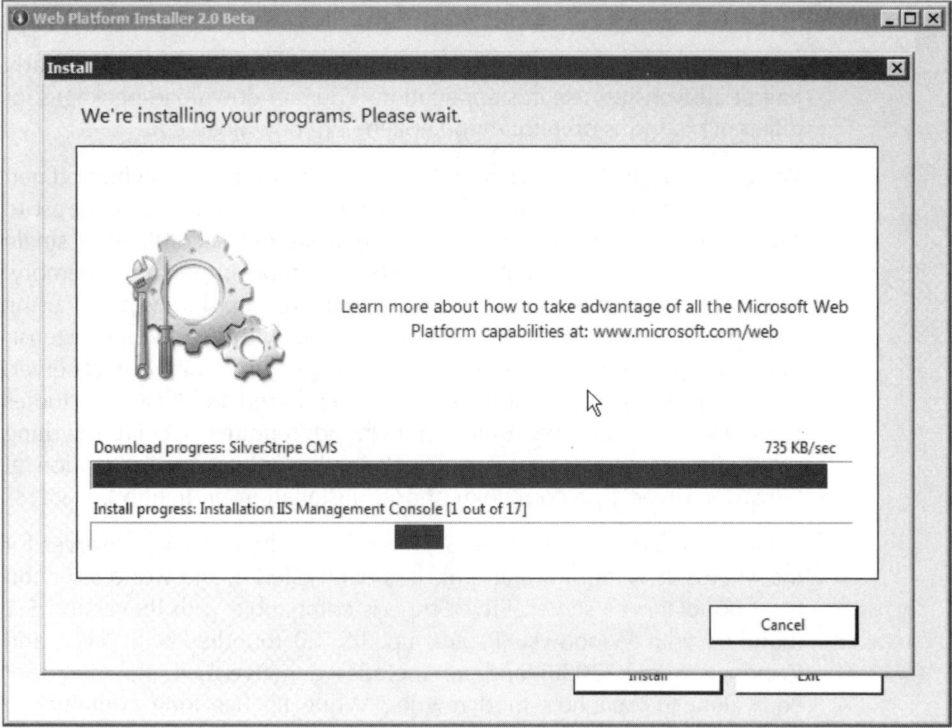

Figure 2.1 Microsoft WebPI Installer in progress.

If you're running Windows XP professional, Windows Vista, or Windows Server (2003 or 2008), you might want to have a look at the *Windows Web Platform Installer*, an all-in one package that downloads the Microsoft IIS webserver alongside with SilverStripe out of the box in a graphical installer. See http://doc.silverstripe.com/doku.php?id=installation-on-windows-pi and http://www.microsoft.com/web/gallery/SilverStripe.aspx for details (sent to Martin via Email).

2.2.2 Webserver as Individual Components

Apart from recommending a package, we of course don't want to keep you from getting to know the components separately. You also might need this when setting up a production environment from scratch. We don't go into much detail about the specific component installations, so please follow the documentation that comes with the downloads. If you download *MAMP* or *WAMP*, you can safely skip this section.

Webserver

Apache is the de facto standard for serving content over HTTP; nearly half of all websites use this application. You can download packages for different platforms on http://httpd.apache.org/download.cgi.

You can get Lighttpd as an alternative to Apache from http://lighthttpd.net/download/. Its architecture is built for high performance; in contrast to Apache it can handle thousands of requests per second on a single process, and saves precious CPU-cycles and most importantly memory. It is commonly used in high traffic scenarios: popular websites using Lighttpd are youtube.com or wikimedia.com. With its modular extensibility and performance, Lighttpd rivals Apache as a mature webserver, and is the fourth most popular webserver based on NetCraft studies from early 2009. SilverStripe on Lighttpd requires special rewriting rules; please refer to the instructions in the online documentation at http://doc.silverstripe.com/doku.php?id=installation-on-lighttpd.

Windows Internet Information Services (IIS) is the official webserver for the Microsoft Windows Platform. It is often cited as the world's second most popular web server. SilverStripe is compatible with IIS version 5.1 (bundled with Windows XP) and up. IIS 7.0 (bundled with Vista and Windows Server 2008) and up includes a native URL Rewriter tool equivalent to Apache's mod_rewrite. While IIS has long contained a content compression feature, there is currently no robust PHP5 byte-code cache for IIS. This means Apache on Windows is likely to offer a faster experience. (see Section 8.5.1, ''PHP: Byte-code Caching''). The most straight forward means for installing SilverStripe on IIS is to use the Microsoft Web Platform Installer mentioned in Section 2.2.1.

PHP5

The scripting language PHP5 is available on http://php.net/downloads.php. Both Apache and Lighttpd access the same libraries, and so differences for the two webservers are rare. Just make sure to select the download matching your operating system.

MySQL

The database server MySQL can be downloaded at http://dev.mysql.com/downloads/mysql/. SilverStripe works with MySQL 4.1 or newer.

2.2.3 SilverStripe Download

The SilverStripe download itself is available at http://silverstripe.org/download/, in the popular tar.gz archive format. You'll also find themes and extension modules on this website.

2.3 Installation

After downloading the packages, you can now either install all components separately, or follow along as we describe installing the *WAMP* package for Windows, *MAMP* package for Mac OS X or the necessary steps for installing on webhosting. As noted before, we assume a local environment, and hence will use http://localhost/ as the webservers address in our examples. If you are using virtual hosts or installing SilverStripe on external webhosting, your address will most likely differ. In any case, ensure to unpack the SilverStripe tar.gz archive into the so-called webroot, the publicly accessible directory on your webserver. The webserver packages usually already have files in the *webroot* – please move those files to a different location to avoid conflicts and unexpected behavior. You should see the SilverStripe system folders *sapphire/* and *cms/* (amongst others) as direct subfolders to your webroot.

Please choose one of the following sections based on your operating system and installation type.

2.3.1 Windows: *WAMP*-installation

Download the installation files from http://www.en.wampserver.com/download.php and execute the installer:

- The installer will ask first and foremost if any existing *WAMP* installation is present on your system. If this is your first time installing *WAMP*, please select 'Yes'. Do the same for the prompt to close all existing windows, and accept the license agreement.

- Now it's time to set the target directory for the installation – in our following instructions, we refer to the suggested default *c:\wamp*.
- After the installation, some parameters need adjustment: Feel free to leave the SMTP configuration empty, unless you have a local email server available.
- You'll find a new WAMPSERVER icon in your task bar (alongside with your system clock). To start Apache and MySQL, left click this icon and choose START ALL SERVICES. Your browser should show some *WAMP* installation data under http://localhost/ now (see Figure 2.2).

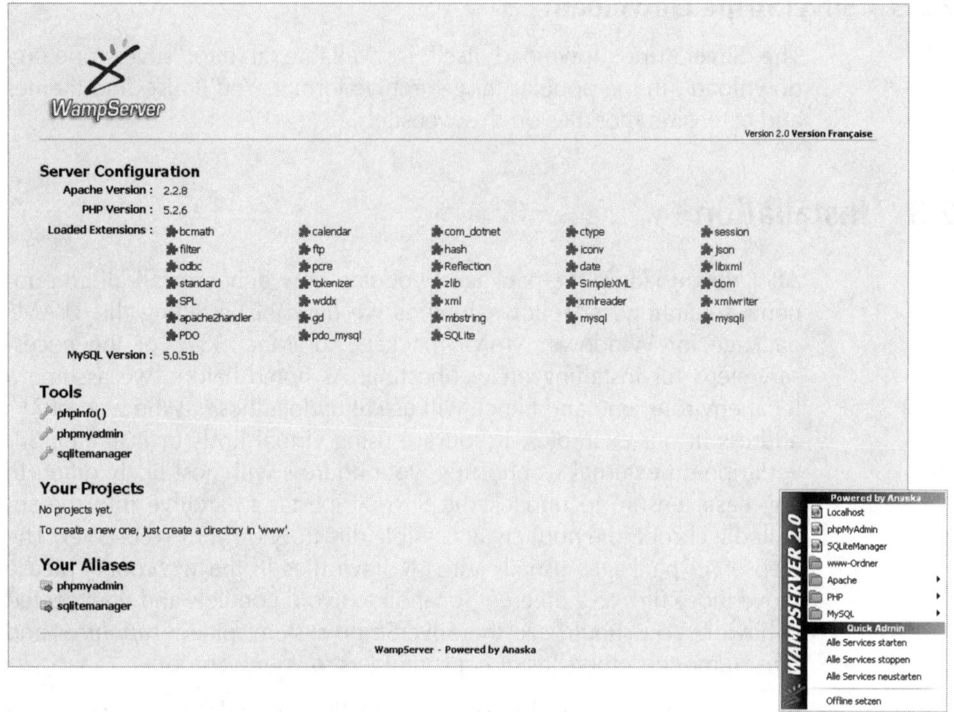

Figure 2.2 *WAMP* start screen and taskbar.

In case you didn't change the target directory during your installation, the webroot should be located at *c:\wamp\www*. Please copy the unpacked SilverStripe directory to this location. Before we can run the web-based SilverStripe installer, some fine tuning is necessary for Apache and PHP:

- We need to enable the *mod_rewrite* module within Apache, which is necessary to view 'friendly URLs' in SilverStripe. Right-click on the

WAMPServer icon in your task bar and select the entry REWRITE_MODULE from APACHE > APACHE MODULE.

- SilverStripe also needs the *cURL* library for connectivity to external services. It can be enabled in the task bar as well, through PHP > PHP-EXTENSIONS PHP_CURL.
- Finally, we need to tell the MySQL database to convert table names lookups to all lowercase, unfortunately a prerequisite on Windows to keep SilverStripe databases portable between platforms. Open the MySQL configuration through MYSQL > MY.INI and append the following directive at the end of the file: `lower_case_table_names = 2`. After saving the file, apply the changes by restarting MySQL through RESTART ALL SERVICES in the task bar.

To run the web-based installer contained in SilverStripe, please skip to Section 2.3.4 'Webinstaller' now.

2.3.2 Mac OS X: *MAMP*-installation

Mac OS X comes out of the box with Apache and PHP, which can be activated with in the SYSTEM PREFERENCES with SHARING > WEB SHARING. Depending on your version of the operating system different releases are available: Mac OS X 10.4 comes with Apache 1.3 and PHP4. Mac OS X 10.5 contains Apache 2 and PHP5. Neither of those base configurations meets the SilverStripe requirements – a manual adjustment would be possible, but only with significant effort and understanding of the underlying techniques. As an alternative we're installing the ready-made (and much easier) package *MAMP*.

MAMP is split up into a free standard edition, and a commercial professional edition. There is only one download on http://mamp.info containing both editions. For our purposes, the free standard edition is perfectly fine, and we'll refer to this edition later on:

- If necessary, stop the built-in Apache webserver in SYSTEM PREFERENCES by deselecting SHARING > WEB SHARING.
- Please download the *MAMP* installer - it totals about 120 MB. If you've installed *MAMP* before on your machine, please read the upgrade notes in the contained document *How to upgrade.rtf*.
- Double click on the resulting download to unpack and mount the disk image (extension: `.dmg`). Copy the contained directory *MAMP/* out of the disk image into your *Applications/* directory. In contrast to other webserver setups and Mac OS X software, all binary executables and configurations are contained in the same location underneath this

directory. The advantage of this approach is an easy removal process: Simply delete the folder to get rid of all *MAMP*-related files.

- After copying the *MAMP/* directory you can safely unmount and close the installer disk image.
- Run the application *MAMP.app* inside the copied directory, which is a small control panel for the most common server settings. Before using the START SERVERS button to start both Apache and MySQL, we have some minor configuration work to do in the Preferences panel.
- Make sure that PHP5 is selected in the PHP tab. While you're here, enable the XCACHE option in the CACHE dropdown. This will significantly speed up your SilverStripe installation (see Section 8.5.1).
- Open the PHP configuration file located in */Applications/MAMP/conf/php5/php.ini,* and search for the `memory_limit` directive. Set it from `8M` to `64M` to meet SilverStripe memory requirements.

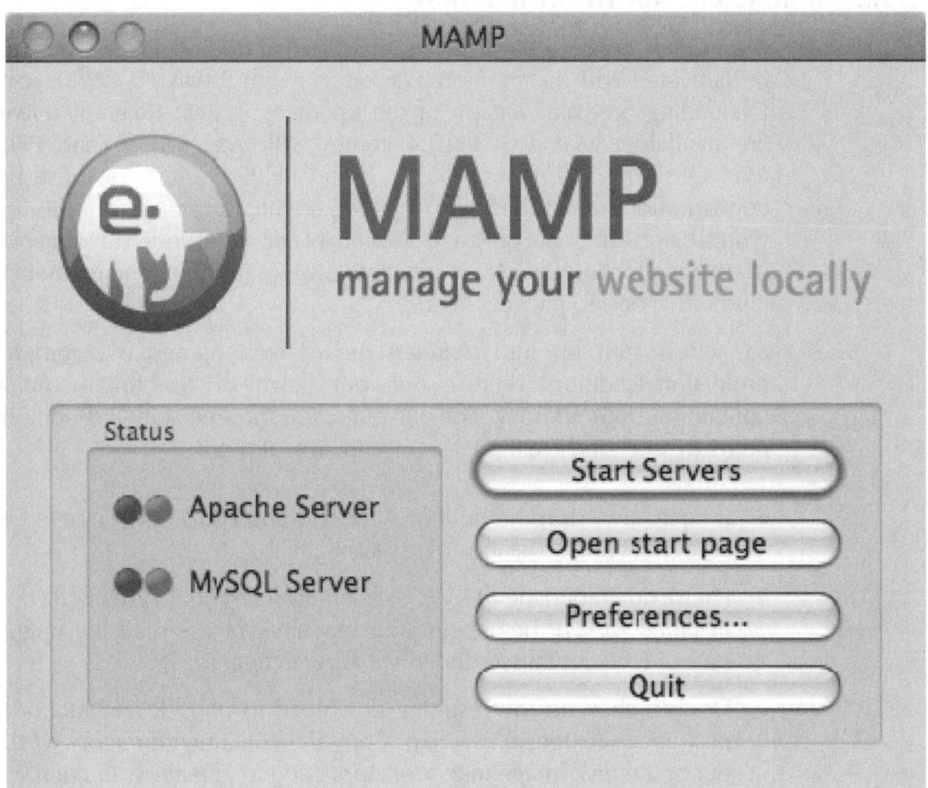

Figure 2.3 The *MAMP* control panel.

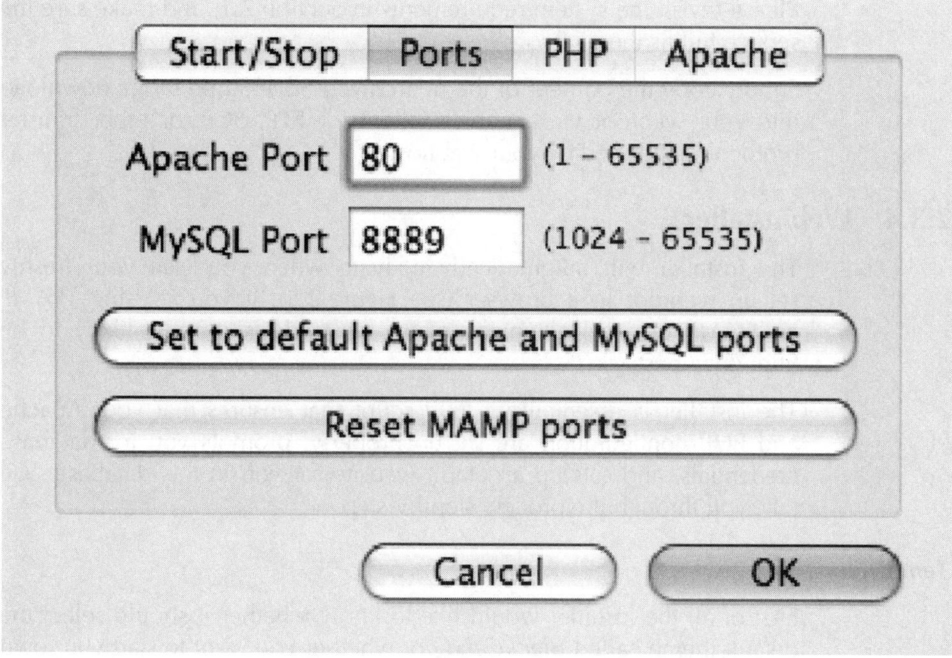

Figure 2.4 Setting the Apache port in *MAMP*.

- Set the default APACHE PORT from 8888 to 80 in the PORTS tab to avoid having to specify the port number on every request to your SilverStripe environment.
- Start your engines: Hit START SERVERS in the *MAMP* control panel. You should be able to see a default *MAMP* page at http://localhost/ now.
- Copy the SilverStripe tar.gz archive that you downloaded in Section 2.2.3, 'SilverStripe download', into your webroot, which is usually pointed to the *htdocs/* folder inside *MAMP*. If you're unsure where to find it, you can find the full path under the APACHE tab in the *MAMP* control panel (see Figures 2.3 and 2.4).

To run the web-based installer contained in SilverStripe, please skip to Section 2.3.4 'Webinstaller' now.

2.3.3 Webhosting

If you want to install SilverStripe on an external webhosting service, you most likely have Apache with PHP and MySQL already installed for you.

Please revisit the system requirements in Section 2.1, and make sure the service fulfills them.

Simply copy the content of the unarchived SilverStripe tar.gz download into your webroot via a transfer client for FTP, SCP, or other transfer protocols supported by your webhost.

2.3.4 Webinstaller

The installer will automatically activate when you visit your freshly set up webroot in a browser (see Figure 2.5). If you're using *WAMP* or *MAMP* on a local environment, the address is most likely to be http://localhost/.

The installer is essentially a PHP script that ensures that your Apache and PHP configuration are set up properly, prompts you for database credentials, and sets up a default website for you in this database. We take you through the process step-by-step.

Template

First of all the installer would like to know whether it should select the default theme called *BlackCandy* or whether you want to start your own templates and stylesheets from scratch. As this is your first encounter with SilverStripe, stick with the default option and use *BlackCandy* as a kickstarter for further development. We'll explain how to customize themes or start your own ones later.

After theme selection the INSTALL SILVERSTRIPE button should be enabled now. If you're using *WAMP* or *MAMP* in the described configuration, you shouldn't need to deviate from the installer defaults. Either way, we encourage you to refrain from hitting the install button just yet, and scroll with us through the remaining installer settings.

MySQL

In this section the installer requires some database credentials: server address, username, and password. If your webhost has predefined database names, you can customize this value as well. The installer defaults to 'SS_mysite'. By clicking RE-CHECK REQUIREMENTS, the installer can validate the credentials, and test that a database connection is possible.

Administration Account

Please enter a username and password combination for the first administrator. This will be your main login to the authenticated CMS interface. Usernames in SilverStripe are usually email-addresses; in this case they can be arbitrary names like 'admin' as well. First name and surname are optional.

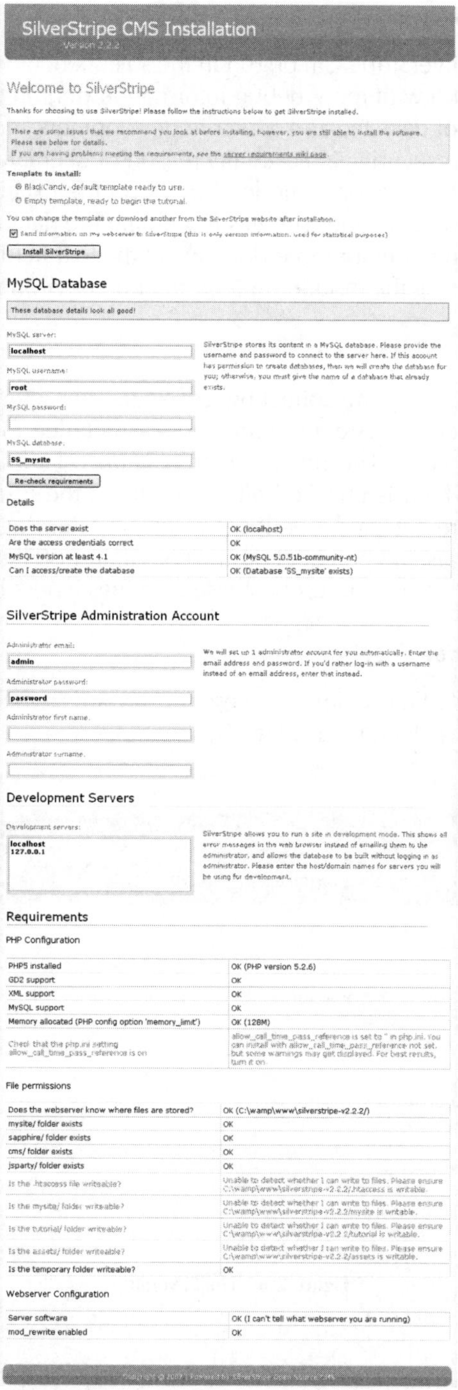

SilverStripe CMS Installation

Welcome to SilverStripe

Thanks for choosing to use SilverStripe! Please follow the instructions below to get SilverStripe installed.

There are some issues that we recommend you look at before installing, however, you are still able to install the software.
Please see below for details.
If you are having problems meeting the requirements, see the server requirements wiki page.

Template to install:

- BlackCandy, default template ready to use.
- Empty template, ready to begin the tutorial.

You can change the template or download another from the SilverStripe website after installation.

☑ Send information on my webserver to SilverStripe (this is only version information, used for statistical purposes)

Install SilverStripe

MySQL Database

These database details look all good!

MySQL server: **localhost**

MySQL username: **root**

MySQL password:

MySQL database: **SS_mysite**

SilverStripe stores its content in a MySQL database. Please provide the username and password to connect to the server here. If this account has permission to create databases, then we will create the database for you; otherwise, you must give the name of a database that already exists.

Re-check requirements

Details

Does the server exist	OK (localhost)
Are the access credentials correct	OK
MySQL version at least 4.1	OK (MySQL 5.0.51b-community-nt)
Can I access/create the database	OK (Database 'SS_mysite' exists)

SilverStripe Administration Account

Administrator email: **admin**

Administrator password: **password**

Administrator first name:

Administrator surname:

We will set up 1 administrator account for you automatically. Enter the email address and password. If you'd rather log-in with a username instead of an email address, enter that instead.

Development Servers

Development servers:

localhost
127.0.0.1

SilverStripe allows you to run a site in development mode. This shows all error messages in the web browser instead of emailing them to the administrator, and allows the database to be built without logging in as administrator. Please enter the host/domain names for servers you will be using for development.

Requirements

PHP Configuration

PHP5 installed	OK (PHP version 5.2.6)
GD2 support	OK
XML support	OK
MySQL support	OK
Memory allocated (PHP config option 'memory_limit')	OK (128M)
Check that the php.ini setting allow_call_time_pass_reference is on	allow_call_time_pass_reference is set to '' in php.ini. You can install with allow_call_time_pass_reference not set, but some warnings may get displayed. For best results, turn it on.

File permissions

Does the webserver know where files are stored?	OK (C:\wamp\www\silverstripe-v2.2.2/)
mysite/ folder exists	OK
sapphire/ folder exists	OK
cms/ folder exists	OK
jsparty/ folder exists	OK
Is the .htaccess file writeable?	Unable to detect whether I can write to files. Please ensure C:\wamp\www\silverstripe-v2.2.2/.htaccess is writable.
Is the mysite/ folder writeable?	Unable to detect whether I can write to files. Please ensure C:\wamp\www\silverstripe-v2.2.2/mysite is writable.
Is the tutorial/ folder writeable?	Unable to detect whether I can write to files. Please ensure C:\wamp\www\silverstripe-v2.2.2/tutorial is writable.
Is the assets/ folder writeable?	Unable to detect whether I can write to files. Please ensure C:\wamp\www\silverstripe-v2.2.2/assets is writable.
Is the temporary folder writeable?	OK

Webserver Configuration

Server software	OK (I can't tell what webserver you are running)
mod_rewrite enabled	OK

Figure 2.5 SilverStripe webbased installer.

Development Server

SilverStripe can be run in the so called 'developer mode', which provides you with more debug information right in the browser. If your domain is not detected as a server in development mode, errors won't be displayed for security and usability reasons, but emailed to an administrator instead. The developer mode also allows the execution of certain administrative functionalities such as rebuilding the database without requiring a login. Enter one or more domains in the text field, or delete the setting if you're using the installer in a production environment.

Requirements

Apart from collecting configuration settings, the installer also checks certain system requirements as detailed in Section 2.1 'System Requirements'. The most common cause of errors here is rewriting of URLs, which is checked after submitting the installer. If missing requirements are detected, you'll see a red error message. Orange text signifies warnings and potential errors, e.g., if an installer can't write to system folders. Please try to resolve these warnings if possible to avoid problems later on.

Install SilverStripe

It's finally time to press the Install SilverStripe button at the top of the installation page (see Figure 2.6).

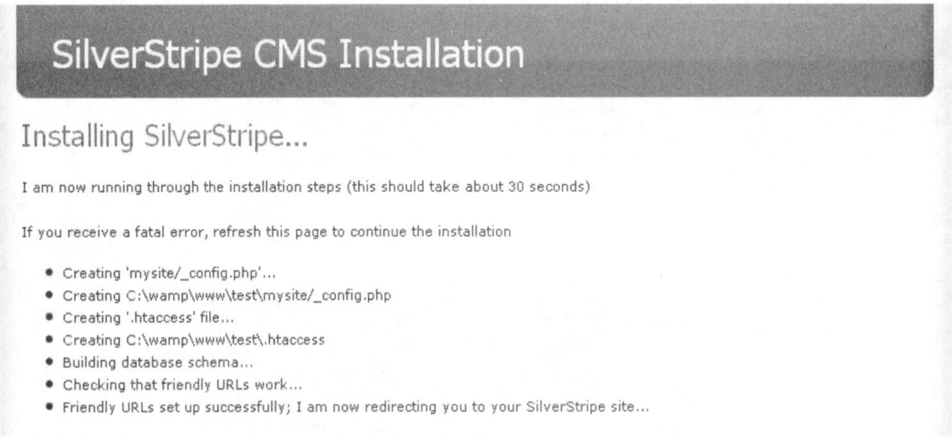

SilverStripe CMS Installation

Installing SilverStripe...

I am now running through the installation steps (this should take about 30 seconds)

If you receive a fatal error, refresh this page to continue the installation

- Creating 'mysite/_config.php'...
- Creating C:\wamp\www\test\mysite/_config.php
- Creating '.htaccess' file...
- Creating C:\wamp\www\test\.htaccess
- Building database schema...
- Checking that friendly URLs work...
- Friendly URLs set up successfully; I am now redirecting you to your SilverStripe site...

Figure 2.6 The SilverStripe installer at work.

SilverStripe takes its configuration from a PHP file called *_config.php*. It's contained in the *mysite/* folder, which holds all your custom code. The configuration file is automatically created through the installer, which prepopulates database credentials as well as setting your selected theme, by default *BlackCandy*. Then the installer writes an *.htaccess* file to allow Apache to rewrite 'friendly URLs' in a format that the *sapphire* framework can process.

If everything went by plan, you should get redirected to the example website and an 'Installation successful' message, as shown in Figure 2.7. For security reasons, you should now delete the installation files as instructed on this page.

Installation Successful

Congratulations, SilverStripe has been successfully installed.

You can start editing your site's content by opening the CMS.
Email: admin
Password: password

For security reasons you should now delete the install files, unless you are planning to reinstall later. The web server also now only needs write access to the "assets" folder, you can remove write access from all other folders.

Click here to delete the install files.

Figure 2.7 Installation successful.

2.3.5 Troubleshooting

In some hosting environments, you might not have full control over your server setup. When the installation doesn't go smoothly, here are some common errors to watch out for. (If your installation succeeded, feel free to skip to Section 2.4.)

PHP5 Extension Handlers

SilverStripe is solely based on PHP5, and is not backwards compatible with PHP4. Some hosting environments assume PHP4 for the normal `.php` file extension, and only use the newer PHP5 with the extension `.php5`. This conflicts with SilverStripe, which only contains files with `.php` extensions. To change this behavior, we tell Apache to use the right PHP version through the *.htaccess* file, which was already created by the installer in your webroot.

```
AddType x-mapp-php5 .php
AddHandler x-mapp-php5 .php
```

Keep in mind that this trick only works if you are allowed to overwrite Apache settings through *.htaccess*. If the change doesn't take effect, please contact your hosting provider.

mod_rewrite

You might need to adjust the *rewriting base* for Apache if your SilverStripe installation is not located at the top level of your webroot. SilverStripe can be installed in a subfolder on your webserver, which is handy to keep multiple installations and projects around.

If you get a 500 SERVER ERROR message after the installation or after moving your SilverStripe directory somewhere else, you need to adjust the `RewriteBase` directive in the automatically generated *.htaccess* file. The base has a trailing slash, but is relative to your webroot – meaning if SilverStripe is located in c:*wamp**htdocs**my-silverstripe-project*\\, the `RewriteBase` should read:

```
RewriteBase /my-silverstripe-project
```

System Information

Most hosting packages should provide the SilverStripe requirements out of the box. If something is missing, it's often hard to pin down the problem in your PHP setup. PHP contains a simple debug command to list its detailed configuration on a webpage called `phpinfo()`. Place a new *phpinfo.php* file in your webroot, and fill it with the following statement:

```
<?php phpinfo(); ?>
```

Now call this page through your webbrowser at http://localhost/phpinfo.php. You should see information about your PHP version, enabled extensions, and your server's environment variables. Please check that you have *cURL* and *GDlib* extensions enabled, and review the value of the `memory_limit` directive.

A word of caution: SilverStripe has an integrated autoloader which includes all PHP files it finds within certain folders. This means you need to be careful with writing code outside of class definitions, because it will be immediately executed on every request. This will get us into trouble with the *phpinfo.php* file – you'll see the PHP debug information on top of every rendered page. Apart from this glitch, it's not suitable to reveal permanently so much internal system information to potentially malicious visitors. We advise you to remove the *phpinfo.php* file after you find what you're looking for.

2.4 Useful Software

Great: SilverStripe and its server are up and running! Before we dive right into the CMS, we'd like to take a quick detour to show some useful tools for exploring and developing with PHP, MySQL, and SilverStripe.

Apart from a server environment, a code editor that does more than just display text can prove invaluable in daily development. In the following sections we present some of our favorite so-called *Integrated Development Environments* (*IDE*). They're all open-source and available across platforms thanks to Java. The list is by no means exhaustive!

2.4.1 Eclipse

Eclipse is actually more of an editor framework than an editor itself, which makes its architecture very extensible. Originally conceived by IBM, its open-source development continues today through the Eclipse Foundation.

The functionality in Eclipse can be extended through plugins. It is traditionally an IDE for Java development, but can be extended to support PHP either through a plugin or a specialized complete package. You can download the basic IDE for Windows, Mac OS X, or Linux at http://eclipse.org/downloads/.

One of the first and most popular plugins for PHP development is called *PHPEclipse*. Strictly speaking, it's a collection of many plugins targeted towards web development. Please follow the download instructions on http://sourceforge.net/projects/phpeclipse/ to integrate the plugins with your existing Eclipse installation.

As an alternative to these steps, an application named *EasyEclipse* combines Eclipse with *PHPEclipse* straight out of the box, which makes it slightly easier to install: http://easyeclipse.org/site/distributions/php.html. *EasyEclipse* comes with a *Subversion*-plugin as well, which we will need later on to check out code from the SilverStripe version control repository. We recommend using *EasyEclipse* over tuning your own Eclipse installation if you can live without the power of upgrading each plugin individually.

The installation of both Eclipse and *PHPEclipse* is so straightforward that we leave it up to the reader.

2.4.2 Aptana

The Californian software company Aptana has developed its IDE Aptana Studio (see Figure 2.8), based on the Eclipse project as well but more geared towards web developers. You have the choice between the free Community Edition and a commercial version that provides more functionality and direct support from Aptana. For our purposes as PHP developers, the Community Edition is a great start: http://aptana.com/studio/download/. Aptana is available for most platforms including Windows, Mac OS X, and Linux.

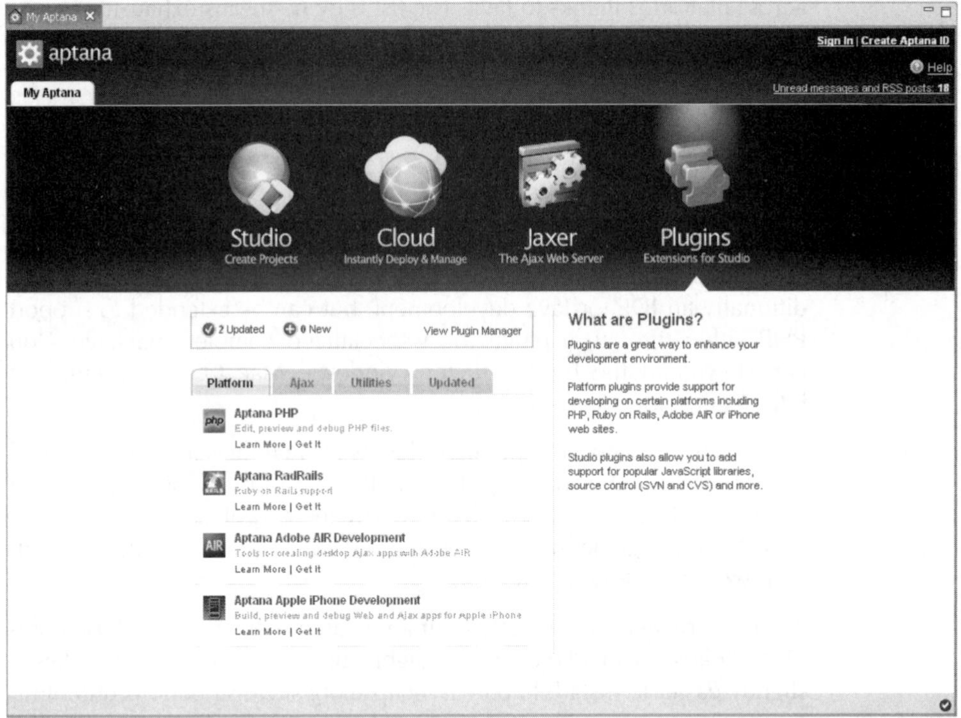

Figure 2.8 Aptana Studio.

Each Aptana download comes with a fairly self-explanatory installer that guides you through the process. At the first start of Aptana, it will present you with a welcome screen called My Aptana. Aptana is a general purpose web development tool, so we'll have to add PHP functionality first. Click on Plugins, choose Aptana PHP, and confirm with Get It. Please click the checkbox Site Providing Aptana PHP on the next page, and finalize the installer. The integrated update manager should now take care of the rest. After restarting the application, Aptana is ready for PHP development.

As a last step, we want to have Aptana recognize SilverStripe template files (extension: `*.ss`) as containing HTML content, and applying the appropriate syntax highlighting and helpers to them. Please open the main preferences menu with Window > Preferences, and choose Aptana > Editors > Generic text. The add button should allow entry of a new file extension 'ss'.

2.4.3 NetBeans

The Netbeans IDE is another popular choice among web developers. The project was initiated around 2000 by Sun Microsystems as a platform-independent open-source tool. Similar to the Eclipse project, Netbeans was originally targeted towards Java development, but thanks to its modular architecture it speaks Ruby, JavaScript, Perl, and PHP just as well (see Figure 2.9).

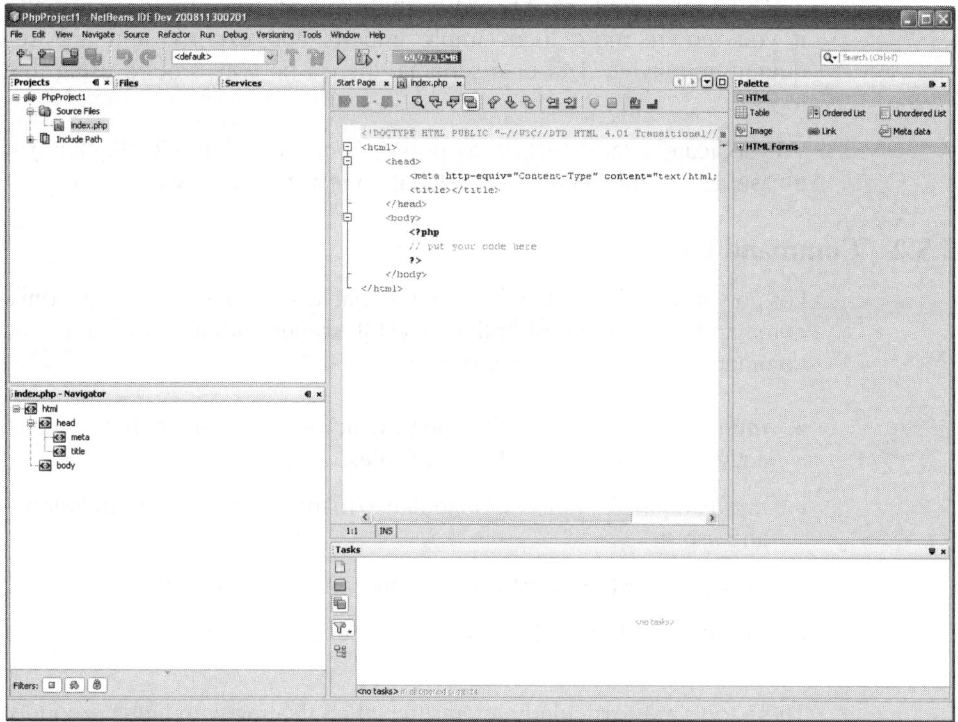

Figure 2.9 NetBeans IDE for PHP.

Download Netbeans at http://www.netbeans.org/downloads/trunk/nightly/latest/. You might need the Java JDK as a prerequisite as well, in case it's not already present on your machine: http://java.com/de.

The installation process is straightforward; there's no need to install additional PHP modules.

2.5 Database Management

Every now and then it might come handy to have direct access to your database and its content without going through SilverStripe or a PHP script, for example to inspect data or modify large amounts of records. We will present some tools to facilitate this step. At the time of writing, SilverStripe only fully supports the MySQL database, hence the tools are specific to this database type.

2.5.1 *phpMyAdmin*

One of the most popular ways to view a MySQL database is through a PHP tool called *phpMyAdmin* (http://phpmyadmin.net/). Especially if you require more than simple imports and exports, and are frequently modifying data or a schema, there's no way around using this tool.

We dedicate a later section to *phpMyAdmin* (Section 8.2, 'Backup') – please refer to this section for installation instructions as well.

2.5.2 Command Line

For power users as well as for any automated scripting, using a text-only command line is the best option. MySQL comes with a couple of useful command line tools, which work very similarly across platforms:

- *mysql:* The official MySQL client, which can be used either in interactive mode, or to read from SQL files;
- *mysqladmin:* Administration toolkit to manage databases, permissions, and users;
- *mysqlimport:* Import data as comma-separated values (CSV);
- *mysqldump:* Export data into SQL, CSV, or XML format.

These tools are particularly interesting when dealing with larger amounts of data, as they are significantly faster than web-based alternatives such as *phpMyAdmin*. More information on how to use the command line tools and available parameters can be obtained at http://dev.mysql.com/doc/refman/5.1/en/using-mysql-programs.html.

2.6 Support

There are a multitude of ways to get your questions and problems addressed: SilverStripe has a very engaged community who is willing to help you out on forums or in chats for free. If you require more solid and prompt support, the creator of the software, SilverStripe Ltd., also provides the option for commercial remote support and paid development - learn more at http://silverstripe.com/.

2.6.1 Forum

SilverStripe hosts an official forum at http://silverstripe.org/forums/, which should be the first point of contact for generic questions as well as very specific problems. It is frequently visited by core developers of the software, but is generally just one of many English-speaking places to get SilverStripe help. The website also contains a community showcase for registered forum members at http://silverstripe.org/showcase/.

2.6.2 IRC-chat

If case your problem is best discussed directly, SilverStripe hosts an official chat channel on the IRC network. This channel is open for everybody, and a good starting point for community gatherings. You can join IRC either via a browser applet on http://irc.silverstripe.com/, or through an IRC client on channel #silverstripe, *server:* irc.freenode.net.

2.6.3 Reporting Bugs

If SilverStripe misbehaves and you discover a bug in the code or interface, please help SilverStripe grow by reporting this error. SilverStripe has an official bug tracker at http://open.silverstripe.com/ which is open to everybody (after a free registration). This is also the place to get information about existing bugs, their status, and any roadmap planning. This is the place to make feature requests and to contribute patches to the core product.

2.6.4 Core Development Mailing List

You can observe and contribute to the core people working on the next version of SilverStripe CMS. While the forums are the best place to ask questions, this mailing list is a useful resource for new people to SilverStripe to read over. Over time, you are encouraged to contribute to core ideas on the direction and decisions being made to the software. See http://groups.google.com/group/silverstripe-dev/.

2.7 Conclusion

In this chapter we've laid the foundation to the following theory and practice: You should have a running SilverStripe installation on your own computer or on a webserver, including the essential tools you need to get started with development. Feel free to have a look around these tools before we introduce some architectural concepts in the next chapter.

3

Architecture

With the previous chapter under our belt, we've finished all the preparations necessary to get to know SilverStripe in a bit more depth. In order to understand the further instructions a little better, you need to be familiar with the underlying paradigms and techniques.

To this end, we describe *Model View Controller* (MVC), *Object Relational Model* (ORM), and other architecture considerations in this chapter. Even if you have gained first-hand experience with these topics in general, we recommend that you read up about their specific implementation in SilverStripe.

3.1 Introduction

Modern development in the software and web arena employs tried and trusted strategies to resolve common tasks. Standardized practices are used for building applications in a modular and efficient fashion, and to create less error-prone and secure code. These strategies are commonly referred to as *design patterns*.

The field of software development has discovered lots of these patterns over the years. Most of them are imperative for everyday programming – you might even use them without knowing about the specific pattern. Choosing a design pattern is always related to the task at hand. First of all you have to identify the task in order to choose an appropriate pattern.

Convention over configuration

For a developer, the expression *convention over configuration* means first and foremost minimizing the (often unnecessary) configuration effort in custom code. Only properties and behavior that deviate from sensible conventions have to be explicitly configured.

One of these conventions is the naming of database tables based on the PHP class names. Although the class needs to be defined in custom code, the naming doesn't have to be repeated for the database – the framework assumes standard settings.

3.2 MVC – Model View Controller

We have hopefully mentioned the MVC pattern enough to make you interested in its details. This pattern is a well-suited basis for web-application architectures and their typical attributes and peculiarities. It's a fundamental concept for the SilverStripe framework. Learning the theoretical basics as well as specific SilverStripe implementations of this pattern are the first step to becoming a great SilverStripe coder.

3.2.1 Theory

The three nouns contained in Model View Controller describe the different logical roles that need to be specified for an application, each of which has a well defined area of responsibility. These logical roles can be separated on the filesystem by different files, or on a PHP level through different classes. Both approaches are relevant and used for SilverStripe. The reasoning behind them comes down to encapsulation: Each of the roles can be developed and tested in isolation, minimizing the side-effects which are typical in less structured procedural code.

One of the most basic requirements of this pattern is the ability to communicate. Each role makes sense only in the context of other roles, therefore they need effective ways to exchange information. The reasons for this separation of concerns are obvious: A task-oriented encapsulation supports more straightforward development with easier code maintenance. Each encapsulated role is also easier to reuse and it's less of a hassle to exchange it with a different implementation. In a team, each team member can use his or her specific skills set on one of the different roles without getting in the way of each other – for example, a template designer would just deal with the view without worrying about where the underlying data comes from.

Early interactive web applications are usually based around two main roles: the presentation or user interface, and data access with attached

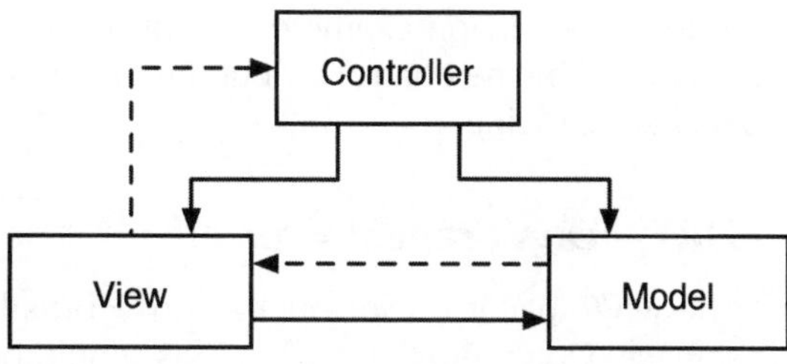

Figure 3.1 MVC design pattern.

business logic. This traditional division has to be regarded in its evolutionary context: In the 'early days' of the Internet, a separation of concerns wasn't a big issue for websites, because they were rarely more than a collection of static pages with the odd form submission and simplistic management interfaces. Unfortunately this architecture tends to scale poorly, as well as the two-tiered code-base becoming unmaintainable on larger projects.

In comparison to the traditional two component architecture, MVC further separates the data access and the business logic into their own roles, forming the trinity of *Model, View,* and *Controller* (see Figure 3.1):

- The *Model* role takes care of defining, storing, and managing data. Models are often connected to persistent storage such as relational databases.
- The *View* role represents this data in a user interface, for example in a browser or the output of a web-service.
- The *Controller* role handles inputs from the view, contains view-specific parts of the business logic, and passes on collected data to the model role if required. In the other direction, a controller can pass on data from the model to the presentation.

So we're dealing with two logical separations here: separating the presentation from the model and separating the controller from the view.

The controller role is the intermediate role, which is a bit harder to pin down: its separation from the view is less important than distinguishing the model role from any presentation. Think of a form submission on your website: The controller would process the data that's entered in your form (the view), and apply certain business logic to it. This business logic will usually result in the data being passed on to the model. This in turn alters the presented data, and the controller is responsible for updating the view.

It's up to the developer which business logic is best applied in the controller, and what should be done on a model role. If you stick with the form submission example, complex server-side form validation will be handled by the controller, but the model will also want to validate its data before saving.

DRY – Don't repeat yourself

The MVC pattern also touches on a broader concept in computer science: Don't repeat yourself. This should be quite obvious, because every new line of code has to be reviewed, updated, and maintained. Given the nature of code, it's very easy to take shortcuts and duplicate slightly modified code. This will make your code harder to follow, and leads to opportunities for making inconsistent behavior. By using common design patterns such as MVC, SilverStripe provides a good basis to avoid unnecessary code duplication.

Particularly in the sector of content management system, there's a trend toward using MVC as the driving architectural pattern: As the systems get more complex, code architecture and maintenance becomes a priority. More specialized and larger project teams beyond the simple designer and an all-knowing webmaster are becoming common. Each of these roles needs tools that match their skills set.

3.2.2 Implementation in SilverStripe

SilverStripe was an early adopter for the MVC pattern, and applies it both for website presentation as well as for the actual CMS application. This is most apparent through the concept of *page types*. Each page in your website is based on a certain type, and therefore has certain data and behavior. The page type is selected within the CMS, which comes with a couple of different types out of the box, ranging from the standard type 'Page' to more specialized types like 'Redirector Page' (see Figure 3.2).

Code-representations of a page type are aligned to the MVC pattern: Each page type consists of a model class, a controller class, as well as one or more templates for the view role. Model and controller classes are both contained together in one PHP file, for example the base class is located in *mysite/code/Page.php*. Template files with the extension **.ss* are typically contained in a theme (we will come to that in a second in Section 3.6, 'Themes'). The names for different page types in the dropdown correspond to their class names in PHP by default, and so the page type PAGE is represented by the class `Page`, in the file *mysite/code/Page.php*.

As you can see in Figure 3.3, the separation of controller and model from the view can also be seen through the folder structure. Your custom controller and model logic is contained in *mysite/code/*, while view

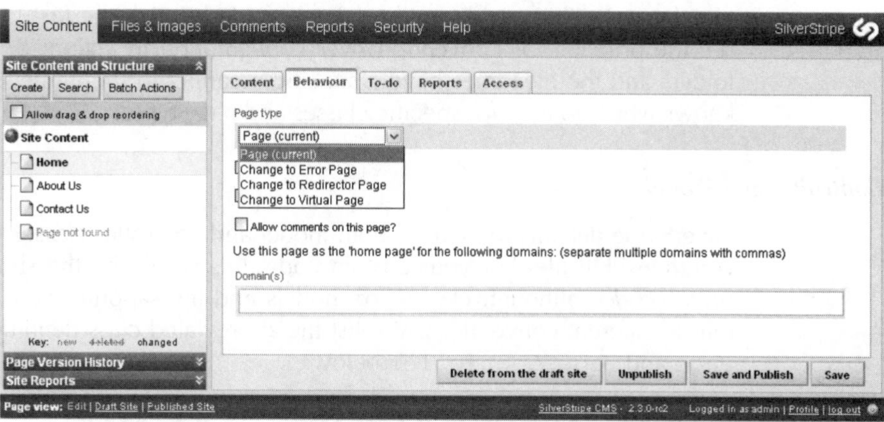

Figure 3.2 Setting a page type in the CMS.

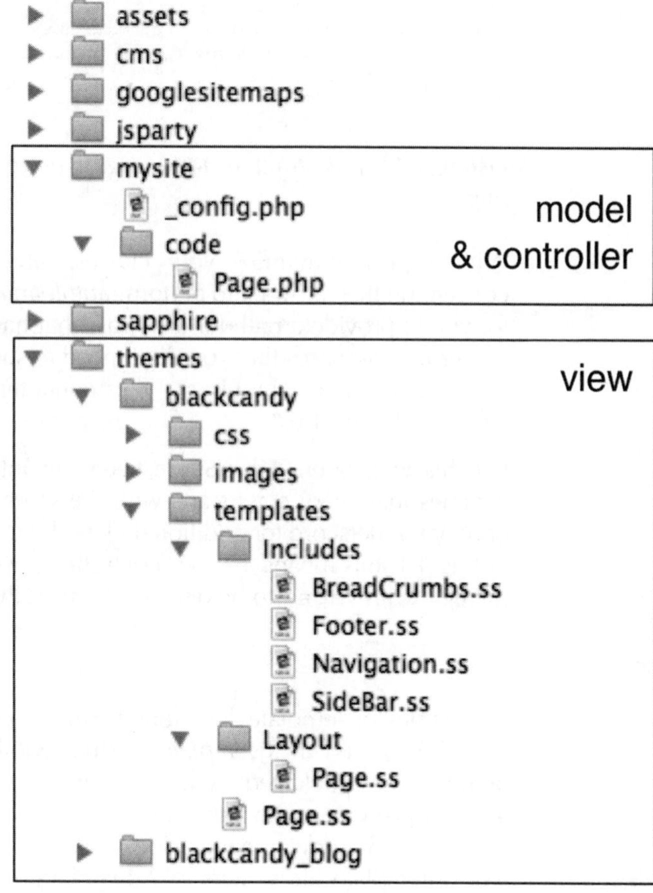

Figure 3.3 MVC in the folder hierarchy.

templates typically reside in the *themes/* folder. This is the first time we see the principle of *convention over configuration* in action: Both the folders and the filenames have a specific meaning to the framework; it knows where to look for specific classes and page types.

Controller and Model

SilverStripe defaults to manage both model and controller classes in one common PHP file. For your custom code, this would be the subfolder *mysite/code/*, although classes for models and the sapphire core might follow different conventions. We list the abbreviated class definitions of `Page` and `Page_Controller` below:

```
<?php
class Page extends SiteTree {
   // Properties and methods for the model
}
class Page_Controller extends ContentController {
   // Properties and methods for the controller
}
?>
```

Listing 3.1 *Class structure for a page type (example: mysite/code/Page.php)*

With respect to naming your classes, SilverStripe follows a naming convention that allows it to perform *autoloading*. PHP5 makes it possible for you to provide a path for any class that hasn't been defined yet. This means in most cases that you don't need to specifically call `include()` or `require()` for any of your files containing the used classes; it just works 'out of the box'.

For this to happen, SilverStripe keeps an internal lookup table which assumes that every class starts with the same name as the file, with an optional underscore for additional class definitions. In our example from Listing 3.1, this means that our controller class `Page_Controller` has to begin with `Page_` to be detected by the SilverStripe autoloader.

View

The names of template files follow similar conventions: They have to be either placed in a *templates/* folder within your *mysite/* directory, or preferably packaged as a reusable 'theme' in the *themes/* folder. SilverStripe comes with a default theme called 'BlackCandy' in the folder *themes/blackcandy/* – have a look around to get an impression on the typical template file structures. A template typically contains the HTML markup displayed on your website, but can also be used for other output formats such as XML. All template files in SilverStripe have to bear the extension **.ss*.

One unique feature of SilverStripe is that the concept of class inheritance is transferred to the template naming as well. Your Page controller in *Page.php* would naturally look for a template called *Page.ss* to render its data, and will find it in *templates/Page.ss* in our theme folder. But it would be quite limiting to have all your markup defined in one single template, particularly when you start to create your own page types with specialized display:

```
<html>
   <head></head>
   <body>
      <div id="Header"><h1>Your Site Name</h1></div>
      $Layout
      <% include Footer %>
   </body>
</html>
```

Listing 3.2 *themes/blackcandy/templates/Page.ss (excerpt)*

The template code in Listing 3.2 doesn't contain all the markup required to render the page; essentially it only outputs 'Your Site Name'. The magic happens in its placeholder `$Layout` and `<% include Footer %>`. They both essentially do the same thing: Include the content from another template file. The dollar sign and angular brackets are both parts of the SilverStripe template syntax.

Besides the main template file *Page.ss*, page types can have a 'layout template', which is based on the name of the page type as well. In this case, `$Layout` is automatically replaced by another *Page.ss* template in the subfolder *templates/Layout/*. This file can contain further markup, template syntax, and its own template includes:

```
<% include Navigation %>
<h2>$Title</h2>
$Content
```

Listing 3.3 *themes/blackcandy/templates/Layout/Page.ss (excerpt)*

The `$Layout` placeholder is a special convention. If you want to include specific template files, use the alternative `<% include %>` syntax. Includes are handy if you want to re-use a specific template in more than one place, as well as logically separate a certain chunk of template code from your other templates. With the placeholder parameter, in our examples `Footer` and `Navigation`, you're actually specifying a filename in the subfolder without the **.ss* extension. For the footer, SilverStripe knows where to look for the file: *templates/Includes/Footer.ss* in our theme folder:

```
<p>Powered by SilverStripe</p>
```

Listing 3.4 *themes/blackcandy/templates/Includes/Footer.ss (excerpt)*

The only placeholder we haven't explained yet is `$Content`. In this case, the SilverStripe template engine doesn't look for a file, but for a property on the underlying model: `Page->Content`. That's our main content field in the CMS, and renders the custom content for this page from the database.

By using certain conventions for the naming and folder structure of files, SilverStripe very rarely requires you to tell it specifically which template you want to use – it's all in the page type. Remember the 'Don't repeat yourself' rule from the beginning of this chapter? That's what we've been talking about.

Template Inheritance

It's quite common for a new page type to have a different layout from the standard page. For example, a page listing your latest customers might want to render an unordered list with small profile pictures, while standard pages render with the content entered in the CMS. The header and footer design for both pages would be the same. The separation into a 'main' and 'layout' template enables us to react to those changes without starting the customer listing template from scratch. Templates mirror the class inheritance, which means they look for templates named after the subclass, but fall back to the parent class hierarchy.

For our example, we would like to create a new page type in PHP called `CustomerPage`, plus its controller `CustomerPage_Controller`. The model extends `Page` and the controller extends `Page_Controller`. You don't have to code this example on your own installation, just bear with us for a moment:

```
<?php
class CustomerPage extends Page {
}
class CustomerPage_Controller extends Page_Controller {
}
?>
```

Listing 3.5 *Defining a new page type: mysite/code/CustomerPage.php*

As the header and footer are identical for the new page type, we just need to create a new 'layout' template called *CustomerPage.ss,* and store it in *templates/Layout/CustomerPage.ss*. For now, we can copy it from the already existing *templates/Layout/Page.ss* file (see Figure 3.4). We will customize its content in the next section.

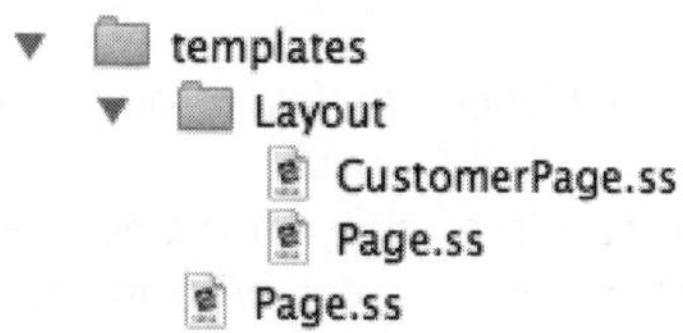

Figure 3.4 Template inheritance.

The CMS will now show a new entry in the page type drop-down. All pages created with this type will now look for *CustomerPage.ss* as their 'main' and 'layout' template. As only the inner 'layout' template exists for this specific type in *templates/Layout/CustomerPage.ss,* the template system will automatically fall back to using the standard *Page.ss* 'main' template for rendering the header and footer.

Communication between the Different Roles

The three different roles in Model View Controller have to be able to communicate with each other. Most importantly, the view templates have to get their data from the controller and model role. In SilverStripe, data accessed through placeholders in the template doesn't need to be explicitly assigned; both public methods and properties on the controller and model are accessible by default. This greatly simplifies the templating workflow – you can just use what's there.

Let's stick with our `CustomerPage` example, and add a method for getting the newest ten customers in the system. The specific syntax isn't important at this point, just bear in mind that `DataObject::get()` returns a collection of objects that can be iterated over in a template. The `Customer` class is part of the example; we aren't defining it here.

```
<?php
class CustomerPage extends Page {
}
class CustomerPage_Controller extends Page_Controller {
   function LatestCustomers() {
      return DataObject::get(
         "Customer",
         "'Customer'.'CategoryID'",
```

```
            "'Customer'.'Created'",
            null,
            10
        );
    }
}
?>
```

Listing 3.6 *Collecting data through the controller*

As you can see, the `CustomerPage` model and the `CustomerPage_Controller` extend from our basic Page classes. The controller is our primary interest at the moment. Even if you don't understand all the code yet, you can see that the `LatestCustomers()` method returns a value. This value comes from a database result as a collection of `Customer` objects, and can be used in our special *CustomerPage.ss* template:

```
<% if LatestCustomers %>
<ul class="customers">
   <% control LatestCustomers %>
      <li>
         <img src="$Image.URL" alt="$Image.Title" />
         Name: $Name
      </li>
   <% end_control %>
</ul>
<% else %>
   <p>No customers found</p>
<% end_if %>
```

Listing 3.7 *Output of controller data through the view*

Even if you don't know much about SilverStripe's templating syntax, the used commands should be fairly self-explanatory. The `<% if %>` clause checks if any customers are returned from our controller, and otherwise outputs 'No customers found' to the template. If customers are returned, they're looped over with a `<% control %>` command: For each returned customer, a new list entry is created. Placeholders like `$Image.URL` or `$Name` are replaced with the specific data from this object. In the case of `$Image.URL`, we're actually working with an image object inside the `Customer` record, which can have its own properties.

You can see that using certain conventions throughout the different MVC roles can help to keep the configuration overhead low: Method names and properties in the controller can be used by the same name in the template.

3.3 ORM – Object Relational Mapping

The model layer in SilverStripe uses a technique called *Object Relational Mapping* (ORM). As the name implies, some mapping is required to translate between the object-oriented approach of PHP classes and a typical relational database such as MySQL. More specifically, SilverStripe uses the *ActiveRecord* design pattern for this process.

Imagine a person object inside an address book application: Apart from simple scalar values such as first name, each person can have a couple of phone numbers and addresses. In an object-oriented fashion, these 'slots' for phone numbers and addresses would be modeled as an array, which can be accessed through the person object. On the other hand, a typical relational database acts on tables with scalar values and fixed columns only. Both on loading and saving, the framework has to convert between the notion of objects and its flexible values and a so-called 'normalized' view of a database table.

3.3.1 Mapping Conventions

Specific concepts in a relational database have to be matched up to types that can be represented in-memory by PHP. There are three simple conventions for this:

- A *database table* maps to a *class.*
- A *database row* maps to a *class instance.*
- A *database column* maps to an *instance attribute.*

Therefore, essentially, most objects in SilverStripe that are stored in the database wrap a row in a database table. These objects extends the base class `DataObject`. Our `Page` class is a `DataObject` as well.

3.3.2 Definition

The definition of the mapping happens in the PHP class, rather than straight in the database. All saveable properties on an object are defined in a static array `$db`:

```
<?php
class Employee extends DataObject {
   static $db = array(
      'Name' => 'Text',
      'Comment' => 'HTMLText',
   );
}
?>
```

Listing 3.8 *Defining the database schema for a custom model*

In this example, the class `Employee` defines two properties: `Name` and `Comment`. SilverStripe automatically takes care of creating a database table named `Employee` with the mentioned properties as table columns. All you have to do is tell SilverStripe to look at all PHP classes and update the database schema accordingly by calling a special admin URL:

```
http://localhost/dev/build
```

Keep this URL in mind because you'll use it a lot throughout the book. Every time you define new classes or properties, the changes reach the database only after this manual refreshing of the database schema.

This URL is only accessible if you either work in 'dev mode' (see Chapter 8, Section 8.1, 'Environment Types') or are logged in to the CMS as an administrator. SilverStripe will redirect you to a login screen if those conditions aren't met.

3.3.3 Object Access

To access rows in the database as an instance of the DataObject class, the SilverStripe ORM provides numerous methods that take care of the low-level SQL calls. The most commonly used ones are:

- `DataObject::get($class,$filter,$sort,$join,$limit)`: Get all objects from a specific class matching the `$filter`, in a specific `$sort` order. Additional tables can be joined via the `$join` parameter, and you can limit the number of returned records through `$limit`. All parameters apart from `$class` are optional.
- `DataObject::get_by_id($class,$id)`: Get a single record by its primary key in the database.
- `DataObject::get_one($class,$filter)`: Get one record based on certain criteria defined in `$filter`.

The ORM saves you from writing direct SQL most of the time, although the optional parameters still adhere to SQL notation. If required, the ORM can be bypassed to execute your own raw SQL queries, although this isn't best practice because you lose most of the benefits of the SilverStripe framework.

3.3.4 Relations to Other Objects

Most applications store their data in multiple tables. As the name implies, rows in a *relational* database can be linked to each other. An order row might have multiple order items and an associated user. In the database schema, these relations are expressed by linking tables based on their primary keys (which in SilverStripe is the `ID` column). This relation can happen in different ways, which we demonstrate below.

The 'has-one' relation

The simplest case is that one row relates to exactly one other row, mostly on a different database table. This is called a *has-one relation*, also known as *1:1*. The owner row of the has-one relation has an additional column which stores a reference to the other row. In database speak, this column is called a *foreign key*. As an example, imagine that an `Author` has exactly one `Profile` where website users can read about him or her. On the other hand, a `Profile` belongs to only one `Author`: To maintain egos, everybody gets his or her own. We illustrate the database tables alongside the class definitions in Figure 3.5.

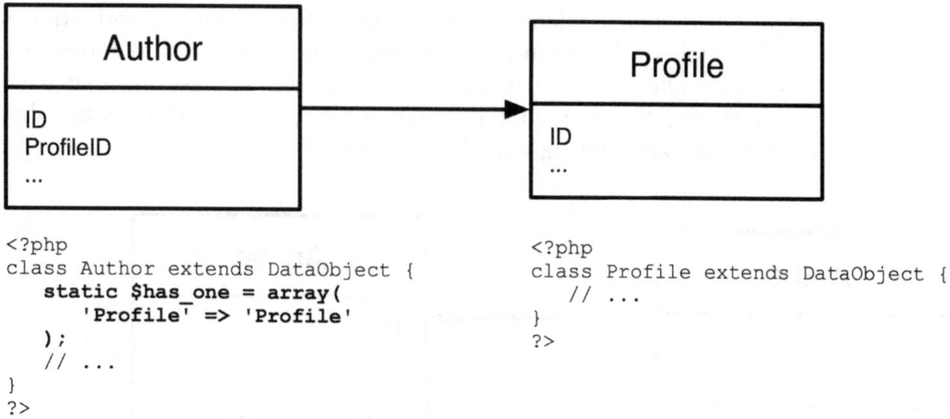

Figure 3.5 A has-one relation.

As you can see, the definition of relations in your SilverStripe class works similarly to the `$db` fields. A static `$has_one` property holds an array of one or more relationship definitions. To keep our examples brief, we aren't defining any additional properties such as an author's name on our objects.

Every entry in the `$has_one` array consists of two parts: the name of the relation as the array key on the left and the associated class as the array value on the right. In this case, both name and class are the same: `Profile`. The relationship name determines the naming of the foreign key database column, plus a suffix to denote its use: `ProfileID`. Note that only one side of the relation has this foreign key.

But more importantly, the name of the relationship is used as a method name in the SilverStripe ORM:

```
$myAuthor = DataObject::get_one('Author', "`Name` = 'John'");
$myProfile = $myAuthor->Profile();
```

As a developer, you don't have to define explicitly this method on your Author class. The framework takes care of this, and knows which database columns to query to get the right row back for you.

Caution: SilverStripe doesn't currently allow the reverse association through method calls in has-one relationships, and so `$myProfile ->Author()` wouldn't work. Strictly speaking, we're handling a *one-to-zero* relation.

The 'has-many' relation

A *has-many* or 1:*n* relation handles a collection of objects, and requires a definition on both 'ends' of the relation. Let's extend our previous example: One `Author` has many `Articles`. We assume that each `Article` on the other hand has only one `Author`: We did mention that our authors are quite egoistical, didn't we? (see Figure 3.6).

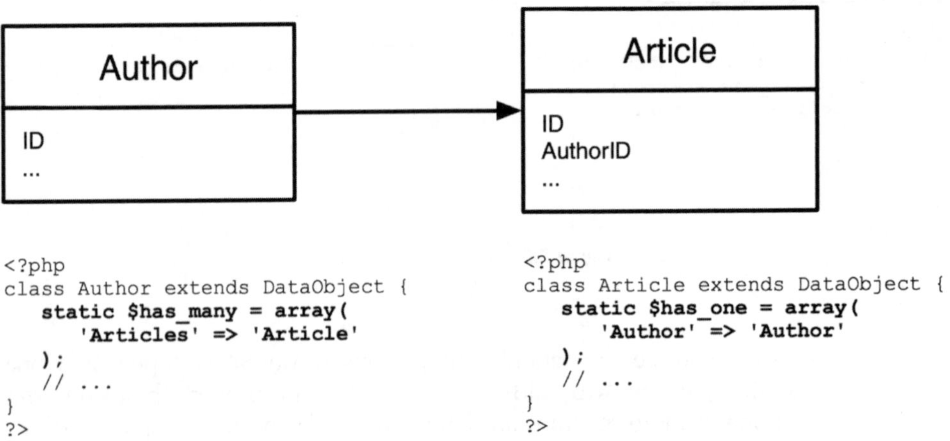

Figure 3.6 A has-many relation.

Seen from an `Article`, we still have a *has-one* relation as previously described. But an `Author` can have many articles, so on this end a single column doesn't cut it – we have to store many references, not just one. SilverStripe knows that it needs to query for the `AuthorID` foreign key to get all associated articles for an author. In terms of accessing the relation through PHP, you can use the relation name on both sides as a method call: `$myAuthor->Articles()` will give you back a collection of Article objects and `$myArticle->Author()` will give you back the Author who wrote the Article. You might have noticed that we're using the plural 'Articles' rather than the class name 'Article' to access the relation – the name of a relation is arbitrary and not bound to the class name.

The 'many-many' relation

The third and last type of relation is connecting many objects to many other objects, a so-called *many-many* or *m*:*n* relation. In our example, a single `Article` could have many `Tags`: Short keywords that categorize its content. `Tags` become useful because of one feature: Other articles can have the same tags, and can therefore be used to categorize and group articles.

In contrast to the other relation types, the database needs a new table to form this connection. Its called a *join table*, which usually doesn't have any content on its own, just a pair of foreign keys pointing to the two ends of the relationship (see Figure 3.7).

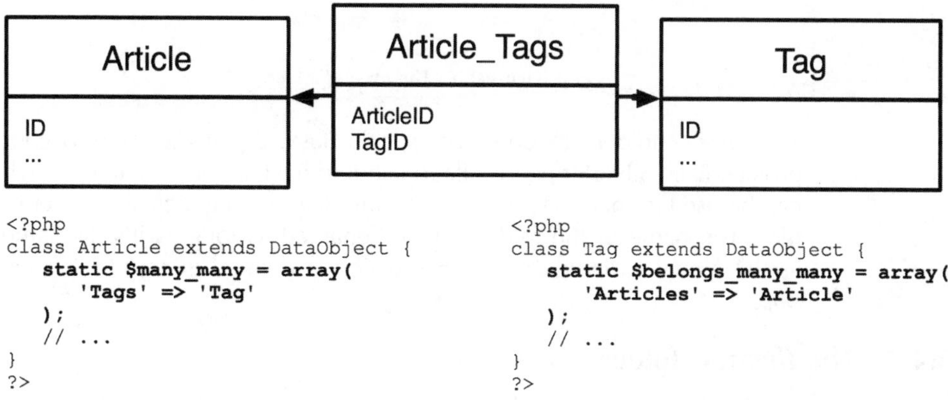

Figure 3.7 A many-to-many relation.

Again, both ends of the relationship have their own definitions, one with a `$many_many`, the other with `$belongs_many_many`. It doesn't matter which variable goes on which class, it just determines the naming of the join table. Both sides have the name of the relationship accessible through a method: `$myArticle->Tags()` and `$myTag->Articles()`.

3.4 Directory Structure

SilverStripe organizes itself mainly on the topmost directory level in your webroot. As a general rule, every directory on the top level stands for a *module*, a piece of encapsulated functionality. Both the CMS and the underlying *sapphire* framework are just modules in SilverStripe, albeit very important ones. We talk a bit more about the concept of modules in Section 3.5, 'Modules and widgets'. For now, let's have a look at important directories in a standard SilverStripe installation.

3.4.1 The *mysite/* folder

This folder contains most of the custom PHP code that you will write when developing a website or application (see Figure 3.8). It's fairly empty by default, but contains one important file: *code/Page.php*, the default page type for all pages in SilverStripe. You'll also find a *_config.php* file, which is created by the SilverStripe installer and contains your database credentials. This file is the starting point for any custom project configuration, which mainly takes place through static method calls to SilverStripe classes.

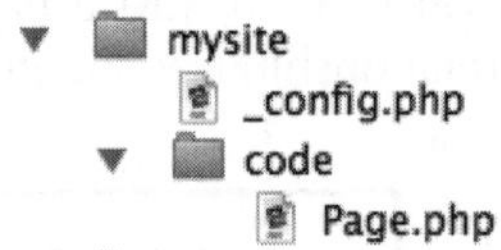

Figure 3.8 The *mysite/* folder.

The *mysite/* folder has one other special task: It gives a name to your project. Each SilverStripe installation should have a unique name, which can be used for naming the database and determining inclusion order of files. The name of the folder can be renamed as long as it's the same as the global variable `$project`, which is defined in *mysite/_config.php*.

3.4.2 The *themes/* folder

In SilverStripe, a theme determines how a website looks, and it's separate from the PHP code that determines its server-side behavior (see Figure 3.9). A theme consists of templates (Extension: **.ss*) that mostly output HTML or XHTML markup, CSS and image files, as well JavaScript files. The *themes/* folder can hold multiple themes in subfolders. By default, SilverStripe comes with the *BlackCandy* theme, contained in the two directories *themes/blackcandy/* and *themes/blackcandy_blog/*. To customize the look of your website, you can either modify an existing theme or start fresh in a new folder. We will explain in Section 3.6, 'Themes', what's involved in creating a new theme.

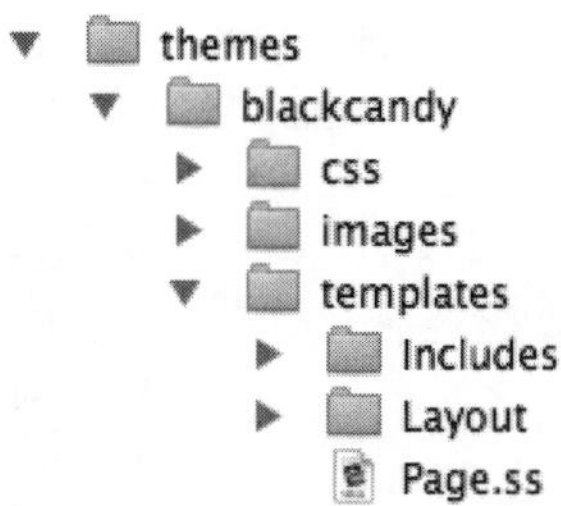

Figure 3.9 The *themes/* folder.

3.4.3 The *assets/* folder

The term assets stands for all the file-based resources that are uploaded by website users or CMS editors (see Figure 3.10). SilverStripe has a special admin interface for managing files and folders in this directory called *Files & Images*. Separating these files from your application logic in *mysite/* and styling in *themes/* makes it easier to track changes and enforce different permissions. From a security standpoint, there's no reason the web-server should be able to write to any SilverStripe directories other than *assets/*. This folder is usually the only place with write permissions throughout the filesystem; all other folders can remain read-only.

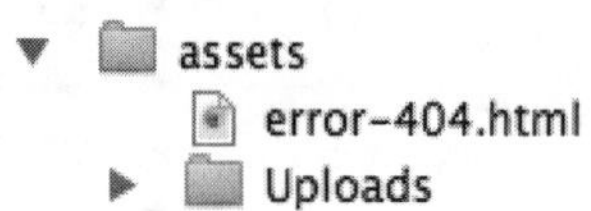

Figure 3.10 The *assets/* folder.

SilverStripe automatically reads-in all files in this directory, which means they can have attached metadata and be treated as normal objects within the framework. If files are uploaded anywhere in the CMS, the framework creates these database records automatically. For all files uploaded through FTP, or copied from elsewhere, SilverStripe will pick them up the next time you load the *Files & Images* section.

3.4.4 The *sapphire/* folder

The *sapphire/* folder is the heart of each SilverStripe application: This folder contains the *sapphire* framework (see Figure 3.11). It's essential for other parts of the system, because it contains core classes used by other modules.

Figure 3.11 The *sapphire/* folder.

3.4.5 The *cms/* folder

This folder contains everything related to the CMS interface (see Figure 3.12). It's dependent on the sapphire framework being in place.

3.4.6 The *jsparty/* folder

SilverStripe has lots of custom JavaScript to drive its rich interface, but it also uses third-party libraries for certain functionality (see Figure 3.13).

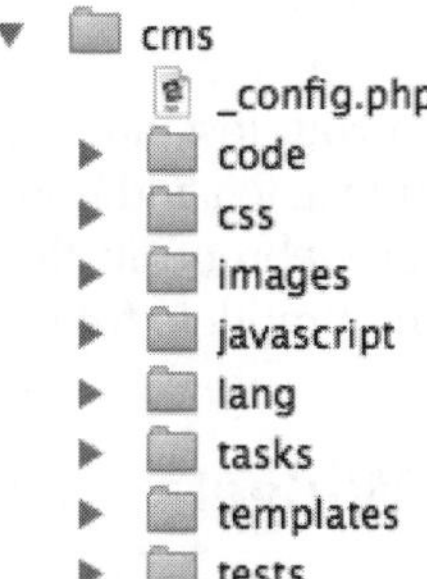

Figure 3.12 The *cms/* folder.

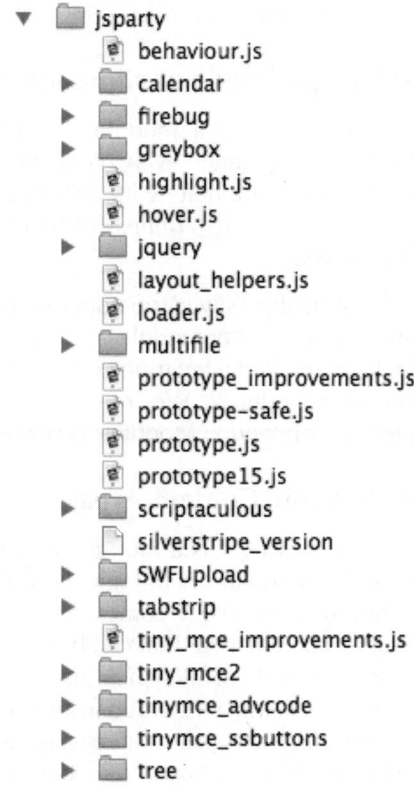

Figure 3.13 The *jsparty/* folder.

The *jsparty/* folder contains these libraries, most importantly the *jQuery* framework with its plugins and interface components, which are used throughout the CMS, as well as the *TinyMCE* content editor.

3.4.7 Other Folders

Depending on your installation, other folders might exist on the top level. As a general rule, each additional module will be contained in at least one folder on your webroot. In the default installation, the *googlesitemaps/* folder contains a module for rendering your sitemap in XML format.

3.5 Modules and Widgets

In SilverStripe-speak, both *modules* and *widgets* are folders that contains encapsulated functionality, for example a blog module or a new form field for editing tags. In other systems, this concept might be called a *plugin* or *extension*.

3.5.1 Modules: Encapsulated Functionality

There's not much to a module in SilverStripe from an architectural perspective. In general, every collection of files in a folder on your webroot can be a module, with only one requirement: The folder needs to contain a file called *_config.php*. Strictly speaking, the *cms/* folder is a module as well.

Have a look at http://silverstripe.org/modules/ for a list of existing modules for SilverStripe. Further modules, mostly in earlier stages of development, can be found in the SilverStripe code repository at http://open.silverstripe.com/browser/modules/. We introduce you to a few useful modules in Chapter 13, 'Appendix: Module overview'.

3.5.2 Widgets: Dynamic Content Areas

Technically, a *widget* is a module as well: It's contained in a top level folder and can contain PHP logic as well as templates and images. The distinction in terminology comes from its more limited use: Widgets are specialized content areas that can be dynamically added to your page via drag&drop in the CMS. A typical use case is a sidebar in your template, which might contain a tag cloud from your blog posts, latest comments – depending on which page the user is viewing. Widgets usually have a limited set of configuration parameters that can be set through the CMS.

Popular widgets are listed on http://silverstripe.org/widgets/.

3.5.3 Installing

Installing both modules and widgets is fairly easy: Just copy a new folder into your webroot and let SilverStripe do its magic. Currently SilverStripe doesn't provide a graphical interface for downloading and managing modules.

Of course, you have to consult the documentation for a specific module, but in general a module installation works as follows:

- Download the module as an archive or check it out from version control.
- Extract the archive into your webroot. The new folder with your module should now be on the same level as *cms/* or *sapphire/*, and have at least one file in it: *_config.php*.
- To tell SilverStripe about the newly available classes and potentially add new tables and columns for the module's data, please refresh the database by calling *http://localhost/dev/build* in your browser.

All classes contained within the module's PHP files should now become automatically available for your own usage, without the necessity to include them in your code. If the module defined new page types, they will show up in the CMS without any further required action. Depending on the module, you might need to explicitly enable its features – please refer to the module documentation for details on how to do this. The *README* file within the module folder is a good start for these instructions.

3.5.4 Uninstalling

Removing a module works just the same: Delete the module folder and refresh the database again. If the module created any database tables that are no longer needed, they'll be marked with the prefix *_obsolete*. This ensures that any data created with the module isn't discarded without your explicit action. If you deleted the module by accident, the data will still be around after you manually rename the table.

3.6 Themes

As mentioned in the earlier Section 3.4, 'Directory Structure', themes form the view role in the MVC design pattern. A theme mainly consists of templates, images, and stylesheets; every part that's necessary to represent your website data to the end user. Ideally a simple configuration change is enough to give your output a completely different look without modifying any PHP by switching to a different theme. Following the MVC pattern, a separate theme directory also provides a better distinction of responsibilities: Designers don't have to deal with PHP code, and developers can focus on the data rather than its presentation.

A theme needs at least one folder within the *themes/* top level directory. This folder name is used to identify the theme throughout the framework.

Have a look at the standard *BlackCandy* themes in *themes/blackcandy/* to get an impression of the structure (see Figure 3.14).

A theme can have multiple *sub-themes*. In addition to *themes/blackcandy/*, you will find a blog-specific folder *themes/blackcandy_blog/*. This is handy for extending an existing theme, because it allows module authors to distribute their templates separately from the theme itself. SilverStripe automatically chooses the most specific template available.

In Figure 3.14, two other themes are listed: 'PaddyGreen' and 'DarkShades'. A SilverStripe project can have more than one theme on the filesystem in parallel, but only one of them can be active for rendering the output.

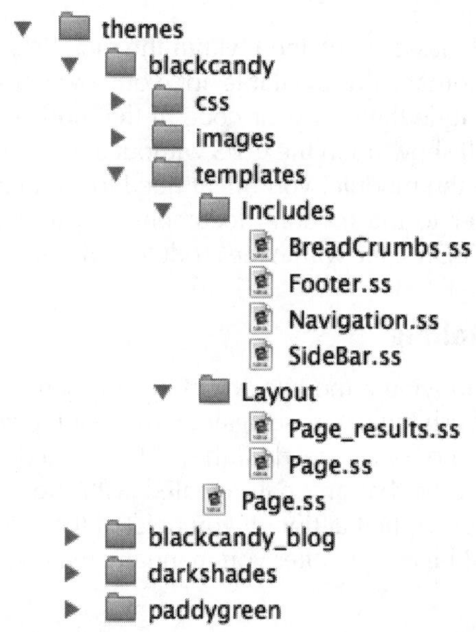

Figure 3.14 Themes folder structure.

Choosing the active theme can be performed in *mysite/_config.php*:

```
SSViewer::set_theme('paddygreen');
```

This activates the theme contained in *themes/paddygreen/*. Most likely, your *_config.php* already has an `SSViewer::set_theme()` directive that you can adjust.

3.7 Configuration

When configuring SilverStripe, you'll mostly find yourself writing simple PHP statements, rather than using a graphical interface. This is a conscious design decision in SilverStripe, and usually seen as an advantage rather than a shortcoming. SilverStripe tries to keep the complexity of configuration away from the typical CMS editor. For developers and administrators, it tries to stay out of their way by allowing configuration through PHP rather than clumsy interfaces. Examples of PHP-based configuration might be choosing a theme or setting the email address of the system administrator.

This paradigm of course excludes certain user-level configuration such as the language you want to display the CMS interface, because every user should be able to pick this herself.

Most of your configuration will go into *mysite/_config.php*. As mentioned before, every module can have its own *_config.php*. These files are the only place in SilverStripe-land where you're allowed to place procedural code that's not encapsulated in a class definition. All *_config.php* files are included on every application call, so all PHP code contained in them gets executed: A desired scenario for configuring the application. This also means that you can have conditional blocks in normal PHP syntax to switch between different settings based on certain factors such as the requested domain.

The downside of PHP-based configuration is that there's no complete documentation of all available configuration settings within sapphire or a specific module. Potentially, every public method or property on a class can be used as a configuration option. We list some of the most common settings in Table 3.1.

Table 3.1 Common configuration settings.

Setting	Description
global $project; $project='<project-name>';	Set the project name. This should match your custom folder name, usually "mysite".
$databaseConfig = array("type" => " ", "server" => " ",	Your database credentials, usually set through the SilverStripe installer. type: The database driver, defaults to "mysql".

(*continued overleaf*)

Table 3.1 *(continued)*

Setting	Description
"username" => " ",	server: Hostname, defaults to "localhost"
"password" => " ",	username/password: Your database credentials
"database" => " ",);	database: Name of your database.
Director:: set environment type (<mode>);	Defines the environment mode. Allowed modes are "dev", "test", and "live". See Chapter 8. Section 8.1, 'Environment Types'.
Director:: set dev servers (array(<domain>));	Set specific domain names or IP addresses to be automatically set into 'development mode'.
PageComment:: enableModeration();	Require approval from a CMS editor before a page comment is shown on your website.
Security:: setDefaultAdmin (<user>,<password>);	Set a default user that doesn't need an account in the database.
SSViewer:: set theme(<themename>);	Set the website theme.
Debug::send errors to (<email-address>);	Send all error notifications to this email address.
Email::setAdminEmail (<email-address>);	Specify the administrator email that should appear as the default sender of system emails, as well as the default receiver of system notifications.

For a more exhaustive list of available settings, please refer to the SilverStripe documentation at http://doc.silverstripe.com/doku.php?id=configuration. You might also want to have a look at the API documentation of a specific class to find potential configuration options through http://api.silverstripe.com/.

You can also configure certain parameters across multiple instances of SilverStripe by a so-called *_ss_environment.php* file. See Chapter 8, Section 8.1, 'Environment Types' for more details on this topic.

3.8 Conclusion

This chapter introduced the concepts of *Model View Controller, Object Relational Mapping,* and their implementation in SilverStripe. A basic understanding of how class inheritance is used both in page types and their templates is crucial to understanding the framework. Although you don't need to worry about database concerns most of the time, it's definitely good to know how objects relate to database tables and their rows.

We also clarified what *modules, widgets*, and *themes* mean in SilverStripe-land, concepts that we will refer to in the next chapter, for example when installing the blog module into our standard SilverStripe package.

The couple of configuration parameters listed in this chapter are just a glimpse of what's possible with the framework, but they should be enough to get you started.

Don't worry if some of these concepts are still a bit confusing, things will get clearer when we start to use them on practical examples. After all this theory, we can finally move on to using the shiny new SilverStripe project you have set up in Chapter 2. Have fun!

4
First Steps

After all the theory of the first three chapters, let's now get our hands dirty. In the pages to come we will create our very first example application.

In this chapter we primarily focus on typical CMS functions. You will learn how to use basic functions, create pages, edit page content, and do some very lightweight coding. Refer to http://userhelp.silverstripe.com/ for a complete guide of CMS backend features. In Chapters 5 'Development' and 6 'CRM', we then venture into deeper waters and extend our example application with custom PHP and HTML code.

4.1 Our Project: Job Portal and User Group

It's not easy to find a good example application to build, because it must cover all relevant parts that encompass a content management system like SilverStripe.

Therefore, what could be a better example than to use the SilverStripe community itself as a starting point? So we build a website that allows SilverStripe developers and contractors to search for and communicate with each other.

Before we get to the practical part, let's discuss the structure of the pages. How should our application look and what should it be able to do?

The following requirements outline the functionality of the application and also reflect the rest of the content of this book.

4.1.1 Display of Static Pages

Our web application should obviously be able to display 'static' pages. By 'static'; we mean text and images that are non-interactive to the public. While they will be managed and editable easily via the CMS, this content will not be changed frequently. Contrast this to news or blog pages that change frequently or can be interacted with by public visitors. However, from a technical perspective the 'static' pages aren't exactly static. Such pages are created by dynamically running PHP and accessing the database rather than serving a static .html file found on the file system.

In our example application we want to provide documents containing general information about the web application.

4.1.2 Comments

Visitors to our website should be able to comment on individual pages. Comments should take a form well known from blogs.

4.1.3 Contact Form

The website should contain a 'contact us' form. SilverStripe has two approaches to forms: the *userforms* module that allows non-technical people to build simple forms, and a set of PHP classes that let developers build more complex and integrated forms. Both approaches are discussed in this book.

4.1.4 Registration and Authentication

A user registration system is a prerequisite for a job portal, because we only want to give authenticated users access to certain parts of the website.

4.1.5 Catalog of Job Posting

The heart of our application is the management of job postings. Non-registered users can use this catalog to browse for open positions. To aid their discovery each job posting should belong to a specific category.

Registered users should be able to post adverts quickly and easily for open positions.

4.1.6 User Group

By providing access to the job postings, we have already opened a channel of communication between the job seekers and companies offering the positions. However, we want to take this one step further and reverse the channel. That is: The seeker should be given the ability to display his or her own profile. Companies can use these profiles to gather preliminary information about the skills and experience of potential new employees and approach them directly.

Now that you know what will be described in the course of this book we can finally focus on beginning actual work on the project. We assume you have a 'fresh' install of SilverStripe with the standard *BlackCandy* theme installed on your system (see Figure 4.1).

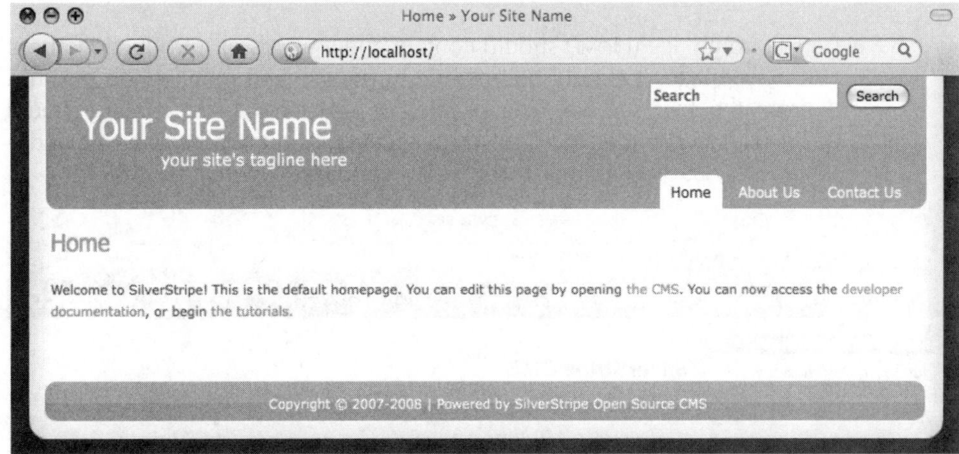

Figure 4.1 SilverStripe front page using *BlackCandy* theme.

If you wish to preview the final result of the development we're going to undertake throughout this chapter, you can do so by viewing the completed project in the *4_first_steps/* folder from the book website. In the *4_first_steps/database.sql* folder you will find an export of the database. You can use database management tools such as *phpMyAdmin* to import this database into your own system. The database will now be pre-configured with an administrator account. Log into this account using the username 'admin' and password 'password'.

4.2 Creating the Page Structure

We now start thinking about the detailed structure and content of the website. However before we do so, let's look and see what SilverStripe has already created for us. Open the front page of your SilverStripe installation at http://localhost/.

You can see three pages already present in the navigation bar of the website: Home, About Us, and Contact Us. (These default pages are created by a fresh install of SilverStripe to make it easier to evaluate and understand the system.) Now let's think about which pages we need for *our* website.

Our job portal should have the following navigational structure:

- Home
- Jobs
- Developers
- Contact

The front page (HOME) should contain a few words of introduction about the webpage. It should be possible to browse and manage job postings from the JOBS section. The profiles of registered programmers should be managed under the DEVELOPERS section. Additionally you will find a CONTACT US as well as an ABOUT US section (see Figure 4.2).

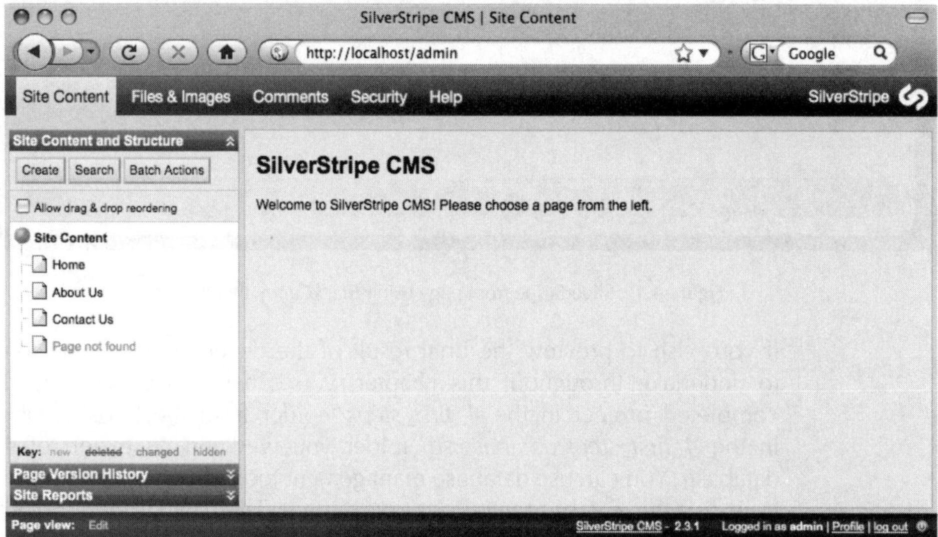

Figure 4.2 SilverStripe CMS after your first login.

4.2.1 The CMS Interface

The first step is to create the site structure using the backend of the SilverStripe system. To do so, please login as the administrator.

The backend is divided into three main areas: the main navigation in the top-most bar, the tree view of pages on the left side, and the content-editing area on the right side, which also contains buttons along the bottom to perform common tasks like saving and publishing pages.

Main Navigation

The main navigation is used to access the basic functions of the system. The contents of webpages can be edited using SITE CONTENT. FILES & IMAGES contains the central document management system, which is used to manage all files referenced in the output pages. COMMENTS is used to manage the comments that users have left on various pages. SECURITY contains the user-management interface. Finally, HELP gives access to the SilverStripe user-guide.

Tree View

Similar to many other content management systems, in SilverStripe you can create and manage pages using a tree view. The framework uses this structure to automatically create the navigation for the website.

At the moment our 'tree' doesn't contain any hierarchy. However, this will soon change. At the moment we have the HOME, ABOUT US, and CONTACT US pages. We will address the PAGE NOT FOUND page a bit later on.

In order to create our desired website structure we need to alter and expand the existing page structure.

4.2.2 First Changes

The first page HOME can stay as it is, because our front page should also use the name HOME (see Figure 4.3). Very nice.

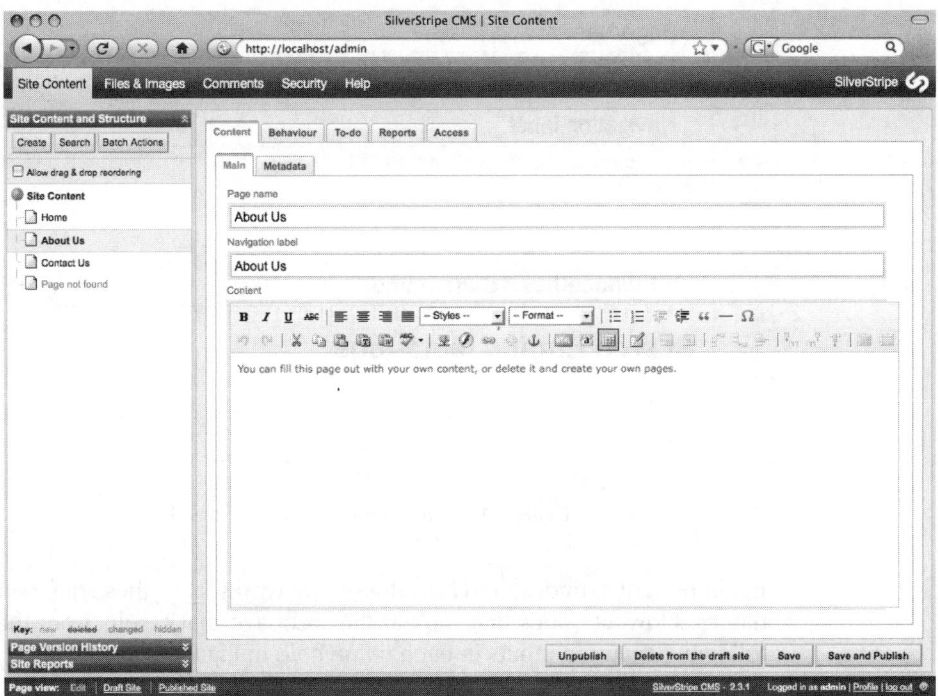

Figure 4.3 SilverStripe backend – Content editing form.

The second page should be called Jobs. This will be our first modification of the existing content. We will use the existing About Us page. That way we will not need to change the sort-order later. Select the About Us page. You will see a number of options for editing the contents and behavior of the page:

The main area is divided into several tabs. To begin with we will concern ourselves with only two of them. These are the Main and Metadata tabs under the Content section.

First we rename the About Us page into 'Jobs'. We will discuss the programming of the logic for the page in the next chapter.

About URLs, Names, Titles, and Navigation labels

SilverStripe works with a total of three different names for a page: Page name, Navigation label, and Title. These names are managed using the Main and Metadata tabs (see Figure 4.4).

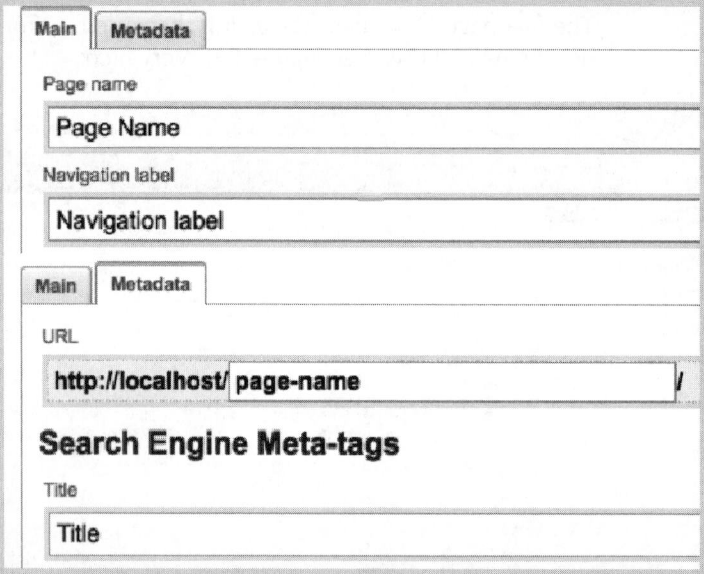

Figure 4.4 Page information in the backend.

It is important to understand how the system works using these different names. However, let's first look at the webpage that results from the following example inputs in each name field in Figure 4.5:

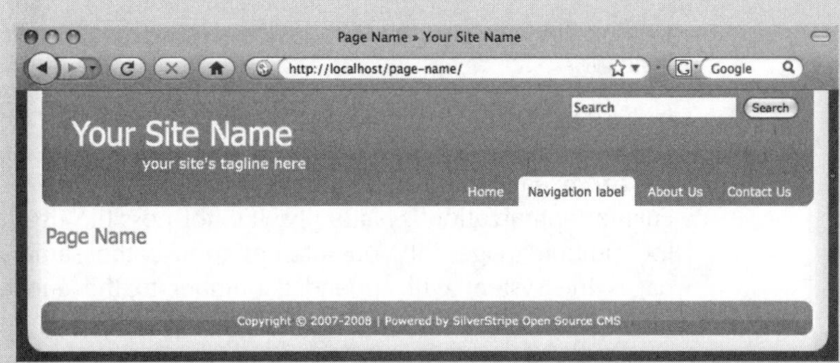

Figure 4.5 Page information in the frontend.

Page Name

This parameter gives the title to a page (dependent on the exact template used, of course). In the *BlackCandy* theme this title is wrapped with a `<h2>` tag. If this field is left blank the value in the NAVIGATION LABEL field is used instead.

URL

SilverStripe, much to the delight of search engines the world over, exclusively uses self-describing, parameterless URLs for its pages. You can access these URLs using the METADATA tab. The system tries to match the page names as closely as possible. As soon as you change the page name and switch to the METADATA tab, SilverStripe queries you whether you want to change the URL to match or keep it as it was. In our case, if we answer the pop-up query with 'yes' after changing the page name to 'Jobs', this will lead to the URL http://localhost/jobs/.

Unfortunately, SilverStripe currently cannot create 'deep' URLs. That is, URLs only exist in a single hierarchical level. However, multi-level hierarchies for URLs is a feature currently being worked on.

Navigation Label

This field is used to generate the labels on navigational links. This is true for the frontend, as well as the backend interface. If this field is left blank, the value from the PAGE NAME field is used instead.

Title

The title of the page can be accessed using the METADATA tab. This value is used exclusively to generate the TITLE tag of the page. If no value is specified for the title, the Page Name field is once again used instead.

Note: It is possible to give the same name to multiple pages. However, this practice is not recommended, even if only because of issues of search engine optimization (see Chapter 5, Section 5.9, 'Search Engine Optimization'). Naturally, it's not possible use the same URL for multiple pages. If you attempt to use the same URL for two pages the system will append a number to the end of one of the URLs.

If you have not done so already, please click on the Page Name field and enter 'Jobs' there. Then correct the URL on the Metadata tab to match. You can either delete the Navigation label field or also change that to 'Jobs'. Both actions have the same result.

You can keep the changes using the Save or Save and Publish buttons on the bottom-right corner of the screen. The difference is that Save creates a private draft copy and Save and Publish immediately makes the changes publicly visible. For now, just click Save and Publish.

Please create the Developers page in the same way as we did for the Jobs page. Do so by renaming the Contact Us page shown in Figure 4.6.

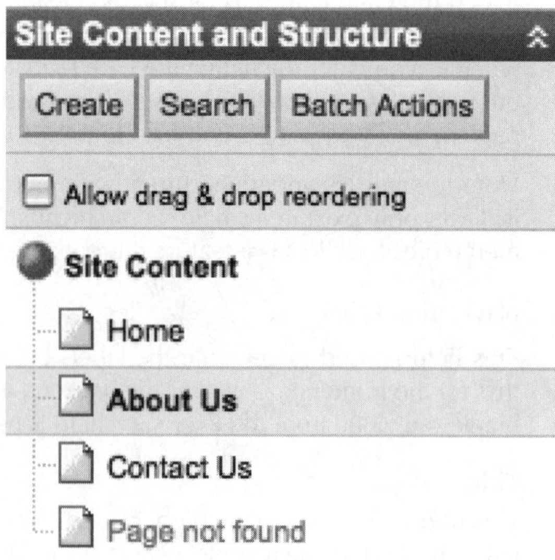

Figure 4.6 Page tree.

4.2.3 Creating a New Page

One more thing needs to be done: We need a contact page. To do this we need to create a new page in the tree under the Site Content and Structure section (see Figure 4.7).

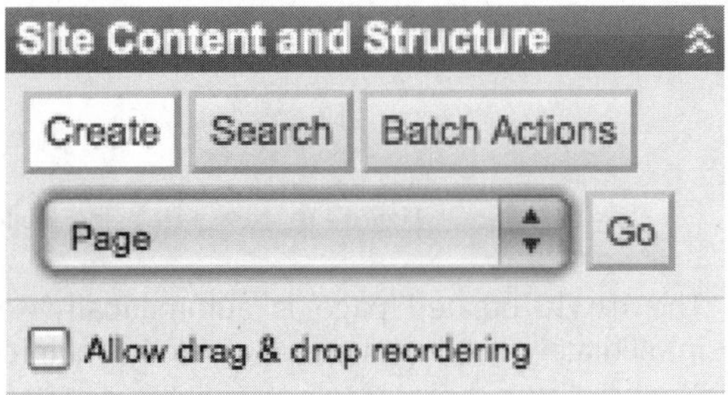

Figure 4.7 Create new page.

Creating a new page is simple. Just click the Create button and a drop-down menu will appear where you can select the page type.

As you might remember from Chapter 3, 'Architecture', Page is the standard page type for a regular HTML pages. We will look at the page type in more detail in the next section.

In order to create a page, please select the page type Page. Now we need to tell the backend system where the new page should be located. To do this click the spot in the tree view below which you want to create the new page. Since we want to create the new page on the same level of the hierarchy as our other pages, we need to select the top-level: Site Content (see Figure 4.8).

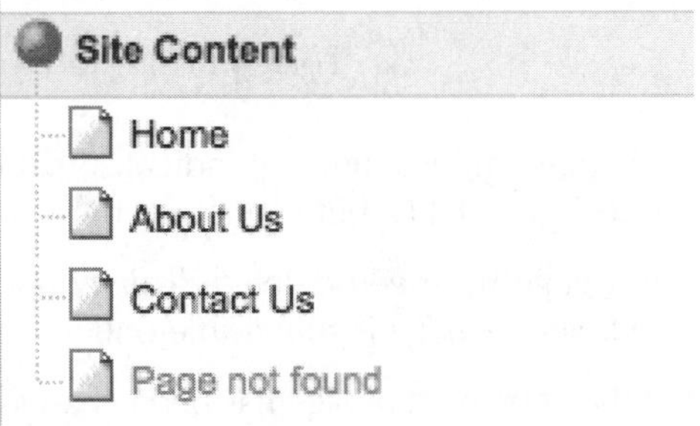

Figure 4.8 Selecting the top-level.

Now click the Go button. A new page will be created below the Site Content element and at the same level as all the other existing pages (see Figure 4.9).

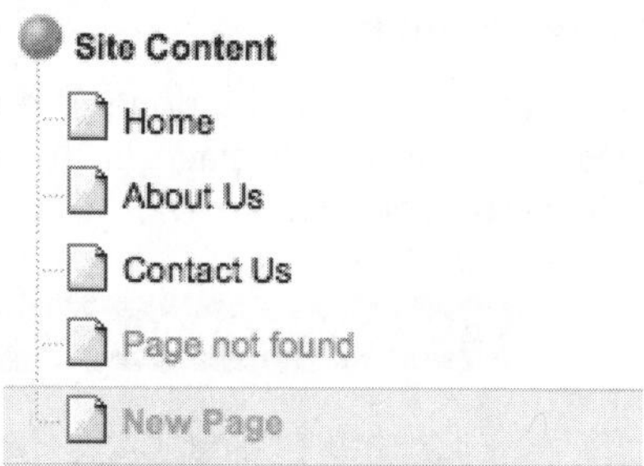

Figure 4.9 New page below the top-level.

The newly created page is automatically selected, so that you can immediately enter data directly into the main content area of the page.

4.2.4 Draft and Publishing

Before we start entering new data, let's take a brief look at SilverStripe's draft feature. You have already encountered the choice between the SAVE and SAVE AND PUBLISH buttons. SilverStripe allows you to save a draft. This draft is only visible to the CMS-editors. Under the hood the SilverStripe system saves each change as a new version. So, a page can exist in parallel in a published and draft version. This feature is automatically available for all page types. It is the foundation for a simple *Workflow* system that allows multiple editors to collaboratively build a website.

You may have already noticed that the newly created page is colored orange. Let's check the legend at the bottom of the tree view to see what this signifies (shown in Figure 4.10).

Figure 4.10 Page tree – legend.

- Orange signifies 'new'. It indicates that the page is existing as a draft (see Figure 4.11), but cannot yet be seen by visitors to the website.
- If a page has been deleted, it first appears crossed out and colored red. Such a page is still visible online.
- If the content of a page has been changed, but the change has not yet been published, the page is colored green in the tree view.

Figure 4.11 Link to the draft version of the website.

The principle here is that if the page has any color other than black, the draft contains different content than is published and visible online.

You can preview changes even if they haven't been published yet. To do so click the DRAFT SITE page view link near to the bottom-left corner of the screen. You'll notice that the URL for a draft page is almost the same as a published page: it just has *?stage=Stage* at the end.

The new, but not yet published, page is already visible in the draft view.

Using Staging

Now we understand what the orange-colored page names signify. You can rename the new page to 'Contact', and then click on SAVE AND PUBLISH button.

Figure 4.12 Save, Publish, or Delete current changes.

The name of the page in the tree view now changes its color to black to indicate that the page has been published and is now visible online (see Figure 4.12).

If you had clicked on SAVE instead of SAVE AND PUBLISH the changes would have gone into a draft and the orange color would have remained. The DELETE FROM THE DRAFT SITE button would have deleted the page completely.

4.2.5 Drag and Drop Page Reorganisation

We have now created our first new page. If you haven't selected anything else in the mean time this new page should still be selected in the tree view.

If you were now to click the GO button again, this would create a new sub-page under the existing new page. So, please first select the top-level (SITE CONTENT) before creating another new page.

If you wish to change the order or arrangement of any of the pages in the tree view, you can do so at any time by checking the ALLOW DRAG & DROP reordering checkbox and using the mouse to drag and drop pages around (see Figure 4.13).

A page can be moved between two existing ones by starting to drag it and dropping it between the two pages. If you drag and drop a page on top of an existing page, it will be moved to become a sub-page of that page. Sub-pages can, of course, easily be moved back to a higher level. Please order the pages as we have discussed before.

Figure 4.13 Moving pages using drag&drop.

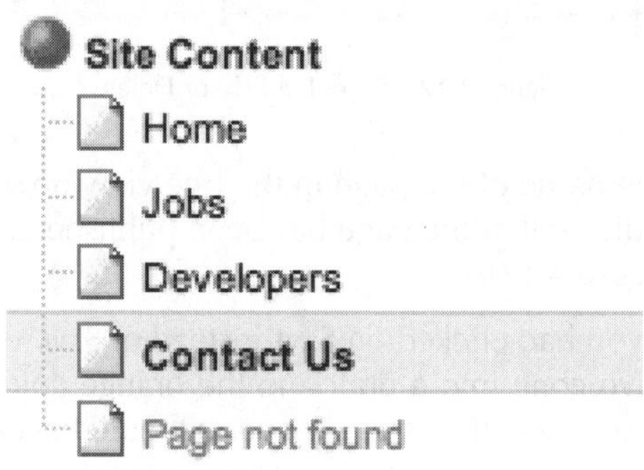

Figure 4.14 Page types.

Now we have created all the pages necessary for our project (see Figure 4.14).

4.2.6 Page Types

Up until now we have not created any special functionality for pages. We have only created pages with the default PAGE page type.

The page type determines which layout and program logic a page uses. As you may remember from Chapter 3, 'Architecture', each page type has a single corresponding MVC definition as PHP code that we'll look at in the next chapter. So, the page type is the mechanism the website editor can use to bridge between the CMS and the MVC-framework.

The page type is set when a page is created, but it can later be changed using the BEHAVIOUR tab.

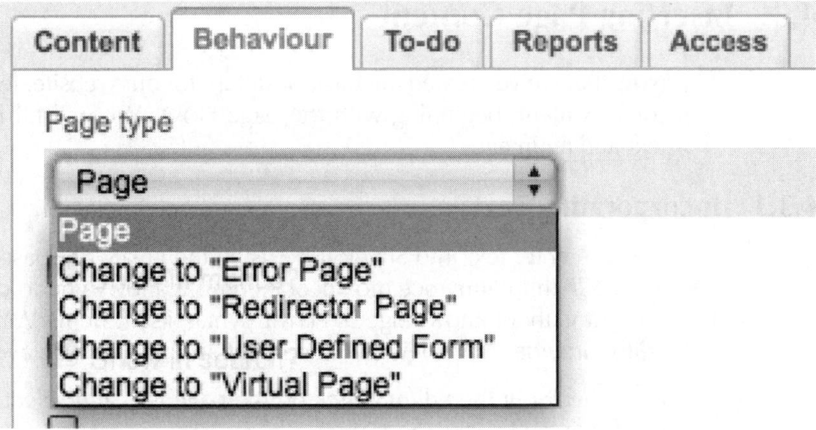

Figure 4.15 SilverStripe – page types.

SilverStripe includes the following page types by default (see Figure 4.15). As you'll learn later, it is very easy and common to create more page types.

Page

Page is the basis for a page to display content to visitors to the website.

Redirector Page

A Redirector Page isn't really a page. It redirects to another page. The Redirector Page creates a direct conduit from itself to the page to which it's redirecting. Requests for the former are automatically passed onto the latter. Chapter 5, Section 5.9.5, 'Metatags' elaborates on SEO and technical issues of Redirector Page.

Virtual Page

A Virtual Page is a copy of another page. The Virtual Page has its own URL, but all content is taken from the original page.

Error Page

You may have noticed the Page not found page in the Site Content tree view. This page has the Error Page page type. As you might imagine, this page is a page that displays an error message. The most common error message will be one with HTTP status code *404 Not Found*. Such errors can be intercepted and displayed with a custom error message. HTTP status codes from 400 to 505 can be intercepted and customized.

4.3 Inserting Page Content

Now that we've created the basic structure for our website, let's fill it with some content, beginning with the page Home. We will fill it with some text and an image.

4.3.1 Incorporating Text

You can enter text into SilverStripe using the JavaScript-based text editor *TinyMCE* (http://tinymce.moxiecode.com). It allows you to create HTML content without knowledge of HTML syntax itself. Being WYSIWYG, the editor provides a preview of the content as it will be displayed later.

Let's check out the editor: Click on the page tree and select Home. Now select the tab Content > Main.

Up until now we've only used the Page name and Navigation label fields. Below that you'll notice the large input field with the example text from the default installation (if you haven't already deleted this text).

You can format this text using the *TinyMCE toolbar,* which is situated above the text (see Figure 4.16).

Figure 4.16 *TinyMCE* toolbar.

Most likely, you're already familiar with most of the icons on the toolbar from using various word processing applications. We will therefore only go over the most important of the options. All icons have *tooltips*, and so just hover the mouse over an icon to learn more about its function.

The first line of the toolbar contains the standard formatting and alignment options. You can also use it to create lists (ordered and unordered), dividing lines, and special characters.

Figure 4.17 *TinyMCE's* clipboard operations.

The second line contains various operations specific to the web. Let's take a look at the clipboard operations (see Figure 4.17). You can use these to, for example, paste in text from applications such as Microsoft Word or OpenOffice.

These operations will be of interest to editors who prefer to write text in traditional word processing applications. Such text can be copied to the clipboard and pasted into the SilverStripe system using one of the following operations.

Paste

This inserts the contents directly from the clipboard in the text area. Various special characters present in the clipboard can potentially lead to problems, which can be avoided by removing all special characters before inserting the text. SilverStripe tries hard to preserve heading styles in pasted content, however your milage will vary depending on the content and your browser.

Paste as Plain Text

The icon with the 'T' symbol pastes text from the clipboard as well, however only as plain text. That is, it removes all non-text symbols from the pasted text like list stylings or colored text. This operation is useful when you want to reformat text in *TinyMCE* that has already been formatted in another application.

Paste from Word

TinyMCE offers a special operation that allows text to be pasted from Microsoft Word. This operation deals correctly with Word-specific symbols and formatting markup. To use this operation click the icon with the 'W' symbol.

Text for our Home Page

Let's now create text for the Home page in a word processing application and paste that into SilverStripe (see Figure 4.18).

In this example we will create text in the freely available OpenOffice word processing application (http://openoffice.org/). Let your creative juices flow freely and create a short introduction text for our Job portal. Copy this text into the clipboard and switch to the SilverStripe backend in your web-browser.

Now paste the text into the text area using the basic Paste operation (text formatted in OpenOffice can be pasted directly without using any special functions) (see Figure 4.19).

TinyMCE should be able to recognize all the formatting and markup and convert it to the web-based view.

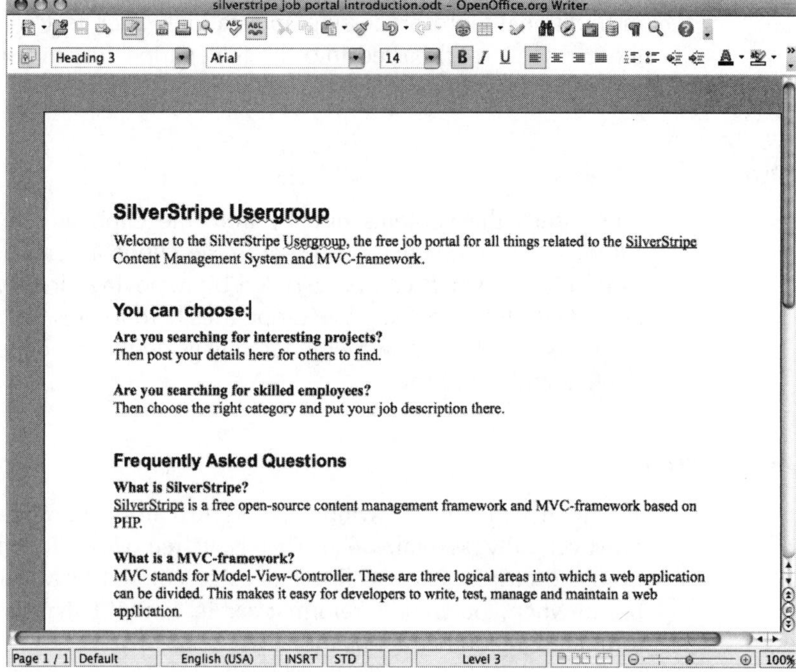

Figure 4.18 Creating text in OpenOffice.

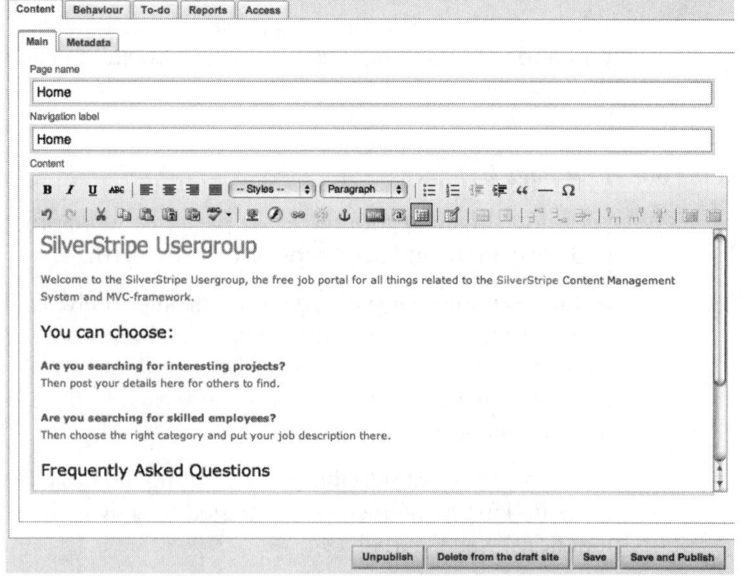

Figure 4.19 Pasting text from OpenOffice.

4.3.2 Hyperlinks

Our text has a few sections that we want to link to specific pages within the website.

To add a hyperlink, highlight the relevant text in the text area (see Figure 4.20).

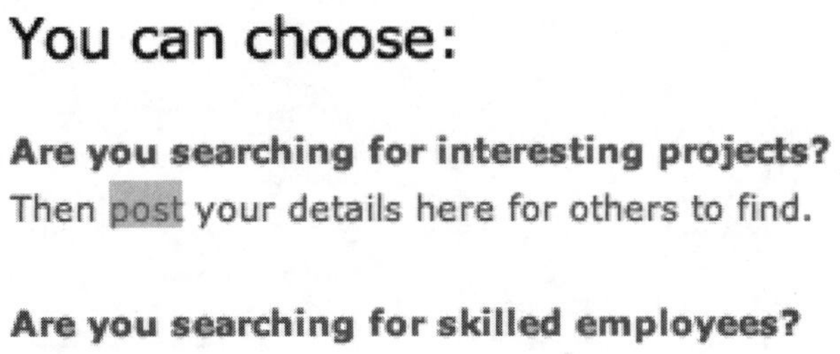

You can choose:

Are you searching for interesting projects?

Then post your details here for others to find.

Are you searching for skilled employees?

Figure 4.20 Adding a link.

Locate the link icon in the toolbar (see Figure 4.21).

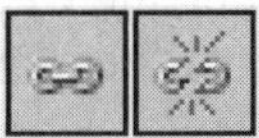

Figure 4.21 Marking text in order to add or remove a link.

Click on the chain-link icon. A new box will open on the right-side of the screen (see Figure 4.22).

This box allows you to set various options for the link. The following options are available.

Page on the Site

This option creates a link to another page already present in the system. An internal link like this will continue to function if you rename the page that is being linked to.

Another Website

This option creates a (static) link to an external URL.

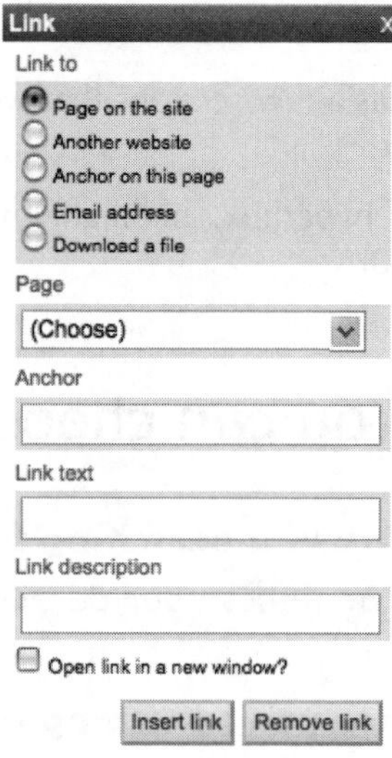

Figure 4.22 Inserting a link.

Anchor on this Page

With this option you can create a link to an anchor tag within the current page. A user visiting the website can use this kind of link to, for example, jump to a section farther down the page.

Email Address

Use this option to insert an email address. This inserts a `mailto:` link which automatically opens an email client on most systems.

Warning: The link to an email address is not encoded. It can therefore easily be read by harvesters that scour the Internet looking for email addresses to bombard with spam. Please use this feature with care.

Download a File

Use this option to create a link to a file that has been uploaded to the system. Uploading files into SilverStripe is explained in the next chapter.

Since we want to link to the Developers page, choose the radio button labeled Page on the site. Use the drop-down box to select the target webpage. Write 'view the developer profiles' into the link description box. This text will be shown as the tooltip when the user hovers his or her mouse over the link. We don't have to enter anything under Anchor, because we haven't specified any anchors yet. We don't want the link to open in a new window, and so we can leave that checkbox unchecked. Now click the button to insert the link.

4.3.3 HTML View

The marked text is now underlined. Let's now quickly check the HTML that *TinyMCE* has generated. To do this, click the HTML button in the *TinyMCE* toolbar (see Figure 4.23).

Figure 4.23 Displaying the HTML view.

The window now displays the HTML equivalent of the text in the editor window (see Figure 4.24).

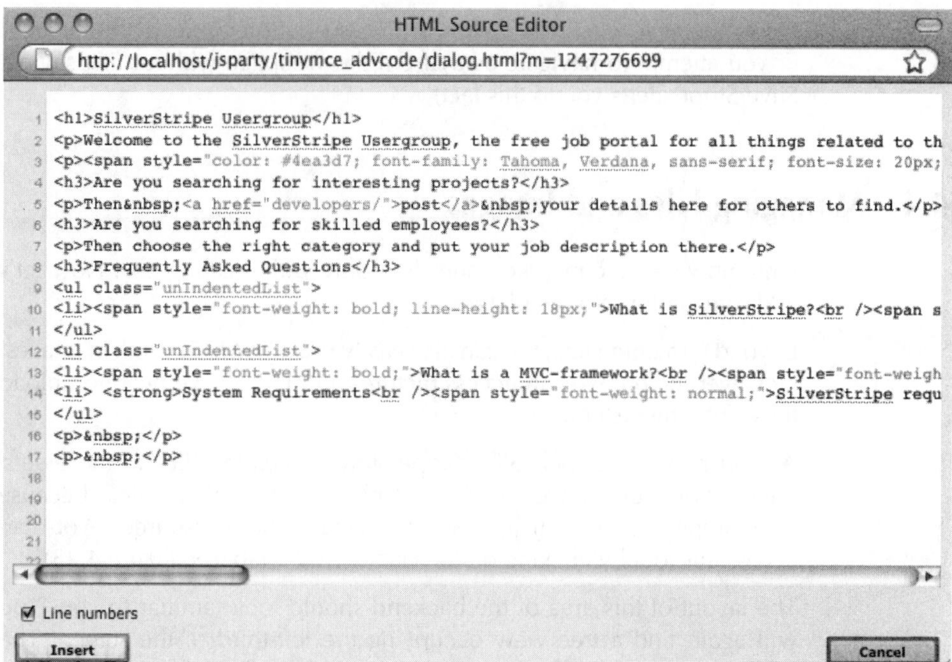

Figure 4.24 HTML view.

As you can see, the link description has been transferred to the title attribute of the link. You can edit the HTML source code. For example, if you wish to remove the link, you can do so by deleting the relevant tag from the HTML. However, it's easier to simply use the *TinyMCE* view. In that view, click the icon of the broken chain-link and that will remove the link.

Valid (X)HTML

TinyMCE tries to create XHTML compliant HTML code. If you manually edit the HTML code, *TinyMCE* may rewrite your code behind the scenes. Moreover, only defined tags are accepted. So, if you use tags that *TinyMCE* doesn't understand, these can lead to unspecified behavior.

However, don't despair, *TinyMCE* can easily be adapted to meet special requirements. See the *TinyMCE* developer webpage at http://tinymcemoxiecode.com/.

Don't forget to click the SAVE AND PUBLISH button to keep the changes (if you attempt to navigate away from the webpage without first saving, SilverStripe alerts you to this fact).

4.4 Managing Files and Images

Until now we've concerned ourselves only with creating text. Now let's add some color into the picture.

Beyond formatting text, we can also easily use *TinyMCE* to link in images. However, before we can access pictures and images we need to upload these into the system.

As you may remember, SilverStripe stores uploaded files in the *assets/* folder. You don't have to use FTP program to upload files, because SilverStripe has its own interface to manage these resources. You can access this tool by clicking on the FILES & IMAGES tab (see Figure 4.25).

The layout of this area of the backend should look familiar to you. You will again find a tree view occupying the left-third of the screen. The folders displayed here correspond to actual folders on the server.

Initially there is only one folder: the */uploads* folder. Click on this folder and the main area on the right-hand side displays information about the files contained within. This area also contains the following tabs: FILES, DETAILS, UPLOAD, and UNUSED FILES.

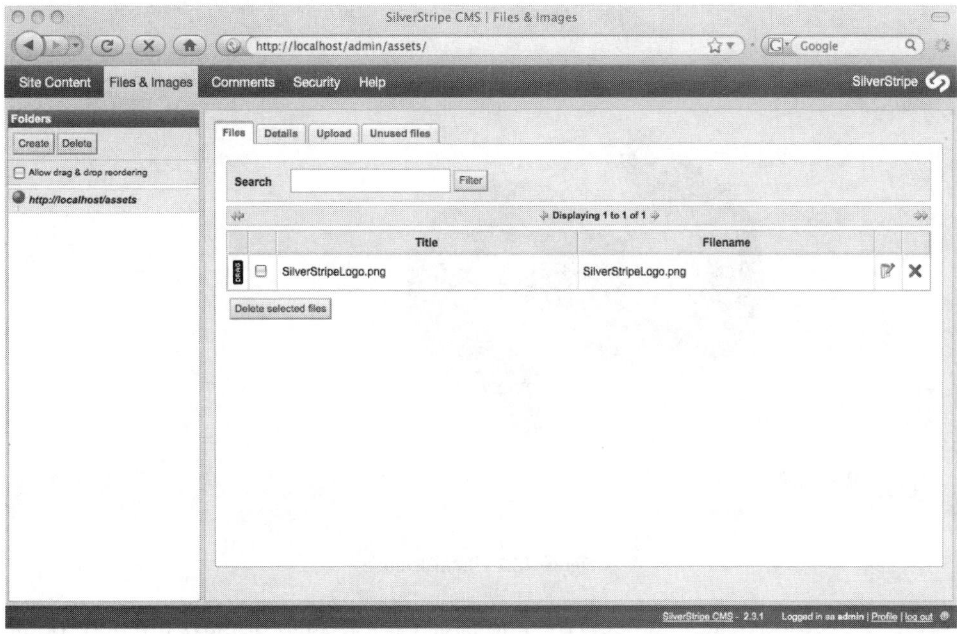

Figure 4.25 Managing files and images.

4.4.1 Viewing and Editing Files

As you might expect, if you click on the FILES tab you see the files in the currently selected folder. At the moment the */uploads* folder should contain only the *SilverStripeLogo.png* file.

You can use the interface to view the file TITLE and FILENAME, as well as to edit and/or delete the resource (see Figure 4.26).

Figure 4.26 Editing or deleting files.

Editing

Clicking on the edit icon brings up a pop-up window. Various metadata is displayed in this window. The exact metadata displayed depends on the filetype. For images you get a preview in addition to the file metadata. To access this preview click the IMAGE tab (see Figure 4.27).

Under the MAIN tab you can edit metadata such as Title, Filename, and Owner (the person who uploaded the file into the system). You can also view file information such as FIRST UPLOADED, LAST CHANGED (last file

Figure 4.27 IMAGE tab.

modification time), TYPE, and SIZE. The LINKS tab displays a report. of all the pages that use this particular file.

Delete

To delete multiple files quickly, you can select the files you wish to delete using the checkboxes in front of each filename and then click the DELETE SELECTED FILES button.

We now switch to the DETAILS tab. Here you can find general information about the currently selected folder (see Figure 4.28).

Moving

You can move files from one folder by dragging the ''drag'' icon and dropping it on the desired location within the folder tree.

4.4.2 Uploading Files

The third tab is interesting: UPLOAD. We can use this to add our own files and images into the system. But not so fast, before we begin uploading our own files let's first create a new folder for them.

First select the top-level of the tree view on the left-hand side of the window, and then click CREATE. If you had accidentally left the UPLOADS folder selected, the new folder would have been created as a sub-folder of the UPLOADS folder (sounds familiar, doesn't it?). You can, of course, always use the familiar ALLOW DRAG & DROP REORDERING feature to move folders around, if you make a mistake.

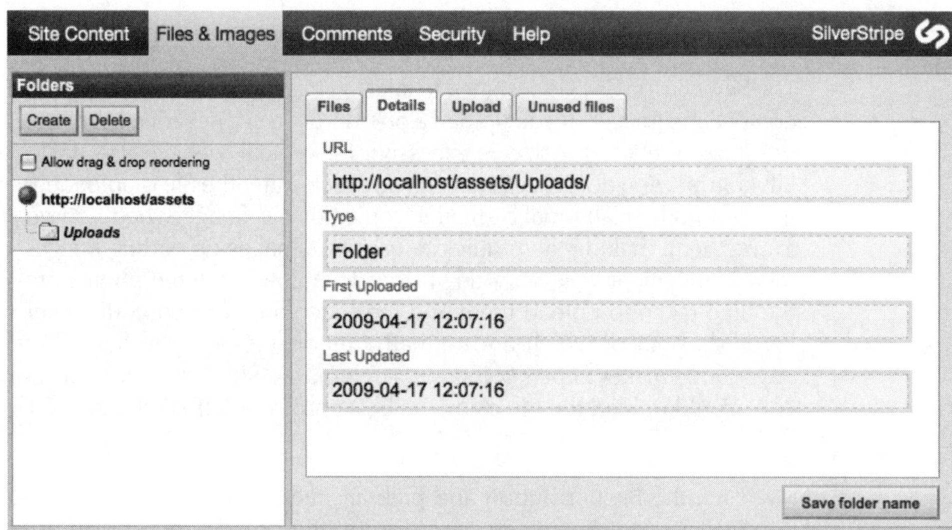

Figure 4.28 File information.

The newly created folder will initially be named *NewFolder*. We should rename it into something more descriptive. Click on the FILES tab to do so.

Type a new name for our folder in the Title field. Let's save our creative energy for later and give the folder the unimaginative 'Images' name. Click the SAVE FOLDER NAME button to keep the change.

Okay, the new folder is created (and hopefully still selected) and we're ready to upload. Please switch to the UPLOAD tab (see Figure 4.29).

Figure 4.29 Selecting images to upload.

Images and file sizes

The SilverStripe CMS is designed to take the hassle away from managing content and images. If you upload a photo from a 10 megapixel camera, the image detail and size is excessive for typical website use. With SilverStripe, you don't need to worry so much. After the file is uploaded, it will automatically make smaller copies of the image when you go to use them, making them quick to use. This makes uploading images more convenient. The only downsides to uploading large photos are the time taken to upload them and the space they use on your server harddisk, both of which are normally minor. Please note that when SilverStripe makes copies of images, it retains the file original format, so you should upload the file using the best choice of GIF, PNG, or JPG.

Now click the BROWSE button and pick an image you would to upload. SilverStripe adds the image to a list of files ready for upload (see Figure 4.30).

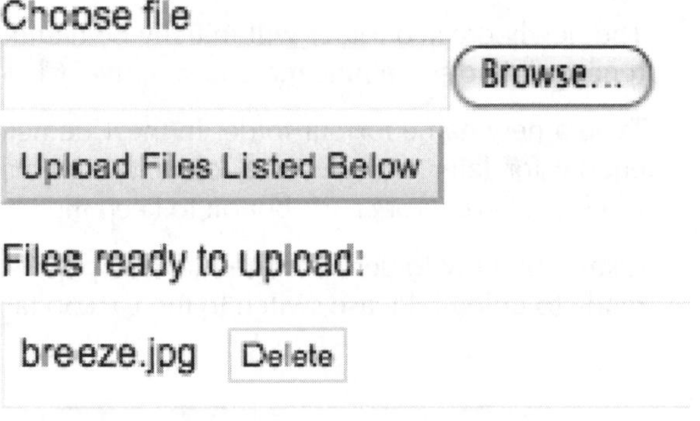

Figure 4.30 Uploading selected files.

We decided to use the *breeze.jpg* file. The used image is licensed under Creative Commons 2.0 Share Alike, and is available at http://www.flickr.com/photos/ronnie44052/539455418. We can add additional files if we want to, but a single image should be enough for now.

You might decide to remove the file you've just marked for upload. To do this merely click the DELETE button next to the unwanted file. Just stick with our file now and click the UPLOAD FILES LISTED BELOW button. All marked files will now be uploaded to the server (see Figure 4.31).

Now, if we click on the FILES tab, we can admire our newly uploaded file in all its glory.

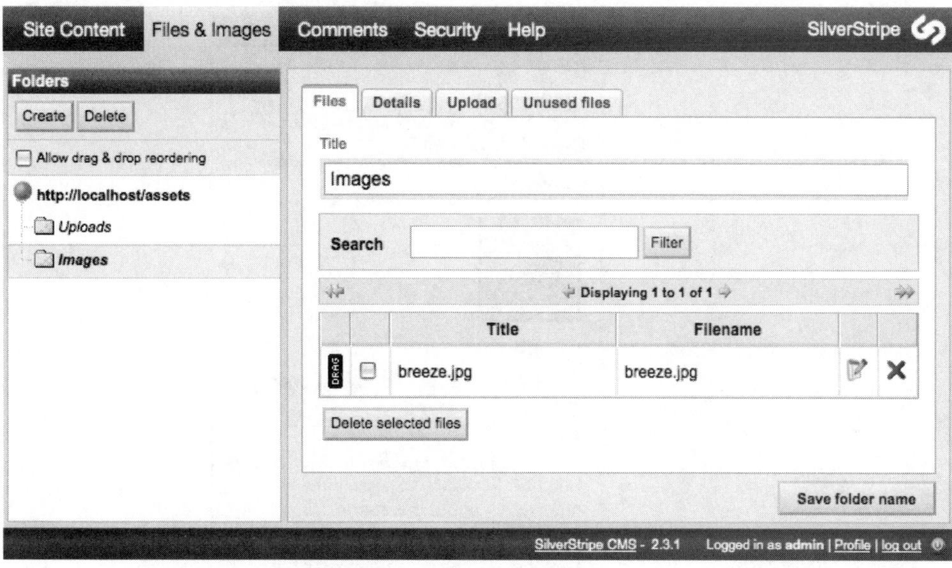

Figure 4.31 Listing of uploaded files.

4.4.3 Inserting an Image into the Content

We want our image to become part of our homepage. To make this happen please switch to the main Site Content tab and select the Home page.

Now go to the Content > Main tab and place the cursor in front of the first heading ('SilverStripe Usergroup' in our case). This is where we want to insert our image. Click the insert image icon in the *TinyMCE* editor (see Figure 4.32).

Figure 4.32 Insert image icon.

The process for inserting images is similar to what you already know from inserting links: a panel opens on the right-hand side of the window. Use the drop-down menu at the top of the panel to select the Images folder. All images in that folder will appear as thumbnail previews.

Since we've only uploaded one image so far, just one thumbnail shows up (see Figure 4.33). Notice the field underneath the image preview. You can use this field to add a description. *TinyMCE* will later use this to add an `alt`-attribute to the image in the HTML.

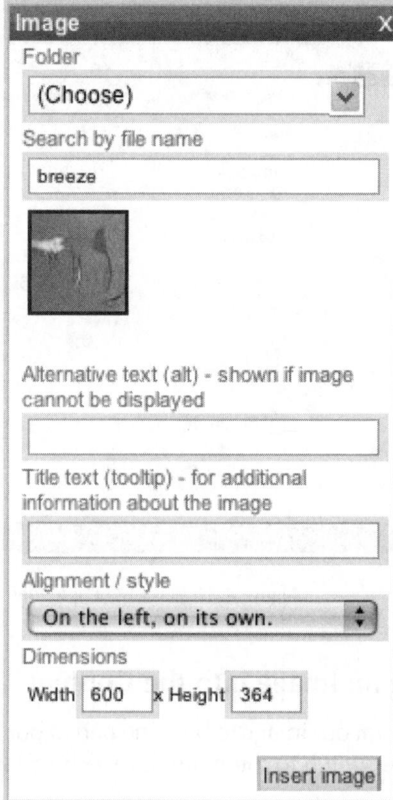

Figure 4.33 Options for inserting an image.

Using the ALIGNMENT/STYLE drop-down, we can choose how to align the image and whether to keep the image on its own or make text flow around it. For now, select ON THE LEFT, ON ITS OWN.

SilverStripe shows you the image's original dimensions. You can easily change these with *TinyMCE* at any time, but leave them unchanged for now.

Now select our picture and click INSERT IMAGE.

Well then, we might even say 'that was a breeze' (see Figure 4.34). Please don't forget to save at this point.

By the way, if you later want to change the size of the picture, do so using the resize handles that appear when you click on the inserted image. SilverStripe doesn't use the original image, but instead cleverly resamples the image to give it the right size. So, don't be afraid: a thumbnail-sized

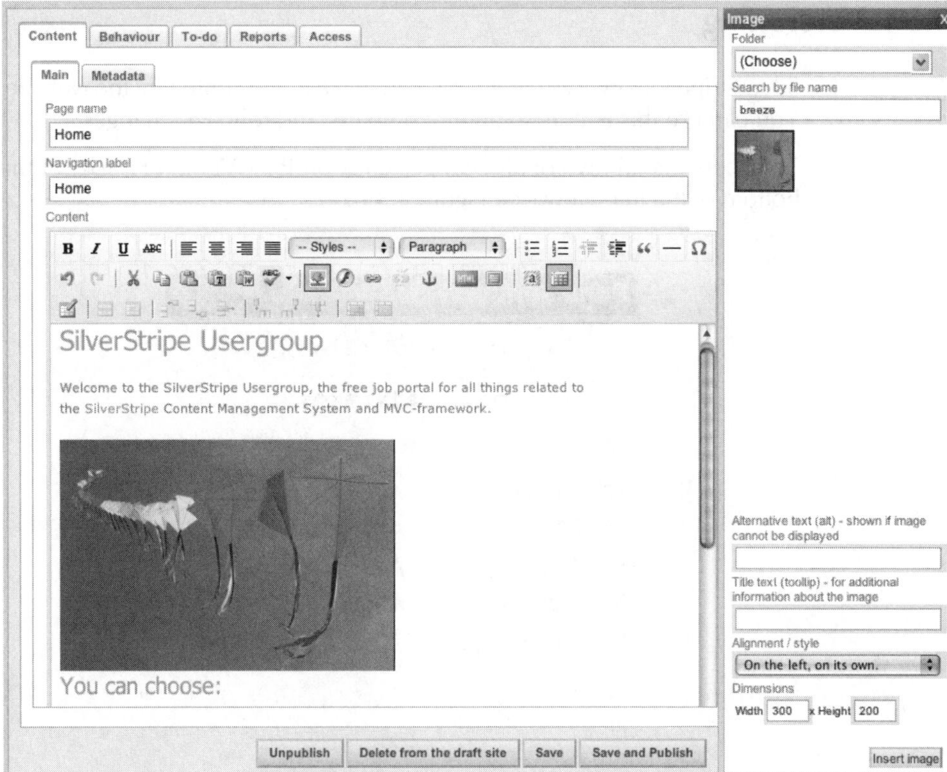

Figure 4.34 Text with inserted image.

preview image isn't using the original high-resolution file and your page doesn't take forever to load because of it.

Let's take a look at the result of everything we have so far in the web-browser (*http://localhost/*). If the display isn't yet 100% convincing, please for now refrain from making changing to cosmetic aspects of the website (you might want to undo these changes later). We first want to use this opportunity to tell you about the versioning system. This feature will make your work much easier in the future.

In-context photo uploading

Depending on your version of the Adobe Flash plugin installed in your browser, the interface shown by Figure 4.33 will also show buttons to create folders and upload images. This makes it quicker to perform these common tasks. This system also lets you select and upload multiple files in one go.

4.5 Versioning

SilverStripe logs every change that you make to the content of the website. You can use this feature to audit, compare, and rollback changes.

To access the archive of all changes click on PAGE VERSION HISTORY at the bottom of the tree view (see Figure 4.35).

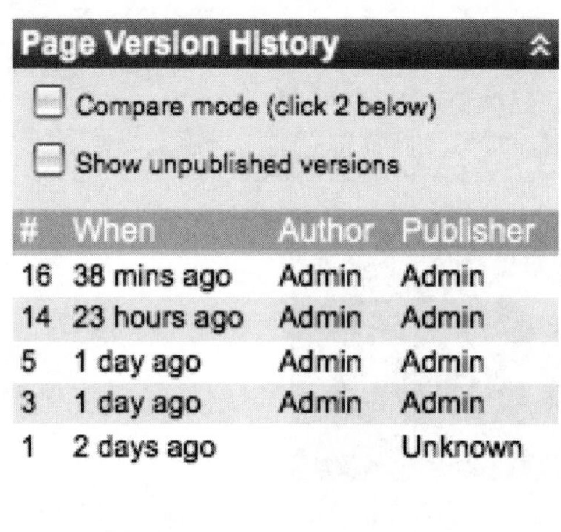

Figure 4.35 SilverStripe versioning.

The version display is always in relation to the currently selected file in the tree view. Every time you save a change, that change is given a version number (as seen in the first column). Versions are sorted in reverse-chronological order. So, the latest change is on top and the oldest change is at the bottom of the list. Additionally, each version lists which user authored the change, as well as who published the content.

As you can see from our example in Figure 4.35, we last saved 38 minutes ago. If you want to view an older version, just click on it in the list. For example, suppose we decide that we would rather not have an image on our front-page. No problem! All we have to do is revert back to a point in time before we inserted the image. Let's go back in time to yesterday and see what happens.

The main area displays the content of the selected version. As you can see, our picture is missing here.

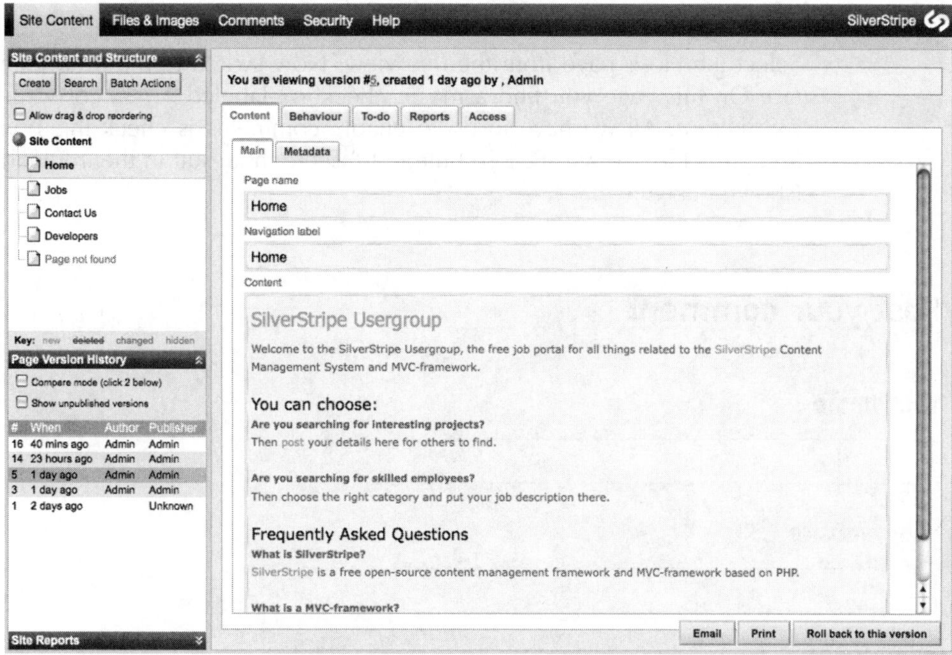

Figure 4.36 Restoring older version.

To restore this version, click the ROLL BACK TO THIS VERSION button (see Figure 4.36).

You can also print data about the older version. Click the PRINT button and SilverStripe creates a printable version of the currently selected version. Additionally, you also get a summary of the content on all tabs under the tree view.

Even though you're browsing an archive of older versions, you can also display an older version in the frontend view. Click the ARCHIVED SITE link located in the footer section of the page.

And finally, and just as clever as everything else, you can send a link to an archived page via email. Just press the EMAIL button. Accessing the archived page will require security rights to the CMS.

4.6 Comments

SilverStripe, like any self-respecting Web 2.0 application, has a comment feature, with blog-style comments being enabled on any page. We want to add a comment form to the bottom of the HOME page of our job portal.

4.6.1 Website Form

Select the Home page from the tree view. Now switch to the Behaviour tab. On this page you find a magic checkbox labeled Allow comments on this page. All we have to do to enable comments is check this box and press the Save and Publish button. Observe the result in the frontend (shown in Figure 4.37).

Post your comment

Your name

Your website URL

Comments

Post

Comments

No one has commented on this page yet.

RSS feed for comments on this page | RSS feed for all comments

Figure 4.37 Testing the comment feature.

As you can see, comments even have their own RSS feed. Let's try them out. Enter your name and write a brief comment in the text box. When you press the Post button your comment will appear as part of the page (see Figure 4.38).

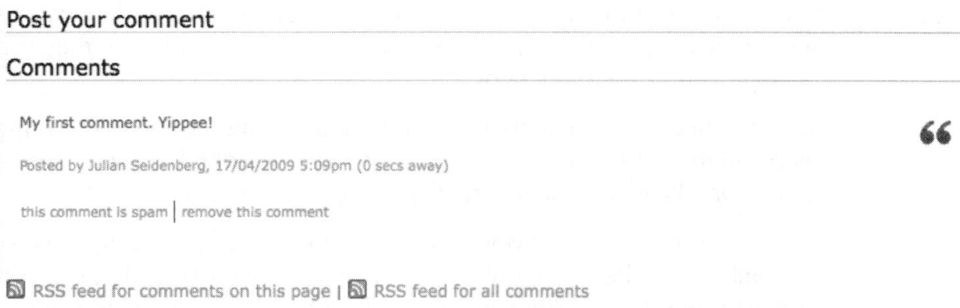

Figure 4.38 Successfully posted comment.

4.6.2 Comment Moderation Using the CMS

Since we're logged in as administrator, we can also moderate comments. We can either mark comments as spam by clicking the This comment is spam link, or we can remove comments completely by clicking the Remove this comment link.

The same thing can also be accomplished in the backend. To manage comments select the Comments tab.

On the left-hand side of the screen, you'll find a folder structure, which allows you to moderate all the comments on the website (see Figure 4.39).

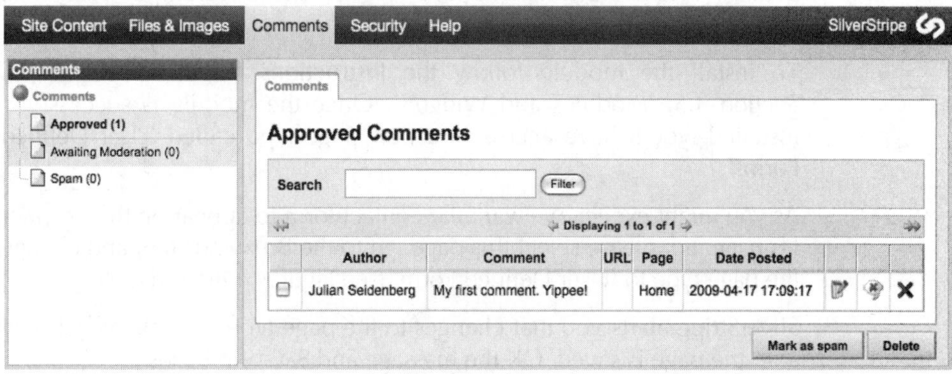

Figure 4.39 Managing comments using the backend.

Approved contains all accepted comments. By default all fully completed comment forms are automatically approved. These settings can be changed using the *mysite/_config.php* file and the following directive:

```
PageComment::enableModeration();
```

If you don't want comments to be approved automatically they can be set to initially go to the Awaiting Moderation folder. From there they can be approved by the moderator.

You can find all comments marked as spam in the folder of the same name on the left-hand side. All comments can be edited, deleted, and (if there aren't labeled as such already) marked as spam.

Please read Chapter 13, 'More Modules' to learn about intelligent ways to combat website comment spam: SilverStripe contains modules that provide support for Mollom and ReCAPTCHA, both of which help reduce the ability of malicious scripts to abuse your website forms.

4.7 Simple Contact Form

We haven't forgotten the changes to the layout we discussed earlier. However, since these require digging into code, let's first explore all the features we can implement using the backend interface. One such feature is the ability to create the ubiquitous contact form found on many websites.

4.7.1 Installing the 'userforms' Module

The SilverStripe module called 'userforms' makes it easy to create such a form. Please download it from the official SilverStripe website at http://silverstripe.org/user-forms-module/.

To install the module follow the instructions found in Chapter 3, Section 3.5, 'Modules and Widgets'. Once the module is successfully installed, you'll have access to a new page type called 'User Defined Forms'.

As you might expect, we want the contact form to appear on the Contact Us page. So, please select this page, go to the Behaviour tab, and change the page type to 'User Defined Form' (see Figures 4.40 and 4.41).

SilverStripe alerts you that changes to the page type will take effect only after the page is saved. OK the message and Save and Publish.

The Contact Us page will be labeled with a new icon in the tree view.

Now, all that's left for us to do is to define our desired fields on the form. The SilverStripe backend provides an effective way of doing so using a simple graphical user interface. No programming required.

4.7.2 Additional Tabs

Four additional tabs have appeared now that we've selected the 'User Defined Forms' page type. The new additions are: Form, Submissions, Email

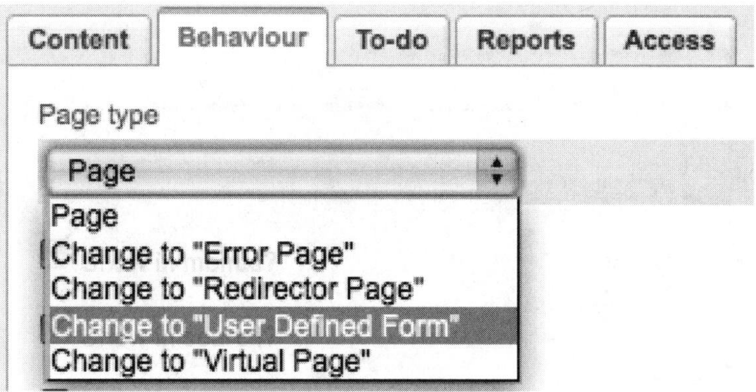

Figure 4.40 Selecting a new page type.

Figure 4.41 Icon for 'User Defined Forms' in the tree view.

RECIPIENTS, and ON COMPLETE. Please select the FORM tab to start creating the form (see Figure 4.42).

We can assemble our form simply by clicking the various interface controls in the input bar.

SilverStripe brings a few special interface controls to the party, beyond those commonly available in HTML (see Figure 4.43).

Checkbox

Use the CHECKBOX control to allow users to answer Yes/No-type questions on your form. CHECKBOX creates a single checkbox and some associated label text.

CHECKBOX GROUP

Lets you ask a single question that has multiple answers, with all the possible answers as presented as checkboxes.

DATE

Asks for a date. Provides the user with a calendar date popup to make choosing a date easier.

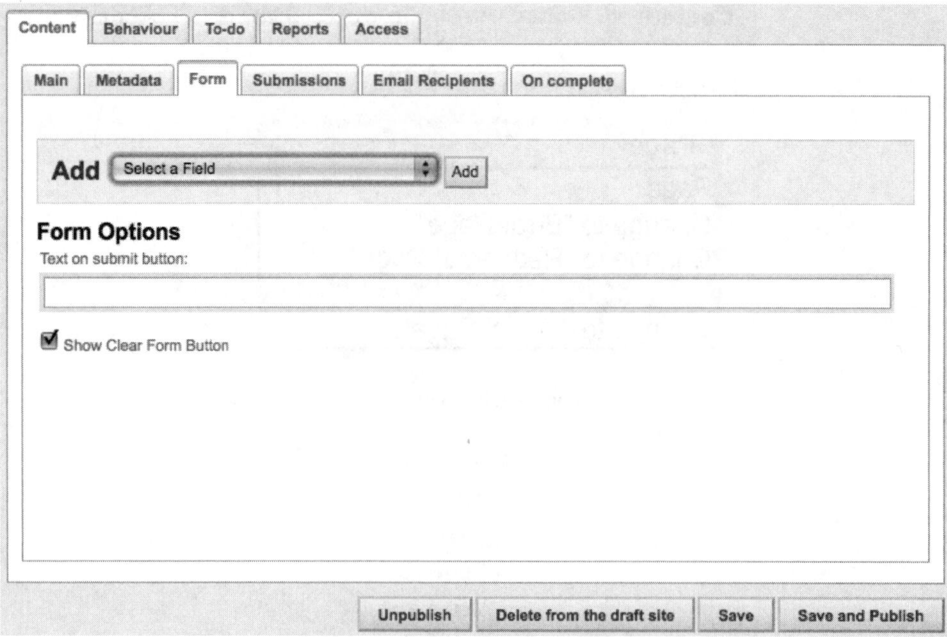

Figure 4.42 Form wizard.

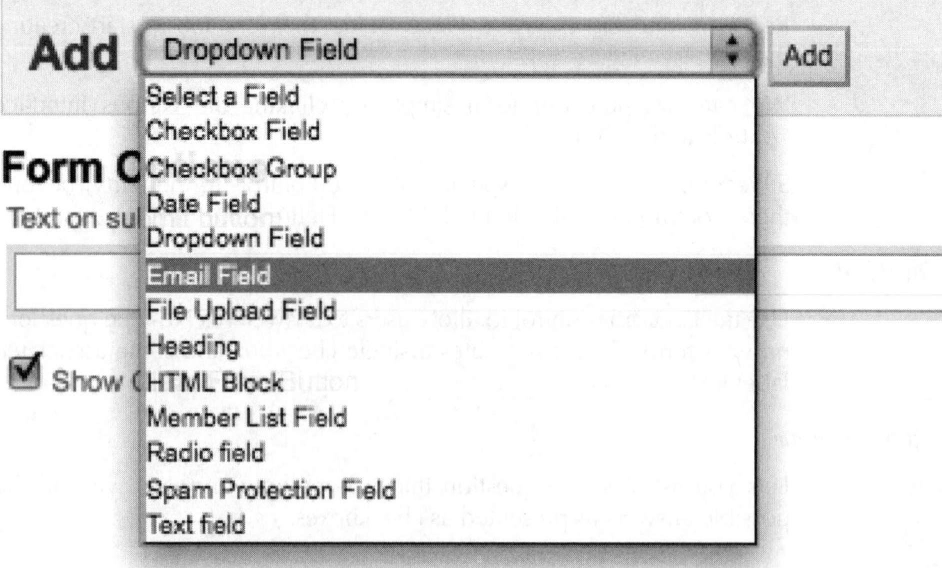

Figure 4.43 Input bar of the form wizard.

Dropdown or Radio

You can allow the user to select between multiple options by creating either the Dropdown or Radio control. The former creates a dropdown menu, whereas the later adds a number of radios buttons onto the form. You can change the order of the available choices using drag and drop.

Email

The Email control validates an input email address. You can also specify whether or not a copy of the form submission should be sent to the email address here.

File

The File control adds upload functionality to your form. By default, the file will be deposited in the *assets/Uploads* folder in the Files & Images tab.

Form heading

This control adds a title to the form.

HTML block

This control allows you to enter a block of arbitrary HTML text to add to the form.

Member list

Shows a list of members contained in a group found in the Security section of the system. Using this, you could create a group for Customer Services staff, and the form could then let people choose the staff member they wish to deal with. (It would simply include the name in the submission – it would not influence where the form is emailed.)

Text

The Text control creates an `<input>` tag or a `<textarea>` on the form. You can specify the minimum and maximum number of characters, as well as the size of the input field.

Spam Protection Field

This control adds a CAPTCHA field to the form to ensure that scripts cannot be used to submit spam using the form.

Adding other types of fields

Some of the modules listed at www.silverstripe.org/modules provide extra types of fields to the userforms module. Examples include the Mollom module and the Google Map Selection Field module. By inspecting the source code of those modules, you can learn how to create your own custom fields, too.

4.7.3 Composing our Form

Now that we know all about the various options we have for creating a form, we can get to work creating our contact form (see Figure 4.44). It will use the following form interface control:

- Name (TEXT)
- Email address (EMAIL)
- Dropdown menu describing message type (DROPDOWN)
- Website rating (RADIO)
- Message (TEXT)

Figure 4.44 First control in the form wizard.

Click on TEXT on the input bar to add the first control.

The new control appears between the two input bars. Now we just need to enter the name of our field: 'Name'.

That's the first control done. Onwards and upwards: now click on EMAIL to add an email control. Title it 'Email address'. We want to require the user to enter his or her email address, and so click the MORE OPTIONS icon to the right of the control.

Check the REQUIRED? checkbox (see Figure 4.45).

Now create a Dropdown control. Give it the 'Message Type' title and open the options. Here you can define the individual options for the drop-down menu. Enter 'Suggestion' in the box and click the green plus icon to add another option. Enter 'Error report' and 'Question' as two additional options for our drop-down menu (see Figure 4.46).

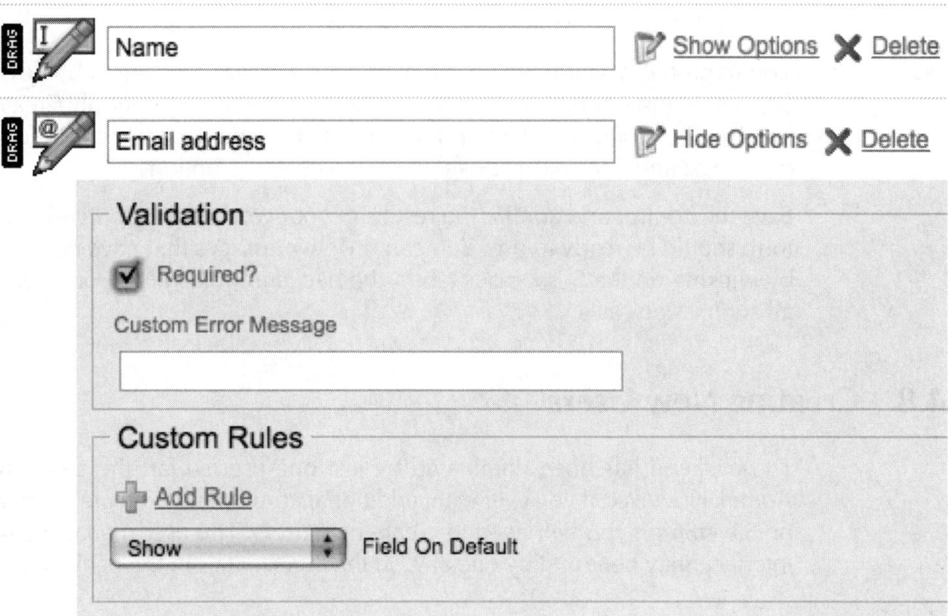

Figure 4.45 Email control options.

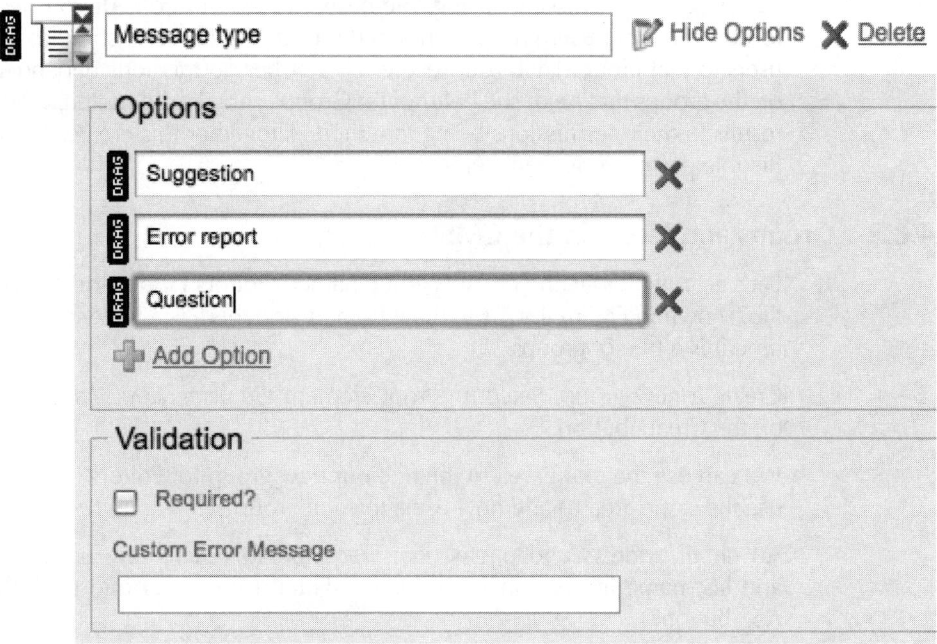

Figure 4.46 Dropdown options.

Create the WEBSITE RATING control (RADIO button) in much the same way as you did for the DROPDOWN. Add the options A, B, C, D, and E.

You're probably getting the hang of this form creation business by now. So, here's just a quick rundown of settings for the last control: Create another TEXT control and enter 'Message' as the title. Enter 30 for LENGTH OF TEXT BOX and 5 for NUMBER OF ROWS in the control's options.

Save the control and admire the results of your work in the frontend. The form should be ready to use. You can review messages that have come in by clicking on the SUBMISSIONS tab in the backend. It also lets you export all submissions as a CSV.

4.8 Creating New Users

The backend has been dominated by just one user so far: the almighty *Admin*. However, if you ever want additional co-workers to create content on SilverStripe you will need to create new users. The user-management interface may be found by clicking on the SECURITY tab in the backend.

4.8.1 Role-based Access Control

SilverStripe makes it easy to set users' access permissions. Individual users can be given permissions using role-based access control. All you need to do is create a user group with a certain set of permissions and assign users to that group. Each user receives his or her permissions dependent on the groups that he or she belongs to. Groups can also be nested, which results in their permissions being inherited. Altogether this creates a very flexible permissions management system.

4.8.2 Groups and Users in the CMS

Let's get right into it and create a group named 'Editors'. Open the SECURITY tab, shown in Figure 4.47. On the left-hand side there is a tree view. This time it is a tree of groups.

Create a new group: Select the root element (SECURITY GROUPS) and click on the Create button.

We can use the main area to rename our new group to 'Editors'. We can use the same area to add new users to each group (see Figure 4.48).

An email address and password is required for each new user. First and last name are optional parameters. Enter a new user and click the ADD button.

A user's information can be edited or even deleted using the familiar icons on the right-hand side.

Figure 4.47 Managing user groups.

First Name	Surname	Email	Password			
John	Smith	john@email.com				
				Add		

Figure 4.48 Creating new users.

4.8.3 User Permissions

We're not quite finished yet. We still need to assign a few permissions to our new 'Editors' group. Click on the PERMISSIONS tab (see Figure 4.49).

You can use the drop-down menu to pick rights and add them to the groups.

SilverStripe allows you to assign group access for each key class of the system. Choose an item from the drop-down and click the green plus icon (hidden under the menu in the screenshot) to add access to it.

Here's a brief description of each item in the list.

CMSMain

A group that has permissions to access CMSMAIN is allowed to view this controller class. In other words, they can edit page content. In addition, in the SITE CONTENT section of the backend, you will notice that the ACCESS

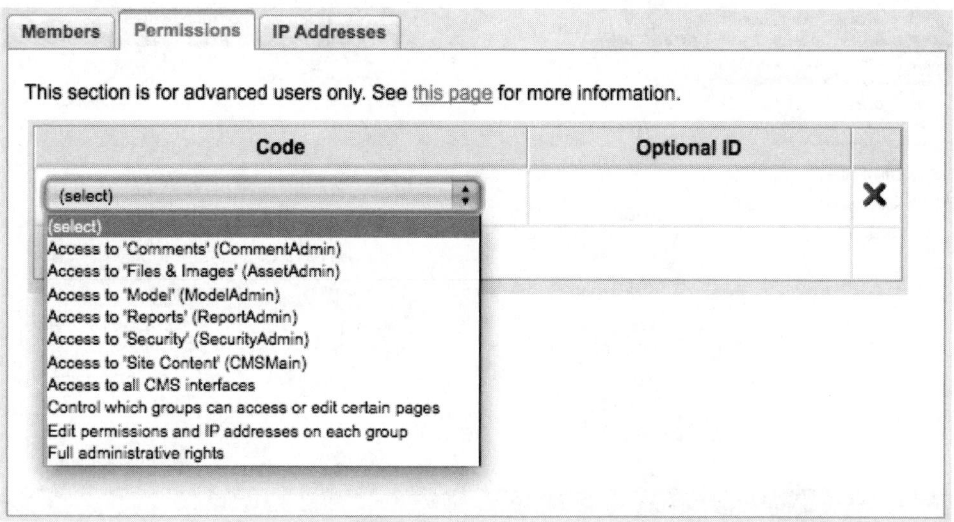

Figure 4.49 Permissions.

tab allows granular view and edit rights for any given page. This means you could limit a user to being able to edit just one page inside the CMS. By installing the Workflow module (see Chapter 13, 'More Modules'), you get further granular rights to in the SITE CONTENT area.

ASSETADMIN

Groups with access to ASSETADMIN can access the FILES & IMAGES area.

SecurityAdmin

If you want a group of users to have access to the SECURITY tab (the one we're using right now), give it access to the *SecurityAdmin* class.

CommentAdmin

This class determines whether or not a user group has access to the comment management functions of the SilverStripe system. Users with these permissions can access the COMMENTS tab.

ModelAdmin

This item in the list of permissions grants a group access to custom user-interfaces created using the *ModelAdmin* class. More information on this topic is available in Chapter 6.

Access to all CMS Interfaces

You don't have to individually assign each permission item to administrators who are to be given universal access to the system. Use this item to give a group access to all areas in one go.

Permissions using group hierarchies

Groups, just like pages, can be organized in hierarchies. That is, one group can be nested inside of another group. If you create a sub-group of another group, the parent group icon changes to the picture of a folder. Groups can be moved around using drag and drop if you activate the ALLOW DRAG & DROP REORDERING checkbox.

A sub-group inherits all permissions from its parent. So, for example, we can give a group of 'Editors' permission to access only SITE CONTENT. A sub-group of 'Editor in chief' inherits these access rights (see Figure 4.50), but we can also allow its members to access FILES & IMAGES, for example.

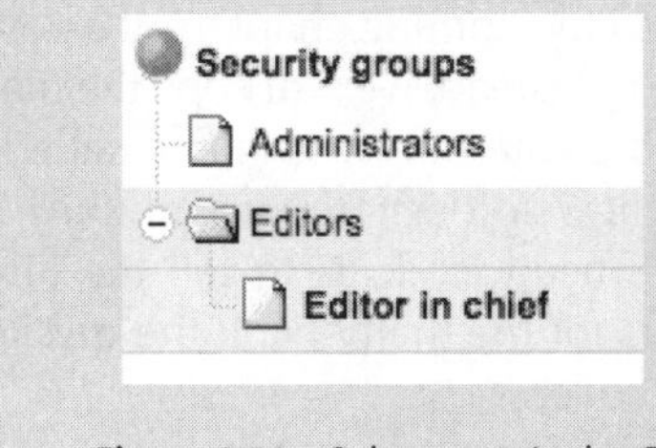

Figure 4.50 Sub-groups in the CMS.

By the way, you can export a list of members as a CSV file, which most data-related applications accept as an input format, most prominently Microsoft Excel.

The above security set up is purely what you get out of the box. With a little PHP, you can completely customise and tailor SilverStripe's user permissions model, which is explored a little in Section 6.9.3, 'Custom Permissions'.

4.9 Themes

Okay, now that we've finished exploring the backend, let's spend some time improving the look and feel of our website.

This subject is intentionally positioned at the end of this chapter. We're leaving the safety of the backend interface and going to edit the same source code for the first time. This is because we're now leaving the mindset and role of a CMS author and into the role of a website developer. As mentioned in Chapter 1, SilverStripe separates the roles of author and developer very deliberately: We'll now being dealing with HTML, CSS, and PHP because this gives developers far more freedom to do their work than a graphical user interface. This will be a nice warm-up for Chapter 5, 'Development' and Chapter 6, 'CRM'. Both these chapters focus exclusively on editing and extending the source code of the system.

All right, it's time to fire up your favorite text editor.

4.9.1 Our Own Theme: 'mysite'

Do you remember where we put the files of the view-class? Exactly! We put them in the *themes/* folder. Up until now we've worked with the standard *BlackCandy* theme located in the *themes/blackcandy/* folder. We could edit this theme directly, but, since we will be adding multiple new templates in the coming chapters, it's better that we leave the *blackcandy* folder as it is. Instead, we will copy the *blackcandy/* and *blackcandy_blog/* folders and create our own theme called 'mysite'. So, we should end up with two new folders: *themes/mysite/* and *themes/mysite_blog/*. Now all that we need to do is to tell the SilverStripe framework to use our new folders for the theme. Edit the *mysite/_config.php* file to include the following code:

```
SSViewer::set_theme('mysite');
```

4.9.2 Changing the Page Title in the Template

Okay, our first step will be to edit the standard layout: Open the *themes/mysite/template/Page.ss* file in your text editor.

Initially we will change the title in the header from 'Your Site Name' to 'SilverStripe Usergroup' (see Figure 4.51). We will also add 'Community, Job portal and more' as a subtitle. To make these changes, look for the <body> tag in the file. Below that you will find a `div` container with `id set to Header`. Change the contents of this `div` as follows:

```
<div id="Header">
   <h1>SilverStripe Usergroup</h1>
   <p>Community, Job portal and more</p>
</div>
```

Listing 4.1 *themes/mysite/templates/Page.ss (excerpt)*

Save the changes and check your browser to see whether you got the desired result.

Figure 4.51 Modified page header.

4.9.3 Changing the Stylesheet

Notice how the title of the page is displayed in blue below the header bar. The *BlackCandy* stylesheet defines size, color, and location of this text. Let's try changing these parameters by modifying the stylesheet.

The parameters in question are contained in the *themes/mysite/css/typography.css* file. Open this file and look for the following text:

```
.typography h2 {
       font-size: 20px;
}
```

Try replacing this code with the following:

```
.typography h2 {
       font-size: 40px;
       text-align: center;
}
```

Reload the page: The title should now be twice as large and in the center of the page.

Naming conventions for theme stylesheets

The *BlackCandy* theme (and our *mysite* clone of it) is organized as follows:

- *themes/mysite/css* contains all the stylesheets for the theme. The stylesheets follow a specific naming convention. You can, of course, define your own CSS files, but you will have to manually reference them from your template files.

- *layout.css* describes the layout of the website. You will find the majority of the CSS content here. SilverStripe templates should use CSS rather than table-based layout, a topic we cover in Section 5.9.3.
- *typography.css* describes the fonts used in the website. *TinyMCE* also loads the CSS in this file so that the fonts shown in the editor are identical to the website – it is supposed to be WYWSYIG (what you see is what you get) afterall! All CSS code in this file should use the `typography` CSS-class, for example: `.typography h3 {color: #f00;}`. Additionally, adding children classes to .typography will add them to the "styles" dropdown in the editor (see Figure 4.16).
- *editor.css* describes any custom formatting you might need in the *TinyMCE* editor.
- *form.css* contains all the CSS for displaying forms and form controls.
- *ie6.css/ie7.css*: Internet Explorer often requires special CSS hacks to get a page to display correctly. Any IE-specific code is contained in these files.

If any of the layout isn't to your liking, please feel free to modify the stylesheets to your heart's content. You should now be armed with enough information to adjust the CSS to meet your requirements.

4.10 Conclusion

We've come a long way in this chapter. We've got to know the SilverStripe backend, created some example content, integrated page comments, designed a contact form, and modified some template code (HTML and CSS). You will now begin to see the separation between SilverStripe's author and developer roles.

Congratulations: You've successfully taken your first steps and are now well prepared for the following chapters. You're well on your way towards mastering SilverStripe.

5
Development: Job Postings

We have created some initial content and our website is starting to look pretty close to how we want it to. Now you might be thinking: 'all that was really easy'. Yes indeed, SilverStripe is very easy to use, and designed to be self-explanatory. Website editors should have no problem finding their way around.

In this chapter we show you how SilverStripe also makes life easy for programmers. We will now leave the beaten path and focus in on the features that bring our job portal to life.

Take a deep breath and try to visualize the system architecture that we outlined during the introduction of the last chapter. Knowledge of the architecture will help a great deal with the next part of our project. We'll create the jobs area through which job postings can be displayed and managed.

You can either follow along as we develop all the necessary code during this chapter, or get a preview of the final result as a full SilverStripe project from the book's website. Extract the downloaded archive, copy everything inside the *5_development/* folder into your webroot and run the SilverStripe installer in your browser as described in Chapter 2, Section 2.3.4, 'Webinstaller'. You will find an example database dump called `database.sql` in the webroot as well. You can use a database management tool such as *phpMyAdmin* to import this database into your own system (see Chapter 8, Section 8.2, 'Backup'). The example database will overwrite any default users set during the installation: it is pre-configured with username 'admin' and password 'password'.

5.1 Job Categories as a Page Type

We created the JOBS page in the last chapter. Now we want this page to display all available job categories. If a user clicks on a category another page should open with a list of all the relevant postings.

Each page has a *Page Type* and it is this type that controls its layout and behavior. You can use the BEHAVIOUR tab in the CMS to change a page's type. In the previous chapter we set the JOBS page to the 'Page' type. That type displays content, but doesn't provide any special functionality.

We need to define a new page type to get our desired functionality. No, wait a minute; we actually need two new page types:

- We need a kind of container for our job categories. Let's call it `JobCategoryHolder`. We will eventually assign this page type to the JOBS page.
- The second page type is for each individual category of job. So, it makes sense to call it `JobCategory`. Pages of this type will later display a list of short previews of each job posting in their category.

To clarify how these page types will look in the CMS page tree, Figure 5.1 shows a screenshot:

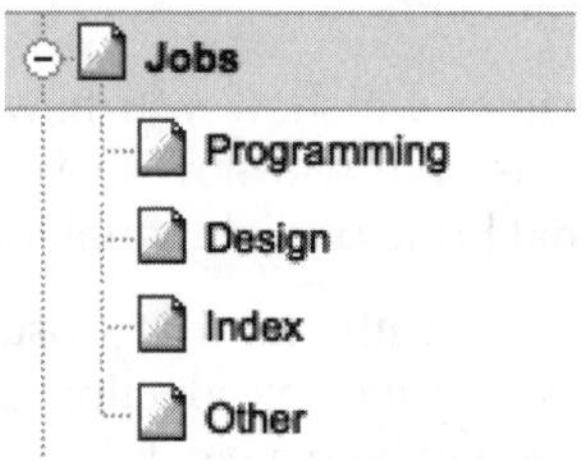

Figure 5.1 Intended architecture.

So let's go over it again: We want the JOBS page to be of type `JobCategoryHolder`. This page is a container for its `JobCategory` sub-pages. Each category is a separate page in the backend. Figure 5.1 shows an example of four such category pages: PROGRAMMING, DESIGN, INDEX, and OTHER.

Page navigation using *BlackCandy*

Hierarchies of pages can be displayed in various ways on the website frontend. Our default *BlackCandy* theme uses a sidebar listing for the second level. We have illustrated this in Figure 5.2 by creating some example children of the DEVELOPERS page.

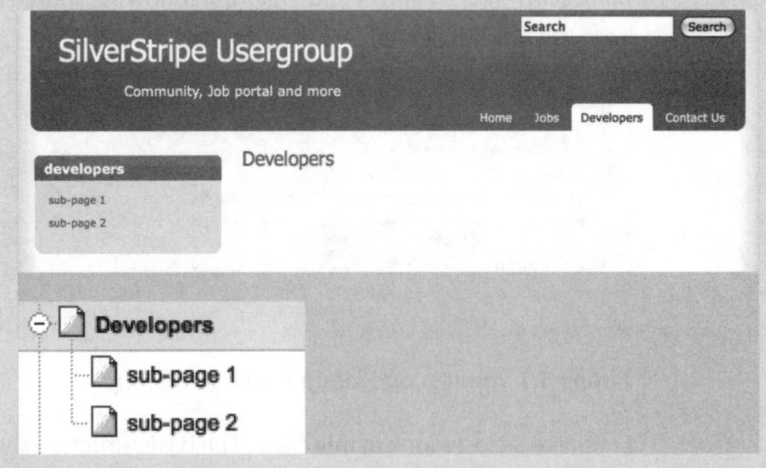

Figure 5.2 Example navigation in the backend.

The result is the output in the frontend as shown in Figure 5.3. We will use a similar design to displaying our job categories, but will adjust the layout and behavior to better suit our new page type.

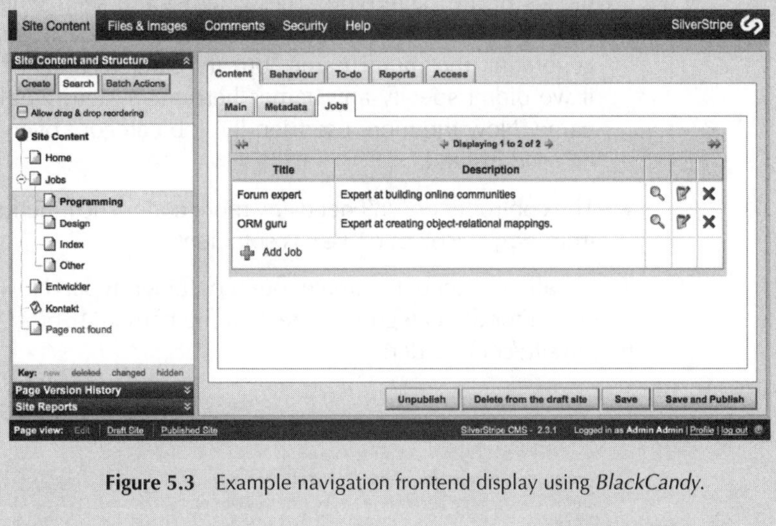

Figure 5.3 Example navigation frontend display using *BlackCandy*.

Please go ahead and create the four sub-pages: PROGRAMMING, DESIGN, INDEX, and OTHER. Give them the 'Page' page type for now.

We will start our programming by creating the container page. For that we need to create a definition for `JobCategoryHolder`. Create a file named *JobCategoryHolder.php* in the *mysite/code* folder (be aware that names are case sensitive) and enter the following source code:

```
<?php
class JobCategoryHolder extends Page {
   static $allowed_children = array(
      'JobCategory'
   );
   static $singular_name = 'Job category overview';
   static $plural_name = Job category overviews';
}
class JobCategoryHolder_Controller extends Page_Controller {
}
?>
```

Listing 5.1 *mysite/code/JobCategoryHolder.php*

Let's take a closer look at this code. The basic structure should be familiar from the previous chapters:

- `$allowed_children` defines that the `JobCategoryHolder` page may only contain sub-pages with the `JobCategory` type. So in the future, the JOBS page will only be allowed to have category sub-pages.
- The next few lines define MVC references for singular and plural names of the page type. These names are seen when selecting the page type in the backend (SilverStripe has basic support for auto-generating the plural name, but it's safer to add it here manually). If we didn't specify any names here the system would use the class name. Now the more userfriendly 'Job category overview' name will be used instead.
- The controller doesn't need any more code. The functionality inherited from `Page_Controller` is sufficient.

That's all we need to create our container type. Now let's create a definition for the categories. Create a file named `JobCategory.php` in the *mysite/code* folder:

```
<?php
class JobCategory extends Page {
   static $singular_name = 'Job category';
   static $plural_name = 'Job categories';
}
class JobCategory_Controller extends Page_Controller {}
?>
```

Listing 5.2 *mysite/code/JobCategory.php*

The JobCategory class, just like the JobCategoryHolder class before it, extends the Page class. Again, custom singular and plural names are defined. Note: It's important to stick to file naming conventions, because the SilverStripe framework automatically selects and references files based on their name.

The Page class: Root of all pages

You might have noticed that we often refer to a page type called 'Page', and subsequently to the Page class in PHP. The Page class is part of the standard SilverStripe installation, and forms the basis of all our page types. It is located in the *mysite/code/* directory, which means it can be customized for your project needs without 'hacking the core'. By default, it's an empty class definition, and is supposed to contain all logic and properties that all your pages will need. For example, the Page class could hold code for generating a site-wide search form that should display on all page types. This way of using class inheritance is a very powerful concept that we'll repeatedly see in the following SilverStripe development.

As you can see from the listing below, Page inherits from SiteTree, a core class the provides the *Model* for your application. Every subclass of SiteTree is required to have its own controller, and so we have a Page_Controller extending the ContentController class.

```
class Page extends SiteTree {
   // ..
}
class Page_Controller extends ContentController {
   function init() {
      parent::init();
      Requirements::themedCSS("layout");
      Requirements::themedCSS("typography");
      Requirements::themedCSS("form");
   }
}
```

Here's a quick run-down of the most important aspects of this code:

- The init() method is called every time a page with page type 'Page' accessed by a website visitor.

The call to parent::init() results in the init() method being called on the SiteTree.

The remaining Requirements::themedCSS (...) calls make sure that the three standard stylesheets are linked into the every page inheriting from Page. See the box 'Requirements: Linking in CSS and Javascript' for more information on the topic.

Requirements: Linking in CSS and Javascript

You can use the `Requirements` class to link JavaScript and CSS-files into an HTML file. The SilverStripe framework makes sure that the specified files are included in your template. However, the actual inclusion takes place within the controller, not the template. The advantage is that all external references can be collected and managed in one place. For example, a form field with autocompletion functionality could load the necessary JavaScript and CSS as requirements, without the need for you as a developer to know about them.

The basic syntax is a set of static method calls with a relative path to the required file:

- `Requirements::javascript("mysite/javascript/myscript.js")`
- `Requirements::css("themes/mysite/css/mystyles.css")`

In addition to linking to external files, you can also directly include JavaScript and CSS code inline. This is useful if the included content contains dynamic variables (see `$name` and `$className` below):

```
Requirements::customScript('alert("hallo $name ...");');
Requirements::customCSS(".tree li.$className {background-image:
  url($icon);}");
```

You can delete previously included requirements with the `Requirements:: clear("<file path>")` syntax. A method call to `Requirements::clear()` without an argument removes all previously included requirements.

You can block specific requirements by calling the `Requirements::block("<file path>")` method. Any file that has been blocked will not be linked to from the page, even if it is specified as a requirement later on in the execution chain. This is useful, for example, if you want to replace a specific Javascript library with your own. Blocking the old library prevents conflicts by ensuring that only your library is included.

Section 8.5.2, 'Compressing Javascript and CSS' details how you can compress files collected through `Requirements` in order to speed up page load time.

5.2 Job as a DataObject

We have successfully created the container for our job postings. Now let's delve a bit deeper: We intend to create an interface to input and edit job postings and make sure that they find their way into the database. Ideally, this should happen in a single file without too much fuss. Does this sounds impossible? Not with our trusty sidekick SilverStripe. Read on.

Please create a file called *Job.php* in the *mysite/code* folder. Let's start by defining the model:

```
<?php
class Job extends DataObject {
}
?>
```

Listing 5.3 *mysite/code/Job.php*

Do you notice anything strange? Right! Up until now we've extended the `Page` class for all our new page types, but now we are extending `DataObject`. We're doing this because we don't want to define a new page type. Instead, we're creating a place to store data so that it can be displayed within the `JobCategory` page.

SiteTree vs DataObject

Objects meant to be saved in the database generally inherit from `DataObject`. This gives them all the basic methods necessary to save and load attributes.

`SiteTree` is a direct subclass of `DataObject`. Any class that inherits from `SiteTree` becomes a page type that can be assigned to pages in the backend. Pages based on such classes can be edited in the CMS and hooked into the page tree. They automatically get an edit form in the CMS interface, which makes it easy to write and manage their content, as well as provide a publication workflow. They can be iterated in the website template to create menus and show their content. Content based on SiteTree can be versioned and viewed in draft mode for publication. So altogether, `SiteTree` provides everything you need to create a stand-alone page.

SiteTree subclasses are great for creating webpages, however they are tied to the CMS interface and might have more functionality that you need for a certain data structure. As a rule of thumb, if your data is not displayed as a standalone page, consider a more specialized and lightweight implementation inheriting directly from DataObject instead of SiteTree. A good example of this split are blog posts versus comments made on those posts. Blog posts are page-based and viewed through URLs, hence an ideal use-case for SiteTree. Comments on the other hand don't need to have their own page, they show within other pages. It would be confusing to show them in the CMS as pages in your site tree. Also, a tree view is less ideal when you are going to manage thousands of items in a flat list, where they would be time-consuming to browse

We will show you more specialized editing interfaces in Chapter 6, 'CRM'.

Our goal over the coming sections will be to create a management interface for our job postings. We want this interface to appear in every job category page in the site tree. Take a look at the screenshot in Figure 5.4 to get a better idea of our end goal.

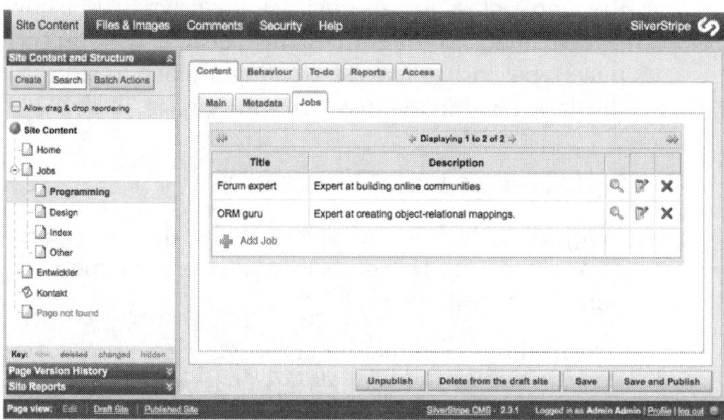

Figure 5.4 Detailed viewer pop-up.

Notice the new JOBS tab in the main area of the screenshot. It contains all the job postings in the selected category. Also notice the familiar icons for adding, viewing, editing, and deleting individual postings in the table on the right.

The next step in achieving our goal is to define the data that is contained within each of our job postings. Each posting should contain the properties `Title`, `Description`, `Location`, and `ExpiryDate`. Update the `Job.php` file to include the following:

```
<?php
class Job extends DataObject {
```

```
    static $db = array(
        'Title' => 'Text',
        'Description' => 'Text',
        'Location' => 'Text',
        'ExpiryDate' => 'Date',
    );
}
?>
```

Listing 5.4 *mysite/code/Job.php*

As you've undoubtedly noticed, the `$db` array now contains our database column names. Or to be more precise, it contains attributes that will be translated into database columns by the ORM layer in SilverStripe.

The array key on the left defines the attribute name and the array value on the right defines the data type.

Available data types

We now take a quick look at the most important data types that the SilverStripe framework makes available. They roughly map to the data types that the underlying database supports, but provide a bit more specialization:

- `Varchar`: A string of variable length (up to 255 characters).
- `Text`: A string up to 2 MB in size.
- `HTMLText`: Stores up to 2 MB of HTML code this type is very similar to the normal data type `Text`, but contains extra methods to create HTML-specific editing scaffolding. It also contains a special summary method that strips out HTML tags.
- `Enum`: One textual choice of multiple values.
- `Boolean`: A Boolean value ('true' or 'false'), stored as `0` or `1`.
- `Int`: Simple signed integer number.
- `Decimal/Float/Double`: A decimal number of varying precision.
- `Currency`: A number with two decimal places, fitting a currency value.
- `Percentage`: A decimal number between `0` and `1`, representing a percentage value. Use the `Nice()` method to show in your templates as a number from 0 to 100.
- `Date/Time/SSDateTime`: Date and time values, optionally combined.

Congratulations. The class that holds the data for our job postings has been successfully created. Onwards to the next task: Defining human-readable names for our new class.

```
<?php
class Job extends DataObject {
   //...
   static $singular_name = 'Job';
   static $plural_name = 'Jobs';
}
?>
```

Listing 5.5 *mysite/code/Job.php (excerpt)*

We don't, strictly speaking, require any of the above code. Our class is already called 'Job' and the built-in plural name generator will automatically append an 's' to the basic name anytime a plural name is required. However, in the interests of keeping our page structure clean and consistent, we have included the code anyway. If in the future we ever decide the change the display name, the code to do it is already there.

The next step is to link the individual categories to the job posting data objects. We don't, after all, want all our job postings to appear in every category.

Default tables in SilverStripe

Every subclass of `DataObject` is mapped to a corresponding table in the database using *Object-Relational Mapping* (as described in more detail in Chapter 3, 'Architecture'). Our new JobCategoryHolder, JobCategory, and Job classes all result in new tables in the database. These join the few dozen tables that SilverStripe creates out of the box.

Here's a brief overview of the standard database tables created by SilverStripe. You might want to use a tool such as *phpMyAdmin* to browse the database structure and gain a first-hand appreciation of how our new tables fit into this overall structure.

- *SiteTree, SiteTree_versions, SiteTree_Live*: The core tables of the CMS. All data belonging to instances of the `Page` class is stored here (because it inherits its data from `SiteTree`). The different tables store representations in the different publication states, as well as track all versions of a page.
- *ErrorPage, RedirectorPage, VirtualPage*: Subclasses of SiteTree that save their unique attributes into separate tables. These classes deal

with displaying error pages, redirecting, and cloning the contents of other pages, respectively.

- *PageComment*: Stores all comments. Blog-style comments can be enabled on any SilverStripe page.
- *File, Folder*: Catalogs all files uploaded into the *assets/* folder in your webroot. The system automatically updates this table whenever the folder is viewed through the *Files & Images* interface.
- *Group*: Records the user groups that are created using the SECURITY tab in the backend. The *Group_Members* table stores many-to-many relations between user groups and individual users.
- *Member*: Contains all the registered users. Personal information, including a hashed password, is stored here.
- *Permission*: Holds the rights assigned that have been granted to various groups.
- *Widgets, WidgetArea*: Stores information related to widgets. 'Widgets' are small visual elements for use in the frontend display. Read more about them in Chapter 3, Section 3.5, 'Modules and Widgets'.

As you can see, each PHP class with `$db` properties has a corresponding database table. For example, `RedirectorPage`, which inherits from `SiteTree`, has an *ExternalURL* attribute stored in its own table. All attributes inherited from `SiteTree` remain stored in the *SiteTree* table.

So, a single class can reference multiple tables, all tied together using a primary key. In 'design pattern speak', this is called *Class Table Inheritance*.

5.3 Relations Between DataObjects

We've already talked a bit about relations in Chapter 3, 'Architecture'. We will now build upon this knowledge while defining the relations between our data objects. So then, let's think about exactly how we want job postings and job categories to interrelate.

5.3.1 Multiple Job Postings Using has_many

An individual job category should obviously be able to hold a number of job postings, but an individual job posting should only be contained in one category. This sounds a lot like a *one-to-many* relation, right? We'll create this kind of relationship between the two entities by using SilverStripe's `$has_one` and `$has_many` definitions.

```
<?php
class Job extends DataObject {
   // ...
   static $has_one = array(
      'JobCategory' => 'JobCategory'
   );
}
?>
```

Listing 5.6 *mysite/code/Job.php (excerpt)*

A quick summary of what we see here: we're telling the `Job` class that it's associated with one (and only one) category. We're using the static variable `$has_one` for this purpose. The left side of the array definition, the array key, stores the name of the relationship. The right side, the array value, holds the class we're referencing. In this case, they happen to be named the same.

That takes care of one side of the relationship. Now let's address the other side: telling the job categories how to relate to job postings.

```
<?php
class JobCategory extends Page {
   // ...
   static $has_many = array(
      'Jobs' => 'Job'
   );
}
?>
```

Listing 5.7 *mysite/code/JobCategory.php (excerpt)*

We again assign an array to a static variable. The array assigned to the `$has_many` variable creates a relation named `Jobs` in the key that references many instances of the `Job` class in the array value.

5.3.2 Notifications Using many_many

It would be nice if a job applicant could subscribe to a job category and receive email updates of any new postings. For now, we'll just create the relationship for this feature, and worry about the emailing details later on.

First of all, let's consider the relationship between the subscriber and the category: A job category can inform multiple users (`Subscribers`) about new postings. Similarly, a user of the job board can subscribe him- or herself to multiple categories (`Subscriptions`). So, we need a many-to-many relationship, also known as `$many_many` in SilverStripe.

```
<?php
class JobCategory extends Page {
   // ...
   static $many_many = array(
      'Subscribers' => 'Member'
   );
}
?>
```

Listing 5.8 *mysite/code/JobCategory.php (excerpt)*

Notice how the name of the relation is `Subscribers` and not `Members`. A relation can be named whatever we like. Only the class on the right-hand side needs to reference a valid subclass of `DataObject`.

The other side of the many-to-many relation is made in the `Member` class. Here the static variable `$belongs_many_many` establishes the reverse relationship. Read the following but don't implement this code:

```
<?php
class Member extends DataObject {
   // ...
   static $belongs_many_many = array(
      'Subscriptions' => 'JobCategory'
   );
}
?>
```

Listing 5.9 *sapphire/security/Member.php (excerpt)*

`Member` is a class belonging to the SilverStripe core. For the sake of keeping your installation easy to upgrade and maintain, modifying core classes like this one is discouraged. The above example is therefore more or less theoretical. See Chapter 12, Section 12.2, 'Core functions extended', for a more elegant way of establishing this kind of relation. For now, just leave the `Member` class as it is. Strictly speaking, we only need one side of the `$many_many` relation in order to establish it in the database.

After refreshing the database structure SilverStripe will create a new table in the database to store the email subscriptions.

In Section 5.7, 'Email Notification', we will show you how to implement the subscription and emailing process.

5.3.3 Creating Relations Using ComponentSet

Our next tasks will be accomplished using the `ComponentSet` class (see Table 5.1).

Table 5.1 ComponentSet methods.

ComponentSet method	**Description**
`add($item, [$extraFields=null])`	Adds one `DataObject` to a relation. You can use the `$extraFields` parameter to pass in an array of additional metadata about the relation. This parameter just applies to a `$many - many` relationship, and stores new columns directly on the join table.
`addMany($idList)`	Add multiple `DataObjects` by way of an array with primary keys.
`remove($item)`	Deletes the relation with the specified `$item`. However, the object itself remains as it is.
`removeMany($idList)`	Batch removal of many relations by an array of primary keys.
`removeAll()`	Removes all objects in a relation.
`removeByFilter($filter)`	Deletes relations that match the `$filter` criteria.

This class provides an easy way to add `$has_one`, `$has_many`, or `$many_many` relations to the database, or remove them accordingly. The SilverStripe framework automatically takes care of finding the relevant tables and executing the necessary database queries. For all intents and purposes you don't need to pay attention to whether you're dealing with a `$has_many` or `$many_many` relation.

Here's an example of how the `ComponentSet` methods can be used in our job portal example:

```
<?php
//Find a single Job category
$myJobCategory = DataObject::get_by_id('JobCategory', 1);
//Find all job postings in a category (using $has_many relation)
$jobs = $myJobCategory->Jobs();
//Find all subscribed Members (using $many_many relation)
$subscribers = $myJobCategory->Subscribers();
//Finding a Member object and adding it
//to the set of subscribers($many_many relation)
$someMember = DataObject::get_by_id('Member', 1);
$subscribers->add($someMember);
?>
```

Listing 5.10 *Using the `ComponentSet` methods*

5.4 Creating the Interface

Let's take a break and reflect on what we've achieved so far. We created the classes for our job categories, generated our database schemas, and established our relations. The only thing missing is an interface to manage the data in the backend. Two features still need to be implemented:

- Listing all job postings in a given category.
- Using a pop-up to view and edit a single job posting.

5.4.1 Listing Records in the CMS

Think back to the page structure in Figure 5.1. When we select one of the job categories in the CMS we want a list of the associated job postings to be displayed. To make this happen we need to edit the `JobCategory` class.

```
<?php
class JobCategory extends Page {
    // ...
    function getCMSFields() {
        $fields = parent::getCMSFields();
        $jobsTable = new ComplexTableField($this, 'Jobs', 'Job');
        $fields->addFieldToTab('Root.Content.Jobs', $jobsTable);
        return $fields;
    }
}
?>
```

Listing 5.11 *mysite/code/JobCategory.php*

Let's go through these additions line-by-line:

- The method `getCMSFields()` is inherited from `DataObject`. It handles the display of editing fields in the backend. By overriding this method we can extend its functionality, in this case to add our jobs table.
- The `$fields = parent::getCMSFields()` statement assigns all the editing fields that have already been created in the parent to the `$fields` variable. This way we extend the parent functionality instead of overwriting it.
- The `$jobsTable = new ComplexTableField (...)` statement creates a new instance of a tabular form field called *ComplexTableField*. We will explore this operation in detail in the next section.

- The `$fields->addFieldToTab('Root.Content.Jobs', $jobsTable)` statement adds the newly created field in a new tab called Jobs. Nested tabs are addressed by a dot notation. The tabs Root and Content already exist in the parent implementation.
- Finally, `return $fields` outputs the object to the framework so it can be used by the CMS form.

That's all we need to do to create our new administration interface. But, as promised, let's take a closer look at some of the details of `ComplexTableField`.

ComplexTableField: Forms Interface for Relations

`ComplexTableField` is a special editing control that SilverStripe uses to display and manage relational data (see Figure 5.5).

The field lists all data fields with standard icons for viewing, editing, and deleting. Clicking on these icons results in a pop-up window for viewing and editing the associated data being displayed.

```
$jobsTable = new ComplexTableField($this, 'Jobs', 'Job');
```

Listing 5.12 *mysite/code/JobCategory.php (excerpt)*

The first parameter is a reference to the controller that's creating the instance. Since we are calling the method from within the `JobCategory`, we can simply pass a reference to `$this`, the current object.

The second parameter `"Jobs"` is the name of the field, in order to have a unique identifier in our form. It's also the name of the relationship we want to show and edit (as defined on *JobCategory.php*). By default, the field will detect this relationship, filter the records accordingly, and add any new records to the correct tables.

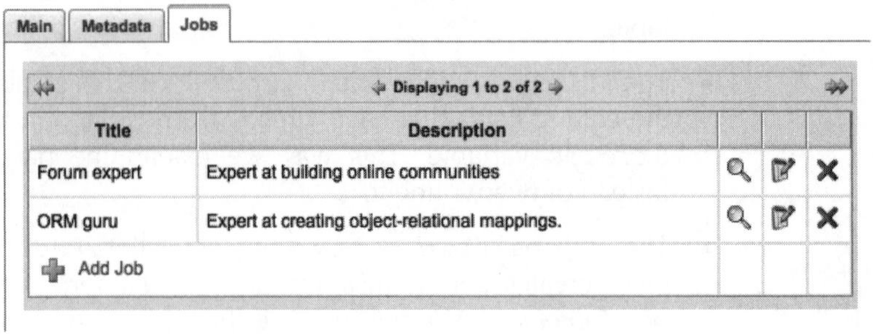

Main | Metadata | Jobs

Displaying 1 to 2 of 2

Title	Description			
Forum expert	Expert at building online communities			
ORM guru	Expert at creating object-relational mappings.			
Add Job				

Figure 5.5 `ComplexTableField`: Tabular view and edit interface.

Lastly, the third parameter defines the type of `DataObject` that the field should handle – in our case a `Job` class. This parameter also determines how the editing pop-up will look like, and which fields to show in the pop-up form. We'll come to that in a second.

`ComplexTableField` is a versatile field with many use cases. It accepts manual filtering in case you're not editing a relationship, allows overriding of the displayed columns, pop-up form fields, and other fine-tuning that might be required.

Adding Tabs in the CMS

We will now focus on the `addFieldToTab()` method that we used previously. This method determines where in the CMS interface a specific form field appears.

```
$fields->addFieldToTab('Root.Content.Jobs', $jobsTable);
```

The first parameter is a path name for our new tab. If we're dealing with nested tabs, the path must be delimited by dots and must start with the `Root` element. You can reference any already existing tab. A new tab will be created if an existing tab of the given name is not found.

In our case, we have selected the existing Content tab and created a new Jobs tab within (see Figure 5.6). The second parameter is the `ComplexTableField` object that we discussed in the previous section. An optional third parameter can be used to denote the position of the new field, by passing in the name of an existing field on this tab. The new field will be placed before it.

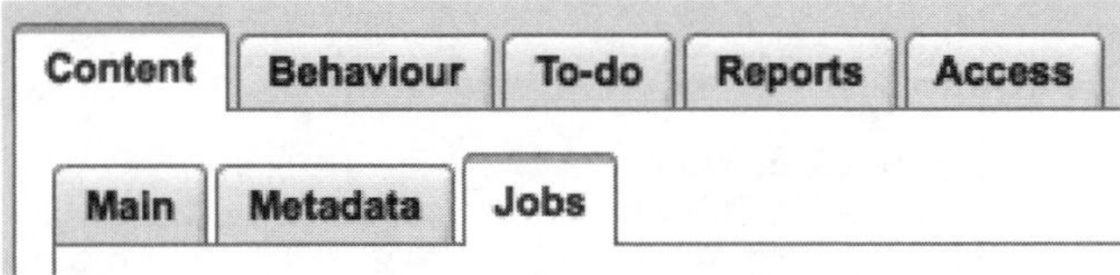

Figure 5.6 Tab structure for 'Jobs'.

You can also use the following notation as an alternative to using dots as delimiters:

```
$fields
  ->fieldByName('Content')
  ->fieldByName('Jobs')
  ->push($jobsTable)
```

Both tabs and a collection of tabs are implemented as PHP classes in SilverStripe, so you can access them as objects and call methods such as `push()` on them.

5.4.2 Detail View in a Pop-up

The `ComplexTableField` class creates an overview listing of job postings and provides buttons to view and edit these postings. However, the viewer and editor pop-ups views are separate interfaces, which must be defined using the `Job` class (see Figure 5.7).

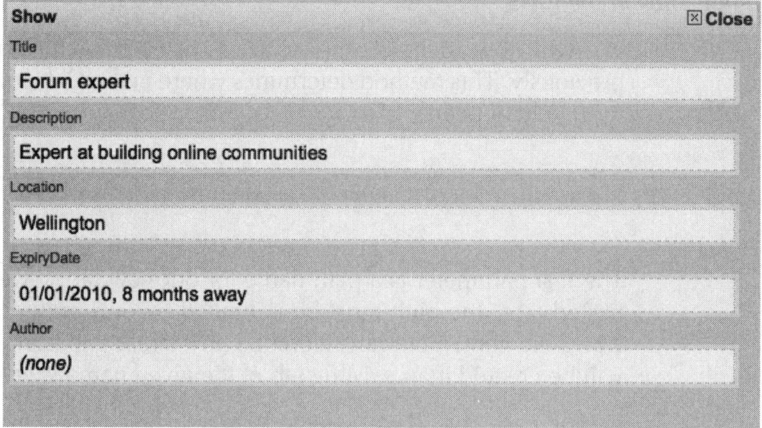

Figure 5.7 Detailed viewer pop-up.

The detailed viewer and editor is defined independently of the category pages. To create it, please open the *mysite/code/Job.php* file and add the following code into the class:

```
<?php
class Job extends DataObject {
   // ...
   function getCMSFields() {
      $fields = new FieldSet(
         new TextField('Title', 'Job Title'),
         new TextareaField('Description', 'Job Description'),
         new TextField('Location', 'Location'),
         new DateField('ExpiryDate', 'Expiry Date')
      );
      return $fields;
   }
?>
```

Listing 5.13 *mysite/code/Job.php (excerpt)*

What's happening here? You are, of course, already familiar with the `getCMSFields()` method. However, in this case we're not using it to extend an existing tab. `Job` isn't a page type, and so isn't using a tabbed interface by default.

We start fresh in the `getCMSFields()` method and create a collection of form fields known as `FieldSet`. The `FieldSet` class is the basis of the SilverStripe forms system. You can pass multiple form fields into its constructor.

A typical form field is instantiated with two parameters: an identifier for the field and an optional label for the field to use when displayed in the interface. If the identifier matches an attribute of the associated `DataObject`, the correct value is automatically pulled out of the `DataObject` and displayed in the form. Any changes are also automatically saved back into the relevant database record.

Let's go through each line in detail:

- `TextField('Title', 'Job Title')` creates a single-line editor field (`<input type="text">`), which edits the `Title` property on our Job class.
- `TextareaField('Description', 'Job Description')` creates a multi-line editor field (`<textarea>`).
- `TextField('Location', 'Location')` creates another single-line editor field for specifying the job's location.
- `DateField('ExpiryDate', 'Expiry Date')` creates an editor field for setting the expiry date for this job posting.

SilverStripe's built-in form fields

SilverStripe has a number of form field types that may be used for a variety of purposes. More fields can be added through modules or custom subclasses. Here's a rundown of the most important types:

- `TextField`: Single-line text input area.
- `TextareaField`: Multi-line plaintext input area.
- `EmailField`: Entry of an email address with format validation.
- `NumericField`: Limits input to numeric values.
- `DateField`: Date input as a single text field.
- `HeaderField`: Creates an HTML heading (not editable).
- `LiteralField`: Displays arbitrary text or HTML (not editable).
- `CheckboxField`: Displays a single checkbox.

- `DropdownField`: A dropdown from an array of options.
- `OptionsetField`: A set of radiobuttons. The value to be selected by default can optionally be passed-in as a second parameter.
- `CheckboxSetField`: A set of checkboxes. This field can optionally save into a relationship.

5.4.3 Linking Overview and Detailed View

'Hey, hang on a minute', you might be saying to yourself, 'just how are the `ComplexTableField` and the detailed pop-up editor view integrated together?'

We've explained quite a bit about the internal workings of SilverStripe over the course of this chapter. However, we didn't need to write a large amount of actual code. Maybe we just forgot to mention how the two interface classes work together?

We didn't, in fact, forget to mention any new code. SilverStripe automatically connects `ComplexTableField` to our pop-up `FieldSet`. How is SilverStripe doing this? Is it somehow reading our mind? Think back to our creating the `ComplexTableField`. The third parameter (`Job`) told the class which `DataObject` to use for the display of data. Unless it's told otherwise, `ComplexTableField` automatically creates links to the detailed editor pop-up view of the `Job` class.

5.4.4 Updating the Database Schema

Up until now we only whetted your appetite with preview screenshots. But now everything is ready. We can update the database schema and actually see our work in action.

As mentioned in Chapter 3, 'Architecture', whenever the database schema (that is: the model) is changed, the actual database must be updated. In order to carry out the update you need to be logged on as administrator or be working in developer-mode. Then type the following into the address bar of your web browser:

```
http://localhost/dev/build
```

The framework will then display the results database refactoring in the browser window. Here's an explanation of what you will see:

- Green entries mean that that particular structure was modified.
- Orange entries are notices or warning. So, for example, if some example data has been auto-generated.

- You should not see any red entries. If you do, there has been some error while executing the refactoring.
- Black entries are tables that have not been modified.

Now that the database refactoring is complete, we still need to do one more thing, namely assign the new page type to each category page:

- The JOBS page should be set to the 'Job category overview' page type.
- The PROGRAMMING, DESIGN, INDEX, and OTHER pages should be set to the 'Job category' page type.

Select one of the category pages in the tree view, click on the CONTENT > JOBS tab, and you should be rewarded with a complete working interface.

Database refactoring without losing data

Once a database table or column has been created by SilverStripe it's never deleted, even if the model is modified. Unused tables are renamed with the prefix '_obsolete'. Unused table columns aren't touched at all. Please keep this fact in mind, because otherwise you might find your application exhibiting unexpected behavior. If you actually want to delete a column you have to do so manually, using a tool such as *phpMyAdmin*.

5.4.5 First Data

Let's create our first job postings. Click the plus icon on the bottom of the form. Presto: a form pops up. Fill out all the fields and see your very first job posting come to life.

5.5 Creating Templates

In this chapter we've come much closer to creating a working job portal. Job postings can already be created, edited, and deleted using the backend.

'Very nice,' you might say, 'but what good does that do for someone visiting the website?'

You're quite right: None of the data is currently output to a view, where visitors to the website might see and interact with it (actually, this is only half-true, as you'll soon see).

Therefore, our next task is to work on the templates. But don't worry. Once again we'll only be writing a very small number of actual lines of code.

However, let's first come back to a bit of theory, so you can understand how everything works together. You'll already know some of the following from Chapter 3, 'Architecture', because that chapter explained the basic principles underlying the template system.

5.5.1 Basic Principles

SilverStripe templates usually contain HTML or XHTML markup, as well as some special commands written in the SilverStripe template language. The template commands can be used to retrieve data from the database. Individual commands can additionally be wrapped in control structures, which allow you to iterate over a set of data.

Flushing the template cache

Once a template has been rendered it's cached in a temporary folder. Usually, *sapphire* clears the cache as soon as it notices that a template file has been changed. You can manually clear the cache by adding *?flush=1* to any SilverStripe URL.

Template Folder Structure

Let's take a look at the templates that make up the standard *BlackCandy* theme. That will give us an understanding of the structure of templates within a theme. You might remember that we copied the *BlackCandy* theme into the *themes/mysite/* folder in Chapter 4, 'First Steps'. If you take a look in the *themes/mysite/templates/* folder you'll find the files and folders shown in Table 5.2.

Table 5.2 Structure of the *BlackCandy* template folder.

Folder/File	Description
Layout/Page.ss	A layout template is generally bound to a page type of the same name. This particular template displays the main content of a page. The relevant text is included using the `$Content` placeholder. Additional page elements such as navigation (*Includes/Navigation.ss* and *Includes/BreadCrumbs.ss*) and sidebar (*Includes/SideBar.ss*) are added to the page via includes.
Includes/BreadCrumbs.ss	Breadcrumb navigation.
Includes/SideBar.ss	Left-hand sidebar (used for second-level navigation).
Include/Footer.ss	Page footer.

Inheritance

Let's now take a look at how the folder structure affects inheritance. When the framework is looking for a theme to apply, it first of all checks in the project folder *mysite/*. Then it checks in the current theme's folder (*themes/mysite/*). The filename of the template must be the same name as the PHP file containing your model and controller class definitions. So, for the page type called `Page`, the corresponding template file should be called *Page.ss*.

Let's say you want to create a new template for the `JobCategory-Holder` page type. This new template should include a (static) introductory blurb at the top of the page. This is easy to achieve: just copy the *templates/Page.ss* file into a new file called *templates/JobCategoryHolder.ss* and add the text into the new template.

But wait, there's a more elegant way to do this. Instead of doing the above, create a copy of the *templates/Page.ss* file into a new file called *templates/Layout/JobCategoryHolder.ss* and add the introductory text to that. So we're working in the Layout/subfolder instead of the main level. The *templates/Page.ss* template will automatically pick up the correct layout template based on the type of page it is displaying. So, the class inheritance also takes place on the level of individual template files. This useful feature prevents code duplication, because it allows you to create a given template element in a single location.

Next we will look into the template language in detail.

5.5.2 Placeholders

Placeholders in SilverStripe work in a similar way to how variables work in PHP. They represent specific data that's included instead of the placeholder when the template is displayed. Placeholders can be displayed anywhere in a SilverStripe template, additional tags are not necessary.

The MVC architecture makes communication between any element in the system very easy. Any method and public property that you create in a controller is immediately available in the view by using the same name. The same is true for properties on the model, meaning that any data we've stored in our database is transparently available in the frontend. All we need to do is create a placeholder for it in the template.

Default Placeholders

The attributes defined in your controllers primarily determine which placeholders are available in your templates. However, SilverStripe already provides some placeholders out-of-the-box and ready for use in any template (inherited from `ViewableData`, `SiteTree`, and `ContentController`. The most important placeholders are detailed in Table 5.3.

Table 5.3 Common placeholders.

Placeholder	Description
`$Form`	Inserts a form, if one has been defined.
`$Content`	Inserts content authored in the backend.
`$Layout`	Inserts code from an associate template in the layout folder. The controller determines which template is inserted. The template with the same filename as the running controller, except with the *.ss* extension, is used.
`$Title`	Inserts the page title.
`$MetaTags`	Inserts the page title, keywords, description text, and metatags in the header section of the page. Add the `false` parameter if you don't want this placeholder to insert the <title> tag: `$MetaTags(false)`.
`$MenuTitle`	Inserts the contents of the NAVIGATION LABEL field. This placeholder is usually used to create the name of the link in the navigation bar of a website.
`$Breadcrumbs`	Inserts a breadcrumb trail that describes the position of the current document in the site hierarchy.
`$URLSegment`	Inserts the path (without the base URL or domain name) to the current page. It represents the URL field in the CMS.
`$BaseHref`	Inserts the base URL of the current site.
`$PageComments`	Inserts the page comments and comment form, if it has been enabled.

Placeholder Casting

Placeholders do more than just insert text fragments. They can actually represent objects that have associated callable methods. This process is called 'casting'. In order to gain a better understanding of how casting on placeholders works, let's take a look at the methods associated with some date-related placeholders. Every `DataObject` (and hence every page) has two built-in date properties: `$Created` is the date on which the current page was created, and `$LastEdited` the point in time it was last saved into the database.

Both properties are of the `SSDateTime` type (see Chapter 4, Section 4.2, 'Creating the Page Structure'). In a template, these simple values such as '2009-01-20 13:30' are actually wrapped in an object of this type, which just contains this value. Various date-related methods can therefore be called on them. For example, to display the creation date of a record in a readable format you use the following method call in your template:

```
$Created.Nice
```

This will call the `Nice()` method of the `SSDateTime` class and output the date in a human-readable format. Note that you don't have to use the round brackets in a template unless you want to pass in parameters.

Table 5.4 Placeholder methods related to dates.

Method	Description
`Nice`	Returns the date in a human-readable format. *Example: '20/01/2009'.*
`Long`	Returns the date in a long format. *Example: 'January 20th, 2009'.*
`DayOfMonth`	Returns the date of the month. *Example: '20'.*
`Day`	Returns the date of the week. *Example: 'Monday'.*
`Range(date)`	Returns a short phrase describing the range between the base date and the date given as a method parameter. *Example: 'January 20th–August 20th'.*
`Format(format)`	Rewrites the date using the *php* `date()` function. *Example: 'Y-m-d'.*
`ShortMonth`	Returns the month in shorthand format. *Example: 'Jan'*
`Year`	Returns the year in four-digit format. *Example: '2009'.*
`Time`	Returns the time in 12-hour format. *Example: '1:30pm'.*
`Time24`	Returns the time in 24-hour format. *Example: '13:30'.*
`Ago`	Returns a string that describes how long ago, or how far in the future, the current the date was or is. *Example: '5 minutes ago', '12 days away'.*
`InPast`	Returns `true` if the current date was in the past.

Table 5.4 details all methods that you can call on instances of `Date`, the superclass of `SSDateTime`. Such methods are of course not limited to the `Date` class. You can define your own placeholder methods, depending on which class they inherit from.

Let's take a look at the implementation of the `Date->InPast()` method so we can get a better understanding of how placeholder methods work:

```
class Date extends DBField {
   // ...
```

```
    function InPast() {
        return strtotime($this->value) < time();
    }
}
```

Listing 5.14 *sapphire/core/model/fieldtypes/Date.php (excerpt)*

`$this->value` contains a reference to the current value of the field in question; in our case the date in SQL-compatible US English date format.

SilverStripe provides methods on other placeholders besides `Date`. For example: `$Image` inserts an associated image object for a record, which can be modified in a variety of ways. `$Image.URL` returns the URL of the image, and `$Image.SetWidth(px)` sets the width of the image to be displayed. Both these methods can be used together, for example: `<a href="$Image.URL">$Image.SetWidth(120)</a>`. Further methods related to images will be discussed in detail in later chapters. For now, all that's important is that you understand what placeholder methods are and how they work.

5.5.3 Conditional Commands

You can specify conditions upon which template code should or should not be output. This is done simply by surrounding the code with an `if`-block. If certain code should be executed when a condition is not met, this should be written in an optional `else`-block.

```
<% if condition %>
...
<% else %>
...
<% end_if %>
```

In many cases, the condition is simply the name of a placeholder. This ensures that the specified placeholder exists and isn't empty or false.

More complex conditions can be constructed using a variety of operators (see box 'Conditional operators'). Please note that placeholders used in conditions must be specified without the usual dollar-sign prefix.

In the following example, the code below the `if`-block is only executed if the date contained in the `Expires` placeholder is in the past:

```
<% if Expires.InPast %> ... <% end_if %>
```

Conditional operators

You can use a variety of well-known operators inside an `<% if %>`-block: Comparison operators: == and != as well as boolean operators: && and ||.

Warning: Statements within conditionals aren't PHP syntax. The SilverStripe template syntax is a custom development and therefore is somewhat limited in what can be expressed. For example, operations can't be chained or grouped using brackets. Comparison operators such as < and > unfortunately can't currently be used.

Template Output for Logged-in Users

You can use an `if`-block to restrict certain template output to be visible only to users who have logged into the system. SilverStripe provides the placeholders shown in Table 5.5 for this purpose.

You might be wondering exactly which methods we can access from `CurrentMember`? It would be boring to list them all. So instead, we just show you how to find them.

`CurrentMember` retrieves the ID of the current user using a cookie. It then looks up all information associated with them from the database. You can access both methods and attributes related to the user using the dot-syntax. This includes directly accessing object properties and relations.

For example, if you want to display welcome text for a logged-in user, you can do so using the following code:

```
<% if CurrentMember %>
  Welcome back, $CurrentMember.FirstName
<% end_if %>
```

Table 5.5 Placeholder information related to logged-in users.

Placeholder	Description
`CurrentMember`	If a user has logged-in, the `CurrentMember` object contains all their user information. User information is accessible using placeholder methods.
`PastMember`	Returns `true` if the user is a registered member of the site.
`PastVisitor`	Returns `true` if the user has visited the website sometime in the past.

`$PastVisitor` and `$PastVisitor` give you a Boolean return value, but, unlike `$CurrentVisitor`, don't provide any methods. Here's an example application of `$PastVisitor`:

```
<% if PastVisitor %>
  Oh, you again...
<% end_if %>
```

Checking the Current Page Type

You can check the page type of the current page. This may sound redundant: Since an individual template can be assigned to each page type, what need would there be to distinguish between page types within a given template?

However, suppose you had a news-summary sidebar that have include on every page. Then imagine you create a NEWS page that lists all news in detail. You don't want to display the summary sidebar on this page. So what do you do? The simplest thing to do is to conditionally display the sidebar only if the current page type is not NEWS. That is:

```
<% if ClassName != News %> ... <% end_if %>
```

Limitations of the template-syntax

The SilverStripe template system works by rewriting the commands within the brackets (`<% %>`) into PHP commands. This limits the number and combinations of commands. However, in most cases you can successfully rewrite a template to overcome the limitations of the template system.

For example, the following is invalid syntax because of too deep nesting:

```
$Person.Image.URL
```

An alternative valid rewriting of the same command is

```
<% control Person %>
   $Image.URL
<% end_control %>
```

You can find a complete listing of the SilverStripe template syntax at http://doc.silverstripe.com/doku.php?id=templates.

5.5.4 Blocks and Loops

Blocks with the `control` statement are essentially loops that you can use to read multiple data sets from a database. These blocks are constructed as follows:

```
<% control parameter %>
...
<% end_control %>
```

The parameter is a reference to a method that can retrieve multiple data sets. Then you can use placeholders within the control block to access specific facets of the data set. If the parameter returns a multiple object, the control block will loop through each returned object.

Placeholders vs control blocks

Placeholders and control blocks are essentially the same. The only difference appears when you are dealing with set of multiple records. If you expect that a database query will only ever return a single record, you can use placeholders and the dot-syntax to achieve the same thing as a control block. This can be helpful to avoid repetition.

Written as a control-loop:

```
<% control CurrentMember %>
   $FirstName
   $Surname
<% end_control %>
```

Written using placeholders:

```
$CurrentMember.FirstName
$CurrentMember.Surname
```

Controls are mainly used to loop through pages. For example, you would typically use them to create a navigation bar. However, their usefulness is quite broad. You can also use them for your own `DataObject` subclasses and collections thereof, the so called `DataObjectSets`.

Defining Your Own Controls

Suppose you had created a `SeniorCustomers()` method in the `Customer_Controller` class:

```
class Customer_Controller extends Page_Controller {
   function SeniorCustomers() {
      return DataObject::get("Customer","Age > 65");
   }
}
```

The `SeniorCustomer` method returns all `Customer` objects with an age greater than 65 from the database. The details of the controller are not important in this case. We are interested in how we can access this data in the view template, by simply opening a control-block with the method name that returns the relevant data:

```
<% control SeniorCustomers %>
   Name: $Name
   Age: $Age
<% end_control %>
```

Note: The parameter, i.e., the name of the method, is specified without using any of the usual PHP dollar- or arrow-syntax. The name of the placeholders within the control corresponds to the names of the attributes within the `Customer` record.

Using Controls for Navigation

The standard *BlackCandy* theme has a number of controls that generate the navigation. Take a look at *Navigation.ss, SideBar.ss,* and *BreadCrumbs.ss* in the */themes/blackcandy/templates/Includes* folder. The available page control types are shown in Tables 5.6, 5.7, and 5.8.

Table 5.6 Navigational controls.

Navigation

Syntax	**Description**
`<% control Menu(level) %>`	Returns the navigation controls at the level which is passed as a parameter. To display the main menu call `Menu(1)` and access the placeholders within the control block.
`<% control ChildrenOf(page-url) %>`	Returns the navigation controls of the sub-pages of the page passed as the `page-url` parameter.
`<% control Breadcrumbs %>`	Returns the breadcrumb trail navigational element.

Table 5.7 Page controls.

Whole page

Syntax	Description
`<% control Level(level) %>`	Returns access to the page specified using the `level` parameter. For example: suppose you're currently at ABOUT US > TEAM > JULIAN. Calling `Level(2)` returns the TEAM page and allows you to access attributes from that page. The same functionality can also be accessed directly without using controls: `$Level(1).Title, $Level(2).Content`
`<% control Page(my-page) %>`	Returns access to the page specified using the URL `my-page`.

Table 5.8 Controls for nested data.

Nested data

Syntax	Description
`<% control Children %>`	Returns all sub-pages of the current page; doesn't return any pages that have been hidden using the BEHAVIOUR > SHOW IN MENUS checkbox in the backend.
`<% control AllChildren %>`	Returns all sub-pages of the current page, including those that have been hidden.
`<% control Parent %>`	Returns the parent page. You can also access the attributes of the parent page directly without using the control. For example: `$Parent.Title, $Parent.Content`.

Controls for DataObjectSets

If you're using a set of `DataObjects` (known as a `DataObjectSets`), you have some additional controls to play with (see box '`DataObjectSet`: A container for your `DataObjects`'). These controls are detailed in Table 5.9.

Instances of the `DataObjectSet` class consist of multiple `DataObjects`. These are roughly analogous to arrays in PHP, but more complex and more powerful.

A special type of `DataObjectSet` is the `ComponentSet`, which is responsible for managing has-one, has-many, and many-many relations between objects.

Table 5.9 DataObjectSet controls.

Syntax	Description
<% if Even %> ... <% end if %>	Code within this conditional is executed only if the output link is an even number.
<% if Odd %> ... <% end if %>	Code within this conditional is executed only if the output link is an odd number.
$EvenOdd	Returns either even or odd, depending on the status of the current line.
<% if First %> ... <% end if %>	The code in this conditional is only executed if the current line is the first line of the set.
<% if Last %> ... <% end if %>	Only executed if the current line is the last line of the set.
<% if Middle %> ... <% end if %>	Only executed if the current line is neither the first nor the last line of the set.
$FirstLast	Returns 'first', 'last', or an empty string, depending on the status of the current line.
$Pos	$Pos contains the sequence number of the current line. This is used, among other things, to determine $Even and $Odd.
$TotalItems	Returns the total number of objects in the current set.
$Top	Normally all placeholders within a control are only able to access content in the context of that control. If you prefix a control by $Top, you break out of the current control block to the one above/surrounding it. For example: $TopURLSegment.

5.5.5 Menu Blocks

Navigation controls give you quite a bit of flexibility with regards to customizing your website menus. We'd now like to show you how to use different styles for different menu states: So, for example, if you want to use a pink-brown dotted background pattern for the currently selected page, SilverStripe should make this easy for you to do (even if you later decide that a rose-mint-toffee pattern look much more stylish).

Menu Status Codes: Link, Section, and Current

SilverStripe provides the following placeholders that can be used to indicate the status of a menu item: `$LinkingMode`, `$LinkOrCurrent`, and `$LinkOrSection` (see Table 5.10).

The navigation is generated from within a control-block. If you use the above placeholders within the navigation control-block, the appropriate status strings will be returned. The return value *section* signifies that this specific page is contained within an active navigation hierarchy, meaning one of its parent or child pages is the current page. A common use case of these values are HTML class attributes that can be picked up by stylesheets: `<li><a href="$Link" class="$LinkingMode">$Title</a></li>`.

Changing HTML Using Status Codes

Although CSS can do a lot, it can't do everything. What would we do if we required completely different HTML for a particular status code? In such a case we can simply use the value of a placeholder in a conditional block to generate the appropriate HTML. In the following example, we don't link the current page, and show it bolded instead.

```
<% control Menu(1) %>
   <% if LinkOrCurrent = current %>
      <strong>$Title</strong>
   <% else %>
      <a href="$Link">$Title</a>
   <% end_if %>
<% end_control %>
```

Table 5.10 Menu status code returns values.

Status code	Description
current	The page that is currently displayed.
section	The parent page of the page currently being displayed.
link	Neither the current nor the parent of the current page: that is, all other pages.

By the way, you can use `<% if InSection(page-url) %>` to execute the code only within the conditional-block if the page specified using `page-url` is the current page, or a sub-page of the current page.

5.5.6 Reuse Using Includes

SilverStripe enables you to reuse code as much as possible, even within the view templates. For this purpose, you can put frequently used snippets of template markup into a separate file and include them wherever you want. You might have heard of this feature from different frameworks under the name *Partials*.

Includes are generally placed in the *themes/mysite/templates/Includes* folder. You can use any filename you wish; in contrast to page type templates, the framework doesn't enforce any specific naming convention for includes. Files do need to end in *.ss*, but you knew that already.

You can access includes with the following syntax:

```
<% include <filename of the include without extension> %>
```

So, if you want include *Navigation.ss* into your site, just write `<% include Navigation %>`. Be aware that names are case sensitive.

5.5.7 Templates for Job Categories

Congratulations! You've now mastered some very important concepts for understanding the inner workings of SilverStripe.

Let's give you a break from learning theoretical concepts and get your hands dirty once again. We return to our example application and create the following templates for the job portal:

- Category overview (Jobs parent page)
- Listing of job posting in a particular category (Job Category page)

Note: If haven't already copied the default *BlackCandy* template into a folder of your own named *themes/mysite/*, please do so now (read Section 4.9.1 'Our own theme: mysite' in Chapter 4 for more information on how to do this).

Category Overview

This isn't a cooking show, but we just have to say it: 'Here is something we prepared earlier'. Please create a new template file in *themes/mysite/templates/Layout/JobCategoryHolder.ss* and enter the following source code. We'll step through it in a second.

```
<div class="typography">
   <h2>$Title</h2>
   <% if Children %>
   <ul class="jobcategories">
   <% control Children %>
      <li class="jobcategory">
         <h3>
            <a href="$Link">$Title ($Jobs.Count)</a>
         </h3>
         <p class="description">$Content</p>
      </li>
   <% end_control %>
   </ul>
   <% end_if %>
   $Content
   $Form
</div>
```

Listing 5.15 *themes/mysite/templates/Layout/JobCategoryHolder.ss*

As the filename implies, this file is the template for the category overview.

With everything you've learnt over the course of the last few sections you should be able to understand what's going on here. However, no harm in giving you a brief run-down:

- The title of the page is displayed using the `$Title` placeholder.
- The conditional-block `<% if Children %>` is then used to check if the current page has any sub-pages (i.e., job categories).
- If there are sub-pages, `<% control Children %>` is used to iterate through all of them.
- Within the control, `<a href="$Link">$Title ($Jobs.Count)</a>` is used within the control to display a link to each job category. The number of jobs in each category is displayed using the `Count` method on the `$Jobs` placeholder. The Count method is a core method that is always available on collections of `DataObject` instances.

Notice how the `$Job` and `$Content` placeholders refer to the sub-page, because they are within the `Children` control-block. So, we're accessing the `JobCategory` pages and not the `JobCategoryHolder` parent page. You might remember that we created a has-many relation called `Jobs` in the job category page model. We're accessing this relation using our view template's placeholders. We will make further use of this ability to directly access the data in a model when it comes time to display the details of each job postings. In fact, that's the next task.

Listing Job Postings

Please create a new file named *themes/mysite/templates/Layout/JobCategory.ss* and type in the following source code:

```
<div class="typography">
   <h2><a href="$Link">$Title</a></h2>
   <% if Jobs %>
   <ul class="jobs">
   <% control Jobs %>
      <li class="job" id="Job{$ID}">
         <h3><a name="Job{$ID}" href="$Link">$Title</a></h3>
         <p class="description">$Description</p>
         <p class="location">$Location</p>
         <p class="expirydate">$ExpiryDate.Nice</p>
      </li>
   <% end_control %>
   </ul>
   <% end_if %>
   $Content
</div>
```

Listing 5.16 *themes/mysite/templates/Layout/JobCategory.ss*

Again, all this should already make sense to you. Nevertheless, let's go through the main points:

- First we use `<% if Jobs %>` to check if the current category contains any job postings.
- If there are postings we open a new control-block by calling: `<% control Jobs %>`. This control references the `Jobs` relation, which we defined within the `JobCategory` model.
- Every job posting contains a primary key. We can access this within the control via the `$ID` placeholder. This serves as a unique identifier for each element in our list.
- The subsequent lines display the values of the `$Title, $Description, $Location,` and `$ExpiryDate` attributes for each Job.
- Finally, the `$Content` placeholder is outside of the control block and therefore refers to the 'normal' content of the page we are editing (as inherited from the `Page` class).

You'll notice Silverstripe has let us write good, clean, semantic HTML and assign CSS classes so that you could later style the appearence of this template. That's it – we've completed the code necessary to display our data.

Now you can see how easy it is to access data using the SilverStripe framework. Just type in the name of the relation and see our glorious job categories rendered in *BlackCandy* (see Figure 5.8).

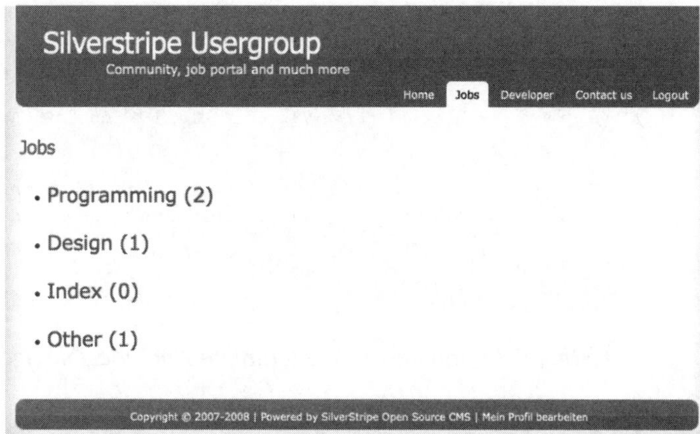

Figure 5.8 Category overview on the website.

As you can see from the figure, we've already created a few job postings in the PROGRAMMING and DESIGN categories.

5.5.8 Login Feature

The next task is to create a different experience for logged-in versus anonymous users. We will start creating the actual user registration system in the next chapter, but you can already test a variety of access rules using your administrator account. SilverStripe differentiates user, editors, and administrators using the user groups defined under the SECURITY tab in the CMS.

We will use the same login form that asked you for your password when you logged into the CMS itself. You can access the login form by going to: *http://localhost/Security/login*. Logging out is accomplished using a similar URL: *http://localhost/Security/logout*.

Naturally users will not just guess these URLs, and so we need to provide appropriate links in the menu bar. The link should be 'logout' for users that are currently logged-in and 'login' for anonymous users who have not yet logged in. We can distinguish between the two cases by using the `CurrentMember` placeholder in the template.

To make this happen we need to edit the *Navigation.ss* template in the *themes/mysite/templates/Includes/* folder. We simply add the appropriate link onto the end of the menu:

```
<ul>
   <% control Menu(1) %>
      <!-- ... -->
```

```
    <% end_control %>
    <% if CurrentMember %>
      <li>
        <a href="Security/logout" title="Logout">Logout</a>
      </li>
    <% else %>
      <li>
        <a href="Security/login" title="Login">Login</a>
      </li>
    <% end_if %>
  </ul>
```

Listing 5.17 *themes/mysite/templates/Includes/Navigation.ss*

5.6 Custom Forms

Our website is looking pretty good already, don't you think? You can enter job postings using a couple of clicks in the CMS and you can nicely view the entered information on the website. But we want to offer more for our future users. We want them to be able to register with the site and create new job postings using the website; that is, without having to access the CMS.

We accomplish this by creating a custom form. We will place the form at the bottom of each category page. This makes the category into which a new job posting is placed self-evident to the user.

Click on one of the example categories such as PROGRAMMING. We will place the form just below the job listing (see Figure 5.9). By now you have a pretty good idea of the structure of a SilverStripe web-application. You might even guess where we're going to integrate this form into the system.

5.6.1 Preparing the Controller

We define the form using a method in a controller and display it using a placeholder in the template.

In which controller should we define the form? Well, do you remember which page was used to display the categories? Right, it was `JobCategory`.

Please open the *mysite/code/JobCategory.php* file and insert the following code:

Silverstripe Usergroup
Community, job portal and much more

Programming

- Forum expert

  Expert at building online communities

  Wellington

  01/01/2010

- ORM guru

  Expert at creating object-relational mappings.

Please send me new job postings in this category by email

Create new job posting

Title

Description

Location

ExpiryDate

Author

(none)

Submit

Figure 5.9 Entry form below the job listings.

```
<?php
// ...
class JobCategory_Controller extends Page_Controller {
   // ...
   function Form() {
      $fields = new FieldSet(
         new TextField('Title', 'Title'),
         new TextareaField('Description', 'Description'),
```

```
            new TextField('Location', 'Location'),
            new DateField('ExpiryDate', 'Expiry Date')
        );
        $actions = new FieldSet(
            new FormAction('doSubmitJob','Submit')
        );
        $validator = new RequiredFields(
            'Title',
            'Description'
        );
        $form = new Form(
            $this,
            'Form',
            $fields,
            $actions,
            $validator
        );
        return $form;
    }
?>
```

Listing 5.18 *mysite/code/JobCategory.php (excerpt)*

Now what does all this code do? It's quite simple, really. We're creating a method named `Form()`, which returns a form object that can display itself as HTML in the template.

We first of all collect a bunch of fields and then pass this data into a new `Form` object, which puts everything together nicely for output. This is very similar to the `Job->getCMSFields()` method that we've previously implemented, but this time we create the form around the fields as well. Let's take a closer look:

- We're already familiar with `$fields = new FieldSet (...)`. The nested constructors within the `FieldSet` object create the layout of the form. `TextField, TextareaField` and `DateField` are the various objects for each of the form's fields. Once again, the first parameter for these objects is the name of the data object and the second parameter is the text that should appear on the form.
- The next step is to create a `FormAction`. That is the method used when submitting a form. It lives within a `FieldSet`, just like the input area of the form (one form can have multiple buttons, by the way). The first parameter of `new FormAction('doSubmitJob','Submit')` is the target method of the submit action and the second parameter is the label on the button.
- It's a good idea to validate the contents of the form before submitting it to the database. We'll keep it simple; in our case we'll just check if the `Title` and `Description` fields have been completed. To do

this we pass a list of the required fields (names of the `DataObjects`) to the appropriately named `RequiredFields` object.

That takes care of collecting the necessary fields, which are then passed into an instance of the `Form` class. Table 5.11 contains a quick overview of the parameters of the `Form` class.

Table 5.11 Form parameters.

Parameter	Description
`$this`	The first parameter is the name of the controller that's responsible for this form. In our case we can simply reference `$this`, because we're creating the form from within the relevant controller.
`'Form'`	The second parameter is the name of the form object. This name serves a double duty as the name of the controller method with which you will later be able to access the form's content.
`$fields`	The third parameter is the object containing the data entry fields.
`$actions`	The fourth parameter is the button class used to submit the form.
`$validator`	The (optional) fifth parameter is the object used for validating the form input.

Saving Form Submissions

Well then, we've prepared our form in the controller. But we aren't finished just yet. Submitted data from the website isn't yet stored anywhere – it will vanish into the digital nirvana.

We did, however, specify a method to deal with incoming data: `FormAction('doSubmitJob','Submit')`. So, all we need to do is create this method and our problems are solved. Please add the following code right below the `Form` method in the controller:

```
<?php
class JobCategory_Controller extends Page_Controller {
   // ...
   function doSubmitJob($data, $form) {
      $job = new Job();
      $form->saveInto($job);
      $job->JobCategoryID = $this->dataRecord->ID;
      $job->write();
      $form->sessionMessage(
```

```
            'Form successfully submitted',
            'good'
        );
        Director::redirectBack();
        return;
    }
}
?>
```

***Listing 5.19** mysite/code/JobCategory.php (excerpt)*

The data of the form arrives in two parts: the `$data` and `$form` parameters of the submission method. The `$data` parameter contains the data that the user entered and the `$form` parameter contains the form object.

First we need to create a place for our form data to go. To do that we create a new instance of the `Job` class.

The `$form` object has a method named `saveInto()`. This method provides a convenient saving of data into a `DataObject` (in our case a `Jobs` object). But how does the method know where to put what data?

Each field on the form needs to have a name, not the least so it can be distinguished from all the other fields on the form. We've labeled each field with the appropriate property names of the `Job` model.

So, if you call the `$form->saveInto()` method, the `Title` field from the form will be written into the `Title` attribute of the `DataObject`. You don't need to worry about saving each individual field. The framework takes care of all that for you. SilverStripe also automatically escapes the data to protect from SQL-injection attacks (for more information, see Chapter 7, 'Security').

You might remember that `JobCategory` and `Job` are in a one-to-many relationship to one another. SilverStripe created a column in the database table `Jobs` named `JobCategoryID` that takes care of this relation. This column contains the ID of the category of each job in the table.

The framework automatically takes care of saving the basic `Job` data into the correct place in the database, but it doesn't know which `JobCategory` to link the job to. We can tell it by using the `$job->JobCategoryID = $this->dataRecord->ID` operation. Here we are using a special 'shortcut' attribute provided by the `Page_Controller` class. Each controller is linked to exactly one page object, referenceable by way of the `$this->dataRecord` attribute. In our case, the reference is to the currently selected `JobCategory` class.

So, let's look at the operation in detail: We created a new instance of the `Job` object earlier in the method. Now we're using `$jobs->`

`JobCategoryID` to reference that column in the `Jobs` table. We then use `$this->dataRecord->ID` to assign the ID of the current job category to the referenced column/attribute.

5.6.2 Preparing Templates

Only one more thing is left to do: We need to actually display our form in the template. Once again all this takes is a few lines of code. Create a new template file in *themes/mysite/templates/Layout/JobCategory.ss* and insert the following code:

```
<div class="typography">
    <!-- ... -->
    $Content
    <h2>Create a new job posting</h2>
    <% if CurrentMember %>
        $Form
    <% else %>
        <p>
            You must be logged-in to create new job postings
            <a href="Security/login">Login</a>
            or <a href="register">Register</a>
        </p>
    <% end_if %>
</div>
```

Listing 5.20 *themes/mysite/templates/Layout/JobCategory.ss (excerpt)*

By now you're probably bored of us explaining these code excerpts in detail. This one doesn't contain anything that you haven't seen already:

- The code for the form is inserted below the main content of the page.
- A conditional block with `CurrentMember` is then used to check whether or not the user is logged-in.
- If the user is logged-in, the form is generated from the `$Form` placeholder.
- If the user is not logged-in, a notice is displayed asking him or her to do so. Including links to the registration form here improves the usability.

Done! In this section you've learnt quite a bit about forms, as well as about saving data. Now that you understand the basic concepts, you'll undoubtedly agree that SilverStripe makes creating database structures and their associated logic extremely easy.

5.6.3 Saving the Author

While you're here, we take the opportunity to tell you a little bit about *Hooks* and *Callbacks*. A hook is an interface that allows you to intercept certain system events and add your own stuff onto them. For example, you can run some custom code every time a `DataObject` is saved to the database. The hooks available for the `DataObject` class and its subclasses are shown in Table 5.12.

We can very elegantly use a hook to save the author of a job posting. Let's think for a moment: SilverStripe already knows who the current user is via `$CurrentMember`. If the user creates a new job posting, wouldn't it be nice if the system could add his or her username into the database for this record?

Each job posting is obviously only published by a single author. Therefore, the first thing we need to do is extend our relation. Open the *mysite/code/Job.php* file and add the following `$has_one` definition for the `Author`:

```
<?php
class Job extends DataObject {
   static $has_one = array(
      'JobCategory' => 'JobCategory',
      'Author' => 'Member',
   );
   // ...
}
?>
```

Listing 5.21 *mysite/code/Job.php (excerpt)*

You already know the `Member` class: It's the base for all users in the system. Our new code has laid the groundwork for linking a `Job` data record to a single Member object. Rebuild the database via `http://localhost/dev/build` and you'll find that the `Job`

Table 5.12 Hooks

Hook	Description
`onBeforeWrite()`	Executes before a record is saved using `write()`
`onAfterWrite()`	Executes after a record is saved using `write()`
`onBeforeDelete()`	Executes before a record is deleted using `delete()`
`onBeforePublish()`	Executes before publication (only for `SiteTree` subclasses)

table now contains a new `AuthorID` column for sorting its associated author.

Now to the hook itself: We want the primary key of the author to be added before a new Job record is written to the database. The following code accomplishes this:

```
<?php
class Job extends DataObject {
    // ...
    function onBeforeWrite() {
        if(!$this->ID) {
            $currentMember = Member::currentMember();
            if($currentMember) {
                $this->AuthorID = $currentMember->ID;
            }
        }
        parent::onBeforeWrite();
    }
}
?>
```

Listing 5.22 *mysite/code/Job.php (excerpt)*

The `onBeforeWrite()` method creates the hook:

- We first use the `if(!$this->ID)` operation to check if the object already has a primary key in the database. This ensures that the hook is only executed the very first time a record is saved to the database.
- Next `Member::currentMember()` copies the data of the potentially logged-in user into the `$currentMember` object.
- `$currentMember` is now checked to see if a user is actually logged-in. Then the user's primary key is retrieved using `$currentMember->ID` and assigned to the `AuthorID` field. The actual save operation can now execute and correctly assign the author ID.
- The final step is to run the `parent::onBeforeWrite()` method. This allows SilverStripe to continue its work and call any other hooks that are waiting in the pipeline.

Note: We're only checking for the existence of a logged-in user at this stage, and not validating the user's security permissions.

Hooks allow you link program logic to database operations consistently and efficiently. They exemplify the *DRY* principle (*Don't repeat yourself*): No matter where a database record is saved, our code will be accessed. This is much more convenient and maintainable than writing the same logic into different form-saving routines and controllers, right?

5.7 Email Notification

Now we tackle the email subscription feature. We want users to be able to choose to receive an email notification of a new job posting. We've laid the groundwork for this feature in previous sections by creating the necessary models.

A quick refresher: A `JobCategory` object can have multiple subscribers of type `Member`. This relation was defined as `Subscribers` and can be accessed using the `$myCategory->Subscribers()` syntax.

We will implement the feature using a template switch. It will only be displayed for users who've logged-in and will allow them to toggle their email subscription on and off for each category. The switch takes the form of a link with two associated states:

- 'Please send me information about new job offers via email' appears when the user isn't subscribed to a certain category.
- 'You are currently subscribed to email updates from this job category. Unsubscribe?' appears when the user is already subscribed to a certain category.

5.7.1 Notification Using Relations

Let's create a method that can tell us whether the currently logged-in user is or isn't subscribed to a certain category. We will later query this method in a template. Enter the following code into the `JobCategory` file and class (not into `JobCategory_Controller`):

```
<?php
class JobCategory extends Page {
   // ...
   function MemberIsSubscribed($member = null){
      if(!$member) $member = Member::CurrentMember();
      $idList = $this->Subscribers()->getIdList();
      return in_array($member->ID, $idList);
   }
}
?>
```

Listing 5.23 *mysite/code/JobCategory.php (excerpt)*

This method takes a `$member` argument and returns a Boolean indicating the status of that member's subscription for a particular category:

- First we check whether a `$member` argument has been passed. If no argument is present, the currently logged-in user is fetched using

Member::CurrentMember(). This design allows the method to be used in a variety of contexts by optionally passing in your own member instance.

- $this->Subscribers()->getIdList() returns a list of subscribers in the form of an array. The list is copied into the $idList variable. $this->Subscribers() accesses the relations database table that the framework has created to handle the relation between categories and members (defined a few lines earlier in the model). getIdList() is a method provided by the ComponentSet class.
- The last line uses the in_array() method to check if the ID of the current user is in the list of subscribers and returns the result.

That covers the database model and query mechanism for email subscriptions. We will get to the template code in a minute, but first let's deal with the process of actually subscribing.

5.7.2 Subscribing

We will once again make use of ComponentSet. It helps us implement two methods: One to subscribe and the other to unsubscribe from email subscriptions. Please add the following code into *mysite/code/JobCategory.php*:

```
<?php
// ...
class JobCategory_Controller extends Page_Controller {
   // ...
   function subscribe() {
      $member = Member::CurrentMember();
      if(!$member) return false;
      $this->dataRecord->Subscribers()->add($member);
      Director::redirectBack();
      return;
   }
   function unsubscribe() {
      $member = Member::CurrentMember();
      if(!$member) return false;
      $this->dataRecord->Subscribers()->remove($member);
      Director::redirectBack();
      return;
   }
}
?>
```

Listing 5.24 *mysite/code/JobCategory.php (excerpt)*

As you can see, ComponentSet makes the process really easy. Both methods work in a similar way. The only difference is that the ID of the subscribing user is written to the database when they subscribe and deleted from the database when they unsubscribe:

- `Member:CurrentMember()` once again retrieves the currently logged-in user.
- If no user is currently logged-in the method returns `false` and thereby aborts this part of the controller execution.
- We use `$this->dataRecord->Subscribers()` to access the relation's `Subscribers` column in the database and then add or remove subscribers using the `add($member)` and `remove ($member)` methods, respectively.
- Finally, the `Director` class is instructed to return back to the original page.

The only really new aspect of this method is the methods to insert/remove the users' IDs.

Now let's deal with the output of all this in the template. We want to display a link that describes the status of the subscriptions and modifies them when clicked on:

```
<div class="typography">
   <!-- ... -->
   $Content
      <% if CurrentMember %>
         <p class="subscribe">
            <% if MemberIsSubscribed %>
               <strong>
                 <a href="{$Link}unsubscribe">
                   Your are currently receiving new job postings
                   by email postings - unsubscribe?
                 </a>
               </strong>
            <% else %>
               <strong>
                 <a href="{$Link}subscribe">
                   Please send me new job postings
                   in this category by email
                 </a>
               </strong>
            <% end_if %>
         </p>
      <% end_if %>
   <!-- ... -->
</div>
```

Listing 5.25 *themes/mysite/templates/Layout/JobCategory.ss (excerpt)*

And now, once again, the code step-by-step:

- The link should only be displayed if the user is logged-in. This is checked using `<% if CurrentMember %>`.
- We then check if the user is subscribed to the current category using the `<% if MemberIsSubscribed %>` method we defined earlier.
- If the user is subscribed, we display a link to unsubscribe: `<a href="{$Link}unsubscribe">...</a>`. We use curly brackets to separate the `$Link` placeholder from the remaining string – this is a little trick that works for all PHP strings.
- If not, we display a link to subscribe: `<a href="{$Link}subscribe">`.

A brief note on these links: `{$Link}` contains a link to the current page. In our case that is the category 'Programming' and the URL *http://localhost/programming/*. Any page can optionally contain an action in its URL, as described in the box 'Mapping URLs and actions with the `Director` class' (below). The action would trigger a method with the same name in the `JobCategory_Controller`, where we defined the `subscribe()` and `unsubscribe()` methods. So, `{$Link}unsubscribe` turns into: http://localhost/programming/unsubscribe.

Mapping URLs and actions with the `Director` class

The SilverStripe framework passes information about controllers, actions and parameters through pseudo-URLs. Behind the scenes, the `Director` is responsible for managing these rules. The system has a couple of predefined rules, but you can add your own ones by using the `Director::addRules()` method.

No custom rule is necessary for our email subscription example, because an existing rule with already map actions for page controllers:

```
Director::addRules(1, array(
   '$URLSegment//$Action/$ID/$OtherID' => 'ModelAsController',
));
```

In this rule, only the `$URLSegment` part is mandatory, all other parts (separated by slashes) are optional. By inspecting the `$URLSegment`, the Director can get to a controller, in our case the `JobCategory_Controller`. It then tries to call a method with the value of the `$Action` part, on our controller this is the `subscribe()` method. `$ID` is available in the method through `$this->request->getParam('ID')` if set through the URL.

For more built-in rules, have a look in *sapphire/_config.php* and *cms/_config.php*.

5.7.3 Sending the Emails

Now the only thing missing is to send the emails. We will implement this by adding a hook in the `Job` class, because we want the email to be sent when each new `Job` is created. Open *mysite/code/Job.php* with your editor and add the following `onBeforeWrite()` method:

```
<?php
class Job extends DataObject {
   // ...
   function onBeforeWrite() {
      if(!$this->ID) {
         $category = $this->JobCategory();
         $this->notifySubscribers($category->Subscribers());
      }
   }
   protected function notifySubscribers($members) {
      if($members) foreach($members as $member) {
         $body = "
            <p>Hi {$member->FirstName}!</p>
            <p>
             A new job posting is available at the following URL:
             {$this->Link()}
            </p>
         ";
         $email = new Email(
            Email::getAdminEmail(),
            $member->Email,
            'job posting notification',
            $body
         );
         $email->send();
      }
   // ..
}
?>
```

Listing 5.26 *mysite/code/Job.php (excerpt)*

What exactly is going on here?

- We check to make sure that the data record doesn't already have an ID, meaning we only execute the following code on the first write request. That way we're sure this is a newly created record.
- Once we're sure the `Job` is a new one, it should notify all subscribed users to tell them about itself. With `$this->JobCategory()` we fetch the category object for this `Job`.
- We then access all subscribed users via `$category->Subscribersw()` and pass them into the `notifySubscribers()` method. The `notifySubscribers()` method should take care of sending the actual emails. As you can see, we use the `protected`

keyword to protect this method from outside access. It would be rather embarrassing if, for example, spammers got control of this part of the system by calling the appropriate URL.

- First we check whether anyone is even subscribed to this category (by checking that `$members` isn't empty). Then we iterate over each subscribed member using a `foreach` loop.
- We now write a message into the `$body` variable. The message is customized using the subscribers name and of course includes a link to the new post. Since we are writing this method from within the `Job` class, we can access the link simply by calling `$this->Link()`.
- Finally, we use `$email = new Email(...)` to prepare the message for dispatch. A call to `$email-> send()` sends the message. `Email` is an internal SilverStripe class that is used to send text or HTML emails. It uses the following syntax: `new Email(<sender>, <receiver>, <subject>, <body>)`.

Hey, wait a minute. We almost forgot to tell you. The `Link()` method used in the email will create a direct link to the job offer. However, the `Job` class is 'only' a `DataObject`, not a page, hence doesn't have a URL by default. We therefore need create a custom `Link()` method so that it knows by which URL it can be reached. Please add the following code:

```
<?php
class Job extends DataObject {
   // ...
   function Link() {
      return $this->JobCategory()->Link() . '#Job' . $this->ID;
   }
}
?>
```

Listing 5.27 *mysite/code/Job.php (excerpt)*

This method returns a link to the category containing the new job posting. To save the user from having to scroll to the actual posting, we add a HTML anchor that directly links to the new posting. The anchor is composed of the `#Job` prefix and the ID of the entry itself (`$this->ID`). This results in a link that looks something like *http://localhost/programming#Job21*.

We've already added the anchor's definition in our template in Section 5.5.7, 'Templates for job categories' with the *JobCategory.ss* template, so this link should work right out of the box.

That completes our email subscription feature. Very nice! Now let's take a break after all this hard work. The next section is about something nice, easy, and fun.

5.8 Integrating the Blog Module

A blog would be something good to add to our example application, don't you think? You can download the blog module from http://silverstripe.org/blog-module/. Get the module and unzip it into the *blog/* folder within your webroot. If you need a refresher on how to install a module, head back to Chapter 3, Section 3.5, 'Modules and Widgets'.

Here's a list of major features for this module while you wait for the download to complete:

- Monthly archive
- Tag cloud
- Spam protection
- Comment moderation
- RSS feeds

Done? Good. Now we can install the module by visiting http://localhost/dev/build. You can tell whether the installation was successful by the appearance of new example pages in the tree view (see Figure 5.10).

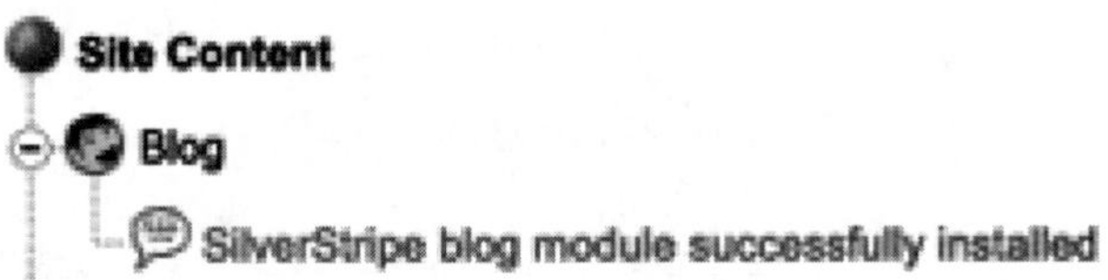

Figure 5.10 Blog module – example page.

The install should have created a page titled 'SilverStripe blog module successfully installed' under the 'Blog' category in the tree view (see Figure 5.11).

Blog Page Types

You now have two new page types available in the CMS: BLOG HOLDER and BLOG ENTRY. This follows the now-tried-and-true formula of the BLOG HOLDER being the page type of the parent BLOG and all individual blog posts having the BLOG ENTRY page type.

Creating New Posts

You can create new blog posts by using the standard 'Create' dialog in the CMS – a blog post is essentially just a new page in the tree. Select the

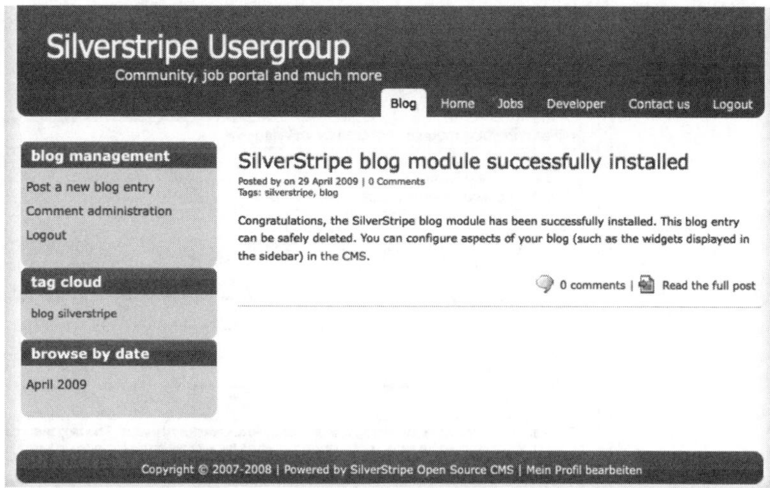

Figure 5.11 Blog module – post overview using the sidebar.

Blog parent page, click the Create button, choose Blog Entry from the drop-down menu and press Go. If you view the blog while logged in as an administrator you will notice that you can alternatively create posts in the front-end, via a stripped-down "bbcode" editor. Visitors to your website can use RSS to subscribe to your blog posts at http://localhost/blog/rss/.

Editing Posts

Select the blog post you want to edit and you can edit its text using the Content > Main tab (see Figure 5.12). If logged in as an administrator, you can also edit posts in the front-end.

Managing Comments

You can manage user comments using the Comments tab in the CMS backend. We've already gone over how to use this feature (see Chapter 4, Section 4.6, 'Comments' for more information). It's a good idea to use RSS to subscribe to a feed contain all comments on your website. This enables you to quickly respond to those communicating on your website. This is available at http://localhost/PageComment/rss/.

The Final Polish

Use drag&drop to move the Blog page to the very bottom of the tree view (so it appears on the far-right of the menu).

You can make some cosmetic changes to the interface by going to the *blog/templates/* folder and editing the template files there. These templates will have default placeholders for displaying tag clouds, monthly

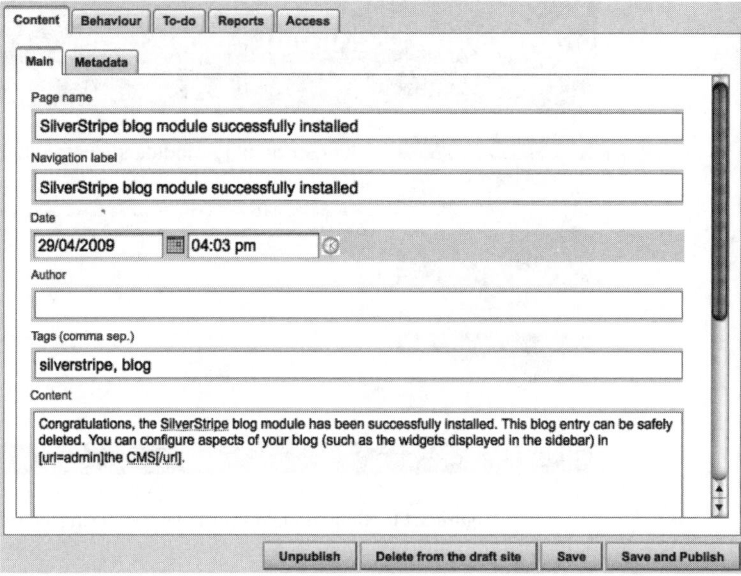

Figure 5.12 Editing a blog post.

archives as well as a paginated list of blog entries. Stylesheets can be found in the *blog/css/* folder. Also, please note that some templates will be overridden by templates in the *mysite_blog* theme. These templates and CSS files are located in the *themes/mysite_blog/templates/* folder.

That's all there is to it. Your blog is now ready for action.

By default, the blog module uses the "bbcode" markup language instead of full HTML for the content of blog posts. This can be reverted to a full HTML WYSIWYG editor by adding the following code to your */mysite/_config.php* file:

```
BlogEntry::allow_wysiwyg_editing();
```

5.9 Search Engine Optimization

Now let's turn our attention to content and its marketing for a while. Although having a technically sound system is a good base, it's just half the battle when it comes to content. The other half is the mighty grip that search engines have on the World Wide Web. Everyone uses them to find stuff. So, we had better know how to optimize our website for a top rank in search results.

One could write a whole book on search engine optimization (in fact, several people have), so there is a limit to what we can teach you in the course of a small section. We'll focus on features of SilverStripe that help you rank well, and what you can do to take advantage of them.

Placing prominently within search engine results can be achieved via two techniques: *Search Engine Marketing* (SEM) and *Search Engine Optimization* (SEO). SEM involves the paid placement of ads in a search engine such as Google. These ads usually appear on a sidebar or in a banner above the search results. SEO refers to measures we take to appear as high as possible in the unpaid search results. Such results are known as *organic* because individual sites generally can't directly influence their ranking.

The following sections deal exclusively with SEO because this is something we can influence directly using the CMS. Please note that we don't make use of any clandestine optimization techniques (so called *Black-Hat SEO*). Also, the criteria for a page's rank in the search results are being continually tweaked by the search companies. We will only focus on more ethnical (called "White Hat") techniques that increase the prominence of desired keywords and aid the indexing activities of search engines.

Black Hat SEO: Invisible content

Using invisible content refers to, for example, placing a large number of common keywords in white text on a white background in the hope that the search engine will pick these up, resulting in one's page occurring more frequently in search results. This technique is frowned upon, because it reduces a searcher's ability of getting objectively-ranked search results. Using such techniques makes it possible for a page that doesn't contain a single genuine reference to the word being searched for to be ranked very highly in a search results. The page might even be completely unrelated to the topic of the search. No search engine can deliver accurate search results if it includes such pages in its catalog. Most of today's search engines will therefore ban websites that are found to be using invisible content from their index. We therefore don't endorse or recommend such manipulations. It's bad for the Internet and ultimately also bad for your website.

Please remember this principle when optimizing your website: Never serve up different content for the search engine than what is served to the human visitor. Both engine and human should be able to see the same thing when accessing your website.

5.9.1 Onsite and offsite SEO techniques

When doing search engine optimization work, you can distinguish between *onsite* and *offsite* SEO techniques:

- *Onsite* refers to the content of your website and how it is structured. Optimizing this involves carefully writing your website content at both the HTML and the human language (e.g. English) level. It also relates to how frequently your content changes, for fresher content can trump stale webpages. We'll expand on a number of such techniques shortly.
- *Offsite* refers to how your website uses hyperlinks to link to other websites, and even more importantly, which websites link to yours. A significant method to ethically improving your page rank is to achieve a high number of genuine links from prominent websites to your website. Achieving this in a 'White Hat' fashion requires contacting the owners of such websites or gaining press, so that they naturally begin writing about you and linking to your website.

Successful search engine optimization addresses both aspects.

5.9.2 Semantic, Keyword-Rich Page Content

Search engines will give preference to websites where the HTML has structure that it easy for machines to digest. This is achieved by carefully choosing HTML elements that convey the *semantics* (or meaning) of the text around them. For instance, it is much more descriptive to use `<h2>` than `<div class="heading2">`. Writing semantic HTML means search engines can separate your page content into varying levels of importance and discover relationships between headings, paragraphs, images, lists and so forth.

Because SilverStripe lets you freely write the HTML and CSS that form templates and because the WYSIWYG editor uses appropriate tags when you choose a heading (see Figure 5.13), it is up to you to make use of the semantics of HTML for the benefit of search engine optimization (not to mention making your content more portable and accessible.)

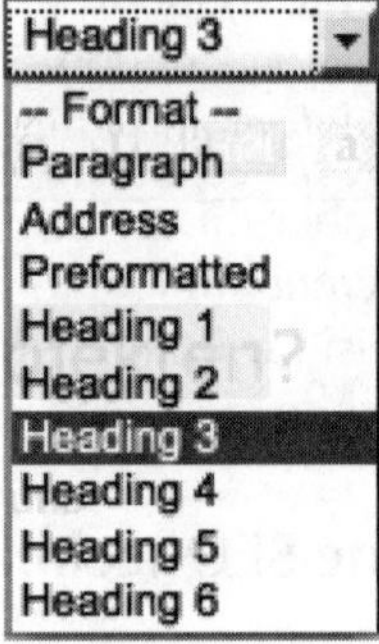

Figure 5.13 Creating headings using *TinyMCE*.

The page title, set by the `<title>` HTML tag, is instrumental to informing search engines of the topic of a page. This title is very important because it is the phrase shown when your website is featured as a search result on Google and other search engines. Therefore it needs to be descriptive. By default in the BlackCandy theme, the title tag is configured to be the combination of the page title (set inside the CMS) followed by "≫ Your Site Name". You should therefore edit the Page.ss template and change "Your Site Name" to a short phrase that communicates what your site does. For example, this is the technique that provides http://silverstripe.org/forums/ with this title tag: `<title>SilverStripe Forums >> SilverStripe.org - Open Source CMS/Framework</title>`

You will also find that your website will benefit greatly from the page content being carefully written in a "SEO friendly" manner. The technique is simply to ensure that your webpages contain the words and phrases likely to be typed as Google searches. It's common sense really: If your pages frequently discuss terms being typed into search engines, then your website will be a logical match for them to promote. What *is* important, however, is that you must use language that is succinct and still makes sense: If you overdo the use of words and phrases then visitors to your website will find your content peculiar and hard to understand. In extreme cases your website rank might be penalized by search engines for exploiting a technique called *keyword stuffing*.

5.9.3 Tableless Template Layouts

We strongly recommend using tableless layouts. Many websites still use tables for layout purposes instead of creating more elegant CSS-based layouts. Search engines still find it quite difficult to analyze text found in table cells, especially if these cells are inside deeply nested tables. Additionally, tableless layouts make it possible to position important aspects of a site's content high in the HTML of a page (where it can easily be found by search engines), and have that content be displayed much lower on the page.

If you study the W3C specification you will notice that the `<table>` element was never intended to be used for layout, but was strictly created to present data that is organised into rows and columns, such as a set of statistics.

By going tableless you support the notion of semantic HTML, and for instance, you make it easier for screen-readers to do a good job of making your website accessible to visually impaired visitors. Note: The *BlackCandy* default theme is proudly tableless.

YAML stands for *Yet Another Multicolumn Layout* and it's a very helpful tool for creating tableless layouts by providing a CSS framework with predefined containers based on CSS floats. Its website features a builder application that can generate a fitting layout for you.

YAML-based layouts display consistently across all major web-browsers and are well tested by its developers. No more battling browsers to get them to display your layout correctly.

Download YAML from http://yaml.de.

5.9.4 Validating Code

You should definitely make sure that your template markup uses valid syntax according to your doctype. For both HTML and XHTML this means: Close your tags properly. If a search engine can't detect where one tag ends and another begins, it will have a very hard time determining which part of your website is most important.

If your website contains HTML and CSS that conforms to the official W3C specification, it is more likely to continue to work with future releases of web browsers. You can check whether your markup is valid by using an online code validator; a common choice is the W3C validator at *http://validator.w3.org/*.

5.9.5 Metatags

Metatags are extra information about a page. They have been greatly misused in the past to manipulate search results. Most search engines therefore don't pay much attention to them anymore. However, the description text of a webpage (`<meta name="description" content="<Your description here>">`) is something that you should be concerned about. Some search engines use this text as the teaser text when displaying search results. You can change a page's description in Content > Metadata > Description.

Duplicate content and redirection

Regardless of how styled, tableless, and valid your site's text may be, please make sure that it's only available from a single URL. Duplicate content can greatly reduce your ranking. Think about it: Why should a search engine index the same text twice? Some of your 'duplicate' pages may be ignored completely.

So, if you want to have the same content appear in multiple locations in the site tree, please do so using the RedirectorPage page type. This redirects a user's web-browser (and search engine robot) to the new page using the friendly HTTP status code '301 - Moved permanently'.

If you really want to, you can mirror a page's content using the VirtualPage type, but this should be used sparingly.

What is important for individual pages is doubly so for a whole domain. If multiple URLs lead to the same website you should choose one address for your content and redirect all requests for the other domain to that site. Once again, status code 301 is the preferred way of doing this.

5.9.6 URL Formats and Links

Many content management systems have the problem that their URLs don't speak for themselves. Often, all pages use *index.php* as their filename and attach a primary key parameter to distinguish one page from another.

The problem is that search engines don't necessarily know that *index.php?id=6652873476* and *index.php?id=329385235* refers to two different pages. They might be the same page with a different affiliate partner ID.

But don't worry: All pages in SilverStripe use human-readable URLs, automatically generated from the page title. So, 'Employment Opportunities at our company' turns into: *employment-opportunities-at-our-company/*. You can modify a page's URL using the Content > Metadata > Url field.

Furthermore, the fact that actual English words (or whatever language your website runs in) show up in the URL provides a search engine more confidence of the intended topic on a given webpage. If someone types in "employment opportunities" into Google, this URL will feature more prominently. Consider this when specifying the URLs for your webpages, but bear in mind that a short page URL like *vacancies/* might be more convenient for humans to type.

Finally, it's good practice to regularly monitor for broken links. Search engines will downgrade a page's rank if it contains a high number of dead links, for good reason: They are of no value to website visitors. The W3C has a link checker that can crawl your website at http://validator.w3.org/check-link/.

5.9.7 Google Sitemap

Google suggests that you use a certain XML format to list every page on your website. This makes it much easier for Google to index your site and ensures that all pages are included. This is especially true for sites that use long parameter-laden URLs. The sitemap file is normally located in the root directory of a site and named *sitemap.xml*.

Having a sitemap-file is useful even if the URL-layout of your site doesn't cause trouble for Google. You can, for instance, use a ping-mechanism to inform Google about new and updated pages via the sitemap.

SilverStripe automatically creates and maintains a sitemap for you. The CMS can also take care of pinging Google automatically when you add or remove pages. This behavior can be enabled by using the following directive:

```
GoogleSitemap::enable_google_notification();
```

5.10 Conclusion

What a day! In the early hours you learnt all about the deep internals of SilverStripe coding, you spent some time blogging over lunch, and in the evening you mastered 'search-engine-fu'.

We have now covered quite a bit of the SilverStripe application. We will bite off the next big chunk in the following chapter.

6
CRM

We fleshed out the job posting features of our job portal in the previous chapter. However, we also want to give job seekers the chance to advertise their own skills. They should be able to create and manage a personal profile. These profiles should then be searchable using a customized search function.

One interesting aspect of this task is the creation of multi-page forms, because SilverStripe has special built-in support for these. Another aspect we will explore is *scaffolding* (see box ''Scaffolding: Automatically generated interfaces'') to create the front- and backend for our profile management interface with relative ease.

Scaffolding: Automatically generated interfaces

Basic interfaces for creating, reading, updating, and deleting data tend to be quite repetitive and boring to write from scratch for all your managed data. Often, you just want to get some data into the system without resorting to tools such as phpMyAdmin.

You've probably heard the term *scaffolding* used in relation to other frameworks such as *Ruby on Rails*. The term refers to the practice of using metadata from your data model to generate interfaces for common administrative tasks. The usual way to accomplish this is to automatically construct the necessary source code files, a practice known as *meta-programming*. True to its name, scaffolding is usually used as a stopgap solution when doing rapid prototyping, with the intention of replacing it with a more polished interface in the final product.

SilverStripe tries to take this idea a step further: The framework doesn't generate any custom code, which will most likely be thrown away later on. Instead, scaffolding plays an integral part in the engineering process towards the final polished interface. It is used as a foundation that automates common tasks in order to let the programmer concentrate on more important matters such as the actual business logic of his or her application.

In this chapter we implement a data model for a simple *Customer Relationship Management* (CRM) system. Although its data model follows the basic rules we learned in Chapter 5, when creating custom page types, it will not be dependent on the CMS interface itself.

At the end of this chapter you will have a CMS to manage content, extended with a CRM to manage people. The CRM will be implemented as an independent interface. It will make deep changes to the way SilverStripe works, while still being entirely separated in terms of its code. Not only that, it will all be pretty easy, too.

We will be modifying and extending code created in Chapter 5 over the coming pages. If you want to follow along as we develop certain features, please continue with your code from that chapter. If you want to get a preview of the results of the work we're about to create, check the *6_crm/* folder in the book website download. It contains the final source code, as well as a sample database called *database.sql*. As usual, an administrator account with username 'admin' and password 'password' is already set up for you.

6.1 Where are we Headed?

Now that we understand the big picture, let's look at some of the details around what we will implement.

6.1.1 Frontend Interface

We want to create an interface that makes it possible for registered users to create and manage a personal profile. Profiles should include the following pieces of information:

- Skills
- Website URL
- References with URL and a screenshot

- Personal introduction
- Location

In Chapter 5, we already started a simple form for submitting job postings. We will build on this work when creating a user registration system, and make sure that only registered and logged-in users are able to submit new postings.

6.1.2 Profile Management in the Backend

In addition to allowing users to manage their profiles from the frontend, we also want to provide a similar interface to administrators of our CRM. We will create a new COMMUNITY area in the main backend navigation bar for this purpose. This will be a completely new section, separate from the existing CMS management features.

6.2 Datamodel

We will get to the source code in a moment, but first let's spend a few minutes considering how our data will be modeled. You might remember how in the last chapter, in order to create our `Job` class, we directly extended `DataObject`, rather than extending the `Page` class. Similarly, in this chapter we will be subclassing `DataObject` directly for all our model classes. The extra features provided by `Page` (e.g., display in the page tree hierarchy) aren't necessary for what we're trying to achieve.

We will create three new classes: `Developer`, `Skill`, and `Reference`. Please don't update the database structure until all three of these are fully defined, because they're mutually dependent on each other.

6.2.1 Developer

The first thing on our to-do list is the creation of a developer record. Much of this functionality is already part of the built-in `Member` class in SilverStripe. However, `Member` doesn't include all of the attributes necessary for our developer profile.

In the interests of not reinventing the wheel, we will subclass and extend the existing `Member` class. As an additional benefit, we will be able to use the standard SilverStripe login forms. This will make login and access control much simpler to implement, because SilverStripe will take care of all the heavy lifting in terms of security and session management.

To get a better idea of what we're talking about, please take a look at some excerpts from the built-in `Member` class:

```
class Member extends DataObject {
   static $db = array(
      'FirstName' => "Varchar",
      'Surname' => "Varchar",
      'Email' => "Varchar",
      'Password' => "Varchar(64)",
      // ...
   );
   static $belongs_many_many = array(
      "Groups" => "Group",
   );
   //...
}
```

Listing 6.1 *sapphire/security/Member.php (excerpt)*

This should look familiar, right? We've used static properties such as `$db` and `$belongs_many_many` to describe attributes and relationships of our own data model before, and built-in SilverStripe classes work very much the same way.

Let's now extend `Member` with the additional attributes we need for our new `Developer` class. Please create the *mysite/code/Developer.php* file and insert the following code:

```
<?php
class Developer extends Member {
   static $db = array(
      'Introduction' => 'Text',
      'Region' => 'Varchar(200)'
   );
   static $has_many = array(
      'References' => 'Reference',
   );
   static $many_many = array(
      'Skills' => 'Skill',
   );
}
?>
```

Listing 6.2 *mysite/code/Developer.php*

There are two new additional attributes: `Introduction` refers to the developer's personal profile description and `Region` is used for locations in which he or she is willing to work.

The last lines define attributes for attaching `Skills` and `References` to a profile. One `Developer` should be able to have multiple `References`. So, we have a 1:n relation (`$has_many`). Additionally, a `Developer` has multiple `Skills` and multiple `Developers` can share the same `Skill`. So, we have a m:n relation (`$many_many`).

The missing subscription relation

As you might remember, we created the `JobCategory` class with a m:n relation to `Members` in the previous chapter. However, we didn't put in the reverse relation from `Member` back to `JobCategory`, because we didn't want to directly modify the `Member` system class. However, now that we have our own `Developer` subclass we can put in the missing relation:

```
class Developer extends Member {
   // ...
   static $belongs_many_many = array(
      'Subscriptions' => 'JobCategory'
   );
}
```

With this little addition we can now query all job categories to which a `Member` is subscribed.

6.2.2 Skills

We want developers to be able to choose skills in the form of *tags*. You might be familiar with this kind of approach from online business networks such as linkedin.com (see Figure 6.1). Tags are essentially chunks of text separated by either a special character like a comma or a simple space character. Tags allow users to collaborate on classifying information themselves, rather than the system impose a rigid structure on them. A system organised by tags is often called a *folksonomy*; a combination of the words folk and taxonomy. Linkedin allows for multi-word tags. However, in order to keep things simple, we will only implement single-word tags, separated by spaces.

Figure 6.1 Example user profile on linkedin.com.

In our planned architecture, we save each tag as a separate object of the class `Skill`. This has a number of advantages: It makes keyword search and the creation of an alphabetical listing easy to implement. Managing keyword objects in the CRM will be a breeze, too. Since each skill is only represented once in the database, data redundancy is minimized. In short, the m:n relation between skills and developers is a clean way of managing this information.

Let us create the `Skill` class in *mysite/code/Skill.php* with the following code:

```
<?php
class Skill extends DataObject {
   static $db = array(
      'Title' => 'Varchar(255)',
   );
   static $belongs_many_many = array(
      'Developers' => 'Developer',
   );
}
?>
```

Listing 6.3 *mysite/code/Skill.php*

This code should be fairly obvious to you. The name of each skill is saved in the `Title` attribute. The `Skill` class is linked to the `Developer` class via a `$belongs_many_many` relation.

6.2.3 References

Each developer should be able to insert a number of references into his or her profile. Each reference should consist of a title, URL, and a screenshot. We will first of all implement the title and URL. Create the */mysite/code/Reference.php* file and insert the following code:

```
<?php
class Reference extends DataObject {
   static $db = array(
      'URL' => 'Text',
      'Title' => 'Varchar(255)',
   );
   static $has_one = array(
      'Developer' => 'Developer',
   );
}
?>
```

Listing 6.4 *mysite/code/Reference.php*

Keeping with the relations we established at the beginning, each `Reference` is only linked to a single `Developer`, and hence we use the `$has_one` relation. We will skip the model code for the screenshot for now, and leave this for Section 6.6, 'File uploads for references'.

6.2.4 Database Schema Changes

We have now created all three classes and their relationships to each other. However, the new schema is not yet present in our database. Remember that whenever a new data class or attribute is defined, the database needs to be notified of this schema change by calling *http://localhost/dev/build/*.

Let us take a quick look at the newly created schema. That will give us a better understanding of what is going on (and allows us to check to make sure SilverStripe is doing its job correctly). Please use a database management tool such as *phpMyAdmin* to locate the new tables.

Table 'Developer'

We extended the `Member` class and added the `Introduction` and `Region` attributes to it. You can find these represented in the database table as shown in Figure 6.2.

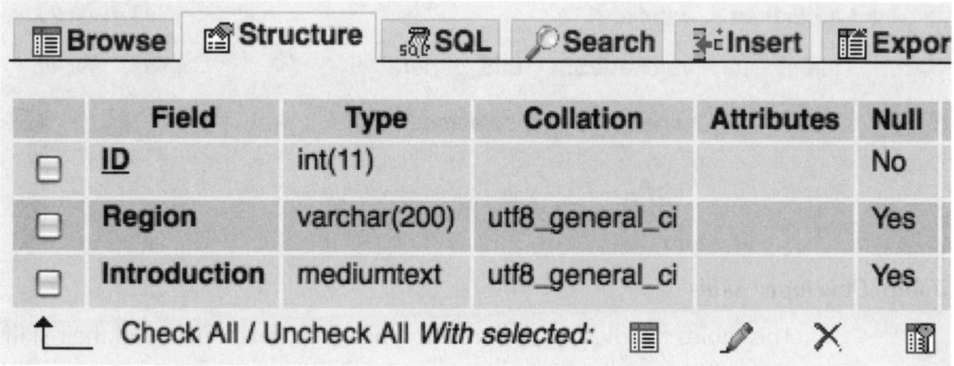

Browse | Structure | SQL | Search | Insert | Expor

	Field	Type	Collation	Attributes	Null
☐	ID	int(11)			No
☐	Region	varchar(200)	utf8_general_ci		Yes
☐	Introduction	mediumtext	utf8_general_ci		Yes

Check All / Uncheck All *With selected:*

Figure 6.2 'Developer' table in *phpMyAdmin.*

Now let's take a look at some of the records in the `Member` table shown in Figure 6.3, which contains the other 'bits' that our developers inherited from their base class.

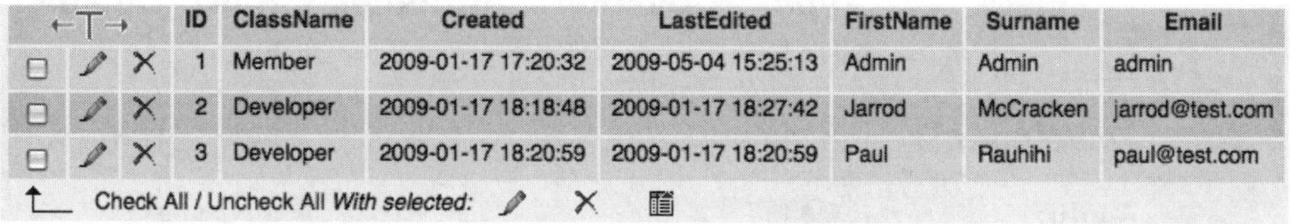

←T→	ID	ClassName	Created	LastEdited	FirstName	Surname	Email
☐ ✎ ✕	1	Member	2009-01-17 17:20:32	2009-05-04 15:25:13	Admin	Admin	admin
☐ ✎ ✕	2	Developer	2009-01-17 18:18:48	2009-01-17 18:27:42	Jarrod	McCracken	jarrod@test.com
☐ ✎ ✕	3	Developer	2009-01-17 18:20:59	2009-01-17 18:20:59	Paul	Rauhihi	paul@test.com

Check All / Uncheck All *With selected:*

Figure 6.3 Contents of the 'Member' table in *phpMyAdmin.*

Notice how the developers are separated from the regular users in the `Member` table. SilverStripe has created a special column named

ClassName. This indicates which class a particular user's record belongs to and tells SilverStripe which additional database to consult to retrieve all of the relevant information.

Table 'Skill'

The names of developers' skills are recorded in the `Title` field, as shown in Figure 6.4.

Browse | Structure | SQL | Search | Insert | Export | Im

Field	Type	Collation	Attributes	Null	Default
ID	int(11)			No	
ClassName	enum('Skill')	utf8_general_ci		Yes	Skill
Created	datetime			Yes	*NULL*
LastEdited	datetime			Yes	*NULL*
Title	varchar(255)	utf8_general_ci		Yes	*NULL*

Check All / Uncheck All *With selected:*

Figure 6.4 'Skill' table in *phpMyAdmin*.

Table 'Developer_skills'

This tables handles the m:n relation between developers and their skills (see Figure 6.5). It records these links with two fields: `DeveloperID` and `SkillID`.

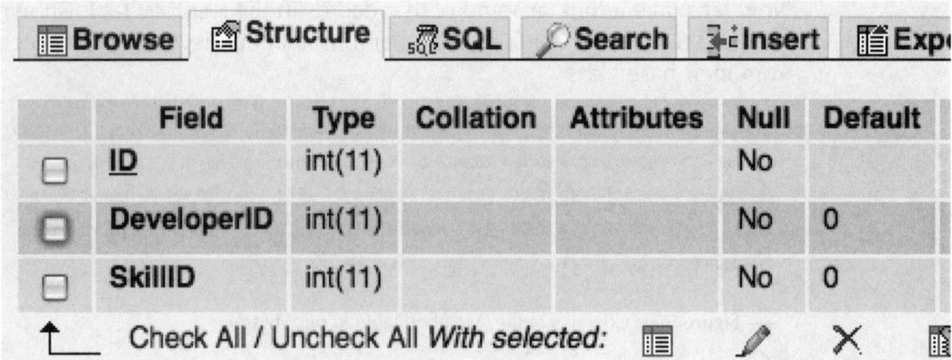

Browse | Structure | SQL | Search | Insert | Exp

Field	Type	Collation	Attributes	Null	Default
ID	int(11)			No	
DeveloperID	int(11)			No	0
SkillID	int(11)			No	0

Check All / Uncheck All *With selected:*

Figure 6.5 'Developer_skills' table in *phpMyAdmin*.

Table 'Reference'

The `Reference` table is shown in Figure 6.6. It records the `URL`, `Title`, and `Screenshot` of each reference. The ScreenshotID property already appears in the figure, but as previously mentioned, will not be integrated fully until later in this chapter.

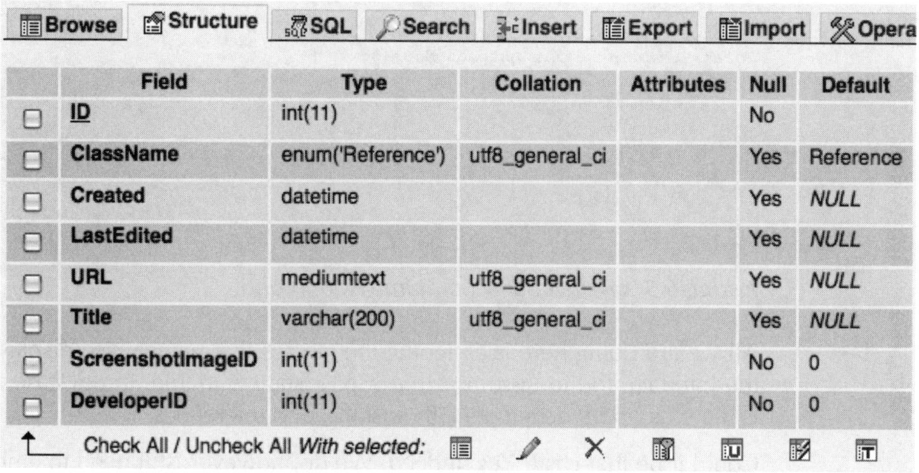

Browse | Structure | SQL | Search | Insert | Export | Import | Opera

	Field	Type	Collation	Attributes	Null	Default
	ID	int(11)			No	
	ClassName	enum('Reference')	utf8_general_ci		Yes	Reference
	Created	datetime			Yes	NULL
	LastEdited	datetime			Yes	NULL
	URL	mediumtext	utf8_general_ci		Yes	NULL
	Title	varchar(200)	utf8_general_ci		Yes	NULL
	ScreenshotImageID	int(11)			No	0
	DeveloperID	int(11)			No	0

Check All / Uncheck All *With selected:*

Figure 6.6 'Reference' table in *phpMyAdmin*.

6.3 Using ModelAdmin for Data Management

Very good; you should now have a good understanding of the underlying data model now. It just needs a way to display and manage this data. We could create a separate page in the CMS for each and every skill and reference, but that would be overkill in this case. In Chapter 5, we already showed you how to extend CMS forms with custom form fields. Now we take this one step further: We will create an entirely new data management interface separate from the main CMS.

If this sounds daunting, don't despair. SilverStripe gives us a helping hand by providing the `ModelAdmin` base class: A generic admin interface that can be used to search, view, and edit records based on DataObject. Just what we need to help us create a sophisticated admin interface with minimal effort.

It works by using a new kind of scaffolding technique. `ModelAdmin` analyzes DataObjects and generates a complete management interface based on the found meta data. The default scaffolding provides the administrator with a way to edit all attributes of each object. You can, however, customize the interface, adding or removing fields as necessary to create a more appropriate backend.

6.3.1 ModelAdmin subclass: CommunityAdmin

All this is possible with just a few lines of code. To start off, we create a subclass of `ModelAdmin` and assign the classes we created beforehand. Let's call our subclass `CommunityAdmin`. Create the *mysite/code/CommunityAdmin.php* file and insert the following code there:

```
<?php
class CommunityAdmin extends ModelAdmin {
   static $managed_models = array(
      'Developer',
      'Reference',
      'Skill',
   );
}
?>
```

Listing 6.5 *mysite/code/CommunityAdmin.php*

All we are doing here is assigning the classes that we want to display in the interface to the `$managed_models` static variable. In our case this is the data about developers, their skills, and references.

Could it be that easy? Yes, indeed. We do, however, still need to embed the interface into the correct place in the backend and make a few modifications to the interface layout. Let's get to it.

6.3.2 Menu Entry and URL Routing

The new backend area should appear in the main navigational menu alongside Site Content, Files & Images, and so forth. We need to extend the menu with a link to the new area. All administrative areas belong under the URL *admin/*, so the choice of URLs falls to *http://localhost/admin/community/*. You can choose the path by defining another static variable in our subclass of `ModelAdmin`. It's called `$url_segment` and defines URLs relative to the *admin/* path:

```
class CommunityAdmin extends ModelAdmin {
   // ...
   static $url_segment = 'community';
}
?>
```

Listing 6.6 *mysite/code/CommunityAdmin.php (excerpt)*

The menu bar title is automatically extracted from the class name unless specified otherwise – in our case COMMUNITY. To change this title, use the `$menu_title` static variable.

6.3.3 Invoking the New Backend

Here we go. Open *http://localhost/admin/community/* in your web-browser and observe the result. The menu bar has a new item and within it you will see the new interface that SilverStripe has built (see Figure 6.7).

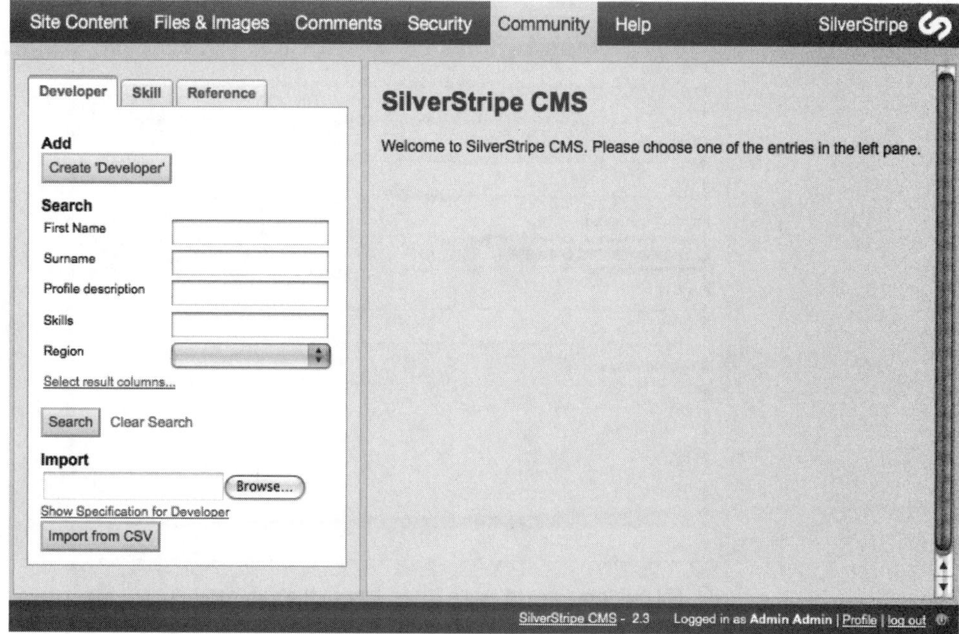

Figure 6.7 ModelAdmin backend.

Observe the two areas that make up the interface: The left-hand side can be used to create new records or search for existing records. The right-hand side displays the relevant data for editing.

Adding Records

Click on the CREATE DEVELOPER button to add your first developer record. This should show a form similar to Figure 6.8.

Figure 6.8 Creating a new profile using `ModelAdmin`.

As you can see, all attributes belonging to `Member`, as well as those belonging to `Developer`, are managed using a single unified form. Enter your personal details to test the system. However, keep in mind that that duplicate users are not allowed by the system. Users are distinguished by email address, so you will have to choose an email address that is not already registered with the CMS.

After saving you will notice that two new tabs appear in the main area: References and Skills (see Figure 6.9). They show all related records in a tabular view, and allow us to create and edit them without leaving the `ModelAdmin` interface. This is handled by a `ComplexTableField`, which we have already used in Chapter 5 to edit job records in a job category holder page.

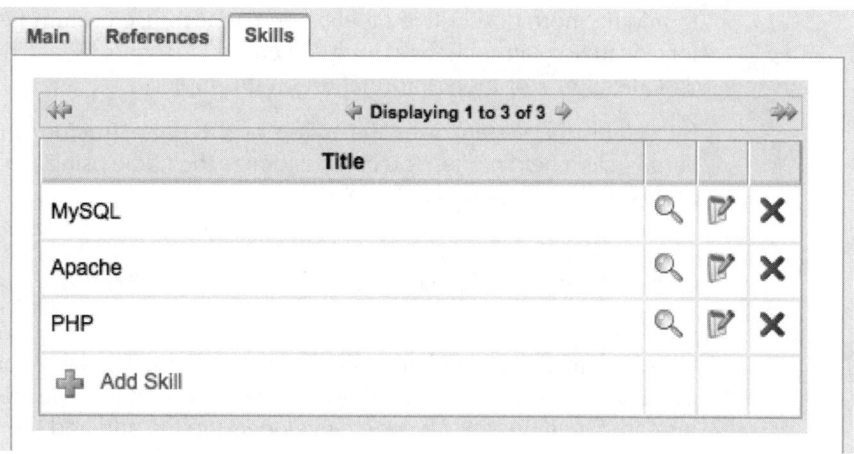

Figure 6.9 New tabs for linked data.

Searching Records

You can use the search boxes on the left-hand panel to search for records based on criteria that you specify. Click the SEARCH button without specifying a search criteria to get a listing of all the developers registered with the system, as shown in Figure 6.10. We will go into detail about how to customize the search behavior in Section 6.7, 'Searching DataObjects'.

Search Results

Displaying 1 to 3 of 3

First Name	Last Name	Email	
Jarrod	McCracken	jarrod@test.com	X
Julian	Seidenberg	julian@test.com	X
Paul	Rauhihi	paul@test.com	X

Export to CSV

Figure 6.10 Listing records in the main area.

Click on one of the records in your search results and you will be taken to a new screen for editing it. Press the red cross next to a record to delete it.

6.3.4 Form Field Customization

You can see from the screenshots in the last section that we have customized some of the field names to be more descriptive. In addition to adding more descriptive labels, you can also use custom field names for localizing an interface to a different language. See Chapter 10, 'Localization', for more information on this topic.

By default the system uses the name of the data structure in the `$db` variable as a field name. You can customize the name using the following syntax in the relevant DataObject:

```
static $field_labels = array(<attribute> => <custom name>)
```

Let's look at one example of using custom names. The label for the field `Introduction` is a bit ambiguous, let's name it 'Profile description' instead. Open the *mysite/code/Developer.php* file and add the following code:

```
<?php
class Developer extends Member {
   // ...
   static $field_labels = array(
      'Introduction' => 'Profile description',
   );
}
?>
```

Listing 6.7 *mysite/code/Developer.php (excerpt)*

Save the file and observe how the labels in the interface change.

6.4 Multi-page Registration Form

The admin interface is working nicely, but what about our website users? We don't want them messing around in the backend. So, the next step will be to make profiles editable on the website. The first step towards this is to let users register and authenticate with our website.

We laid the groundwork for a registration system in the previous chapter, but didn't actually implement it. Now we will create a multi-page registration form that will allow users to create their own profiles. Both job seekers and employers will be using the same basic interface.

We split the form into two separate pages because there is a lot of information to enter: One page for personal information and a second one for references. Luckily, SilverStripe has built-in support for forms that are spread across multiple pages. Once again, scaffolding will help us out. There's no need to define our forms manually, but instead we can have them scaffolded from existing metadata, very much like the edit forms we've already seen in ModelAdmin. This enables a more rapid development, and has less potential for errors as well as lower maintenance overhead.

6.4.1 First page: User Details

The first page should be used to gather personal details about the user (take a look at Figure 6.11). Most fields are simple text entry areas, which we will not talk about in detail.

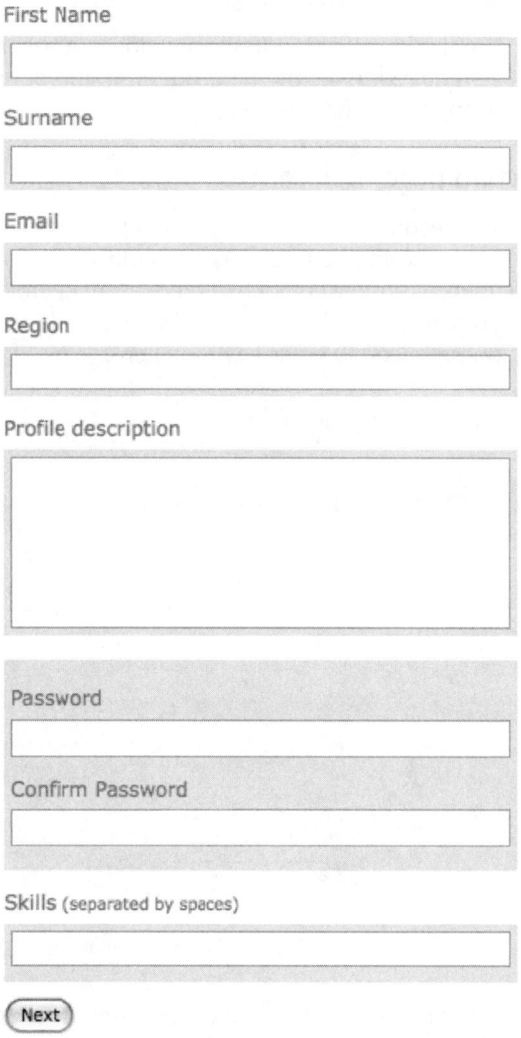

Figure 6.11 Registration form: first page.

The Password field requires a confirmation field, and will automatically take care of hashing the password in a suitable format for storage in a `Member` record.

As previously mentioned, we want to represent skills as tags. The Skills field looks like a simple text input. We want our web-application to check whether a given skill is already in the database and auto-suggest the field name if this is the case. So, for example, if a user starts entering 'My' as a skill, 'MySQL' should show up below the field. The user then just has to click the suggestion and the field will be filled without having to finish writing it. All of this would, of course, only work if a different user has previously entered 'MySQL' as a skill.

We'll add validation to those fields in a second, and mark some of them as required. Note the Next button at the bottom of the form: It will lead us to the second form page.

6.4.2 Second page: References

The second page should record a first reference for the registering developer (see Figure 6.12). Again, nothing is unusual beyond standard text fields. A screenshot for a reference can be uploaded in a standard browser upload field. All fields will be optional, so a user without references doesn't need to enter anything here.

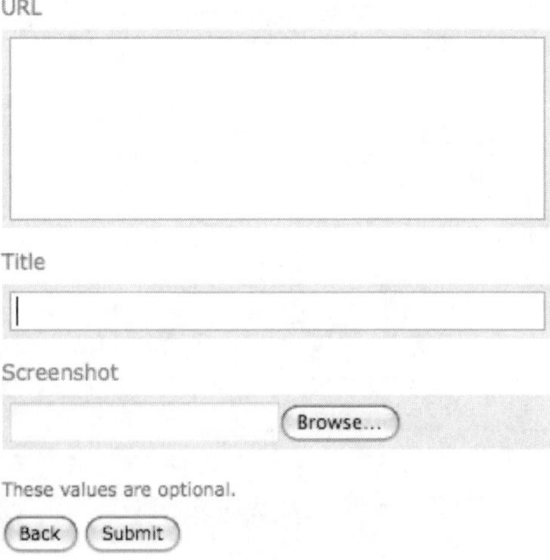

Figure 6.12 Registration form: second page.

We will use some modules that aren't part of the standard SilverStripe distribution in order to make this form interface come to life. Check out Chapter 3 for help on installing modules.

6.4.3 The 'Multiform' Module

The *multi-step form* module helps us to spread the registration across two pages. Technically, it consists of two components: the `MultiForm` and `MultiFormStep` classes. Generally, you can integrate a multi-step form into your code just like any other form. However, there is a twist: Fields and actions aren't defined directly on your form. Instead, `MultiForm` manages multiple `MultiFormSteps`, which are the individual form pages. We can customize the functionality by subclassing the two classes.

The `MultiForm` class saves each form page in a temporary database table. This makes it possible for a user to jump back and forth between multiple form pages without losing any submitted data. Each page knows which page is coming next, or if it is the last page in the set. Once all pages have been completed, `MultiForm` takes care of saving all of the collected data. We are just using two pages for our example, but you can create forms with an arbitrary number of pages following the same pattern.

You can download and install the module from the following URL: http://silverstripe.org/multi-form-module/. To install, copy the *multiform* folder into the SilverStripe webroot and update the database by opening *http://localhost/dev/build/* in your browser.

6.4.4 RegistrationMultiForm

Enough talk, let's see some action! First we will create a class for the multi-page form. We will call it `RegistrationMultiForm`. Create and open the *mysite/code/RegistrationMultiForm.php* file and enter the following code:

```
<?php
class RegistrationMultiForm extends MultiForm {
   protected static $start_step = 'RegistrationDetailsStep';
}
?>
```

Listing 6.8 *mysite/code/RegistrationMultiForm.php*

Each step in our form is represented by a specific class. As you can see, we have only defined the first step in the process using the `$start_step` static variable, a class called `RegistrationDetailsStep`.

6.4.5 RegistrationDetailsStep

Our first form step is called `RegistrationDetailsStep`, and is a subclass of `MultiFormStep`. It takes the name, email address, and other common fields from our user, as described in the preceding section. Scaffolding will take care of most of the work for us.

Create the `RegistrationDetailsStep` class in a file called *mysite/code/RegistrationDetailsStep.php*:

```
<?php
class RegistrationDetailsStep extends MultiFormStep {
   protected static $next_steps = 'RegistrationReferenceStep';
   function getFields() {
      $fields = singleton('Developer')->getFrontendFields();
      return $fields;
   }
}
?>
```

Listing 6.9 *mysite/code/RegistrationDetailsStep.php*

Let's go through this code step-by-step:

- The `$next_steps` static variable defines the next form on the page. In our case, this is a class called `RegistrationReferenceStep`, which we will define soon.
- We use the `getFields()` method to collect all of the fields for display on the form. The `getFrontendFields()` method is a built-in method that automatically creates the right form fields for us. This method returns a `FieldSet` object, which contains form field elements for all editable attributes of the DataObject on which it was called. So, a form for editing all aspects of a developer is dynamically created based on the model structure of the underlying object.
- You will undoubtedly have noticed that we're using the *Singleton* design pattern here. For the purpose of generating the form fields we only need a generic object, without an associated database record. The `singleton()` method always returns an instance of the same basic object. "The Singleton design pattern" for more information.

The Singleton design pattern

Singleton – just like *Model View Controller* – is a design pattern. The general principle is quite simple: A singleton only allows a single instance of a particular class to exist at any given time. Access to the class is provided globally without having to instantiate any new object. This reduces memory requirements and increases execution speed of the application.

```
// two instances of the same class
$inst1 = new MyClass();
$inst2 = new MyClass()
// two references to the same instance
$s1 = singleton('MyClass'); // creates new instance
$s2 = singleton('MyClass'); // gets existing instance
```

The `singleton()` method works by first checking whether an object of the `MyClass` class already exists. Since no such objects exist, it creates a new instance and assigns this to the `$s1` variable. The same procedure is run through the second time the method is called. However, this time there is already a `MyClass` object, and so no new instance needs to be created. Instead, the existing object is assigned to the `$s2` variable.

Now we want to make sure that certain required fields are filled in. The system would, after all, not know what to do with a name-less, email-less developer.

```
<?php
class RegistrationDetailsStep extends MultiFormStep {
   // ...
   function getValidator() {
      return new Member_Validator(
         'FirstName',
         'Surname',
         'Email',
         'Password'
      );
   }
}
?>
```

Listing 6.10 *mysite/code/RegistrationDetailsStep.php (excerpt)*

The `getValidator()` method can be used to validate any form input. We want to do a basic check for required fields in our form and we use the built-in `Member_Validator` class, which is part of the `Member` class. This validator is instantiated and returned by the `getValidator()` method. The parameters passed to the validator are those form fields that must be completed for a form to be accepted. The validator also checks for duplicate email addresses, and so we don't need to perform this check separately.

That takes care of the first page of the form. The next page should be easy as pie for you.

6.4.6 RegistrationReferenceStep

We already specified the name of the second form page in the first form page class. It was to be called `RegistrationReferenceStep`. So, please go ahead and create the *mysite/code/RegistrationReferenceStep.php* file and insert the following code:

```
<?php
class RegistrationReferenceStep extends MultiFormStep {
   protected static $is_final_step = true;
   function getFields() {
      $fields = singleton('Reference')->getFrontendFields();
      return $fields;
   }
}
?>
```

Listing 6.11 *mysite/code/RegistrationReferenceStep.php*

The static variable `$is_final_step = true` tells the system that this is the last page of the form. `$next_steps` is obviously not used in this class. The `getFields()` methods works in much the same way as it does on the first page. It returns the form fields for the developer's references. Since all fields on this page are optional, no validation is required.

Displaying form fields in different contexts

SilverStripe is similar to most web applications in that multiple users with differing access rights are operating on the same data. The separation typically takes place in terms of the interface that users use. Administrators use the CMS (backend) and have full access; regular users interact with the website (frontend) and can perform only a limited set of tasks. This also has implications on the allowed form fields in these different contexts.

Each `DataObject` has two build-in methods to make this separation possible: `getCMSFields()` for working in the CMS and `getFrontendFields()` for display on the actual website. Both methods internally call `scaffoldFormField()`, but can do so with differing parameters. You can override these methods to change which information is displayed in a particular context, or even to define your own contexts. You might, for example, want to create two different registration processes: A quick registration with limited fields and an alternative, more detailed, procedure. Section 6.4.8 explains this further.

6.4.7 Integration with RegistrationPage

Now that we have prepared the multi-page form we need to integrate it with the actual site. Up until now, with no public registration system, only administrators with backend access could create new job postings. Integrating the registration form will make it possible for all users to register and interact with the system.

Our registration form should be accessible from a new page on the website, which has to know how to instantiate the right form, and pass through any submissions to it. Let's create a new page type for the form. Create the *mysite/code/RegistrationPage.php* file with the following code:

```
<?php
class RegistrationPage extends SiteTree {
}
class RegistrationPage_Controller extends Page_Controller {
   function Form() {
      return new RegistrationMultiForm($this, 'Form');
   }
}
?>
```

Listing 6.12 *mysite/code/RegistrationPage.php*

We override the existing form creation method called `Form()` in our newly created RegistrationPage page type. This method instantiates and returns the `RegistrationMultiForm` class we just defined. This form, just like any other form, needs a reference to the controllers (`$this`) and the name of the form (`'Form'`).

Save your changes and rebuild the database using *http://localhost/dev/build/*. Then login to the CMS and create a new page with the Registration Page type, name the page 'Register' and move it to the bottom of the page tree (that way it will appear on the right on the menu bar in the frontend). Take a look at *http://localhost/register/* and try out the complete registration form that now lives there. Isn't it amazing that we didn't have to explicitly define any of the fields? The framework's scaffolding feature took care of most of the work for us.

6.4.8 Fine-tuning the Form Fields

Naturally, the framework doesn't know which attributes we may not wish to display or allow to be editable when scaffolding a form. The standard `Developer->getFrontendFields()` method manifests all attributes of a developer, even the password. We will need to do some fine-tuning here. The `getFrontendFields()` method internally uses the `scaffoldFormFields()` method of the `DataObject` class. That method does the actual heavy-lifting of extracting and creating the various form fields. It can be called with an optional parameter of an array with only those fields we want it to output.

The method `getFrontendFields()` is built into every `DataObject`. Since we want to limit the data that is displayed about a developer to include only first name, surname, email address, and region, this is the place make it happen. Open the *mysite/code/Developer.php* file and insert the following code:

```
<?php
class Developer extends Member {
   // ...
   public function getFrontendFields() {
      $fields = $this->scaffoldFormFields(array(
            'restrictFields' => array(
               'FirstName',
               'Surname',
               'Email',
               'Region',
            ),
            'fieldClasses' => array(
               'Email' => 'EmailField',
            )
         )
      );
      return $fields;
   }
}
?>
```

Listing 6.13 *mysite/code/Developer.php (excerpt)*

We are overriding the inherited `getFrontendFields()` method with our own code. This method will look very similar to the original version. We are accessing `scaffoldFormFields()` and passing an array of those attributes we want displayed on our form in `restrictFields`.

The email address is stored as a regular string in the database, and usually edited by a simple text field. However, we want to activate the special validation that occurs to prevent duplicate email addresses. To do this we need to specify that `Email` is a field of type `EmailField`. The `fieldClasses` array parameter references an associative array with attribute name keys and values that specify the associated field type.

Security in form fields

Displaying only a subset of all available fields is certainly useful for the purposes of usability. However, a much more important consideration is the security of the web application. Users can edit only those attributes of an object that are displayed in forms. They don't have access to anything else. If a form were to display the `DeveloperID` attribute for linking between a user and his or her references, malicious users could overwrite this field to hijack other user's references.

So please always keep security in mind while developing your application. Be careful what you expose to users. SilverStripe as a framework can provide you with the means to apply security practices, but it can't predict all possible contexts for locking down certain fields.

We have now carefully limited what is displayed in the first form page. Onwards to the second page. We will also limit what attributes of the Reference class are displayed. Open the *mysite/code/Reference.php* file and insert the following code:

```
<?php
class Reference extends DataObject {
   function getFrontendFields() {
      $fields = $this->scaffoldFormFields(array(
         'restrictFields' => array(
            'URL',
            'Title',
            'ScreenshotImage'
         )
      ));
      return $fields;
   }
}
?>
```

Listing 6.14 *mysite/code/Reference.php (excerpt)*

This code follows the same mold as the `Developer` class. We are limiting the display to include only the `URL`, `Title`, and `ScreenshotImage` attributes.

6.4.9 Saving the Form Input

The one thing missing is a way to save the entered form data. Let's look at the architecture of multi-page forms to work out how best to do this. Unlike a normal form, the saving of multi-page form data occurs in two stages: First the data from the individual form pages is collected into a session object on a temporary database table; and second, after all data has been collected, it is saved into the correct database tables by a different process.

We will implement this finalization process as part of the `MultiForm` class. SilverStripe looks for a method classed `finish()` when saving multi-form data. Therefore, let's create this method. Open the *mysite/code/RegistrationMultiForm.php* file and insert the following code:

```
<?php
class RegistrationMultiForm extends MultiForm {
   // ...
   public function finish($data, $form) {
      parent::finish($data, $form);
      $detailsStep = $this->getSavedStepByClass(
         'RegistrationDetailsStep'
      );
      $developer = new Developer();
      $detailsStep->saveInto($developer);
      $developer->write();
      $developer->logIn();
      $referenceStep = $this->getSavedStepByClass(
         'RegistrationReferenceStep'
      );
      if($referenceStep->loadData()) {
         $reference = new Reference();
         $referenceStep->saveInto($reference);
         $reference->DeveloperID = $developer->ID;
         $reference->write();
      }
      return $this->controller->customise(array(
         'Form' => false,
         'Content' => '
            Thanks for registering!
            You are now logged-in.
         '
      ))->renderWith('Page');
   }
}
?>
```

Listing 6.15 *mysite/code/RegistrationMultiForm.php (excerpt)*

This code reads the data that the user entered on the two pages of the multi-step form and saves it into the main database:

- The `finish()` method is called after the user submits the second and last form page. At this point the system has not yet processed the data from that final form page. The first line of the code in the listing takes care of doing that: `parent::finish($data, $form)`.
- Calling `$this->getSavedStepByClass('RegistrationDetailsStep')` returns all data contained within a single form page. All we need to do is call this method with the name of the relevant class of the form page. We then assign the data to the `$detailsStep` variable.

- `$developer = new Developer()` creates a new developer object.
- We then earmark the data from the first page of the form to be saved into the newly created developer by calling `$detailsStep->saveInto($developer)`.
- The save is executed by calling `$developer->write()`.
- The user who has just registered him- or herself into the system is signed in automatically by calling `$developer->logIn()`.
- Now we move onto the dealing with the second page of the form. We collect the entered reference data by calling `$this->getSavedStepByClass('RegistrationReferenceStep')`.
- Since this data was optional, we need to use `if($referenceStep->loadData())` to check whether any data exists in the first place.
- If we have data, we can create a new `Reference` object and earmark the data to be saved into that object. Note that we need to associate the reference with the Developer that it belongs to (using the Reference's `DeveloperID` field).
- Once everything has been saved the last few lines of the code generate a success message for the user.
- Let's look at that last line again in greater detail. The output page is referenced using `$this->controller`. The `customise()` method on the controller can then be used to modify the output. Any placeholder in the template can be overridden by passing in an associate array with the relevant keys. In this case, we use `Form => false` to tell the controller not to output a form (because the user just submitted the form). We also insert a status message into the `'Content'` placeholder. Please make sure that you don't mistakenly use the American spelling of 'customize'. SilverStripe uses the British spelling for this method 'customise' (as indeed it uses 'behaviour' and not 'behavior'.
- Finally, `renderWith('Page')` creates the output page using the *Page* template.

That's it! We have successfully implemented a multi-page form.

File paths in SilverStripe templates

You may have noticed that we did something new in the previous code example. Instead of the template being selected automatically according to the page type's filename, we explicitly set the page's template using PHP code.

`$obj->renderWith('<template-name>')` allows us to programatically select any template for a given page. The folder of the current theme, as well as the current project's folders are searched for the specified template name. If you want to diagnose what's going on in greater detail, just add *?debug_request=1* to the end of the URL. The `renderWith()` method is defined in the `ViewableData` class. This class is the basis of all Controller and DataObject instances. This allows you to mold most 'viewable' classes in the framework into your desired HTML or any other output format.

By the way, you can also pass an array with multiple templates into the `renderWith()` method. The system will use the first valid template it finds.

6.5 Skills as Tags

You will remember that we had planned to do something special for the skill input interface. We want every skill to be a separate tag, separated by spaces. We also want tabs to offer as-you-type suggestions for possible tabs, a feature also known as *autocomplete*.

Skills are saved as `Skill` DataObjects via a many-many relation. For example, suppose we enter three skills 'MySQL', 'Apache', and 'PHP'. These skills would be saved as three separate `Skill` objects. This has the advantage that our generic ModelAdmin backend will be able to access this data seamlessly, as well as allowing us to quickly and easily generate links for each specific tag suggestion. But don't worry. You won't have to create the interface for this task all by yourself.

We will use a module known as 'TagField' for this purpose. Please download the module from the following webpage: http://silverstripe.org/tag-field-module/. Install the module in the usual way. The module automatically searches for and displays relevant tags. It is based on a plug-in for the *jQuery* JavaScript framework (http://jquery.com/) known as 'tag suggest' (http://plugins.jquery.com/project/tag-suggest/).

Since we're using a module, creating our desired functionality isn't very difficult. We start by looking at the `getFrontendFields()` method. We previously used this method to customize which data entry fields were displayed on the form. Now we will add the field for entering tags. Tags belong to the personal attributes of a developer, and so we add the tag field to the first page of the form. Please open the existing *mysite/code/Developer.php* file and insert the following code:

```
<?php
class Developer extends Member {
   // ...
   public function getFrontendFields() {
      // ...
      $tagField = new TagField('Skills');
      $tagField->setTagTopicClass('Developer');
      $fields->push($tagField);
      return $fields;
   }
}
?>
```

***Listing 6.16** mysite/code/Developer.php (excerpt)*

Installing the module has given us access to a new class of form field called `TagField`. Let's look at the `getFrontendFields()` code in detail:

- We initialize the `TagField` by giving it the name of the relation (`Skills`) from which it will draw its autocomplete suggestions.
- The call to `$tagField->setTagTopicClass('Developer')` sets the base class that has relations to the `Skills`.
- `$fields-> push($tagField)` attaches the new field to the existing fields.
- `return $fields` outputs the form fields with the newly included `TagField` field.

And that's it. Try it out. The best way to test the functionality is to create two new users. Enter 'MySQL' as a skill of the first user. Then register another user and enter 'PHP mys' into the skills field. 'PHP' and 'mys' will be identified as a separate tags and any matching existing tags will be displayed below the field.

Since 'MySQL' is already present in the database, 'mys' is matched against that and 'MySQL' is suggested as a possible tag, as shown in Figure 6.13 and 6.14.

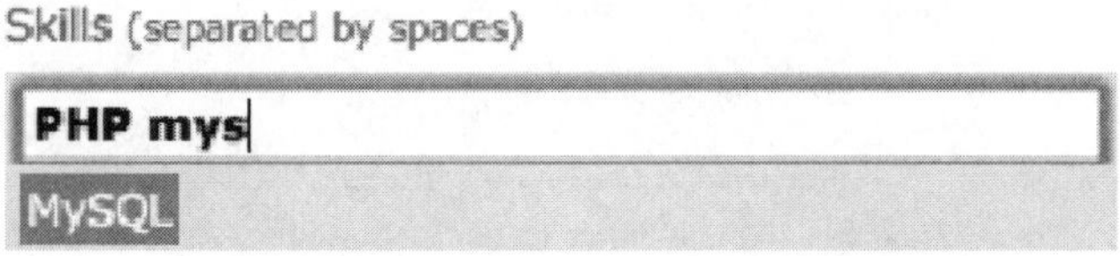

Skills (separated by spaces)
PHP mys
MySQL

Figure 6.13 Entering a tag and getting a suggestion.

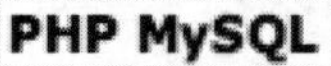

Figure 6.14 Inserted suggestion.

As you can see, SilverStripe makes it possible to create powerful functionality with relatively little effort.

6.6 File Uploads for References

The next issue we will tackle is uploading images: Developers should be able to upload screenshots of websites that they have created to go along with their references.

Every file within the *assets/* directory in SilverStripe is also an instance of the `File` class. That is: Each file is represented both in the file system and in the database. The framework takes care of synchronizing the two places of storage. For example, if you upload an image into the *assets/* folder via FTP and visit the FILES & IMAGES section of the backend, SilverStripe automatically adds this file into the database.

In the case of our screenshots we need to use a subclass of the `File` class called `Image`. This class can be used to manipulate images in a variety of ways. It does this by using the GD library (*http://php.net/gd*), which is integrated into most PHP distributions.

6.6.1 File as a Has-one Relation

As files are just rows in a database table, they can be related to other objects. Generally this is done using a has-one relationship. In our case, we want to display a reference with its associated screenshot. Open *mysite/code/Reference.php* and insert the following code:

```
<?php
class Reference extends DataObject {
   // ...
   static $has_one = array(
      // ...
      'ScreenshotImage' => 'Image',
   );
}
?>
```

Listing 6.17 *mysite/code/Reference.php (excerpt)*

We called the relation `ScreenshotImage`, which is an arbitrary name for the relation. The value of the array makes sure that the relation is linked to an object of type `Image`.

6.6.2 Uploads Through a Form Field

Now let's create a form field that makes it possible for the user to upload a screenshot into the system. SilverStripe provides a variety of fields for this purpose, as displayed in Table 6.1.

Table 6.1 File Upload Fields.

Class	Description
`FileField`	Simple field for standard forms (`<input type="file">`).
`FileIframeField`	Upload using an *iFrame*, i.e., an independent HTML page embedded within another page. This form offers a choice between selecting an existing file on the server or uploading a new file from the user's hard disk. This method of uploading is suited only for use in the CMS backend.
`SimpleImageField`	Similar to `FileField`, but limits the file selection to allow only common image file formats (jpg, gif, png).
`ImageField`	Similar to `FileIframeField`, but limits the file selection to allow only common image file formats. This field also generates a preview thumbnail on-the-fly after upload. This method of uploading is suited only for use in the CMS backend.

File Uploads: Security considerations

If we allow any kind of file to be uploaded to the server, we might create a security vulnerability. Please observe the following guidelines to minimize the risks:

- Limit the file size of the upload so that the storage capacity of the server can not be exhausted, whether by accident, or as a results of a maliciously user. Limiting the file size is easily done by editing the *php.ini* configuration file and editing the `upload_max_filesize` directive. You can alternatively limit the upload file size on a form-by-form basis by setting a parameter on the file input field. For example, to limit any uploads with a specific field to 2 MB, use the following method call: `$myFileField->setAllowedMaxFileSize(2000*1024)`.

- Limit the file types that a user is allowed to upload. You might want to handle only files with a *.txt or *.doc extension. You can set the file types that an input field accept by calling `$myFileField->setAllowedExtensions(array('txt','doc'))`. It is particularly important to disallow the upload of any extensions that are interpreted as scripts by your web server. If your web server allows you to limit script execution by directory, please ensure not to execute any files stored in *assets/* as a precaution.
- Only allow uploads into a single fixed folder location. This mitigates the *directory traversal* security vulnerability of reading or writing from other folders by using a special folder or file name. By default SilverStripe deposits all uploads into the *assets/Uploads* folder. You can read more on this topic in Chapter 7.4, 'Directory Traversal'.

6.6.3 Image Editing and Thumbnails

We already mentioned that SilverStripe makes uses of the GD-library when editing and converting images. Users should be able to upload high-resolution screenshots to the server when they register. However, we don't want the full-sized screenshots to be displayed in all views. They would take too long for the user to download and take too much screen real estate. We will therefore generate and use thumbnail images on the fly.

Every image file is associated with an instance of the `Image` class, which comes with lots of useful graphic conversion methods out of the box. We want a specific size for our thumbnails with a width of 400 pixels. It is very easy to subclass Image in order to extend it with this specific thumbnail logic. Every thumbnail is associated with a reference, and so we will declare the new class `Reference_ScreenshotImage` in the *mysite/code/Reference.php* file. Please open this file and insert the following code:

```
<?php
// ...
class Reference_ScreenshotImage extends Image {
   function generateWebsiteThumbnail($gd) {
      return $gd->resizeByWidth(400);
   }
}
?>
```

Listing 6.18 *mysite/code/Reference.php (excerpt)*

These few lines limit the width of an uploaded image to 400 pixels with `$gd->resizeByWidth(400)`. The height is adjusted automatically to keep the same image ratio. Note that the name of the `generateWebsiteThumbnail()` method is not arbitrarily chosen, but conforms to a SilverStripe naming convention. Read more on this issue in Section 6.6.4, 'Operations on Image Objects'.

Autoloading and prefixes for class names

When you're creating new classes, be sure to name them in such a way that they can be found by the class *autoloader* in SilverStripe. This autoloader is called whenever a class is first accessed in your PHP code, and makes direct `require()` or `include()` calls unnecessary. Classes must take their name from the name of the file they are contain within. In our case the file is called 'Reference.php', and so our thumbnail class must start with the 'Reference_' prefix.

In order for our new thumbnail to be actually used for the output display we now modify the has-one relation we created a while back. We initially created a relation to the `Image` class. Now, however, we will replace that with a reference to the `Reference_ScreenshotImage` class:

```
<?php
class Reference extends DataObject {
   // ...
   static $has_one = array(
      // ...
      'ScreenshotImage' => 'Reference_ScreenshotImage',
   );
}
?>
```

Listing 6.19 *mysite/code/Reference.php (excerpt)*

Conceptually, each instance of an Image can contain more than one representation of an image. The original might be in a high resolution, while smaller thumbnails are created on the fly, and are cached in the file system. Our thumbnail image is created in much the same way. The actual resized image is stored in the cache, but can nevertheless be used exactly as if it were the original image referenced by the `Image` class through its own placeholder in a template.

Since we are using scaffolding to generate our form fields, we don't need to specify explicitly which form field type a form should use. The scaffolding automatically selects the most appropriate method. Take a look at the more advanced upload form field used in the admin interface in Figure 6.15, and a more simple field type used on the registration form (see Figure 6.16).

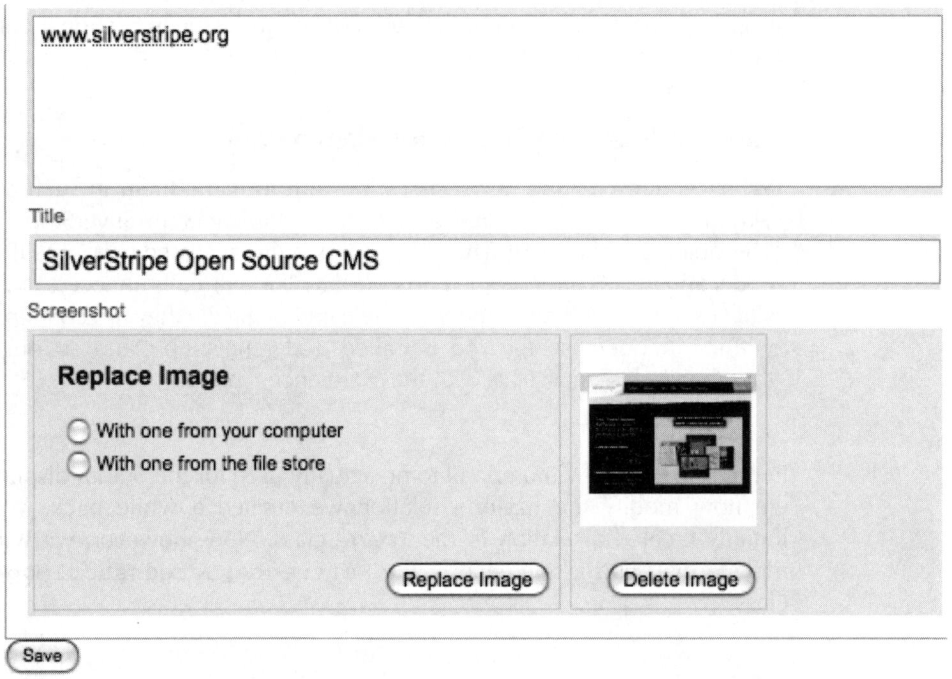

Figure 6.15 Uploading a screenshot in the backend, using FileIframeField.

Figure 6.16 Uploading a screenshot in the frontend, using SimpleImageField.

The last step we need to complete is to modify the registration form to ensure that it accepts only files with valid extensions and appropriately limits the file size. To do this we need to assign a `Validator` to the multi-step form. We already used `RequiredFields`, a subclass of `Validator`, on the first page of the form. However, the fields on the second page are optional, and so a simple `Validator` is all we need to trigger validation appropriately for our uploads.

```
<?php
class RegistrationReferenceStep extends MultiFormStep {
   // ...
   function getValidator() {
      return new Validator();
   }
}
?>
```

Listing 6.20 *mysite/code/RegistrationDetailsStep.php*

6.6.4 Operations on Image Objects

SilverStripe wraps the functionality of the PHP graphics library, which is quite difficult to use on its own and limited in the API it provides. The SilverStripe `GD` class offers a higher level of abstraction and its operations can be applied directly on `Image` objects. Some of them are listed in Table 6.2.

The `GD` class also provides a few 'magic methods'. PHP5 makes it possible to override the behavior that occurs when accessing an invalid method. Normally an error message would be returned, but a custom action can be programmed to occur instead. SilverStripe uses this feature to enable dynamic access to objects via snippets of method names. In the Image class, these magic methods have to start with 'generate'. In our case we named one of our methods `generateWebsiteThumbnail()`. The identifier `WebsiteThumbnail` can then be used to access the dynamically generated image from within a template or using PHP code:

```
<% control MyReference %>
$ScreenshotImage.WebsiteThumbnail
<% end_control %>
```

Listing 6.21 *Using a dynamically generated image within a template*

```
$thumb = $myReference->ScreenshotImage->WebsiteThumbnail;
echo $thumb->URL;
```

Listing 6.22 *Using a dynamically generated image in PHP code*

Table 6.2 Image operations.

Method	Description
`resize(width, height)`	Stretches or compresses the image to the specified dimensions.
`resizeRatio(width, height)`	Preserving aspect ratio, reduce the image so that it will just fit within the specified dimensions. If the aspect ratio doesn't match the new width and height, one edge of the image will reduce one of the dimensions.
`paddedResize(width, height, [background])`	Preserving aspect ratio, reduce the image so that it will fit within the specified dimensions. Space around the image will coloured 'background', which if omitted is ''FFFFFF'' (white).
`croppedResize(width, height)`	Crops the image to the specified dimensions, using the center as a reference point.
`resizeByHeight(height)`	Resizes the image to a given height, keeping the original aspect ratio.
`resizeByWidth(width)`	Resizes the image to a given width, keeping the original aspect ratio.
`greyscale([r],[g],[b])`	Convert the image to greyscale. You can optionally provide values for r, g, and b (from 1 to 100). This alters the default emphasis of the how red, green and blue are converted into greyscale.
`getHeight()`	Returns the height of the image.
`getWidth()`	Returns the width of the image.

6.7 Searching DataObjects

You will have noticed that the backend search form shown earlier in Figure 6.7 is 'somehow' automatically created. Behind the scenes the system collects all the basic attributes known to it and makes them searchable. In the DEVELOPER tab, for example, currently only those attributes that are inherited from `Member` are searchable (`FirstName`, `Surname`, and `Email` are already declared searchable in the `Member` class). Now we will show you how to go beyond the automatically searchable attributes and define your own fields.

6.7.1 Defining a Searchable Attribute

We want to make the `Region` and `Skill` attributes searchable along with the rest of the information about a developer. Please open *mysite/code/Developer.php* and add the following code:

```
<?php
class Developer extends Member {
   // ...
   static $searchable_fields = array(
      'FirstName',
      'Surname',
      'Region',
      'Skills.Title',
   );
   static $field_labels = array(
      'Skills.Title' => 'Skills',
      // ...
   );
}
?>
```

Listing 6.23 *mysite/code/Developer.php (excerpt)*

The static variable `$searchable_fields` is used to tell SilverStripe which attributes to include in the search. The first two fields (`FirstName` and `Surname`) were already included as searchable fields from the parent class. We have now added our own `Region` field.

Each `Skill` is its own separate DataObject accessed using the `Skills` relation. Attributes from relations can be accessed using a dot notation. `Skills.Title` accesses the `Title` attribute using the `Skills` relation and makes that field searchable.

If we want to change the name of a given search field in the user interface we can do so by using the `$field_labels` static variable. An array of attribute identifiers and the names that we want to appear on their labels should be assigned to this variable.

`SearchContext` and `SearchFilter`

The heavy lifting of creating the interface and executing the search is handled by the `SearchContext` class. This object contains various instances of `SearchFilter`, each of which is responsible for one attribute of each searchable object. Searching therefore doesn't require a single SQL command, or even a call to `DataObject::get()`. `SearchContext` creates the search interface mostly by using standard fields like `TextField` and various drop-down menus and checkboxes. It is therefore a very capable platform upon which extended search functionality can be built.

Each `SearchContext` instance can be tuned to search a specific DataObject class. Each DataObject can have different `SearchContext` classes, depending on the context of the search. This makes it possible to provide customized search interfaces for different users and different purposes. This might be a simple search for website visitors and and power-search for administrators.

6.7.2 Custom Search Behavior using SearchFilter

The `SearchFilter` class can be used to modify the search behavior of a particular field. By default every search does a partial match on the search text. As long as a search term occurs somewhere within a searchable attribute, it will be found. However, you might want to have exact matching of search terms on certain fields, such as for example, on dates. You can use the search filters listed in Table 6.3 to make this happen.

Table 6.3 Search filter classes.

Class	Description
`PartialMatchFilter`	Does a partial match using the following SQL syntax: `LIKE '%searchterm%'`. This is the standard filter for all text-based attributes.
`ExactMatchFilter`	Matches the complete text of the search against the searchable fields.
`GreaterThanFilter`	Selects numeric attributes that are greater than the number being searched for. This filter can also be used to search for dates.
`LessThanFilter`	Selects numeric attributes that are smaller than the number being searched for. This filter can also be used to search for dates.
`ExactMatchMultiFilter`	Matches the complete text of several possible comma-separated search terms against the searchable field. Returns results if one of those terms matches.
`FulltextFilter`	Full-text search using the SQL command: `MATCH AGAINST`.
`NegationFilter`	Selects those attributes which don't include the searched text.
`StartsWithFilter`	Select those attributes that start with the text of the search.
`EndsWithFilter`	Select those attributes that end with the text of the search.
`SubstringFilter`	Matches parts of a string, rather than searching across words.

We will now use what we have learned about customizing search behavior in our example application. Let's tweak the pop-up suggestion that appears as a developer enters a skill. Up until now entering 'SQL' would result in 'MySQL' appearing as a suggestion. We want to prevent this from happening. We only want a suggestion to appear if it exactly matches the search term. Add the following to the *mysite/code/Skill.php* file:

```
<?php
class Skill extends DataObject {
   // ...
   static $searchable_fields = array(
      'Title' => 'ExactMatchFilter'
   );
}
?>
```

Listing 6.24 *mysite/code/Skill.php (excerpt)*

Unlike the array assigned to the `$searchable_fields` static variable in the `Developer` class, you see the `Title` keyword associated with the `ExactMatchFilter` class.

6.7.3 Drop-down Menu for Searching Regions

`SearchContext` is a very flexible class that can easily be customized to your specific needs. We will use it to create a drop-down menu for our search form. We want to make it possible to search for developers by selecting a region from a drop-down. This drop-down should be populated with all regions entered in the user profiles so far. This behavior is not available by default, but is quite straightforward to implement.

Our community admin search form uses the `getDefaultSearch-Context()` method of each DataObject class to generate its interface. This method builds the input fields for interface. By default `TextField` controls are used in most places, but we want to change this so we have to override this method. First of all, we call the same method on the parent class to generate the default interface: `parent::getDefaultSearchContext()`. Then we remove the `TextField` from the 'Region' attribute and replace it with our own drop-down menu. Following that, the drop-down menu needs to be populated with all the region attributes from all the `Developer` objects. Let's look at the code. Insert the following into *mysite/code/Developer.php*:

```
<?php
class Developer extends Member {
   // ...
   public function getDefaultSearchContext() {
      $context = parent::getDefaultSearchContext();
      $context->removeFieldByName('Region');
      $regions = self::get_regions();
      if($regions) {
```

```
            $regionMap = array_combine($regions,$regions);
        } else {
            $regionMap = null;
        }
        $regionField = new DropdownField(
            'Region',
            'Region',
            $regionMap
        );
        $regionField->setHasEmptyDefault(true);
        $context->addField($regionField);
        return $context;
    }
    public static function get_regions() {
        $devs = DataObject::get('Developer');
        if(!$devs) return array();
        $regions = array_unique($devs->column('Region'));
        sort($regions);
        return $regions;
    }
}
?>
```

Listing 6.25 *mysite/code/Developer.php (excerpt)*

Okay, those are quite a few lines of code. Once we go through them step-by-step it will all make sense:

- The original context is grabbed from the parent class using `$context = parent::getDefaultSearchContext()`.
- The `$context->removeFieldByName('Region')` command removes the automatically generated 'Region' field.
- At this point `$regions = self::get_regions()` is used to read out all region associates with all the developers. The `get_regions()` method is defined a bit later in the listing, we will get to that in a minute. For now just assume it generates an array with all the regions in the system.
- We now check to make sure at least one regions exists using `if($regions)`. If we have some regions, we create an associative array using the `$regionMap = array_combine($regions, $regions)` command. The array has the same elements as both keys and values.
- Instantiating the `DropdownField` object creates our actual drop-down menu ready for display.
- In case someone wants to execute a search without specifying any particular region, we need to add an empty field to the drop-down. This is

done by calling `$regionField->setHasEmptyDefault(true)`. The empty field is also made the initial default choice of the drop-down.

- `$context->addField($regionField)` adds the new field into the existing interface, and `return $context` returns the completed object to the calling method.
- Now let's take a closer look at that `get_regions()` method. It first of all fetches all developers by calling `$devs = DataObject::get('Developer')`. Either there are no developers and we return an empty array, or we have some developers and can read all their region attributes into an array by calling `$devs->column('Region')`. We remove any duplicates using the `array_unique()` function. Finally, we use `sort()` to organize the array into alphabetical order.

As you can see, defining a search form is quite similar to any other form in SilverStripe. We didn't have to use a drop-down menu to create our region selector. Any input control can be used in a search form; for example, a `DateField` can be used to input a date.

6.8 Generic Views Using CollectionController

'That's all fine and dandy,' we can hear your say, 'but what about the search feature for the users of my system?' You are, of course, right to demand a nice search interface for the users of your system. In fact, this kind of customized search interface is one of the core features we want to offer with our community portal. This section will therefore focus on implementing such a feature.

We want to create an interface that makes it possible for users to find other users by name, region, and skill. The search results should be paginated, meaning that if there are dozens of results, they are split across multiple pages. We also want a details page that comes up when the searcher clicks on a search result. This page should show the profile data and references of a user on a single page. This page should also include a profile editor, which a user can use to edit his or her own information.

Displaying data from DataObject should be child's play for you. We covered that extensively in Chapter 5 (creating templates to display the `Job` class, etc.). So this time let's do things a little differently. We will introduce you to a new module called *Genericviews*.

6.8.1 The Genericviews Module

The Genericviews module is similar to the `ModelAdmin` class that we've already covered. It provides scaffolding to automate the display of typical views and functions. However, unlike the backend views of `ModelAdmin`, Genericviews are meant for frontend display. The following classes make up this module:

- `CollectionPage` is a new kind of page type for use in the page tree. We will later use it to display various different views.
- `CollectionController` is used to execute the search. It creates listings and manages various objects for display.
- `RecordController` is responsible for displaying a single record. It also provides a form interface for editing data.

All we need to do to start using these classes is to create the appropriate page in the page tree and assign a DataObject to it. Please download and install the 'Genericviews' module from http://silverstripe.org/generic-views-module/. The installation process is the same as usual. Please remember to update the database schema after the installation.

6.8.2 CollectionPage for Developers

We want to place our search feature on a new page type. Now that you have installed the module, you should have access to the new *CollectionPage* page type in the CMS. Please create a new *CollectionPage* and name it 'Developers'.

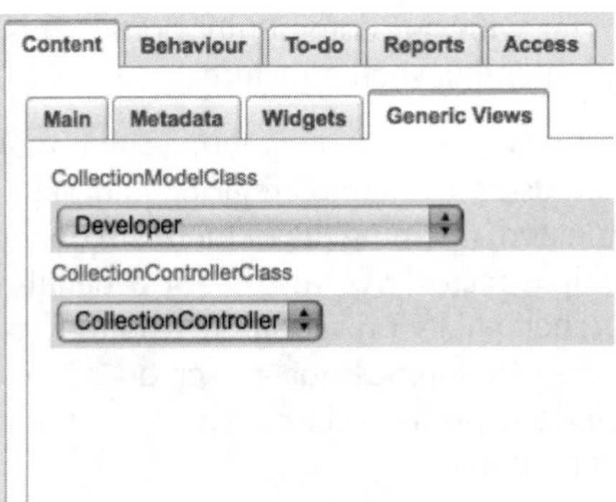

Figure 6.17 CollectionPage.

Now we need to tell the new CollectionPage which data it should manage. To do that select the CONTENT > GENERIC VIEWS tab and choose DEVELOPER from the COLLECTIONMODELCLASS menu. It should look like Figure 6.17.

Save and Publish the page and take a look at it in the frontend. You see a ready-made search form, as shown in Figure 6.18.

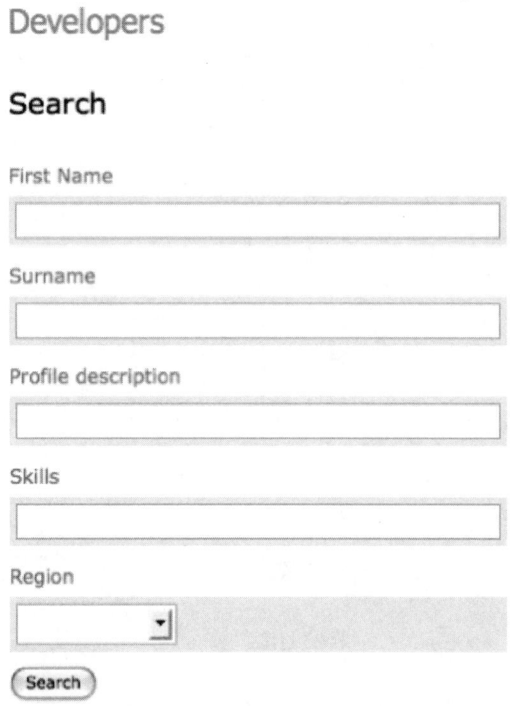

Figure 6.18 CollectionPage with search field in the frontend.

The fields of the search form were once again generated from the model's `$searchable_fields` variable. We already customized this variable when implementing the `CommunityAdmin` interface, so everything should appear exactly as we expect it to.

The `CollectionPage` labels each item in the search results by calling the `getTitle()` method of the appropriate DataObject. `Developer` inherits this method from the `Member` class, which returns titles in the 'Surname, First name' format. Consequently, our search feature will list results using this same format (see Figure 6.19).

All search results are links. Clicking on a result will lead you to a detailed view as shown in Figure 6.20. By default, the detailed view is read-only, but we will change that soon by creating our own template.

But first, let's take a look at the URL of a detailed view:

http://localhost/developers/Developer/2/view

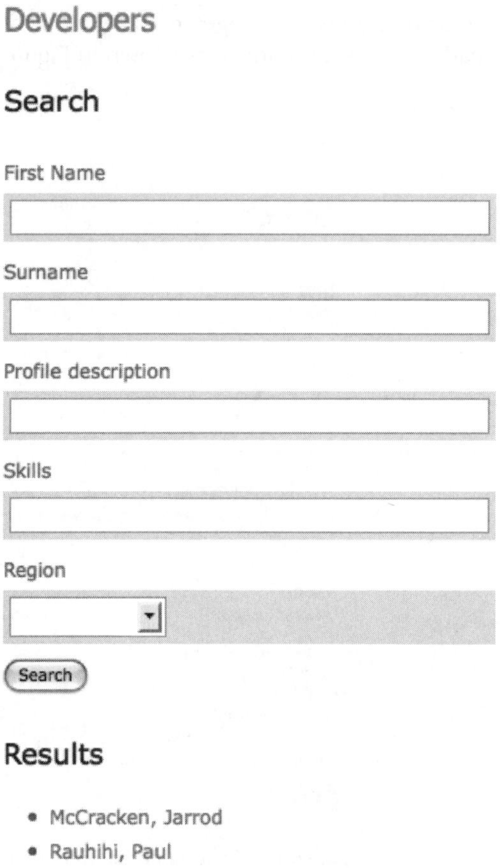

Developers

Search

First Name

Surname

Profile description

Skills

Region

Search

Results

- McCracken, Jarrod
- Rauhihi, Paul

Figure 6.19 CollectionPage with search results in the frontend.

The underlying pattern here is: <page name>/<class name>/<ID>/<action>. Try replacing 'view' with 'edit' and see what happens. Aha, there's our editable view. If you're a little naughty you may have already tried also changing the ID. A user can now view and edit any profile in the system – not very secure. We definitely need to change some things here, and will deal with limiting access permissions in the next Section 6.8.3, 'CollectionPage for References'.

But before we get to that, let's first integrate the profile editor into the rest of the website. If a user is logged in, we want him or her to see a link to the footer titled 'edit my profile'. Please open the

Developers

First Name

Paul

Surname

Tester

Email

paul@test.com

Region

Wellington

Profile description

A brilliant developer

Skills

MySQL PHP Java

References

- SilverStripe Open Source CMS

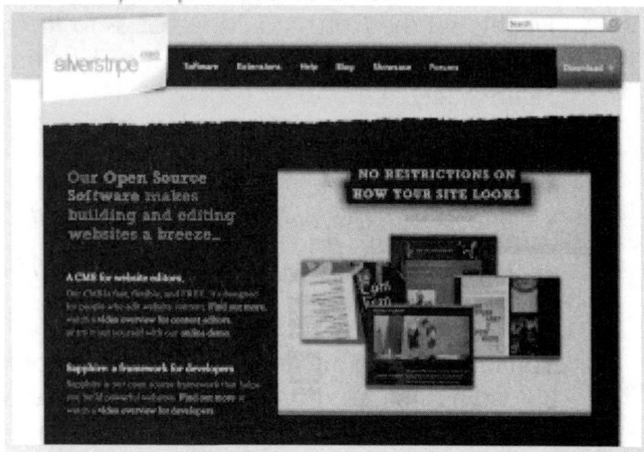

Figure 6.20 Profile view.

themes/mysite/templates/Include/Footer.ss file and insert the following code:

```
<p>
Copyright <!-- ... -->
<% if CurrentMember %>
   | <a href="developers/Developer/$CurrentMember.ID/edit">
      Edit my profile
   </a>
<% end_if %>
</p>
```

Listing 6.26 *themes/mysite/templates/Includes/Footer.ss*

The website footer should now look like the image shown in Figure 6.21.

Figure 6.21 Footer with link to the profile editor.

6.8.3 CollectionPage for References

Up until now users could only create a single reference when registering. Now we want to make it possible for them to create additional references using the profile editor.

But wait a minute: Can we even view a reference in detail? Oops, that's not yet implemented. We quickly fix this oversight using the Genericviews module again. Create a new `CollectionPage` page in the CMS and call it 'References'. Make this page a sub page of 'Developers'. Finally, set the CollectionModelClass to Reference. We now have a nice interface for viewing, searching, and editing references, as shown in Figure 6.22.

The URL patterns are similar to the ones for interacting with Developers:

- *http://localhost/references/Reference/<ID>/view*
- *http://localhost/references/Reference/<ID>/edit*

You'll notice that the detailed view has automatically obtained a form for uploading images. If you've already uploaded images, you'll see these with thumbnail previews on the details page. Note that the thumbnails aren't generated using our custom `generateWebsiteThumbnail()` method, but instead created by the `Image` class using its integrated `generateThumbnail()` method.

Figure 6.22 Profile editor.

6.8.4 Customizing the Detailed View

Clicking on a search result should bring up the detailed view with a developer's profile information, together with a list of his or her references on the same page. We don't want our users to piece together references and developers purely by URLs. References should appear as links to the reference detailed view.

All this is quite easy to implement. We don't even need to write any PHP code. All we have to do is extend a few templates. The Genericviews module uses normal SilverStripe templates for displaying its pages. You can find them in the *genericviews/templates/* folder. Note that we will make use of a specific new naming convention when extending these templates (see the following box).

Naming convention for Genericviews templates

Up until now we have used only a single template for each page type. A template is used for displaying the content coming from a controller of the same name. If we had multiple differently named templates they wouldn't know which controller to get their data from, right?

Well, not quite. SilverStripe provides an additional way that templates can be linked to controllers and visa-versa. This method allows every method (action) in a controller to be linked to its own template. The linking is once again done using a specific naming convention. We use the usual class name and add the method name using an underscore. The result looks as follows:

<classname>_<methodname>.ss

This features makes it possible for us to create separate templates for the different actions associates with a `Developer`. Therefore, the 'view' and 'edit' actions can use different layouts: *Developer_view.ss* and *Developer_edit.ss* respectively.

First of all we extend the developer detail view with a listing of references. Do this by creating the *themes/mysite/templates/Layout/Developer_view.ss* file and inserting the following code into it:

```
<div class="typography">
      <div id="Content">
      <h2>$Title</h2>
      $Form
      <% control currentRecord %>
         <h3>References</h3>
         <% if References %>
         <ul class="referenceItems">
         <% control References %>
            <li>
               <a href="$URL">$Title</a><br />
               $ScreenshotImage.WebsiteThumbnail
            </li>
         <% end_control %>
         </ul>
         <% else %>
            <p class="message">No references found</p>
         <% end_if %>
      <% end_control %>
      </div>
</div>
```

Listing 6.27 *themes/mysite/templates/Layout/Developer_view.ss*

What exactly have we done here?

- The actual displaying of the record is done by `$Form`. As previously described, this outputs a read-only form. We could, of course, not have used $Form at all and created our own custom output display, but instead we chose to re-use the built-in mechanism for the sake of convenience.

- <% control currentRecord %> makes sure that all placeholder references within the loop refer to the data of the record to be displayed.
- <% control References %> references the has-many relation from the developer to its references. Each reference's URL and screenshot are displayed within this loop.

The $ScreenshotImage.WebsiteThumbnail placeholder requires a bit of explanation. You might remember how we created a class named Reference_ScreenshotImage within the *mysite/code/Reference.php* file. We created this class to generate a custom-sized screenshot image. We called the method to do this generateWebsiteThumbnail(). The 'magic' keyword generate was used to allow WebsiteThumbnail to masquerade as an object. We could, for example, get the URL of a screenshot by calling $ScreenshotImage.WebsiteThumbnail.URL.

In our case, we're directly referencing $ScreenshotImage.Website Thumbnail from within a template. In this case, SilverStripe automatically inserts a HTML image tag into the output. Once again, the CMS is making things easy for us. We can just add the reference and rest easy knowing that the formatting will be taken care for us.

6.8.5 Customizing the Form

Now that the detailed profile view is complete we want to adjust the edit view as well. Once again, we want a developer's profile information and references to be displayed, but below that we will add a listing of References with links to edit each reference and a link to add a new reference (see Figure 6.23).

References

- SilverStripe Bits (edit)
- My Profile (edit)

Add Reference

Figure 6.23 Customized links to edit and add references.

Create the *themes/mysite/templates/Layout/Developer_edit.ss* file and insert the following code:

```
<div class="typography">
    <div id="Content">
    <h2>$Title</h2>
    $Form
    $ExtraForm
    <% control currentRecord %>
        <h3>References</h3>
        <% if References %>
        <ul class="referenceItems">
        <% control References %>
            <li>
                <a href="$URL">$Title</a> 
                <a href="references/Reference/$ID/edit">
                    (edit)
                </a>
            </li>
        <% end_control %>
        </ul>
        <% else %>
            <p class="message">No references found</p>
        <% end_if %>
    <% end_control %>
    <p>
        <a href="references/Reference/add">
            Add a reference
        </a>
    </p>
    </div>
</div>
```

Listing 6.28 *themes/mysite/templates/Layout/Developer_edit.ss*

As you can see, this code is very similar to the code for viewing the profile. Once again `$Form` is used to display the form, although of course this time editing is enabled. There are only two differences to the previous listing:

- In the `References` control block we added a link after the title of each reference to the `CollectionPage` for editing that reference.
- In the last few lines of the file we create a link to `references/Reference/add`, which adds a new reference.

And with this template, we're done. The Genericviews module provided us with an agile and flexible means for rapidly implementing our interface. We could have used the tools and techniques from Chapter 5 to create everything we just did from scratch, but I hope you'll agree that using the scaffolding approach saved us a lot of time.

6.9 Defining Access Permissions

Okay, to tell the truth, we're 'almost' finished. We still need to deal with some security issues in our publicly available editor interfaces. SilverStripe's framework provides a set of methods as part of the DataObject class for this purpose.

6.9.1 Methods Within DataObject

Security is handled in SilverStripe using various 'magic methods' that can be queried to determine whether a given user group has the necessary rights to perform a given action. As usual, you can override these methods with your own custom code to adjust them to your own needs and preferences.

Permission codes

The framework organizes access permissions using *Permission Codes.* These take the form of fragments of text that represent the permission to execute a certain action. Each permission code can be assigned to one or more security groups using the SECURITY tab in the backend. For example, the permission code 'ADMIN' grants access to all functions in the CMS, and this code is assigned to the 'Administrators' security group. This group in turn has the default user 'admin' as one of its members. Users can belong to multiple security groups and security groups can have more than one permission code.

Permission codes can be queried using `Permission::check('<code>')` or `Permission::checkMember($myMember, '<code>')`. The basic check without the `$myMember` parameter uses the currently logged-in member. Both methods return a Boolean indicating whether a user does or doesn't have a given permission.

Permissions are solely group-based. Complete *Access Control Lists (ACL)* for assigning record-specific permissions to individual users haven't been implemented in SilverStripe. However, groups can be organized into hierarchies using the SECURITY tab in the backend. Child groups inherit their parent group's permissions. This feature makes it possible to craft quite sophisticated permission settings.

Permissions for accessing the backend are restricted to administrator users by default. However, the permissions system isn't integrated into every aspect of the framework, so any new code you write won't necessarily require administrator rights to access. It's therefore important that you know how to add security measures into your code.

Take a look at the `Developer` class. We want to make it possible for every registered user to view existing developers and create new records belonging to this class. However, a user should only be able to edit his or her own record, unless he or she is an administrator as identified by the permission code `ADMIN`. Every record has an owner ID, so it isn't too difficult to do a check to see if the current user is trying to access his or her own record. We have to modify the `Developer` class a bit in order to add the above security features. Let's get started. Open the *mysite/code/Developer.php* file and add the following code:

```
<?php
class Developer extends Member {
   // ...
   public function canView($member = null) {return true;}
   public function canCreate($member = null) {return true;}
   public function canEdit($member = null) {
      if(!$member) $member = Member::currentUser();
      if(!$member) return false;
      return (
         Permission::checkMember($member, 'ADMIN')
         || ($member && $member->ID == $this->ID)
      );
   }
   public function canDelete($member = null) {
      return $this->canEdit($member);

   }
}
?>
```

Listing 6.29 *mysite/code/Developer.php (excerpt)*

SilverStripe recognizes the `canView()`, `canCreate()`, `canEdit()`, and `canDelete()` methods. Most controllers check these methods every time an instance of this class is accessed for these operations. If a method returns `true`, the permission to perform the respective action is granted (the default behavior on most core classes is to return `true`, only if the current user has 'ADMIN' permissions). You can probably guess what each method does from its name, but Table 6.4 contains descriptions, just in case.

Table 6.4 Methods for checking DataObject permissions.

Method	**Description**
`canView()`	Can the user view this record?
`canCreate()`	Can the user create new records of this type?
`canEdit()`	Can the user edit this record?
`canDelete()`	Can the user delete this record?

These methods are generally called with the current user as a parameter. If no current user exists, the `$member` variable defaults to `null`. As you can see from the code listing, `canView()` and `canCreate()` always return `true`, so any logged-in user can perform these actions. The `canEdit()` method is a little more tricky. We need to retrieve the ID of the current user and compare it to the owner ID of the record. Editing permissions should be granted only if the two IDs match. The same rule should apply for deleting the record; if we're allowed to edit it, we should also be allowed to delete it. So we just call the `canEdit()` method from the `canDelete()` method.

6.9.2 Securing Jobs

It looks like we're on a roll here, right? Let's implement some security for our job postings in much the same way. Please open the *mysite/code/Jobs.php* file and insert the following code:

```
<?php
class Job extends DataObject {
   // ...
   public function canView($member = null) {return true;}
   public function canCreate($member = null) {return true;}
   public function canEdit($member = null) {
      if(!$member) $member = Member::currentUser();
      if(!$member) return false;
      return (
         Permission::checkMember($member, 'ADMIN')
         || ($member && $member->ID == $this->AuthorID)
      );
   }
   public function canDelete($member = null) {
      return $this->canEdit($member);
   }
}
?>
```

Listing 6.30 *mysite/code/Job.php (excerpt)*

6.9.3 Custom Permissions

If you find that the default codes are insufficient for what you're trying to do, you can create custom permission codes. Here's an example of such a case: Suppose you have a web-community that has a problem with spam postings where users keep uploading 'objectionable' images. You want to solve the problems by recruiting volunteers to go through your website and remove the offensive content. Naturally, you don't want to give full administrator permissions to these volunteers. So what to do?

The simple answer is to create a new custom permission code. Let's call it `EDIT_ALL_REFERENCES` and assign it to a new group called 'Helper'. Open the *mysite/code/Reference.php* file and insert the following code:

```
<?php
class Reference extends DataObject implements PermissionProvider {
   // ...
   public function canView($member = null) {
      return true;
   }
   public function canCreate($member = null) {
      return true;
   }
   public function canEdit($member = null) {
      if(!$member) $member = Member::currentUser();
      if(!$member) return false;
      return (
         Permission::checkMember($member, 'ADMIN')
         || Permission::checkMember($member, 'EDIT_ALL_REFERENCES')
         || $member->ID == $this->DeveloperID
      );
   }
   public function canDelete($member = null) {
      return $this->canEdit($member);
   }
   public function providePermissions() {
      return array(
         'EDIT_ALL_REFERENCES' => 'Edit all references'
      );
   }
}
?>
```

Listing 6.31 *mysite/code/Reference.php (excerpt)*

This code is very similar to the previous two listings, and so we won't go through it line-by-line. However, three things deserve highlighting:

- In addition to checking whether the user attempting to perform the edit is the owner or has administrator permissions, we also check for the `'EDIT_ALL_REFERENCES'` permission code.
- We have added a new method called `providePermissions()`, which returns an array with the new permission code.
- We declare that the `Reference` class implements the `Permission-Provider` interface. This makes our new permission code accessible in the framework, i.e., it now shows up as an option in the drop-down menu under the PERMISSIONS tab in the SECURITY backend.

Make sure to add a new group in /admin/security/ and assign the newly available permission code to it.

6.10 Web Services Using RESTfulServer

Access to a website's data isn't limited to viewing HTML. SilverStripe also provides access to data via *web services*. This programmatic access makes it easy to use the data in different contexts and combine it with data from other sources, a concept usually referred to as a *mashup*. You could, for example, write an application that collects job postings from partners' websites and provides an overview listing. SilverStripe makes such things a breeze with a built-in *RESTful API*, a special flavor of web service that works on top of the HTTP standard. This section teaches you how to use this API to access data within the CMS.

6.10.1 REST Architecture

REST stands for *Representational State Transfer*. It was introduced by Roy Thomas Fielding in his PhD thesis in the year 2000. REST was originally envisioned as a means of accessing remote data and executing remote procedure calls, but is now primarily used for web-services.

A web application that's built using the principles of REST is called *RESTful*. One central principle of such RESTful applications is that they have uniquely identifiable *resources*. That is: Every data item should be addressable by a *URI*. REST, in contrast to the *SOAP* protocol, doesn't have its own transport layer. It instead uses the existing HTTP standard for all its communication. HTTP has worked brilliantly for the web since its inception, so why not use it for web-services as well? In SilverStripe every page has its own URL, so it makes sense that data items like users and job postings should also be accessible in that way. Why should we reinvent the wheel?

The way this is works in practice is that we use *HTTP-verbs* (*POST* and *GET* being the most common) to tell the system what to do. That makes it possible to do basic CRUD data management tasks. All verbs defined in the HTTP 1.1 standard are described in Table 6.5. Note that *PUT, DELETE*, and *HEAD* are disabled by default on most servers, and so most RESTful applications don't use these verbs.

Table 6.5 HTTP verbs.

HTTP verb	Description
POST	Creates new data
GET	Queries existing data
PUT	Updates existing data
DELETE	Deletes data
HEAD	Previews data

REST has a number of advantages when compared with SOAP. For one, REST calls are a lot more concise than the equivalent SOAP requests, which improves request performance. Another advantage is that you already have a great tool for viewing REST data: your web-browser. Writing data using REST does, however, require using some specialized applications or PHP libraries.

REST is format neutral. In SilverStripe, you can choose either XML or JSON (see http://json.org/) for inputting and outputting data. You specify the format you want by either using a pseudo-file extension, or using a special HTTP-header.

Table 6.6 Querying data using REST.

Querying	
GET/api/v1/<class>/<id>	Outputs the specified data object
GET/api/v1/<class>/<id>/<relation>	Outputs the specified relation(s) of the particular data object
GET/api/v1/<class>?<field> = <val>	Outputs data objects according to a particular filter criteria

Table 6.7 Creating and updating data using REST.

Creating and updating	
PUT/api/v1/<class>/<id>	Updates a data object
POST/api/v1/<class>/<id>	Creates a data object

Table 6.8 Deleting data using REST.

Deleting	
DELETE/api/v1/<class>/<id>	Deletes the specified data object
DELETE/api/v1/<class>/<id>/ <relation>/<foreign-id>	Removes the connection between two data objects, without deleting either of them

Table 6.9 Calling methods using REST.

User-defined methods	
POST/api/v1/<class>/<id>/<method-name>	Calls a particular method on the specified data object

Any SilverStripe model can be enabled for RESTful access. REST is disabled by default as a security precaution, so you need to enable it explicitly for a specific model class. Tables 6.6, 6.7, 6.8, and 6.9 give you an overview of the supported verbs and URI structures. You'll notice that all URIs start with */api/v1/*: This is the URL namespace for all API calls.

In order to make full use of REST we recommend that you put all your data manipulation logic into the model, and leave as little as possible to the controller. The reason for this is that the framework's `RESTfulServer` class provides its own controller for models accessed using REST, which means any custom controllers won't come into play. Take our registration form: You might want to ensure that a given email address is unique in the database. This check isn't specific to the context of a registration form, but should be performed on all create actions for this object. This check belongs in the model. If you implement the check in the form controller, a user may, accidentally or maliciously, skip the check when you enable REST.

6.10.2 Opening Objects

As we remarked in the previous section, we need to explicitly enable REST access on a specific model class. This is done by setting a static variable: `$api_access`, a technique which should be very familiar to you by now. One thing you can do is simply set the variable to a Boolean value, `true`. This enables REST access for all HTTP verbs and attributes. By default, RESTfulServer will query the permission methods on your subclass for access checks: `canView()`, `canCreate()`, `canEdit()`, and `canDelete()`. However, we want to be a bit more specific and will therefore use an array to specify exactly which actions and attributes we want to enable for REST access. The following code shows you how to do this. Please insert it into the *mysite/code/Developer.php* file:

```
<?php
class Developer extends Member {
   static $api_access = array(
      'view' => array(
         'FirstName',
         'Surname',
         'Region',
         'Introduction',
         'References',
      ),
      'edit' => array(
         'FirstName',
         'Surname',
         'Region',
         'Introduction',
      )
   );
   // ...
}
?>
```

Listing 6.32 *mysite/code/Developer.php (excerpt)*

As you can see, we created a multi-dimensional array and assigned it to `$api_access`. It contains two top-level elements `view` and `edit`, which in turn contain arrays listing the names of all the attributes for which we want to enable access. This code enables RESTful viewing of a developer's basic profile information and references. However, only the basic profile information is editable. We have specifically *not* enabled RESTful editing for the references.

It goes without saying that you should never enable RESTful access to any attributes that will compromise the system's security. Specific care has to be taken when setting foreign keys to other objects, as well as viewing and editing sensitive information such as password data.

6.10.3 Read Access

You can use your web browser to perform a quick and easy check to test if you have successfully enabled REST. Just enter one of the URIs listed in Table 6.10 into your browser's address bar and observe the results. It should look similar to Figure 6.24, although results will vary depending

Table 6.10 REST calls using URIs.

REST call	Description
http://localhost/api/v1/Developer	Overview of all developers in the system
http://localhost/api/v1/Developer/4	Developer with the ID 4
http://localhost/api/v1/Developer/4/References	All reference relations of the developer with the ID 4

This XML file does not appear to have any style information associated with it. The document tree is shown below.


```
- <Developer href="http://localhost/6/api/v1/Developer/3.xml">
    <FirstName>Paul</FirstName>
    <Surname>Tester</Surname>
    <Region>Wellington</Region>
    <Introduction>A brilliant developer</Introduction>
    <ID>3</ID>
  - <References linktype="has_many" href="http://localhost/6/api/v1/Developer/3/References.xml">
      <Reference href="http://localhost/6/api/v1/Reference/3.xml" id="3"/>
      <Reference href="http://localhost/6/api/v1/Reference/4.xml" id="4"/>
    </References>
  </Developer>
```


Figure 6.24 XML representation of a Developer in the browser.

on which web browser you use. By the way, you don't need to write any templates for your REST requests: SilverStripe generates these for you automatically from the available metadata.

Insert the following into the *mysite/code/Reference.php* file in order to make references accessible via REST:

```
<?php
class Reference extends DataObject {
    static $api_access = array(
        'view' => array(
            'URL',
            'Title',
            'Developer'
        ),
        'edit' => array(
            'URL',
            'Title',
        )
    );
    // ...
}
?>
```

Listing 6.33 *mysite/code/Reference.php (excerpt)*

Once you have enabled RESTful access to this class, please try the example queries in Table 6.11 to test whether everything is working correctly.

Table 6.11 Querying references using REST.

REST call	Description
http://localhost/api/v1/Reference	Overview of all references
http://localhost/api/v1/Reference/1	Reference with ID 1

SilverStripe's RESTful server currently supports two output formats: XML and JSON. The server returns the appropriate format depending on the Content-Type that is specified in the HTTP request's header. Alternatively, you can use a pseudo-file extension to request the server to return a specific output format (see Table 6.12).

Table 6.12 Querying references using JSON.

REST call	Description
http://localhost/api/v1/Reference/1.json	Reference with ID 1 in JSON format

The reason why we can seamlessly use the browser to test these REST queries is that REST queries take the form of HTTP GET requests. Browsers use the GET request when regularly accessing websites. However, POST, PUT, and DELETE requests are more difficult to perform using a browser. You can create a POST request by submitting a form, but the other two HTTP verbs aren't supported by most browsers. We need some extra help, which comes in form of a specialized REST-client application.

REST clients are available in a variety of forms. The important part is that these applications don't need to be tailored towards a specific API, because all RESTful interfaces use the same standard set of well-defined HTTP operations. Some are web-based and are implemented using PHP, Flash, or JavaScript. Others clients are stand-alone applications written in Java or C++. We recommend a free Java-based client software program for testing REST services. You can download it from: http://rest-client.googlecode.com/files/restclient-2.1-jar-with-dependencies.jar.

Adding a Reference

We will now attempt to create a new reference using the REST client. Enter *http://localhost/api/v1/Reference* into the address bar and choose POST as the HTTP Method (see Figure 6.25). As you can see, we're using the same URL that we used for querying. The only difference is that we're using the POST verb instead of GET.

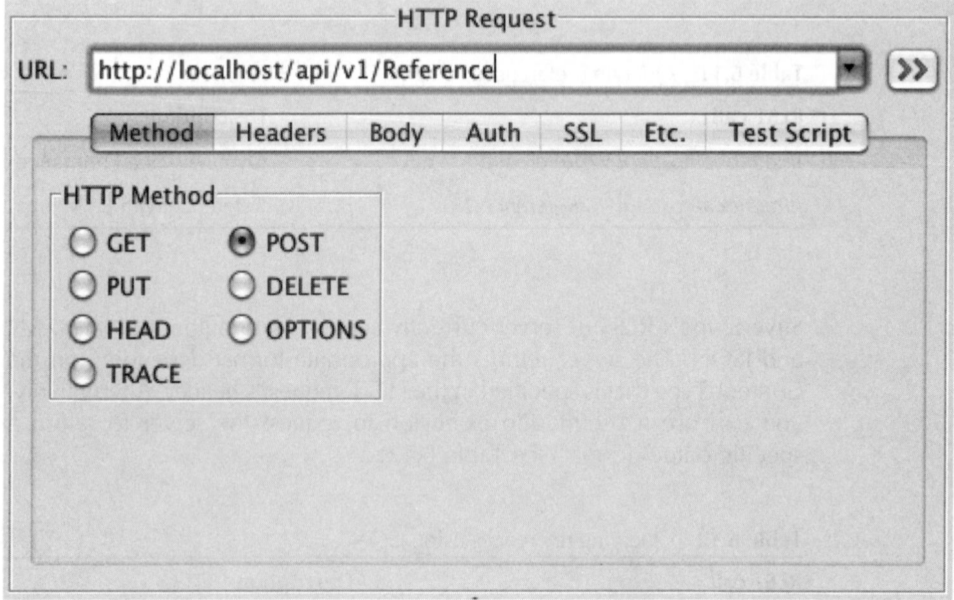

Figure 6.25 REST client: Creating a new reference.

A few more things are left to do before we send off the POST request: we need to switch to the Body tab and change the Content-Type from text/plain to application/xml, so that the server knows which format it should respond in. Now the most important part: the reference itself. Enter the following text into the main text area on the Body tab:

```
<Reference>
<URL>www.silverstripe.com</URL>
<Title>New reference</Title>
</Reference>
```

Notice how the structure of this XML is exactly the same as the XML that you got back when querying for data. Click the green double-arrow icon to submit the POST request. If all goes according to plan, you should get back a `201` status code confirming the newly created reference, as shown in Figure 6.26.

Figure 6.26 Status message after successfully creating a new reference.

If the creation was successful, the Body section of the HTTP Response should show you the newly created record in XML, also containing the ID property.

Depending on how you configured your security permissions, you might be asked to authenticate yourself by entering a username and password before the POST is accepted.

Editing a Reference

We can edit a reference in much the same way. However, we will need to append an ID onto the end of the URL, in order for the server to know which data item we intend to modify. We also need to use the correct REST verb. Please use a valid reference ID, for example the one we just created in the previous section. Append it to the URL (*http://localhost/api/v1/Reference/<ID>*), and change the HTTP Method to PUT (as shown in Figure 6.27).

Once again, also change your Content-Type to application/xml and enter your desired new data into the body text area using an XML syntax, as shown in Figure 6.28. As edit actions are limited to logged-in users with the `EDIT_ALL_REFERENCES` permission, we also need to pass our

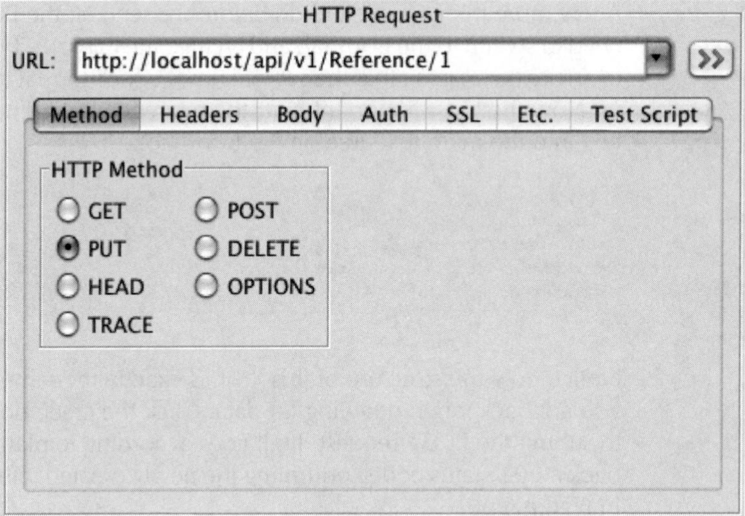

Figure 6.27 Using the REST client to modify an existing reference.

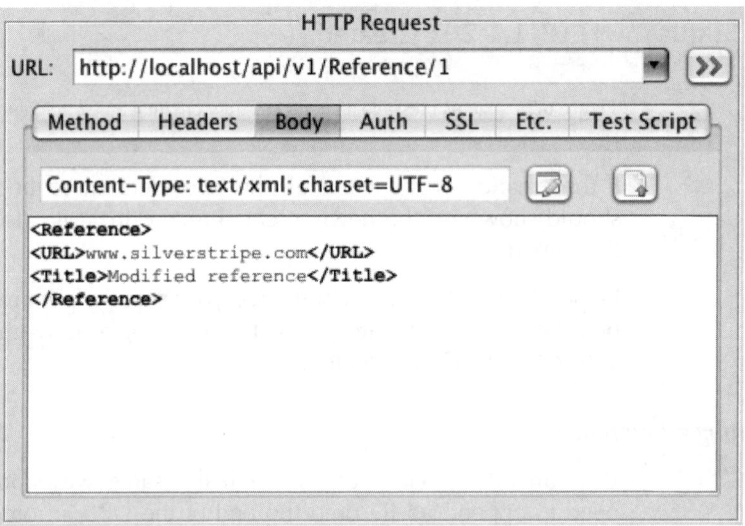

Figure 6.28 Setting the new data that will replace the existing reference.

credentials along. Navigate to the Auth tab, enable BASIC Auth Type, and enter the correct Username and Password.

We hope that this short introduction to SilverStripe's RESTful web-services has shown you how you can use REST to provide your data in a useful way. Everything we did using the REST client can be done equally well programmatically using your favorite scripting language. SilverStripe has a built-in client for hooking into other APIs with the `RESTfulService` class. REST and XML are easy ways of pushing and pulling data from a SilverStripe-based webservices, but not the only possible solution. For alternative web service paradigms, have a look at the SOAP protocol. SilverStripe provides a light-weight SOAP wrapper around RestfulService, see http://doc.silverstripe.com/doku.php?id=soapmodelaccess for further information. Let your imagination run wild.

6.11 RSS Feeds for Jobs

Just to round things off a bit, here's another way you can make your custom data accessible in a different format: Listing jobs on a website is a good start, but wouldn't it be great if interested visitors could subscribe to them via a RSS feed? This format allows structured content to be consumed by a wide variety of applications. It's surprisingly simple to output any model object in this notation through SilverStripe.

We want to have RSS feeds specific to each job category, and so we need to implement the feature on the `JobCategory` controller. Open the existing file *mysite/code/JobCategory.php* and add the following code:

```
<?php
// ...
class JobCategory_Controller extends Page_Controller {
   // ...
   function init() {
      parent::init();
      RSSFeed::linkToFeed($this->Link(). 'rss');
   }
   function rss() {
      $feed = new RSSFeed(
         $this->dataRecord->Jobs(),
         $this->Link() . 'rss',
         "Jobs in {$this->dataRecord->Title}",
         "New Job Postings for SilverStripe Developers",
         'Title',
         'Description'
      );
      return $feed->outputToBrowser();
   }
}
?>
```

Listing 6.34 *mysite/code/JobCategory.php (excerpt)*

That wasn't too bad, was it? Let's step through the code:

- The `init()` method in our controller triggers a static method on `RSSFeed` called `linkToFeed()`. This will add the following HTML to the <head> section of your template in order for web browsers to show an RSS icon in the address bar:

```
<link rel="alternate" type="application/rss+xml"
title="Jobs in ..." href="/jobs/rss">
```

- The `rss()` method instantiates a new `RSSFeed` object. The feed takes a collection of DataObjects as a first argument; in our case all `Job` objects related to this page.
- The following parameters give information about the feed URL, as well as some description. With `'Title'` and `'Description'` we define which attributes should be used as the main content elements for each job entry.
- Lastly, `$feed->outputToBrowser()` returns the rendered content with the right content type to our visitors.

Only one slight modification has to be performed on the `Job` class itself: It needs a `Link()` method so that the RSS feed knows where to point each entry. As `Job` extends `DataObject` and not `Page`, it doesn't have its own URL by default. We cheat a little bit by including an anchor link to the job in the job category page instead. Open *mysite/code/Job.php* and add the following code:

```
<?php
class Job extends DataObject {
   // ...
   function Link() {
      return $this->JobCategory()->Link() .
         '#Job' . $this->ID;
   }
}
?>
```

Listing 6.35: *mysite/code/Job.php (excerpt)*

RSS feeds come in different standards, by default the RSSFeed class in SilverStripe produces output compliant to the RSS 2.0 standard.

Incidentally, we've already included the necessary anchors in our *Job-Category.ss* templates when we created it back in Chapter 5. If you visit one of the job category pages created through the CMS, your browser should automatically detect an available feed. In Mozilla Firefox, this is noted by a small icon towards the right of the menu bar.

6.12 Conclusion

In this chapter we covered many of SilverStripe's advanced features. Developing the CRM interface led us into using scaffolding for rapid development of sophisticated interfaces. We also touched on techniques for direct data manipulation using REST and alternative representations using RSS.

There is one feature that we purposely did not describe, because we're confident that by now you're able to implement it all by yourself. See your 'homepage' as making it possible for a developer to upload and insert a personal portrait into his or her profile. Hint: Take another look at the `Reference_ScreenshotImage` class.

7
Security

This chapter describes some malicious attacks against websites, which unfortunately are all too common these days. We will discuss the principles behind each attack pattern, tell you how SilverStripe attempts to protect you, and highlight gotchas to watch out for when programming your web application. We also cover security for the user's browser, secure data processing in PHP, and secure database storage.

We refer to various user access permissions used within SilverStripe. You might want to re-read Section 6.9, 'Defining access permissions,' as a refresher. Please see this chapter as a first-steps guide to help you start securing your web application. It is not meant as a complete compendium. SilverStripe itself will try to help you wherever possible by using good out-of-the-box conventions. However, it can't protect you in every conceivable circumstance. You will have to take active responsibility for ensuring that your website remains secure.

7.1 Cross-site Scripting (XSS)

Cross-site scripting is a security vulnerability where malicious code is secretly inserted into a webpage seen by a visitor. This code might then be used to grant unauthorized access, mislead the visitor, or steal his or her identity through session information. Cross-site scripting techniques are often used in *phishing* attacks, and pose the vast majority of security vulnerabilities on the web.

The vulnerability typically occurs when a user can provide data through a form submission or URL parameter, and this data is displayed on the browser without first being checked for malicious HTML and Javascript. Take the example of a search box, which might re-display the entered search term on a results page. The search logic has to ensure that any code apart from the plaintext search term is either stripped out or escaped before display.

7.1.1 Field Types

SilverStripe allows us to specify the *field type* of database fields using the `static $db` attribute variable of a DataObject. Several field types are available for storing strings. Their main difference is the length of text that a field can store: `Varchar` is used for short strings up to 255 characters and `Text` stores up to 2 MB of text on a typical MySQL database. These types should be used for plaintext content only, any HTML content is escaped by default when passed through a SilverStripe template. If you want to explicitly allow HTML content, use the sub-types `HTMLText` and `HTMLVarchar`.

For example, suppose we store `<strong>bold&heavy</strong>` into a field. `Varchar` and `Text` will show the unformatted content by escaping special characters such as angular brackets. The output for these two fields will be `<strong>bold&heavy<strong>`. Both `HTMLVarchar` and `HTMLText` will output the content without conversion, showing the text as bold in your browser.

You have to decide which field type to use in a certain context, and when to trust your users with entering HTML content. Keep in mind that HTML markup can be used to insert JavaScript content if not escaped, meaning an attacker is able to actively change the content and behavior of any output. If we use `HTMLText` as a field type, the following code could replace the contents of the webpage with malicious content:

```
<script>document.body = '<h1>Your site has been hacked!</h1>';</script>
```

The `HTMLText` type is used internally by SilverStripe for its `$Content` field, which stores the main page text. No security protection is used because SilverStripe assumes that only trusted parties will have access to the backend and be able to enter page text. In the next section, we show you ways to escape data manually before storing it or outputting it to the user.

7.1.2 Escape Types

We can ensure that input or output is appropriate for a certain use case by converting it using a specific *escape-type*. Some input has to be escaped before it's written to the database, whereas other data might need special conversion before displaying it to the user. Each `DBField` type has built-in getters for their value in different escape types, as shown in Table 7.1. Alternatively, you can use static methods on the `Convert` class to convert any string value.

Table 7.1 Escape types.

DBField method	Convert method	Description
`RAW()`	–	Shows the unfiltered content of the field.
`XML()`	`raw2xml()`	Safe for use in HTML and XML. Any special characters are converted to their HTML entity names (e.g., '`&`' becomes `&`).
`SQL()`	`raw2sql()`	Safe for use in a SQL query string. Any quote characters are escaped with backslashes.
`JS()`	`raw2js()`	Safe for use in a Javascript string, which means escaping quotes and newlines.
`ATT()`	`raw2att()`	Can be used inside an XML or HTML-attribute such as `NAME` or `ID`. Only basic letters, dashes, and numbers are allowed. All other characters are removed.

These methods are available both in your PHP logic and within a template. For example, if you want to prepare the first name of a member of field type `Varchar` for a particular use, you can do so as follows:

```
<a href="#" title="Biography of $FirstName.ATT" />
   $FirstName.XML
</a>
```

Note that although `$FirstName.ATT` is necessary here, writing `$FirstName.XML` is actually redundant: By default, all fields apart from `HTMLText` and `HTMLVarchar` use `XML()` as their template output. Please note that XML is used synonymously with HTML and XHTML in this context, because they escape essentially the same characters.

On `DataObject` and other subclasses of `ViewableData`, you can get the property as an object rather than its string representation, and call the `XML()` method on it:

```
$myMember->obj('FirstName')->XML();
```

7.1.3 Alternative Markup Languages

Due to the nature of HTML markup, it's astonishingly complicated to filter out malicious code such as any inserted JavaScript. On the other hand, you often want to allow you visitors to enter formatted text, e.g. for a comment or forum post. If you want to allow your users to format their input text safely, alternative markup languages with a more well-defined and locked-down syntax are a good compromise. Examples of these languages are different wiki notations, Textile (`http://textile.thresholdstate.com/`), or Markdown (`http://daringfireball.net/projects/markdown/`). SilverStripe comes with a built-in parser for the *Bulletin Board Code* (*BBCode*) markup language. It's extensively used as a markup language in webforums and wikis.

Suppose, for example, that someone wants to make a text snippet bold. They can easily do so by writing `[b]bold&heavy[/b]`. BBCode uses square brackets instead of the angle brackets, which are typical for HTML. Most HTML tags have BBCode equivalents, although the exact details of the markup will vary between individual implementations. Table 7.2 shows a few examples of BBCode as it can be used within SilverStripe.

Table 7.2 BBCode examples.

BBCode	HTML equivalent
`[b]bold[/b]`	`<b>bold</b>`
`[i]italic[/i]`	`<i>italic</i>`
`[center]centered[/center]`	`<center>centered</center>`
`[color="color"]Text [/color]`	`<font color="color">Text </font>`
`[list] [*] First [*] Second [/list]`	`<ul> <li>First</li> <li>Second</li> </ul>`
`[url=bsp.com]link text[/url]`	`<a href="bsp.com">link text</a>`
`[img]bsp.com/picture .jpg[/img]`	`<img src="bsp.com/picture .jpg" />`

SilverStripe uses the `BBCodeParser` class in the *blog* and *forum* modules. You can also enable BBCode in page comments. It is also available in your own custom fields by setting the field to the `Varchar` or `Text` type, both of which allow BBCode markup. The only thing left to do then is to make sure that the output text is appropriately parsed. Do so by replacing the `$Content` placeholder in the template with the following code:

```
$Content.Parse(BBCodeParser)
```

7.2 Cross-site Request Forgery (CSRF)

Cross-Site request forgery involves unauthorized requests from a user that the website or application trusts. Most of the time, the user doesn't even know about this action, because the request is made through his or her browser in the background by visiting a different malicious website. For example, the browser could try to load an image that actually points to a different trusted website to which the user has previously logged-in. To the application, it looks like a normal request from the user, and can be used to modify personal data such as passwords, and ultimately to hijack the account.

The distinguishing feature of this kind of attack is that while the user's browser executes the script, the actual malicious code comes from a different website to the one being attacked. In most cases neither the user nor the web application notice anything amiss.

A good general rule for mitigating CSRF exploits is given by the HTTP-standard. It states that all GET requests (and therefore all links on a website) should not be able to perform any destructive or modifying actions. POST requests such as form submissions can be secured through a so-called *Shared Secret* to prevent CSRF exploits.

A Shared Secret is a randomly generated ID that's saved in the user's session and also placed in a hidden form field. When such a form is submitted the system can be sure that the logged-in user submitted the form and not a malicious script. This is done by comparing the ID on the form with the ID from the user's session variable. If they match, the submitted data is saved and associated actions are executed. Because the session is likened to the user, a malicious attacker is usually unable to fake this verification token.

SilverStripe automatically inserts a hidden field with a Shared Secret ID into all forms:

```
<input type="hidden" name="SecurityID" value="1744666706" />
```

Naturally, this kind of measure is only effective if all measures for mitigating *Cross-site scripting* have been taken (see Section 7.1), because otherwise the Shared Secret could be found by a malicious script, making the security precaution useless.

If for some reason you don't want the Shared Secret ID to appear in your form, you can disable it by calling `$myForm->disableSecurityToken()` when defining the form.

7.3 SQL Injection

SQL injection is an attack in which a malicious user tries to manipulate a SQL command to his or her benefit. The attack tries to exploit a server which is not sufficiently checking client input before using it as part of a SQL command. Potentially problematic inputs are typically caused by form submissions or URL parameters, but also include cookie values and even HTTP-headers.

Let's look at an example. Suppose you have implemented a search form that searches for users' names in the following unsafe way:

```
$sql="SELECT * FROM Member WHERE name = '".$_POST['search']."'";
```

Instead of searching for a normal name like 'Smith', an attacker could attach additional malicious code into the SQL statement:

```
Smith'; UPDATE Member SET type="admin" WHERE name='Attacker' --
```

An unchecked search query like this would result in the following SQL statement being executed:

```
SELECT * FROM Member WHERE name = 'Smith';
UPDATE Member SET type="admin" WHERE name='Attacker' --'
```

The double-dash starts a comment and prevents any SQL after it from being processed as part of the command (in our case the single quote, which closes the SQL statement). The result is a valid SQL statement that secretly upgrades the attacker's account to an administrator.

7.3.1 Validation

One possible way to prevent such an exploit is to validate the input. All validation must be performed on the server-side. Browser-based validation is insufficient, because it can be easily circumvented, for example by turning off Javascript. Validation is primarily used to ensure that the input uses a valid syntax; for example, ensuring that an email address contains an @ symbol.

7.3.2 Automatic Masking

Apart from applying robust validation techniques, a more effective way of mitigating SQL injection is to mask any symbols relevant for a SQL statement. This makes an SQL injection attack next to impossible. Potentially problematic symbols are replaced with a so-called *escape-sequence*. The following operations automatically use SQL escaping:

- `DataObject::get_by_id()`
- `DataObject::update()`
- `DataObject::castedUpdate()`
- `DataObject->Property = <val>`
- `DataObject->setField(<name>,<val>)`
- `DataObject::write()`
- `Form->saveInto()`
- `FormField->saveInto()`
- `DBField->saveInto()`

That covers the major methods that a developer might use to write data to the database. So, if you simply use the standard ways of saving form data, such as `Form->saveInto()`, you don't need to worry about masking/escaping SQL. SilverStripe takes care of that for you automatically.

7.3.3 Manual Masking

SilverStripe doesn't perform SQL escaping everywhere; certain arguments are assumed to be escaped by the developer, granting him or her more flexibility. These methods are primarily used for direct queries or fetching user input:

- `SQLQuery`
- `DataObject::get()`
- `DataObject::get_one()`
- `DB::query()`
- `Director::urlParams()`
- `Controller->requestParams / HTTPRequest->requestVars()`
- `Controller->urlParams / HTTPRequest->params()`

This list is not exhaustive, please check the method documentation for expected input escaping whenever passing SQL strings as an argument. You can use the `Convert` class described above to perform SQL masking manually. Using this class ensures that the code for escaping SQL is defined in a single central location. Masking should be done in any place where user-submitted text forms part of an SQL command. Both read and write operations should be masked.

7.3.4 Casting in PHP

You probably know that PHP isn't too fussy about the typing of data. It will 'decide' for itself whether `42` is a text string or a number. If it's a string it might be 'the answer to the ultimate question of life, the universe, and everything' (a quote from the novel *Hitchhiker's Guide to the Galaxy* by Douglas Adams), or if interpreted as a number, it might just be a somewhat less than healthy body temperature. This ambiguous typing can sometimes cause unwanted and unexpected behavior.

Luckily, you can tell PHP which type a given piece of data has by prefixing a variable with its type in parentheses. This 'casts' the type as the one specified. All available casting operators are shown in Table 7.3.

The use of casting can reduce the risk of an SQL injection attack. For example, if a SQL statement inserts a numeric ID value, we can explicitly cast this value via `(int)` and thereby ensure that the variable doesn't contain any potentially dangerous text fragments. The following example gives you an idea of how to do this:

```
$SQL_categoryID = (int)$request->getVar('category');
// No SQL injection: $SQL_categoryID is casted as an "int"
$obj = DataObject::get(
   'CaseStudy',
   "CategoryID = $SQL_categoryID"
);
```

Table 7.3 Casting in PHP.

Data type	Description
`(int), (integer)`	Only accepts whole integer numbers. Example: `42`
`(bool), (boolean)`	Only accepts Boolean values. Example: `true`
`(float), (double), (real)`	Only accepts floating point values. Example: `2.3`
`(string)`	Only accepts text strings. Example: `'illusionless warmup'`
`(array)`	Only accepts arrays. Example: `array('one',2)`
`(object)`	Only accepts objects. Example: `new Page()`

7.4 Directory Traversal

Directory traversal is a security exploit in which the attacker gains access to a folder on the server's file system, which was ordinarily not meant to be displayed. This can potentially reveal important configuration information and passwords to an attacker. Dynamically constructed pages and upload forms are vulnerable to this kind of attack.

7.4.1 Access Rights

The first layer of protection against *directory traversal* should be the server's file system. Any commands executed through the web application will be executed in the context of the user running the web-server. This user should therefore not have access to sensitive files such as system password information. Shared hosting providers already implement this security precaution, if only to protect themselves.

Note: If you're running PHP in CGI-mode and not as an Apache module, you might be using a different user for PHP than you're using for Apache, which could lead to a security vulnerability (see `http://www.php.net/manual/en/security.cgi-bin.php` for more information).

Let's take a look at the file system permissions inside the SilverStripe root folder. The web-server user shouldn't have write access to the *cms/* and *sapphire/* folder. Only the *assets/* folder, which is used for uploads and other user data, should be writable. As an added security precaution, the *assets/* folder shouldn't allow the execution of scripts (see Section 7.4.4, 'Deactivating PHP in subfolders').

Temporary files generated by PHP or any other script should be stored outside the SilverStripe webroot folder. They are located in the default PHP temporary file locations determined by the `sys_get_temp_dir()` or `tempnam()` functions.

7.4.2 Limiting Data-type Access Permission

When a user uploads files from his or her web browser onto the server, that person has some degree of write access to the server's file system. After all, the file has to end up somewhere, right? Every upload is a potential security vulnerability, if not properly checked.

One way of mitigating this vulnerability is to limit the allowed file types for uploads, e.g., to allow only upload images with the extensions **.jpg*, **.gif*, or **.png*. Listing 7.1 shows you how to create a restricted upload field suitable for insertion into a SilverStripe form:

```
$fileField = new FileField('MyFile');
$fileField->setAllowedExtensions(array('jpg','gif','png'));
$form = new Form(
   $this,
   "UploadForm",
   new FieldSet(
      $fileField
   ),
   new FieldSet(
      new FormAction('upload', 'Upload')
   )
);
```

Listing 7.1 *Limiting uploads to picture files*

If the user now tries to upload anything that's not an image according to its extension, SilverStripe will not accept the file. This is particularly important for any files that might have active script content, most prominently files with a **.php* extension.

7.4.3 Filtering File Paths

As a best practice, we only want users (and editors, for that matter) to be able to save files in the *assets/* folder and its subfolders. All files should be referenced relative to this folder; no absolute pathnames should be allowed. Any user-submitted filename should be filtered through the `basename()` function in order to ensure that the user can't sneak a file into an unwanted file system location.

The standard upload form fields such as `FileField` and `SimpleImageField` take care of this kind of protection automatically. They only allow images to be saved into the *assets/* folder or its subfolders, as set by the `FileField->setFolderName()` method (default: *assets/Uploads/*).

7.4.4 Deactivating PHP in Subfolders

SilverStripe only permits user-submitted files to be saved into special folders, and so it makes sense to prevent PHP files in that folder from being executed. After all, we don't want users finding ways to upload and execute scripts on our server. We can disable the PHP parser for the *assets/* folder by creating a *.htaccess* file with the text in Listing 7.2 and placing it inside this folder. However, keep in mind that this will trigger the web-server to deliver those files as plaintext, meaning they will be readable by anybody.

```
php_flag engine off
```

Listing 7.2 *Configuring Apache through assets/.htaccess*

In order to be able to influence the PHP configuration at runtime using *.htaccess* files, you need to have PHP installed as an Apache module. If you're using shared hosting, that's very likely to be the case. Additionally, the directive `AllowOverride All` informs Apache to accept configuration changes from *.htaccess* files, and so you may also need to set this directive in order to get your custom *.htaccess* file to work. More information on this topic is available at: `http://www.php.net/manual/en/apache.configuration.php` and `http://www.php.net/manual/en/configuration.changes.php`.

If you're not using PHP as an Apache module, or you're not allowed to override the *.htaccess* configuration, you can create a virtual host in your Apache configuration file as follows:

```
<VirtualHost *:80>
   ServerName 127.0.0.1
   DocumentRoot /path/to/webroot
   <LocationMatch assets/>
      php_flag engine off
   </LocationMatch>
</VirtualHost>
```

Listing 7.3 *Configuring Apache through httpd.conf*

7.5 Sessions

Sessions enable a web-server to uniquely identify a user across multiple requests. For example, when the second page of a multi-page order form asks for a user's address, it also needs to remember that user's name from the first page. Sessions make this kind of 'memory' possible.

The HTTP protocol is stateless. Webpages are sent from the server to the requesting clients using this protocol. Without additional measures, the server doesn't know that a client's second request for a page is actually connected to the first one; for all it knows, the client could be someone entirely new.

Logically linking multiple pages presents a problem. A web application can only track a user from page to page if that person sends a consistent identifier with each page request. The server can then link this identifier to a unique user identity. This unique *session identifier* is assigned to the user when he or she logs in.

So, the identity of a user depends on the session identifier. If attackers can somehow get this identifier, they could pretend to be a different user and gain all the security permissions of the original user.

7.5.1 Session Hijacking

One method of an attacker taking control over a user's account is called *session hijacking*. In this scenario, it's next to impossible to guess a session identifier, and so an attacker has to use other means of gaining access.

If the attacker has access to the physical network and the connection is not SSL secured, he or she can sniff the packets being sent over the network and read out potential session identifiers. Another means of hijacking is to use *Cross-site scripting* to retrieve a browser cookie that might hold session information (see Section 7.1, 'Cross-site scripting').

There's no complete protection again session hijacking because not all factors are under the web-server's control. The most you can do is do your best to mitigate XSS vulnerabilities and encrypt any important data connections. That will hopefully make it impossible, or at least very difficult, for an attacker to compromise your server.

7.5.2 Session Fixation

Session fixation is another way of compromising a server. An attacker using this technique doesn't try to steal the valid session identifier of the user, but instead tries to trick a user into logging in using a session identifier known to the attacker.

Almost every modern web application needs to use sessions when offering its services. In most cases, this means storing the session identifier in a cookie on the user's computer. However, some users are afraid of all the security vulnerabilities associated with cookies and disable cookies in their web browser. Many web-servers therefore sometimes offer an alternative means of transmitting the session identifier between pages, by attaching the identifier to every link on the page. This means it will be transferred alongside any subsequent request.

Unfortunately, this kind of URL-based session transmission makes it much easier for an attacker to use session fixation against an unsuspecting user. Therefore, we see that disabling cookies gives a false sense of security. In fact, it can make one more vulnerable to attack.

If a web application accepts session identifiers as parameters in a GET or POST request, it becomes possible to use session fixation to hijack a session. Suppose the following link is sent to an unsuspecting user by email, and note how it contains a specific session identifier '1234':

```
http://example.com/login.php?PHPSESSID=1234
```

If the user clicks this link and logs into the website, the attached session identifier might be used for the remainder of the session. The attacker could therefore hijack the user account and play around to his or her heart's content.

Preventing this kind of attack is difficult, because it requires that the user is educated and aware. He or she should frequently check whether encrypted (SSL) connections are used when performing sensitive operations. Additionally, users should choose not to use options that offer to 'remember me next time'. The longer the user remains logged-in this way, the higher the chance that their session ID will be compromised and their account hijacked. By the same token, it is important to logout from a service after using it, because the active session usually gets removed, thereby making hijacks impossible.

In PHP, sessions are initiated through `session_start()`, which either creates a new session for the current user or resumes an existing one. Using this method without additional measures makes you susceptible to session fixation. SilverStripe uses the `session_regenerate_id()` function to generate its session identifiers. This function generates a new identifier every time the login form is displayed. It also creates a new session identifier if a user signs-in using 'auto-login'. This technique prevents a potential attacker from figuring out a user's session when that person is logging in.

See the following website for more information about session fixation and other security vulnerabilities: `http://shiflett.org/articles`.

7.6 Conclusion

As long as networked systems exist, people will try to gain unauthorized access to them. A system administrator and developer has no choice but to face the danger and implement as many protective measures as possible. Unfortunately, too many systems and services today are still extremely vulnerable to attacks.

In this chapter we summarized a few of the most important measures you can take to secure your systems. Please take this advice into account when planning and deploying your web applications. There is nothing quite as aggravating and potentially costly as a hacker compromising your website.

8
Maintenance

The previous chapter was all about defending a website from external attackers. This chapter, in contrast, is all about ensuring the smooth operation of your system. It will teach you about server maintenance. Armed with this knowledge you won't despair when your site's performance is compromised, or even if it goes down completely. Instead, you'll know were to look to solve the problem.

8.1 Environment Types

SilverStripe can be run in three different *environment types: dev, test,* and *live*. The choice of mode determines how SilverStripe behaves in regards to displaying error messages and other maintenance operations. You can change the mode by editing your *mysite/_config.php* file and inserting the following line with the appropriate mode:

```
Director::set_environment_type(<mode>);
```

Dev

You should choose developer mode if you want error messages to be displayed directly in the browser. SilverStripe automatically defaults to developer mode when certain URLs are used to access it. In particular, if *http://localhost/* or *http://127.0.0.1* are used, SilverStripe assumes that a privileged developer is accessing the site. This assumption makes sense because these URLs shouldn't be accessible to remote visitors. You can add to this white-list of domain names using the `Director::set_dev_servers()` command.

Alternatively, SilverStripe can be forced into developer mode for a single request: simply add *?isDev=1* to the end of any URL. Note that you need to be logged in as an administrator for this to work.

This mode also allows the *dev/build* script to update the database schema to be run without being logged in as an administrator.

More information on debugging SilverStripe web applications can be found in Chapter 9.

Test

In this mode, SilverStripe displays generic error messages in the browser. As its name implies, this mode is suitable for testing a site just before it's due to be deployed in live mode.

Live

We don't want a live site to display ugly plaintext error messages, right? Not only would our website look unprofessional, but also it might expose sensitive data about the underlying system. Live mode therefore suppresses error messages and doesn't display them in the browser. However, developers can still review detailed error messages; currently the only available notification mechanism is through sending error emails to a dedicated admin address. If you don't specify the mode that SilverStripe should use, and it doesn't detect any white-listed domains for specific modes, live mode is the default case.

To determine which mode SilverStripe is currently using, the `Director` class has easy checks:

- `Director::isDev()`
- `Director::isTest()`
- `Director::isLive()`

These methods are very useful for adding conditional configuration in your *mysite/_config.php* based on the mode in which you're running.

8.2 Configuration of Multiple Environments

SilverStripe supports the configuration of multiple SilverStripe projects through a single file, which is useful for anybody with more than one SilverStripe project on the same server or development machine. Typically, some configuration overlaps between these installations. A common example of shared configuration is your database credentials – they most likely differ on your production environment and development machine, but are the same for all projects on this environment.

8.2.1 Environment File Locations

Environments are defined in a file named *_ss_environment.php*, usually stored in the folder containing different SilverStripe webroots (see Figure 8.1).

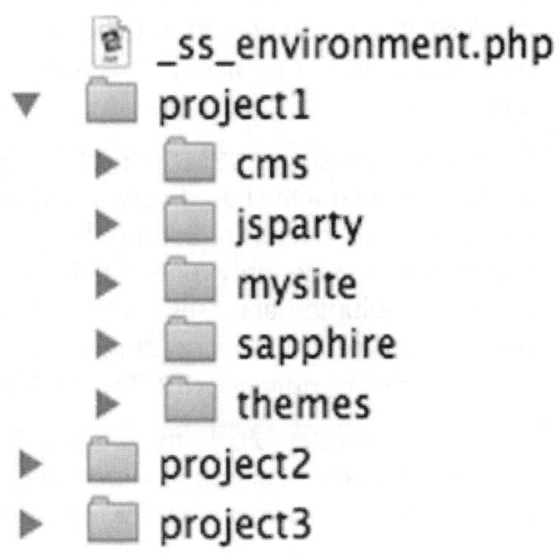

Figure 8.1 Example directory structure.

You can of course still use the *mysite/_config.php* file to configure a specific project across environments. Such settings might include an administrator's email address, which is project specific but doesn't really change between a development and production environment. In summary, *mysite/_config.php* should look the same on every server, whereas *_ss_environment.php* may vary depending on the environment details.

The environment file consists of various PHP constant definitions which are picked up by SilverStripe automatically:

```
<?php
define('SS_ENVIRONMENT_TYPE', <type>);
define('SS_ENVIRONMENT_STYLE', <style>);
define('SS_ENVIRONMENT_ID', <id>);
define('SS_DATABASE_SERVER', <uri>);
define('SS_DATABASE_USERNAME', <user>);
define('SS_DATABASE_PASSWORD', <password>);
define('SS_DATABASE_CHOOSE_NAME', <database>);
?>
```

Listing 8.1 *_ss_environment.php*

Let's go through the parameters one-by-one:

- `SS_ENVIRONMENT_TYPE` should be familiar to you already. You can use this parameter to set the mode in which the site should run ('dev', 'test', or 'live'). This value is internally passed on to `Director::set_environment_type()`.
- `SS_ENVIRONMENT_STYLE` is useful when multiple developers are working off a single shared server and each developer wants to use his or her own database. Setting this parameter to `single` instructs SilverStripe to use only one database. However, if you set it to `shared`, multiple databases can be used. The particular database to be used is determined according the following naming convention: `SS_<project_name>_<SS_ENVIRONMENT_ID>`.
- `SS_ENVIRONMENT_ID` is the unique ID that's used to distinguish between different users on a shared development server. The ID can be a number or arbitrary text, for example 'debian_test_server'.
- The usual settings for connecting to a MySQL database are settable in the environment file. They are: `SS_DATABASE_SERVER`, `SS_DATABASE_USERNAME`, and `SS_DATABASE_PASSWORD`.
- `SS_DATABASE_CHOOSE_NAME` is an optional parameter that can be used to set the database name independent of the `SS_ENVIRONMENT_ID` parameter.

To have the *_ss_environment.php* file picked up by your PHP installation, include the following line in your *mysite/_config.php*:

```
require_once("conf/ConfigureFromEnv.php");
```

8.3 Version Control using Subversion

If you've ever programmed in a team you'll undoubtedly be familiar with tools for version control. They help manage the work of multiple team members in a central place and collate all their contributions into a working application. These tools help when merging multiple developers' modifications into the same file. Even the smallest project benefits from using a version control system. Indeed, a single developer working by him- or herself can benefit from a version control system's ability to rollback to previous versions of a file.

The 'grandfather' of version control is probably *Concurrent Versions System* (CVS, http://nongnu.org/cvs/), which lost popularity over the last few years to a more versatile system known as *Subversion (SVN,* http://subversion.tigris.org/). Both systems rely on a central repository to which clients can connect for reading and writing data, mostly source code.

More recently, distributed solutions such as *Git* (http://git-scm.com/) and *Bazaar* (http://bazaar-vcs.org/) have been gaining traction. These projects allow for a better collaboration on large community-driven projects by a decentralized architecture.

SilverStripe primarily uses Subversion for source control, so we focus on this architecture in the following descriptions.

8.3.1 Terminology

A Subversion system is comprised of a server and various clients. The server manages all versioned files and folders and stores them in its *repository*. The repository can be browsed and managed similar to a normal filesystem.

Clients are individual computers that establish temporary connections with the server in order to exchange modified files with it. Your local machine can be both a client and a server at the same time. We limit our description of the SilverStripe Subversion repository to client-side operations.

Using Subversion involves just three operations, at the most basic level: *checkout, commit,* and *update. Checkout* copies data from the repository to the local computer. It should be your first operation when initially starting work on a project. Once you have made some changes to files you should contribute these back into the repository for other team members to see and use. This can be done using the *commit* command. You should periodically check that you're working with the latest files, by running the *update* command. This checks the repository for any changes made by other users and updates your local files to match the latest snapshot.

There's a lot more information available on the topic of configuring and using Subversion. We recommend reading the free e-book *Version Control with Subversion* by Ben Collins-Sussman, Brian W. Fitzpatrick, and C. Michael Pilato, available at http://svnbook.red-bean.com/.

8.3.2 Software

Subversion clients are available on every major platform. A couple of prominent clients include:

- Subclipse (http://subclipse.tigris.org/): A plug-in for the *Eclipse* platform.
- TortoiseSVN (http://tortoisesvn.tigris.org/): A client that integrates with *Microsoft Windows Explorer.*

A full list of clients is available at http://subversion.tigris.org/. Let's reiterate once again that you don't need to setup your own server to use Subversion. All you need is a client application.

8.3.3 The SilverStripe Repository

We will get into checking out files in a moment, but first let's take a look at the SilverStripe repository. The SilverStripe project uses Subversion to manage all of its source code. Read-only access is publicly available, and is an alternative to the archived downloads obtained from http://silverstripe.org/. This is particularly interesting because it allows an interested developer to download and review the 'bleeding edge' of SilverStripe without waiting for a release – with a lesser degree of stability, of course. For information on downloading SilverStripe through Subversion, see http://silverstripe.org/subversion/.

You can find the SilverStripe repository at http://svn.silverstripe.com/open/ and can access it in a number of ways. You have the options of using a graphical Subversion client to browse the repository, listing its contents using the command-line, or simply using your web-browser to obtain a view of the files. The folder structure should be as follows:

```
modules/
phpinstaller/
themes/
thirdparty/
tools/
```

This folder contains all the files comprising the SilverStripe platform. The *modules/* folder contains all the modules, as well as the core in the *cms/*

and *sapphire/* subfolders. The *phpinstaller/* folder contains the installer, some basic files, and a few other system folders.

You will find three folders within each subfolder: *trunk/*, *branches/*, and *tags/*. These represent the basic building blocks of the version control system:

- *trunk/*: contains the main working copy of the files in that folder. For example, *sapphire/trunk* contains the newest code from the core of SilverStripe.
- *branches/*: contains past releases and experimental features that haven't yet been migrated into *trunk/*.
- *tags/*: contains copies of files from *trunk/* or *branches/* in the form of snapshots labeled with easy to understand names. This folder also contains a list of current and past snapshots named according to their version numbers.

Copying the current version from the repository

If you want to copy the newest version of SilverStripe from the repository onto your local computer, you can do so using the following command (written in a single line):

```
svn checkout http://svn.silverstripe.com/open/phpinstaller/trunk/
   SilverStripeSite
```

The `checkout` command copies the complete set of files into the *SilverStripeSite/* folder on your local hard drive.

Try performing the checkout. You'll notice that some files appear in the target folder that didn't directly exist in the repository folder. This is because externals were taken into account. Subversion externals can be used to link to other paths within the repository. In any case, after the checkout process completes you will have the latest version of SilverStripe on your hard drive.

8.3.4 Subversion in Eclipse

It takes only a few steps to install a Subversion client for Eclipse or for a development environment based on *Eclipse* such as *Aptana Studio*. If you have *EasyEclipse* installed, you don't have to install anything, because it already contains a Subversion client.

If you're using Aptana Studio, select Help > Software-Updates > Find and Install and click on the Search for new features to instail button. In the following window select Subclipse, and then click Next and Finish to start the installation process. Wait until the installation process finishes and restart the application. Now you should be able to open the SVN-repository explorer by going to WINDOW > OPEN PERSPECTIVE > OTHER. Click OK and the repository explorer will be available from the icon on the top-right corner of the window:

You can integrate a repository by clicking on the ADD SVN REPOSITORY icon (see Figure 8.2).

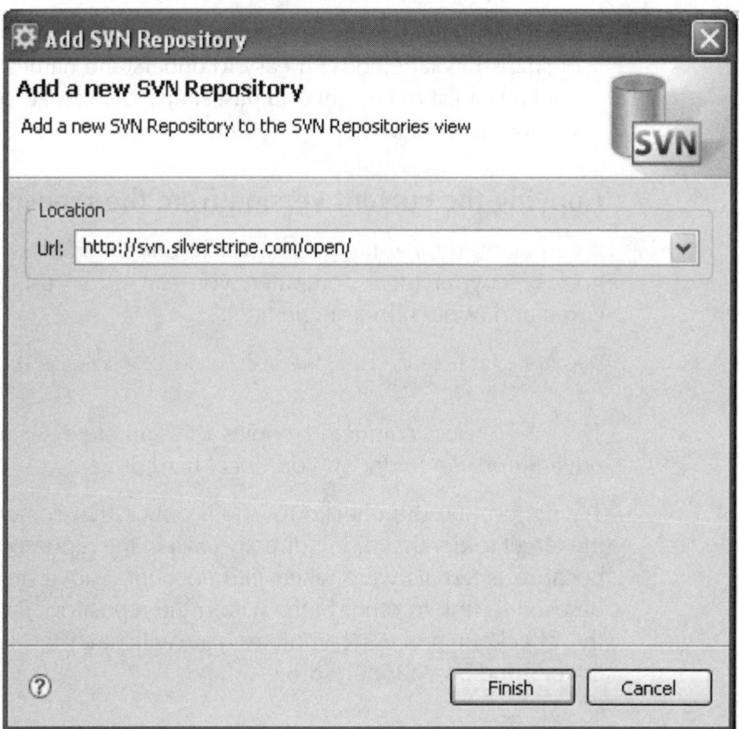

Figure 8.2 Using SVN within Aptana Studio.

Enter the URL of the SVN-repository to which you want to connect into the LOCATION field (for SilverStripe this is: http://svn.silverstripe.com/open/). After clicking FINISH, you'll be able to browse the data within the SVN (as shown in Figure 8.3).

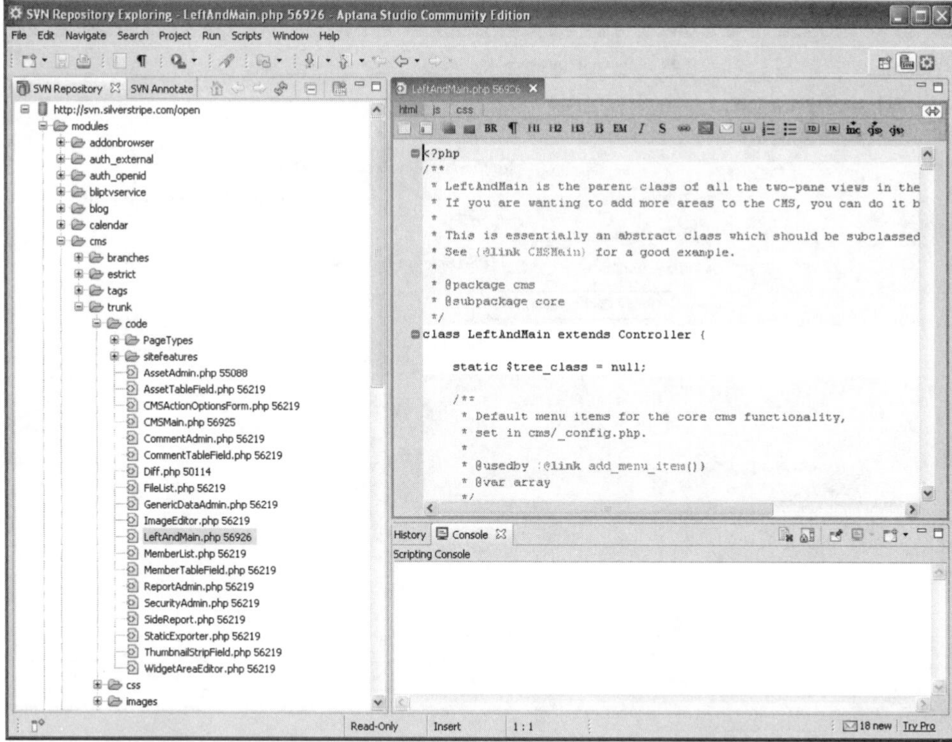

Figure 8.3 Browsing an SVN repository within Aptana Studio.

8.3.5 Subversion in Netbeans

In order to use Subversion within Netbeans you first need to install the *subversion command-line client*. If you haven't already done so, you should download it from the Subversion website (http://subversion.tigris.org/).

You will need to restart your computer after installing the command-line client in order for Netbeans to be able to access it. You can then enter the address of an SVN repositories by going to VERSIONING > SUBVERSION > CHECKOUT (see Figure 8.4).

Click on the BROWSE button and you'll see an overview of the folders within the repository. Select the folder you want to check out and click OK.

NetBeans will start the checkout process and download the necessary files onto your computer. It will then ask you where you want the files to be stored and whether you want to create a new project.

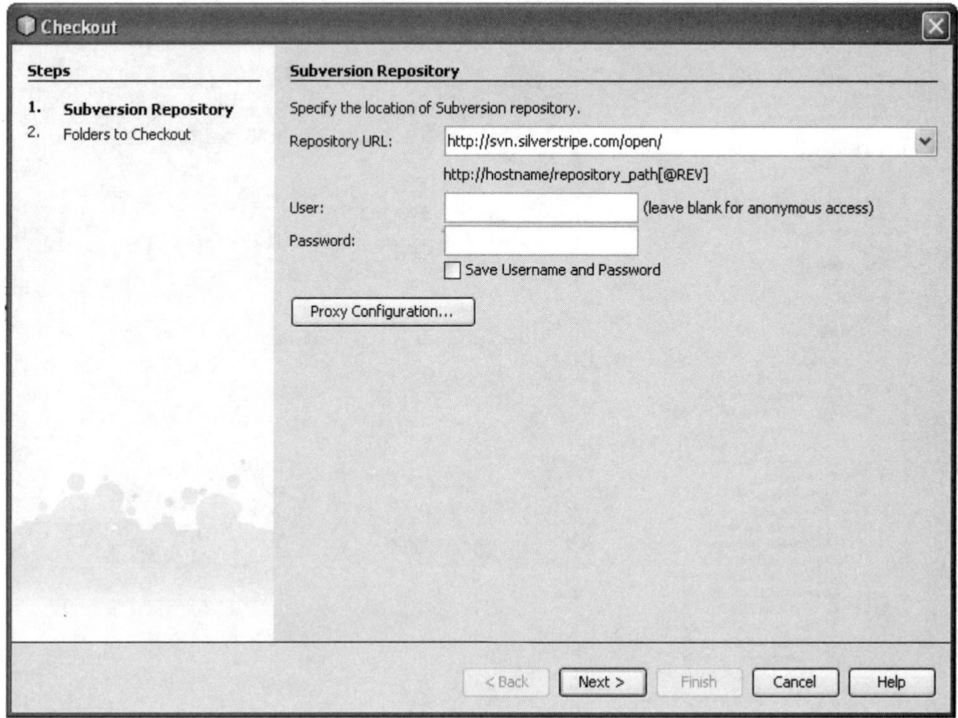

Figure 8.4 Setting up SVN in Netbeans.

8.4 Backup

Even the best website or web application is no use if your hard disk crashes. Better be safe than sorry and make external copies of both your database and the SilverStripe webroot folder. You should also make a backup before updating to a new version, changing the data model, or running a destructive SQL operation. Besides the obvious benefit of recovering from data loss, backups can also be useful for the purpose of analyzing the progression of a project.

SilverStripe is designed as a portable system which can be easily migrated between different servers and platforms. There's no explicit export/import workflow beyond the described database and filesystem backup to store all relevant data for a specific installation, and restore it identically later on.

8.4.1 Database

In Chapter 2 (Section 2.5, 'Database Management'), we introduced you to tools such as *phpMyAdmin* and the MySQL command line. Many inexpensive shared-hosting providers provide *phpMyAdmin* access to your database. Some of the packages for installing PHP locally, such as WAMP and MAMP, also include *phpMyAdmin* by default. We will therefore not go into detail about installing database administration software. If you run into any problems, or have further questions, please consult the *phpMyAdmin* project's homepage at: http://phpmyadmin.net.

From here on we will assume that WAMP or MAMP are installed on your machine and *phpMyAdmin* is accessible at http://localhost/phpmyadmin/.

Export

To perform a quick backup of the database schema, call up *phpMyAdmin* and select the database you want to backup from the navigation bar on the left-hand side of the screen. The default SilverStripe database name is *ss_mysite*, unless you changed the name in the installation process. Select the EXPORT tab in the right panel (see Figure 8.5).

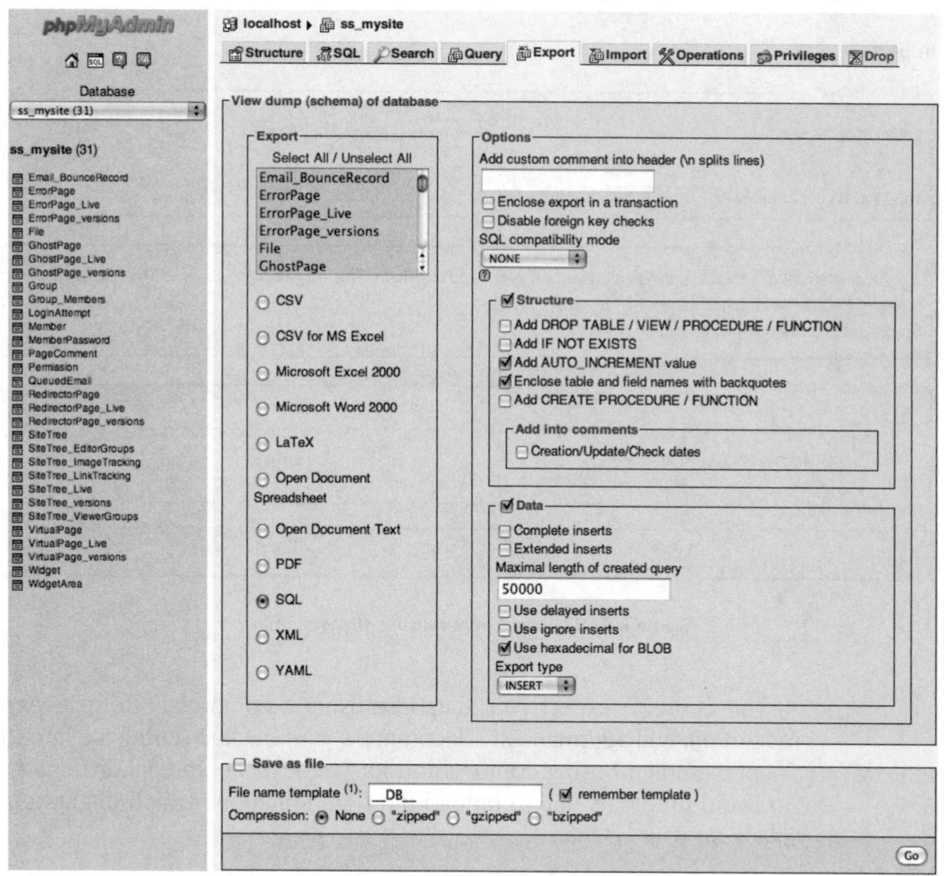

Figure 8.5 Database export using *phpMyAdmin*.

The EXPORT field-set allows you to select which tables you want include in the export. By default all tables will already be selected. You can also select the export format you wish to use; for database backups the default SQL option will be fine. In the OPTIONS area you can select whether you want to export just the structure/schema, data, or both. It's also a good idea to tick the SAVE AS FILE checkbox, because *phpMyAdmin* will otherwise output any generated SQL straight in your browser.

Import

If you want to re-import data, select the IMPORT tab and click the BROWSE button in the FILE TO IMPORT area and select the file you just exported (see Figure 8.6).

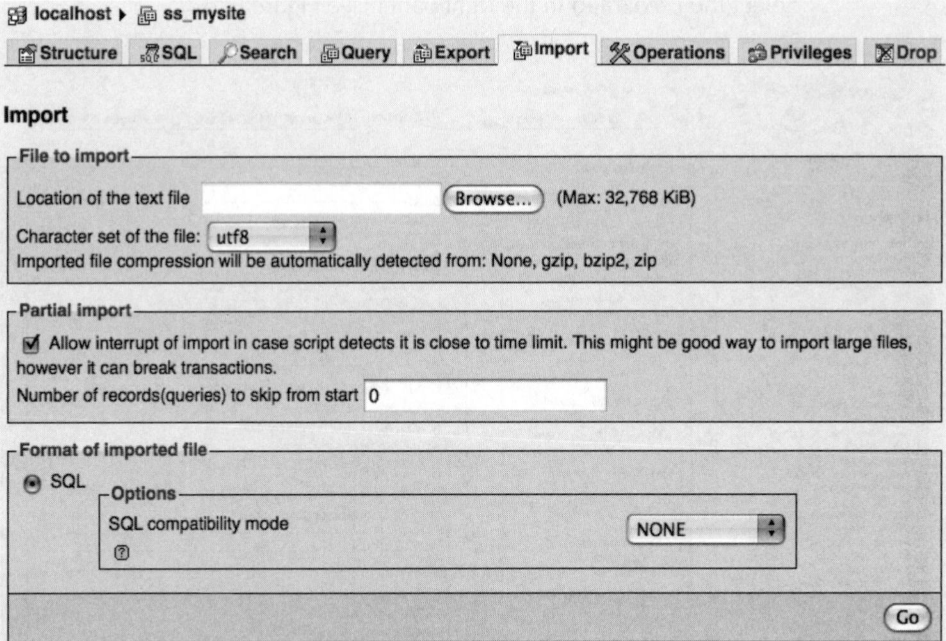

Figure 8.6 Database import using *phpMyAdmin*.

If you chose to export your database using a compressed format, *phpMyAdmin* will automatically decompress your backup during the import. We recommend using compression for larger database backups, mainly to avoid problems due to upload file size limitations which might be in place on your web-host.

MySQLDumper

phpMyAdmin processes each operation within a single PHP request. This can lead to timeouts in script execution and poor performance, particularly with tasks such as backing up large databases. Increasing script execution time or other performance requirements might not always be allowed (for example, shared hosting providers usually limit all your scripts to around 30 seconds). *MySQLDumper* presents a nice alternative if you want to export a particularly large database. It's an application based on PHP and Perl, but works a bit differently to *phpMyAdmin*.

Every backup and import of large data sets is segmented into smaller pieces, each of which is small enough to be processed within your host's performance limitations. Segments are processed sequentially, one after the other.

In addition to this neat little trick for getting around script time limits, the tool also provides a range of sophisticated settings for configuring your backups.

You can download *MySQLDumper* at http://mysqldumper.de/en/.

MySQL on the Command-line

Both *phpMyAdmin* and *MySQLDumper* are useful utilities for a development workflow, but not well suited for automation and backups of production data. MySQL comes with a command-line utility called *mysqldump*, which produces SQL exports. Together with scheduling services such as *crontab* on Unix and other system administration tools it forms a solid base for regular production backups.

Usage of *mysqldump* is beyond the scope of this book, you can find an overview of parameters and examples at http://dev.mysql.com/doc/refman/5.1/en/using-mysql-programs.html.

8.4.2 Filesystem

An instance of SilverStripe is composed mainly of the files in the server's webroot folder (see Chapter 3). The only related files outside of this folder are temporary files that don't need backing up, because they'll be re-created as necessary. However, there is one other important file that you might miss: The SilverStripe webroot folder contains a hidden *.htaccess* file. Please make sure to include this and other hidden files in your backups. In particular, *.htaccess* contains the access permissions for various file types and folders and it's important to preserve them when backing up.

When backing up production data, consider using well-known tools such as *tar* to create compressed archives and *rsync* to copy backups to a different location. As so often, automation is key when backing up: ensure that you have the right tools for the job.

8.5 Upgrade

Generally, open source software should be kept as recent as possible, particularly when considering patches for security issues. In the interest of stability, you should generally wait for a new release before upgrading. These releases are usually announced on the SilverStripe blog at http://silverstripe.org/blog/.

If you're more adventurous and keen to try out unreleased 'cutting edge' versions of SilverStripe, check them out from the official Subversion repository. Alternatively, the so-called *daily builds* offer a convenient way of getting newer versions without requiring any additional tools such as a Subversion client (see box 'Daily builds – state of the art')

Daily builds – state of the art

Every day http://dailybuilds.silverstripe.com/ is updated to contain the newest version of SilverStripe, which makes it very easy to stay up-to-date. The website distinguishes between the core system and optional modules. Additionally, you can choose to either download individual files of the source code or download everything packed in a *tar.gz* archive.

To give you a better idea of what's changed, each folder contains a file called *changelog.xxxx.today* and *changelog.xxxx.sincestable*. These files list the changes made since yesterday and those made since the last stable release, respectively.

It's a good idea to backup your data before upgrading your database. To conduct the upgrade you should first delete existing core and module folders, which ensures that there are no older files conflicting with the new code. Delete everything except the *assets/* containing user-uploads, your *mysite/* project folder, or any folders you created yourself. Extract all system folders (mainly *sapphire/, cms/* and *jsparty/*) from the new release archive and place them in your webroot. Finally, visit http://localhost/dev/build/ to update the data schema to the latest version.

Upgrade checklist

- Check if all used modules are compatible with the new version of SilverStripe. This should be noted in their documentation on http://silverstripe.org/modules/.
- New versions of SilverStripe may contain changes to the core API. Confirm that any custom code still works with the new version. Unit testing can help in this effort. Check the *changelog* at http://open.silverstripe.org/wiki/Changelog/ to see if there have been any changes that may affect you.
- Check if any HTML, CSS, or Javascript has been changed.
- Read the online documentation and upgrade guide for the new version: http://doc.silverstripe.com/doku.php?id=upgrading.

The upgrade process is generally quick and easy provided that you haven't made any changes to the SilverStripe core files. These changes will be undone by the upgrade and would need to be re-implemented. If your project requires changes to the core, there are cleaner ways that don't necessitate modifying core files (see Chapter 12).

8.6 Error Handling

In the previous parts of this chapter we describe how to configure SilverStripe's error message handling. We now look at reasons why a given error may have occurred and what can be done to fix it.

The first thing to do when a web application is misbehaving is to take a look at the log files. There are three different levels of logs that are of interest: Apache, PHP, and SilverStripe.

8.6.1 Apache

The lowest level of error occurrences may be found by looking at the web-server log files. The exact location of these files will vary according to the details of your particular operating system and installation. Most Unix distributions place these files in */var/log/apache/* or */var/log/apache2/*. A WAMP installation generally makes these log files accessible from the context menu in the Windows start bar.

You will want to inspect the Apache log files if you suspect that requests aren't reaching a SilverStripe PHP process to begin with. For example, an 'Internal Server Error (500)' might be related to the `mod_rewrite` rules for rewriting URLs defined in the *.htaccess* file of a SilverStripe webroot. In such cases looking at the Apache *error_log* file can help you diagnose and fix the problem.

8.6.2 PHP

If you're sure that the server is passing requests to SilverStripe, inspect PHP error logs. SilverStripe has its own *error-handler,* which catches and displays most recoverable errors occurring within PHP, and quits the process in an orderly fashion with a userfriendly error message. However, the error-handler can't catch a *fatal error.* You should check the PHP-logfile if you're getting such errors. WAMP/MAMP's server menu once again provides access to this file.

If you're running a live site you'll generally want to suppress fatal errors from being displayed in the user's browser, mainly to avoid exposing sensitive information. You can do this by modifying the *php.ini* configuration file, as follows:

```
display_errors = Off
log_errors = On
error_log = /path/to/errorlog
```

This ensures that error messages are saved for review in the appropriate log file, but not displayed to any visitors.

You can also set these parameters on a site-by-site basis in your *mysite/_config.php* file, as long as your Apache configuration allows for this:

```
ini_set("display_errors", "Off");
ini_set("log_errors", "On");
ini_set("error_log", "/path/to/errorlog");
```

Keep in mind that fatal errors might still occur before these configuration changes take effect, so the preferred approach is a global configuration through *php.ini.*

8.6.3 Logging in SilverStripe

If neither Apache nor PHP are causing the error, finally look into error handling in SilverStripe itself.

Error levels in PHP

PHP and SilverStripe distinguish between three different types of *user errors* that can be raised through `trigger_error()`:

- `E_USER_NOTICE` errors are meant to inform the developer of something. A notice might tell the developer that he or she is using a deprecated method, or that a minor syntax error has occurred.
- `E_USER_WARNING` is an severe but recoverable error, meaning that it doesn't halt the execution of the PHP script.
- A regular `E_USER_ERROR` is a fatal problem that forces the script to abort and display the error message.

You can find a complete list of all error levels and their various meanings at http://php.net/manual/en/function.error-reporting.php.

SilverStripe provides developers with a very detailed error report, including URL, stack-trace, and detailed parser error message. You can view this error report using a variety of channels.

Standard Output

As described earlier in this chapter, you can view SilverStripe error messages directly through the PHP standard output stream (mostly displayed in your browser) for specific environment types, which is particularly useful while debugging. However, a live site shouldn't display such detailed error messages because of security concerns. We don't want to grant a malicious user insight into the deepest innards of our application code.

To enable this browser-output, you need to switch your environment type to '*dev*' or '*test*', by adding the following line to the *mysite/_config.php* file:

```
Director::set_environment_type(<type>);
```

Log File

By default, SilverStripe doesn't record errors in its log file. You can activate error logging by added the following line to the *mysite/_config.php* file:

```
Debug::log_errors_to(<logfile-name>);
```

Note: The file will be automatically stored one level above the web-root, to avoid it being readable by unauthorized parties. Internally, the built-in `error_log()` function is used; see http://en.php.net/manual/en/function.error-log.php.

Email

You can have SilverStripe send error messages via email to a dedicated administrator account, by adding the following line to the *mysite/_config.php* file:

```
Debug::send_errors_to(<email-address>);
```

Keep in mind that email notifications might quickly fill up your inbox, depending on the popularity and complexity of your website. This way of debugging is only feasible for low traffic SilverStripe installations.

8.6.4 Custom Error-pages

The default error message for visitors to your live website is generated by the `Debug::friendlyError()` method, which returns a rather terse statement: 'The website server has not been able to respond to your request.' You may wish to customize this message to be more friendly and/or informative.

These kinds of error messages are implemented as static HTML pages located in the *assets/* folder. SilverStripe automatically outputs there when an error occurs in 'test' or 'live' environment types.

Error pages follow a particular naming convention; the error-handler selects error pages based the error-code of the error. Error pages should be named according to the *error-*`<error-code>`*.html* pattern. For example, if no page is found under a certain URL, SilverStripe will redirect to *assets/error-404.html* (see the later box 'Common HTTP status codes' for a description of some error codes).

It's somewhat tedious to manually create an error page for each error type. Doing so would also result in lots of duplicate HTML-code. There is an easier way: Apart from the dreaded 'fatal error', all other recoverable errors can be handled through the standard SilverStripe templating engine.

Create a new page with the `ErrorPage` page type. Select the error code for which you want the page to be responsible from the drop-down menu on the CONTENT > MAIN section of the page. The default SilverStripe installation already contains an error page for 'Page not found', linked to HTTP error code 404. And here is the kicker: Every time you publish an error page SilverStripe generates a static HTML version of the file and deposits it into the *assets/* folder.

In case the error does simply state that a given URL wasn't found, the remaining SilverStripe functionality is still available to you on this page. This means you could implement an automated search for alternative pages with a similar URL, searching for alternative spelling of the page name or providing a full text search field.

Common HTTP status codes

The status of a page is transmitted with HTTP headers, bundled with the actual content visible in the browser. A status code generally consists of a human-readable description as well as a more machine-friendly numeric code. The following status codes are common and we suggest that you create custom error pages for them:

- **404 Not Found**: The most common server error message, usually occurs when a visitor mistypes the URL or a previously existing URL has been removed from the system. Search engines may also retain these outdated pages in their indexes resulting in visitors reaching it by mistake. Keep in mind that unpublishing a page in the CMS will make the URL unavailable to visitors.
- **500 Internal Server Error**: The error that's returned if Apache is misbehaving or a PHP script is abruptly terminated due to an error. We also recommend that you craft a custom error page to make this error less scary for your visitors.

Certain errors can completely stop a PHP script from executing, preventing SilverStripe from recovering with a friendly output – in PHP this is called a fatal error, which is generally represented by the HTTP status code '500 Internal Server Error' through a web-server. For this error, we have to start a bit lower in the toolchain and modify the Apache configuration by adding the following line to your *.htaccess* file:

```
ErrorDocument 500 assets/error-500.html
```

Apache now uses your custom page instead of its own default error page.

8.7 Performance

Performance is an important factor, which permeates all the way from choosing a solid language and framework over coding practices through to infrastructure decisions. Particularly in a web-application context, it is a difficult beast to measure, because it depends just as much on relatively central server tuning, as well as various parameters within the browser environment of your visitor.

In terms of web-server load, even the smallest blog site can experience unexpected usage spikes, because it might be featured on a high-volume link portal – the so called *slashdot-effect.* Generally every seemingly insignificant website should have basic precautions that help sustain performance under increased load.

Many of these measures relate to infrastructure setup and general best practices, and are well beyond the scope of this section. Therefore, we stick mostly to selected SilverStripe and PHP specific tools of optimization.

8.7.1 PHP: Byte-code Caching

The simplest way to speed up a SilverStripe site is to use a PHP *byte-code cache.* This cache saves the compiled byte-code of a PHP script. That way, a page will load more quickly in subsequent calls, because PHP already has some of the necessary source code in a compiled form. Depending on the complexity of the code in question, the page's speed can increase by a factor of 5 (see http://xcache.lighttpd.net/wiki/Introduction).

These caching systems can be seamlessly installed using a PHP extension; you don't need to modify your own application in any way. You do however need to have access to the configuration of your web-server. If you're using a shared host, your provider might already use some kind of byte-code caching system. If you're running your own server, a number of open-source caching systems are available for you to use. You can find a comprehensive list on http://en.wikipedia.org/wiki/PHP_accelerator.

We've found that XCache (http://xcache.lighttpd.net/) works well with SilverStripe. Installing it is as simple as adding a few lines into your *php.ini* file. See the official documentation at http://xcache.lighttpd.net/wiki/InstallingAsPhpExtension/ for detailed installation instructions.

8.7.2 Client: Reducing Download Size

You may have noticed that SilverStripe uses quite a bit of JavaScript. This Javascript is often included in multiple files, each loaded one after the other. It is best practice in SilverStripe to use the `Requirements` class to manage these includes, rather than writing them into a template by hand. You'll already have encountered this class in the standard `Page_Controller` class:

```
<?php
class Page_Controller extends ContentController {
   function init() {
      parent::init();
      Requirements::themedCSS("layout");
      Requirements::themedCSS("typography");
      Requirements::themedCSS("form");
   }
}
```

Listing 8.2 *Using requirements in mysite/code/Page.php to insert Javascript and CSS files*

SilverStripe searches for the specified themes and inserts them into the document by generating the following HTML code:

```
<link rel="stylesheet" type="text/css"
   href="themes/blackcandy/css/layout.css" />
<link rel="stylesheet" type="text/css"
   href="themes/blackcandy/css/typography.css" />
<link rel="stylesheet" type="text/css"
   href="themes/blackcandy/css/form.css" />
```

You can insert Javascript into your pages in very much the same way. For details on using Requirements, see the box 'Requirements: Linking in CSS and Javascript' in Chapter 5.

Each of those requirements will cause a separate HTTP request, though. Unfortunately, most browsers won't process all these requests in parallel, but instead open a limited number of connections to the server and download the necessary files sequentially. Depending on the amount of CSS and JavaScript in your website or application, this can cause significant delays.

GZIP Compression

The easiest measure to reduce actually-transferred bytes for your website is to compress data on-the-fly within the web-server. A commonly used compression mechanism for this purpose is GZIP, which can compress data to about a quarter of its original size. It's widely supported by modern browsers, who will announce their support in any HTTP request.

Compression is usually easy to integrate in most web-servers: Apache uses *mod_gzip* for Version 1.x (http://sourceforge.net/projects/mod-gzip/) or *mod_deflate* for Version 2.x (http://httpd.apache.org/docs/2.2/mod/mod_deflate.html). These modules can be configured to apply compression to certain files – ideal candidates for us are any HTML, JavaScript, and CSS files. Images are already compressed in GIF, PNG, or JPG format, which makes compression less feasible. Of course any compression means additional workload for both server and client, but it's usually negligible compared to the speed increases in network delivery.

Dynamic Aggregation

One approach for solving the problem of slow page loading due to too many different files is to reduce the number of HTTP needed by combining several files into one. SilverStripe helps you do this by providing a handy method called `Requirements::combine_files()`. You can specify any desired files and the method dynamically combines them into a single file and then caches it by saving it onto the filesystem. This combined file is available for use when loading included content from other pages.

The file containing the collection of other files is re-created every time one of the original files is changed. SilverStripe uses a time-stamp to tell when it has changed.

The `Requirements::combine_files()` method takes two parameters: The name of the new file (without path) and an array with the relative path to each file that should be combined. New requirements are generally specified in the controller's `init()` method, but can in principle be inserted anywhere in your controller logic. Here's an example:

```
<?php
// ...
class MyPage_Controller extends Page_Controller {
function init() {
   parent::init();
      Requirements::combine_files(
         'script_ab.js',
         array(
             'mysite/javascript/script_a.js',
             'mysite/javascript/script_b.js',
         )
      );
   }
}
?>
```

Listing 8.3 *Combining multiple JavaScript files*

In our example we combine the contents of the *mysite/javascript/script_a.js* and *mysite/javascript/script_b.js* files to create a new file called *script_ab.js*.

A second example shows how we can combine cascading stylesheet files in much the same way:

```
<?php
// ...
class MyPage_Controller extends Page_Controller {
   function init() {
      parent::init();
      Requirements::combine_files(
         'style_ab.css',
         array(
            'mysite/stylesheet/style_a.css',
            'mysite/stylesheet/style_b.css',
         )
      );
   }
}
?>
```

Listing 8.4 *Combining multiple CSS-files*

Please be mindful of the order of the files that you specify for combining. The combined file is assembled with the exact order of the files in the array. As inclusion order has an impact on both CSS rules and JavaScript logic, this can lead to unwanted behavior. Also, keep an eye on which files to combine: Not all files might be necessary for each page, which means combining too many files into one can actually have the reverse effect and increase the downloaded size.

Minifying JavaScript

When using `Requirements::combine_files()`, SilverStripe also makes use of the *JSMIN* library (http://www.crockford.com/javascript/jsmin.html). This library is a filter that cuts out unnecessary baggage from Javascript code, a process called *minification*. It removes comments, whitespace, and line breaks and thereby reduces the file size of most files without affecting functionality.

Note that if you want to prevent minification, you can deactivate it by calling `Requirements::combine_js_with_jsmin = false;`. One reason to avoid minifying Javascript is to make the code easier to debug.

Placing Code in the HTML Body

External files are usually included in the `<head>` part of an HTML document, which ensures that all necessary client-side logic and styling are available before rendering anything in the browser. Sometimes, though, it makes sense to show content a bit earlier – not all external assets might be crucial for rendering an initial representation of the HTML.

This will usually improve the speed perception for your visitors, even if the overall download time stays roughly the same.

You can trick browsers into this behavior by moving all references to external CSS and JavaScript files as close to the bottom of your HTML document as possible. SilverStripe can do this for your with a single command in the appropriate SilverStripe controller class:

```
Requirements::write_js_to_body = true;
```

Other Clientside Performance Tips

The optimization tricks suggested in the preceding sections just scratch the surface of client-side performance. You can find more suggestions and tricks at http://developer.yahoo.com/performance/rules.html.

8.7.3 Generating Static Pages

The biggest performance problem with dynamically generated webpages is exactly that they are dynamically generated. Every request requires the PHP parser to start up, compile the SilverStripe code, and then run through the entire framework, gradually generating the complete HTML document until the page can finally be output to the browser. Static documents are much easier for the server to serve up, and might be the single most effective optimization step you can perform.

Most of the content on a webpage changes far less often than it's requested, e.g. when a new article is published. If only the framework was able to know when a page has changed, it could use a static version of the page whenever regenerating the complete page was unnecessary. And guess what? SilverStripe can do exactly this. With a bit of configuration effort, it can create static HTML representations for every page in the system, and automatically re-create them when required. Besides improved performance, a purely static website removes a lot of attack surface by not exposing dynamic (and potentially insecure) scripts.

A word of warning: Using this technique isn't for the faint of heart, because it requires extensive configuration to 'teach' SilverStripe the content dependencies between your pages. It should only be attempted if you're creating a large website that will be subject to a great deal of load. Completely static webpages might also not be feasible depending on the use case – partially dynamic features such as a simple page comment form can become a nightmare to maintain.

SilverStripe uses the `StaticPublisher` and `FilesystemPublisher` classes to create static pages. To enable caching, add the following line to your *mysite/_config.php* file:

```
Object::add_extension(
    "SiteTree",
    "FilesystemPublisher('cache/', 'html')"
);
```

Static pages will now be created in the *cache/* folder relative to the webroot. Generated pages will use an *.html* extension. If you're logged in as an administrator you can create the static files for all webpages in the CMS by running the following command:

```
http://localhost/dev/buildcache
```

First you need tell your web-server to serve up pages from the static cache instead of asking SilverStripe to generate them by adding more rewriting rules to your existing *.htaccess* file. The directives contained in this file are quite lengthy, so we don't list them in this book. You can find a listing as part of the `StaticPublisher` documentation at http://doc.silverstripe.com/doku.php?id=staticpublisher.

The trickier part is to teach SilverStripe when a page has changed. Most page content is not only shown on its own page. For example, publishing content like a new blog entry might impact a number of different pages: archive pages listing blog entries by date, all pages with a sidebar showing the newest entries, etc.

Some user-defined output might also be too diverse to feasibly cache, for example result pages from a full-text search. They need to be generated at runtime. As you can see, things can get a bit complicated when you venture into the world of static pages. But all the effort is worthwhile when you see your website able to handle dozens or even hundreds as many requests.

Things get really exciting when you start distributing static pages across multiple different web-servers. SilverStripe can do this with the `RsyncMultiHostPublisher` class. This core class allows SilverStripe to integrate with a large *Content Delivery Network* (*CDN*). The CDN can then deliver pages to users from servers in the same geographic location as them, which results in extremely low latency and the ability to handle several orders of magnitude more requests. The `RSyncPublisher` class assumes a Unix environment with the *rsync* tool installed, and is based around *SSH* access to transfer files to other servers. Please refer to the documentation for further details: http://doc.silverstripe.com/doku.php?id=staticpublisher.

8.8 Conclusion

In this chapter we discussed several tools and techniques for improving the maintenance and security of your web applications. You should now be able to implement these measures at the flip of a hat. We also showed you how to keep up-to-date with the latest version of SilverStripe, and covered error handling, with friendly errors shown to your visitors, while preserving a more detailed log for developers. Finally, we gave a few hints on how to improve your applications' performance. This should give you a head-start in the world of performance tuning and researching further techniques that might not be directly related to SilverStripe.

9
Testing

We've written quite a few lines of code so far. Among other things, we created a complete job-portal. By now you're probably itching to dive in and start adapting and changing things. You might even have customers knocking on your door asking for new and improved features. Pretty soon you'll no longer be able to test all your new features (and their potential side-effects) simply by clicking around in your web-browser.

You might find yourself walking on thin ice: One tiny innocent looking change will completely mess up your whole application, manifesting itself in a seemingly unrelated part of the code. Now you have two options: you can either spend many hours chasing the gremlins in your code, while your project goes over budget and your customers beat down your door. Or, you can choose to work a little more proactively, more efficiently, and a little less frantically: by writing automated test cases.

In this chapter we write a few tests for our sparkly new job-portal that we created in Chapters 5 and 6. Our aim is to test assumptions we had about how the system was supposed to work, and verify that the code holds true to these assumptions. For example, suppose we have assumed that 'the currently signed-in user is automatically assigned as the author of a newly created job'. As long as we ask the right question, one that can succinctly be answered with 'yes' or 'no', and the job of creating the actual test becomes relatively easy.

SilverStripe's unit testing infrastructure is built upon two established open-source testing frameworks: PHPUnit (http://phpunit.de/) and SimpleTest (http://simpletest.org/).

9.1 Test-driven Development

Automated tests are very useful to verify existing behavior from a previous development phase. On the other hand, it's far too easy to let things slip this way, maybe because the development budget is exhausted, or because things 'seem to work fine' at the moment.

A different way of looking at the problem is the practice of *test-driven development*. It comes from a software development methodology known as *Extreme Programing (XP)*. That may sound very outlandish but is actually very much 'common sense programming'. XP advocates writing tests before the implementation. That way tests will be in place to catch bugs as they occur. Testing nonexistent classes and interfaces may seem strange at first, but in time test-driven development will become as natural as project planning and implementation.

This methodology helps developers see tests as part of the project specification. A traditional paper specification is printed out and then most likely left to rot on someone's desk. In XP the specification become a living, breathing part of the development process through tests. Everyone quickly notices when the implementation and spec get out of sync, because the tests start failing.

Writing tests is an iterative process, just like coding. Tests should ensure that if a given bug is fixed, the same bug doesn't occur again. Tests should also ensure that features keep working as the code-base evolves over time.

Test-driven development in this book

The code examples outside of this chapter don't use test-driven development. We intentionally didn't want to overwhelm you with having to learn the testing framework at the same time as learning SilverStripe. Code examples are easier to comprehend if you don't need to worry about also understanding the associated test cases. We do, at the same time, recommend test-driven development for any major software project. You might want to implement some tests for the existing job-portal application, as an exercise.

Regardless of when you decide to write tests during your development process, they are an important tool that should be part of every developer's toolbox. It's one of the few ways that a developer can be certain that a feature works (and continues to do so), as well as a good verification mechanism for other stakeholders on a project.

You can find information about Extreme Programming and Agile Software Development at http://agilemanifesto.org/.

Continuous integration

Tests are only useful if they're checked regularly. It's a good start to rely on developers running tests on any code modifications they perform. In addition to manual checks, automated runs on a separate machine can help to identify failures early on and notify the development team. Modern multi-core processors make it quite feasible to have tests running continually on a dedicated testing machine. This practice is known as *continuous integration* (CI).

If a version control system is being used, tests only need to be run when a check-in occurs. Extreme Programming advocates that changes should be kept small and checked into version control as soon as possible. This practice keeps the feedback-loop between changes and bugs as short as possible. Bugs can then be fixed very early in the lifecycle, when the cost of fixing them is low.

Another interesting aspect of CI is the social dynamic it creates. A CI server usually informs all developers if a test fails due to a specific change, and points out the culprit. This results in developers thinking twice about submitting buggy code, because their name will be associated with any failed tests that result from it.

A variety of software is available for implementing continuous integration:

- Buildbot (http://buildbot.net/, Python)
- CruiseControl (http://cruisecontrol.sourceforge.net/, Java/.NET/Ruby)
- TinderBox (https://developer.mozilla.org/en/Tinderbox/, Perl)

By the way, the SilverStripe project also uses continuous integration. You can see the status of the most recent builds at http://buildbot.silverstripe.com/.

9.2 Installing PHPUnit

We will use *PHPUnit* (http://phpunit.de/) as the foundation for testing our data model. This third-party PHP library isn't installed by default in SilverStripe; you need to download it separately. The easiest way to do this is to use the package manager PEAR from the command-line (see the following box).

PEAR: PHP extension and application repository

PEAR is an online library and package manager for PHP code implementing commonly used functionality. You can find packages on PEAR for parsing XML, encoding emails, encrypting data, database abstraction, and much more.

All packages are available at http://pear.php.net/ as downloadable archives. Alternatively you can use a special application to manage all packages installed on your local machine, using either the command-line or a web-interface. New packages and their dependencies can be downloaded with a simple command. Existing packages can be updated to the latest version just as easily. All downloaded packages are stored in a central location and ready to be linked into any of your web projects.

PEAR is included with PHP by default, so you probably already have it installed on your machine. If you followed our installation instructions in Chapter 2 and have WAMP or MAMP installed, you can find it at the following paths:

- WAMPServer (Windows): *C:\wamp\bin\php\<php-version>\pear.bat*
- MAMP (Mac OS X): */Applications/MAMP/bin/php5/bin/pear*

After having the `pear` command-line tool available, you need to inform it of the PHPUnit server URL:

```
pear channel-discover pear.phpunit.de
```

Then type the following command to download and install PEAR:

```
pear install phpunit/PHPUnit
```

More information about PHPUnit, including a more detailed installation guide, is available at http://www.phpunit.de/pocket_guide/3.2/en/installation.html.

9.3 Running Tests

Now that we have equipped ourselves with PHPUnit we are ready to go. Let's start by running some existing tests already present in the SilverStripe core. There are two ways of running tests, through a web-interface or with slightly more effort through the command-line. Both methods run the same tests, the only difference is the output format and interface used to configure the tests.

The basic component of any test is a *test case*, which should test one isolated aspect of system logic. One or more test cases can be collected in a *test suite*. Test cases are expressed as methods in PHP code; a suite is represented by a class. For example, the method `testDelete()` on the suite `DataObjectTest` verifies that deletion of DataObjects is correctly handled.

9.3.1 Web Interface

Every SilverStripe installation contains a web interface that can be used to run any found tests, as well as some other useful functions. This interface is accessible at *http://localhost/dev/tests/* (as shown in Figure 9.1). The following options are available for running tests:

- List all tests (all suites are automatically discovered and listed here): *http://localhost/dev/tests/*
- Run all tests: *http://localhost/dev/tests/all/*
- Run a single specific test: *http://localhost/dev/tests/<test-class>*

Try it yourself: Run a test and see what happens. After a few seconds you should get a status screen telling you which tests passed (labeled in green) and which failed (labeled in red).

Note: Running all tests using *http://localhost/dev/tests/all/* can take quite some time and requires a lot of memory, and therefore may exceed the limits set for these resources in your PHP configuration. We recommend that you increase these limits in your *php.ini* configuration:

```
maximum_execution_time = 240
memory_limit = 128M
```

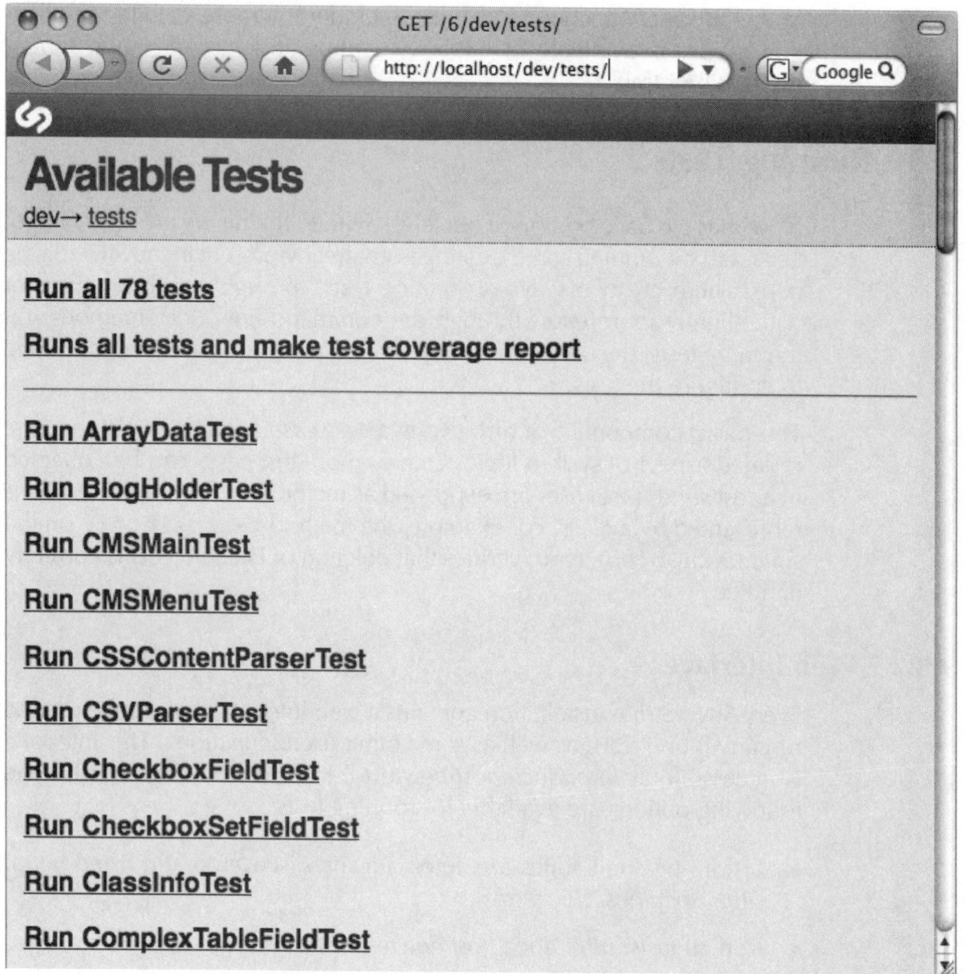

Figure 9.1 Web interface for running tests.

9.3.2 Command-line

The second means of running tests is to use the command-line. It might not look as snazzy as the web-interface, but it makes integrating tests with other tools and scripts quite easy. One common use case is a continuous integration server, as explained in Section 9.1, 'Test-driven development'. For this purpose, SilverStripe comes with its own lightweight command-line tool called *sake* (see the following box).

Sake: SilverStripe's command-line utility

Sake stands for 'Sapphire Make'. The name refers to the UNIX command-line utility for compiling code. SilverStripe's utility doesn't do any compiling, but does have a few useful tricks up its sleeve. The tool essentially runs a SilverStripe URL through a command-line invocation. For example, *sake dev/build* will perform the same logic as opening *http://localhost/dev/build/* in your browser. This makes makes it easy to automate SilverStripe's system functions.

The sake tool is currently only available on UNIX-based system. You can install it into your system path by typing the following on your command-line:

```
sudo <silverstripe-webroot>/sapphire/sake installsake
```

This will copy the sake script into */usr/bin/sake*, which makes it available in every SilverStripe installation on your system.

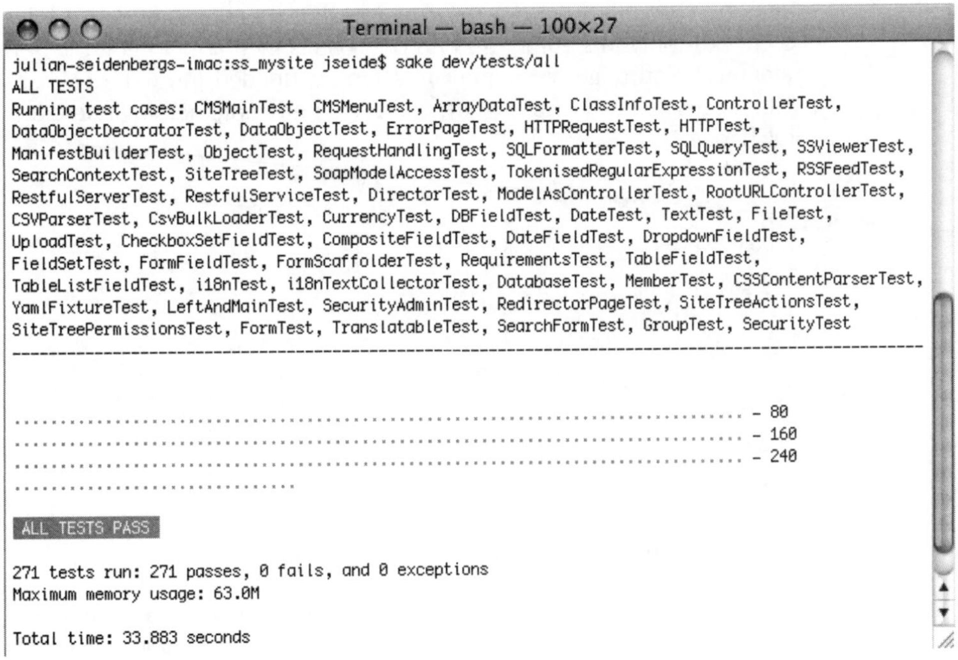

```
Terminal — bash — 100×27
julian-seidenbergs-imac:ss_mysite jseide$ sake dev/tests/all
ALL TESTS
Running test cases: CMSMainTest, CMSMenuTest, ArrayDataTest, ClassInfoTest, ControllerTest,
DataObjectDecoratorTest, DataObjectTest, ErrorPageTest, HTTPRequestTest, HTTPTest,
ManifestBuilderTest, ObjectTest, RequestHandlingTest, SQLFormatterTest, SQLQueryTest, SSViewerTest,
SearchContextTest, SiteTreeTest, SoapModelAccessTest, TokenisedRegularExpressionTest, RSSFeedTest,
RestfulServerTest, RestfulServiceTest, DirectorTest, ModelAsControllerTest, RootURLControllerTest,
CSVParserTest, CsvBulkLoaderTest, CurrencyTest, DBFieldTest, DateTest, TextTest, FileTest,
UploadTest, CheckboxSetFieldTest, CompositeFieldTest, DateFieldTest, DropdownFieldTest,
FieldSetTest, FormFieldTest, FormScaffolderTest, RequirementsTest, TableFieldTest,
TableListFieldTest, i18nTest, i18nTextCollectorTest, DatabaseTest, MemberTest, CSSContentParserTest,
YamlFixtureTest, LeftAndMainTest, SecurityAdminTest, RedirectorPageTest, SiteTreeActionsTest,
SiteTreePermissionsTest, FormTest, TranslatableTest, SearchFormTest, GroupTest, SecurityTest
----------------------------------------------------------------------------------------------------


................................................................................ - 80
................................................................................ - 160
................................................................................ - 240
...............................

ALL TESTS PASS

271 tests run: 271 passes, 0 fails, and 0 exceptions
Maximum memory usage: 63.0M

Total time: 33.883 seconds
```

Figure 9.2 Command-line interface for running tests.

To get all tests running with sake, some additional configuration steps are required, as outlined in the SilverStripe online documentation at *http://doc.silverstripe.com/doku.php?id=sake.*

With sake installed, switch your working directory to the webroot folder of the SilverStripe instance you want to control and type the following to run all tests (as shown in Figure 9.2):

```
sake dev/tests/all
```

9.4 Unit Tests for the Model

Now that we know how to run existing tests, we can get into creating some tests of our own. Writing tests for the complete job-portal is beyond the scope of this book, but we will write a few tests to show you the ropes. Our first test checks if newly created references automatically have the currently logged-in user assigned as its author. We also want to check if only this author and no one else is then able to edit the new reference. You might remember that we overloaded the write callback with `Reference->onBeforeWrite()` when implementing references in Chapter 6.

```
<?php
class Reference extends DataObject {
   // ...
   function onBeforeWrite() {
      if(!$this->ID) {
         $this->DeveloperID = Member::currentUserID();
      }
      parent::onBeforeWrite();
   }
   // ...
}
?>
```

Listing 9.1 *mysite/code/Reference.php (excerpt)*

Keep in mind that the test cases in this chapter rely on code that was written in Chapters 5 and 6. The book website should get you started with a complete example project download in *6_crm.zip.*

9.4.1 A Simple Test Case

Okay, let's get into testing the `Reference` class. The first thing we need to do is create a subclass of `SapphireTest` called `ReferenceTest`.

SapphireTest is a core class that provides a gateway to the PHPUnit testing framework.

As a convention, test classes should be stored in a subfolder *tests/* on the module they are testing, which in our case would be the *mysite/tests/* folder. Please create this folder and add a new file *mysite/tests/Reference-Test.php* with the following code:

```
<?php
class ReferenceTest extends SapphireTest {
    function testAuthorIdSetOnFirstWrite() {
        $reference = new Reference();
        $reference->write();
        $this->assertEquals(
            $reference->DeveloperID,
            Member::currentUserID(),
            'Developer ID is automatically set on first write'
        );
    }
}
?>
```

Listing 9.2 *mysite/tests/ReferenceTest.php*

As you can see, the ReferenceTest class contains only one method called testAuthorIdSetOnFirstWrite(). SilverStripe's testing framework will only recognize and run methods prefixed with 'test', all other methods are discarded.

The method creates a new reference instance and writes it to the database. After that we get to the interesting part: $this->assertEquals() is used to test an *assertion:* We assert that the DeveloperID of the new reference is equal to the ID of the current user. The third parameter is optional; it allows us to express the assumption we're testing in words. This can be helpful when later reviewing failed tests and trying to figure out what they were testing. The assertEquals() method is one of many little helper methods provided by PHPUnit (see the later 'PHPUnit Conventions' box for more information).

Try running the new test using the web-interface:

http://localhost/dev/tests/ReferenceTest/

You should see a page with a green box telling you '1 passes, 0 fails', indicating that our assumption was true and the test passed (see Figure 9.3). If one of the assertions was to be false, you would get a test failure as shown in Figure 9.4.

You might be wondering about the choice of the testAuthorIdSetOnFirstWrite() name for the test method. Although it seems quite

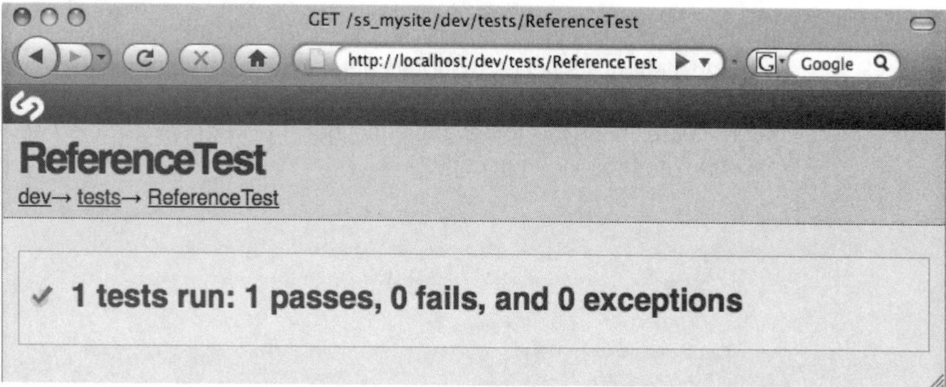

Figure 9.3 Our first test passes.

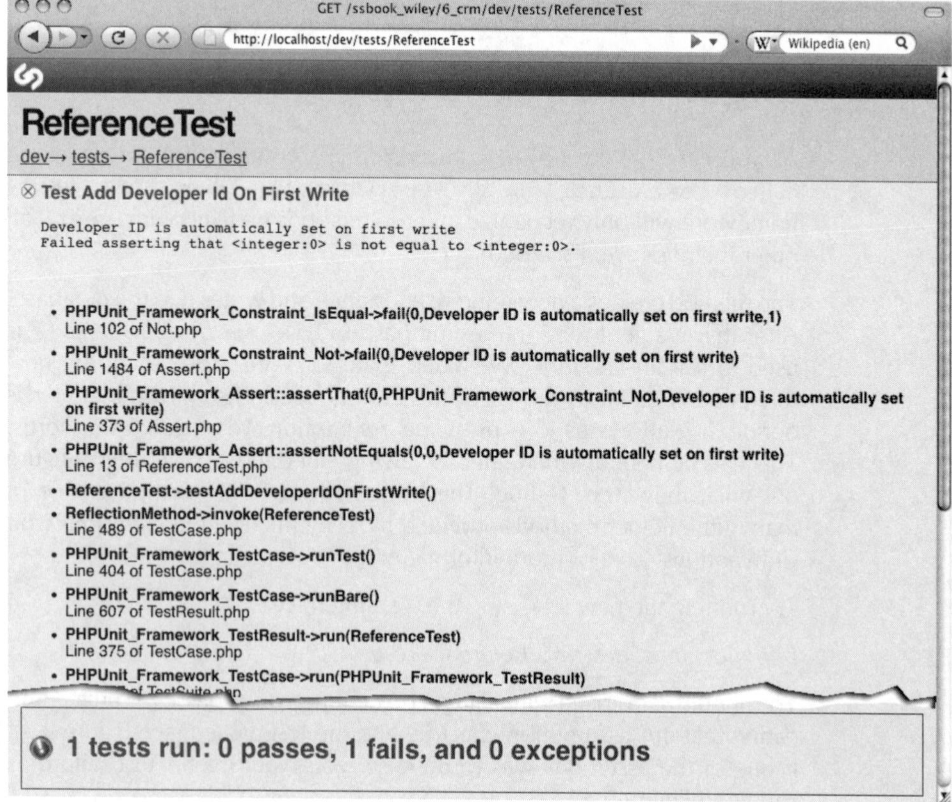

Figure 9.4 Test failure.

verbose in a normal programming context, there is method to this madness: We have named the method to describe the assumption we're testing as accurately as possible. This brings us closer to the code being a 'living specification'. Ideally, a new programmer only needs to read the name of the test method to immediately get an idea of what the tested class was meant to do.

Clever as you are, you're undoubtedly wondering about what will happen to the reference we just wrote to the database. Will it become visible as a real record on our website? Don't worry. SilverStripe uses a separate database for all its tests and this database is emptied as soon as a test run is complete. So there is no chance of tests causing any unintended side-effects on your precious production database.

PHPUnit conventions

Not all assumptions can be expressed as a comparison of two numbers. The PHPUnit framework therefore provides a number of different methods for a variety of different assertions. These methods have one thing in common: They all return either `true` or `false`, which makes them very easy to evaluate. Here are some examples:

```
assertEquals($val1, $val2, $msg)
assertTrue($condition, $msg)
assertFalse($condition, $msg)
assertContains($needle, $haystack, $msg)
assertNotContains($needle, $haystack, $msg)
assertType($expected, $actual, $msg)
assertSame($expected, $actual, $msg)
```

The complete documentation is available at the following URL: http://phpunit.de/manual/current/en/api.html#api.assert.

9.4.2 Fixtures: Sample Test Data

Our next test will be a bit more sophisticated, and check the access permissions on a reference. It should only be editable by a user with the permission code `EDIT_ALL_REFERENCES`. You might remember how we implemented this constraint in the `Reference->canEdit()` method in Chapter 6.

In order to write this test we need to add an additional method to the `ReferenceTest` class. Let's call it `testCanEdit()`. It will test the access permission for three different classes of users:

- `$randomUser`: A user with no access permissions
- `$refOwner`: The owner of the reference

- `$refEditor`: An administrator who has the permission code `EDIT_ALL_REFERENCES`

This poses a problem though: Because test runs work on a separate empty database, these users and their necessary group associations don't exist. It's fairly common for test runs to assume certain conditions based on an existing set of sample data. These testing records are known as *Fixtures*. SilverStripe tries to make things easy for us here: We don't need to create any records in PHP code, but can rather define our fixtures in a separate file. Fixtures can be loaded for a specific test suite by using the `$fixture_file` static variable. All objects created through this fixture are available in our tests by calling the `objFromFixture()` method.

We will explain exactly how all this works in a moment. First, take a look at the new code for `testCanEdit()`. Reopen the *mysite/tests/ReferenceTest.php* file and add the following code:

```
<?php
class ReferenceTest extends SapphireTest {
   static $fixture_file = 'mysite/tests/ReferenceTest.yml';
   // ...
   function testCanEdit() {
      $ref = $this->objFromFixture(
         'Reference',
         'reference1'
      );
      $randomUser = $this->objFromFixture(
         'Member',
         'random_user'
      );
      $refOwner = $this->objFromFixture(
         'Member',
         'reference_owner'
      );
      $refEditor = $this->objFromFixture(
         'Member',
         'reference_editor'
      );
      $this->assertTrue($ref->canEdit($refOwner));
      $this->assertTrue($ref->canEdit($refEditor));
      $this->assertFalse($ref->canEdit($randomUser));
   }
}
?>
```

Listing 9.3 *mysite/tests/ReferenceTest.php (excerpt)*

If you assume that the `objFromFixture()` method returns DataObject instances of the class specified by the first parameter, and ignore where these actually come from, the test should be fairly self-explanatory:

With `assertTrue()` and `assertFalse()` we verify that the correct permissions are set on a reference.

Fixtures are defined in YAML (http://yaml.org/) format, a standard for serializing data. YAML is easy to read and write with minimal overhead. In fact, we only need to use colons and indentation to define our test fixture data. This data can be defined on three separate levels: class, instance, and attribute. Each level is accessed by appropriately indenting the text. Indentation in YAML means that three 'space' characters don't work.

To create a sample reference fixture called 'reference1', the following code is sufficient:

```
Reference:
   reference1:
      Title: Reference 1
      Developer: =>Member.reference_owner
```

The first level symbolizes a class, in our case `Reference`. All following indented records will be of this type.

The second level creates and names the instance of the object: `reference1`. Names of instances work just like IDs of database records. However, they're much easier to use. All you need to do is write some instance names into the YAML file. Behind the scenes SilverStripe creates a database row with the actual data, and keeps track of the mapping between database IDs and fixture identifiers. Calling the following method retrieves the instance of the `Reference` class named `reference1` from the test database, ready for us to use in our test:

```
$this->objFromFixture('Reference', 'reference1');
```

The third level is used to create the `Title` and `Developer` attributes. `Title` is a simple text field. However, `Developer` is a has-one relation and therefore can't just be set to a string of text. Instead, we assign a pointer to a different fixture called `Member.reference_owner`, which translates into an instance of the `Member` object named `reference_owner`.

Let's complete our YAML fixture file. We need to create definitions for the three types of users and assign each of them to a specific security group. Each security group needs to have certain permission codes, represented as a relation to an instance of the `Permission` class. The finished *mysite/tests/ReferenceTest.yml* file look as follows:

```
Permission:
   reference_edit_permission:
      Code: EDIT_ALL_REFERENCES
Group:
   reference_editors:
      Title: Reference Editors
      Permissions: =>Permission.reference_edit_permission
Member:
   reference_editor:
      FirstName: Reference Editor
      Groups: =>Group.reference_editors
   reference_owner:
      FirstName: Reference Owner
   random_user:
      FirstName: Random User
Reference:
   reference1:
      Title: Reference 1
      Developer: =>Member.reference_owner
```


Listing 9.4 *mysite/tests/ReferenceTest.yml*

Run the test at *http://localhost/dev/tests/ReferenceTest/*. You should now see the message: '2 passes, 0 fails'. This tells you that both our previously defined tests, `testAuthorIdSetOnFirstWrite()` and `testCanEdit()`, were executed and passed. Great!

9.5 Functional Tests for the Controllers

Suppose that you've written a perfect unit-test for every method of every class in your web application. Can you now delight in the thought that your site will work perfectly? Unfortunately not. A system is usually more complex than the sum of its parts. Every class may work exactly as intended in isolation, but all of them taken together can still malfunction. We need a different kind of testing in order to prevent this kind of compound error. It is called *functional testing,* sometimes also known as *integration testing.*

Next on our list of things to test is the form for submitting new job postings on the job board. You might remember how signed-in users were allowed to create new job postings and then assign them to specific job categories.

9.5.1 Testing Template Output

Create a new subclass of `FunctionalTest` and call it `JobCategory-Test`. The `FunctionalTest` class provides us with methods that can be used to simulate an HTTP-client. With it we can request webpages from within our test, search these pages for certain HTML fragments, and extract and compare them with our expected results. So, we can, for example, check to see whether the job postings form is only accessible to registered users. Write the following code in a new *JobCategoryTest.php* file:

```
<?php
class JobCategoryTest extends FunctionalTest {
    static $fixture_file = 'mysite/tests/JobCategoryTest.yml';
    function setUp() {
        parent::setUp();
        $this->useDraftSite();
    }
}
?>
```

Listing 9.5 *mysite/tests/JobCategoryTest.php*

The above listing is the initial skeleton of our functional test. You will notice the `setup()` method. The testing framework automatically runs this method before starting the actual tests in order to set the stage for the upcoming evaluation. Conversely there is also the `tearDown()` method, which 'clears the stage' by removing anything that was created during the setup.

In our case, we call the `useDraftSite()` method in our setup. This is a neat little trick that removes the need to publish every page before evaluating it. Although not strictly necessary, it's useful because it helps speed up testing by skipping an unnecessary step.

The fixture file is quite short. We only need to create a single test user and a page of the `JobCategory` page type. We make the page accessible via the *developer-test-url* URL. All these objects are, once again, created in a separate database. No one outside of the testing framework will ever see them.

Create the *JobCategoryTest.yml* file and insert the following code:

```
JobCategory:
    developers_category:
        Title: Developers Category
        URLSegment: developers-test-url
Member:
    testmember:
        FirstName: Test Member
```

Listing 9.6 *mysite/tests/JobCategoryTest.yml*

Now the fun part: the actual test code in form of the `testAddJobFormVisibility()` method. In this method we request the page created in the fixture file by calling `$this->get('developers-test-url')`. We do so twice: once as an anonymous user, without a valid login and once logged in as the Test Member. Please extend your *JobCategory-Test.php* file as follows:

```
<?php
class JobCategoryTest extends FunctionalTest {
   function testAddJobFormVisibility() {
      $testMember = $this->objFromFixture(
         'Member',
         'testmember'
      );
      $response = $this->get('developers-test-url');
      $this->assertNotContains(
         '<form id="Form_Form"',
         $response->getBody(),
         'Form doesnt show without valid login'
      );
      $this->session()->inst_set(
         'loggedInAs',
         $testMember->ID
      );
      $response = $this->get('developers-test-url');
      $this->assertContains(
         '<form id="Form_Form"',
         $response->getBody(),
         'Form show for logged in members'
      );
   }
}
?>
```

Listing 9.7 *mysite/tests/JobCategoryTest.php (excerpt)*

`$this->get()` returns an `HTTPResponse` object. Calling `$response->getBody()` extracts the contents of the response, i.e., it gives us the body of the HTML page. Next we call `assetContains()`, which tests if the string passed as the first parameter is contained in the object passed as the second parameter. In our case, we check to see if a form tag is present in the returned HTML-code.

Try running the test using the web-interface. Load the following URL:

http://localhost/dev/tests/JobCategoryTest/

9.5.2 Submitting a Test Form

Okay, we're now sure that the correct user is seeing the right kind of form. However, we don't yet know whether the form actually works. Once again, SilverStripe can help us. We can use the testing framework to send test form submissions and check the results. Let's do just that by creating a new test method called `testSubmitJob()`. Re-open the *JobCategoryTest.php* file and add the following code:

```
<?php
class JobCategoryTest extends FunctionalTest {
   // ...
   function testSubmitJob() {
      // ...
      $jobData = array(
         'Title' => 'Test Title',
         'Description' => 'Test Description',
      );
      $this->submitForm('Form_Form', null, $jobData);
      $response = $this->get('developers-test-url');
      $this->assertPartialMatchBySelector(
         'li.job h3 a',
         'Test Title',
         'Submitted job title displays in overview'
      );
   }
}
?>
```

Listing 9.8 *mysite/tests/JobCategoryTest.php (excerpt)*

The `FunctionalTest` class remembers the last page requested (the JobCategory page with the form that we created in the *JobCategoryTest.yml* fixture). The form on this page can be identified by the HTML-fragment `<form id="Form_Form">`. This means we can use the same ID find and submit the form. The call to `$this->submitForm('Form_Form', null, $jobData)` does just that (the unused second parameter is for choosing the correct submit button when a form has multiple submit buttons). It sends the `$jobData` test array to the server using the same submission mechanism that an actual user would use. If everything is working correctly the result should be that a new record is created in the test database.

So, now we should check whether the new record is actually there. First, we reload the page by calling `$this->get('developers-test-url')` again. Then we search for the data we just submitted. We don't want to search the entire page, because the string 'Test Title' might appear elsewhere and confuse our test; nor do we want to search only a specific block or tag, because a slight modification to the template could break our test.

So, we use the `$this->assertPartialMatchBySelector()` method to search only the text with the appropriate CSS styling. We know that the job posting will be a linked title in a list, and so we can use the `assertPartialMatchBySelector()` method to search all occurrences of text with the `li.job h3` a style for the 'Test Title' string. If the string is found, the test passes.

9.6 Conclusion

In this chapter we created some *Unit Tests* and *Functional Tests* for the code from earlier chapters. Of course, we managed to cover only a small part of the code with our tests. You'll certainly be able to come up with countless other areas that would benefit from automated testing.

You can see how even a relatively small amount of test code can lead to great benefits, such as improving security, verifying functionality, and ensuring that existing functionality doesn't break in the future. Instead of having to re-test manually a code-base that has potentially grown over several years and developers, automated testing gives you simple means to save time and money in the long run.

We encourage you to give up the old stereotype of what testing is. It shouldn't be a tedious activity that you'd rather avoid. Instead, try and see it as the first step in any development activity. Test-driven development makes finding bugs easier (even in an automated fashion) and helps structure your code nicely. It should therefore become a central part of your day-to-day code-writing workflow.

10

Localization

The topic of *localization* describes the adaption of computer systems to the language and regional differences of its users. You might also know this process as *internationalization* or *globalization* (see box 'L10n, i18n, and g11n'). For a content management system, this primarily concerns everything that's presented to users in an application- or website context. English-speaking users should see labels, dates, and content in the format and language they expect; Japanese visitors, for example, have completely different language, character sets and formatting conventions.

Technically speaking, localization can be applied to database content, templates, PHP code, and even JavaScript. We explain in this chapter how SilverStripe can support you in adapting your website to different cultures and languages.

L10n, i18n, and g11n

As we all know, programmers tend to be pragmatic people – they hate repetition and redundancy. They can also be quite lazy writers. This leads to some curious constructs of abbreviations, which count the removed letters in a word: Localization becomes *l10n*, internationalization becomes *i18n*, and globalization is shortened to *g11n*.

In terminology, i18n means that a computer system is prepared to process and display content in different languages and cultures. SilverStripe as an *internationalized* system provides its developers with easy means for *localizing* a product.

Caution: Localization support in SilverStripe is fairly young; currently there is no out-of-the-box support for localizing dates or currencies in the database, or when processed through a form. Thanks to the encapsulation of these features into classes, this problem can be resolved by subclassing and custom implementations in the meantime.

10.1 Character Sets and Unicode

Before we start with the practical examples, we need to address some basics to help you navigate the deep and sometimes stormy waters of localizing anything stored in bits and bytes.

SilverStripe stores and processes all characters in a specific *character set* called *Unicode* or *UTF-8*. This is the baseline for easy out-of-the-box support for non-western languages. But what are character sets, and why do you need to choose one?

10.1.1 The Legacy: ASCII and ISO 8859

ASCII was the first standardized character set widely used in computers. Given its history of being used by mostly western scientists eager to preserve their scarce computer resources, it was limited to 7 bits of storage per character, and hence allowed only 128 different characters. These mapped a part of western alphabets, plus a couple of symbols and specific control characters. Anything written in nonwestern alphabets was pretty much out of luck, and had to fall back to its own implementations.

To counteract this, the *International Organization for Standardization* (ISO) has released 15 different character sets under the group name *ISO 8859*. This specification reserves 8 bits of storage for each character, which results in 256 addressable characters. Not all that much, when considering everything from Roman, Arabic, Cyrillic, and other languages. To solve this dilemma, different variations of ISO 8859 exist. *ISO 8859-1* contains characters for western Europe and all characters required for English, *ISO 8859-7* is dedicated to Greek, *ISO 8859-11* for Thai, and so forth.

The first 128 characters of the ISO 8859 standard are identical with their ASCII equivalents, to preserve backwards compatibility. The crux with these overlapping variations is that there's no real way to determine which variation is used by looking at a sequence of bytes. This has led to a lot of headaches for anybody dealing with more than one character set, and increases the complexity of any software dealing with it.

10.1.2 Unicode: A Unified Standard

A newer standard called *Unicode* tries to remedy the ambiguities and restrictions of ISO 8859 and assign a unique identifier to every character used in written languages around the world. Unicode is a widely accepted standard which is supported by most modern operating systems and other software. The Unicode character set can be represented in encodings, the most commonly used one being called *UTF-8*. This encoding can use more than one byte to store a single character, hence having a lot larger range of supported characters – over 100,000 individual items have been identified by this standard (`www.unicode.org/versions/Unicode5.1.0/`).

Particularly in the web context, the *World Wide Web Consortium* (W3C) recommends Unicode for all web content (`www.w3.org/International/tutorials/tutorial-char-enc/`), and can be displayed correctly by all modern web browsers. To let a browser or other HTTP client know that your content is encoded with UTF-8, the HTTP standard provides an attribute called *Content-Type*. This can be either sent directly with the *HTTP response header* or stored inside your document through a `<meta>` tag:

```
<meta http-equiv="Content-type" content="text/html; charset=utf-8" />
```

SilverStripe uses UTF-8 throughout the whole content process, and automatically delivers and denotes the correct encoding to browsers, and so usually you don't have to worry about setting these properties manually. It is automatically inserted through the `$MetaTags` template placeholder in your main *Page.ss* template. If you need to change your encoding, either overload the `MetaTags()` method on your custom page type or consider using the `ContentNegotiator` class (see box 'Content-Type with the ContentNegotiator Class').

In XHTML documents, a third place to denote your character encoding is the `<xml>` tag on top of your document:

```
<?xml version="1.0" encoding="UTF-8"?>
```

UTF-8 content is stored differently from ISO 8859 or ASCII, and would necessitate conversions when mixing encodings. To avoid this step, we need to ensure to consistently use UTF-8 wherever content is stored.

This includes templates, PHP, and JavaScript files, as well as database content. You should be able to set the default encoding in your IDE or text editor. Be careful with any data you import into the database: by default no encoding conversion is applied to database dumps in SQL format or CSV files.

Content-Type with the ContentNegotiator Class

The ContentNegotiator can be used to alter all content served through the SilverStripe templating system. The main use case is automatic conversion between the different markup conventions for HTML and XHTML. Through a set of text replacements, it allows you to convert self-closing tags, as well as automatically insert the correct *DOCTYPE* definition. By default, your template is delivered as-is, but this class can be a handy utility to ensure all markup is complying to some basic rules for the standard you intend to follow.

Apart from different HTML standards, the ContentNegotiator is set to deliver UTF-8 content, and alter the HTTP response. If you use this class, ensure that you switch your content type as well in *mysite/_config.php* with the following directive:

```
ContentNegotiator::set_encoding("iso-8859-1");
```

10.1.3 HTML Character Escapes

If you have ever looked through HTML source code, you might have noticed that some content seems a bit 'garbled' with ampersands and hash characters. This is an alternative way to encode special characters within XML or HTML in decimal or hexadecimal notation. This is partially a work-around to display characters that have a special meaning within HTML and XML, such as the angle brackets '<' and '>'. Decimal notation is expressed with the character sequence &#DD, where DD can be a variable length number referencing this character in the Unicode character set. Hexadecimal notation works similarly with the format &xHH, with HH being a variable length of hexadecimal digits.

For some selected characters, a simpler notation can be used: An opening angular bracket '<' can also be written as <, the equivalent closing bracket '>' is represented by >.

This is relevant here, because the *TinyMCE* rich text editor in SilverStripe is used for the main page content, and encodes some characters in this notation before storing them in the database. You can find a complete reference of replaced characters in *TinyMCE* at http://wiki.moxiecode.com/index.php/TinyMCE:Configuration/entities.

10.2 Translating Templates and Code

There are two ways to store natural language content within SilverStripe: In the database or in text files on your file system. We'll come to database content in a second; first, let's have a look at what's required to make templates, PHP code, and even JavaScript files translatable within the SilverStripe framework.

In previous examples we have often 'hardcoded' content that is shown to the website user, e.g., the label of a form field in your controller, or previous/next labels for paging a long list of elements in your template. You might want to present your content in different languages, depending on the preference of your visitors.

We need to give the framework a starting point to handle these strings dynamically. To achieve this, we write these strings as a parameter to a global function called `_t()`. This enables us to exchange the string by finding another representation for it in the so called *language tables*. In general, the `i18n` class takes care of code- or template-based translations.

10.2.1 Configuration

Translation capabilities are automatically enabled in SilverStripe, and are set to English language in the region of North America by default. This is captured by a so called *locale*, in this case *en_US*. See box 'Languages, Locales, and Cultures' for information about locale values. You can set a different global default by adding the following setting to your *mysite/_config.php*:

```
i18n::set_locale('de_DE');
```

This would set your locale to `de_DE`, which represents German language in the region of Germany.

Languages, Locales, and Countries

Languages in computer systems are identified by standardized short forms: English can be expressed as `en`, German is marked as `de`. This code is often used to identify a geographic region. But there's more to specific visitors than their language code: For example, German is not only spoken in Germany, but also in Austria and other countries, each with different writing rules and dialect. Due to this, a so called *locale* is used to more accurately represent this combination of language and region: *German-Austria* is marked as de_AT, *German-Germany* as de_DE.

But the differences don't stop with language: Regions have certain standards for writing currencies or formatting their dates, and a myriad of other subtle differences in treating written information. Most of this can be captured by the locale setting.

For more information on available locales and details on their usage, the W3C has compiled an overview at http://www.w3.org/International/articles/language-tags/. A selection of common locale values is preset in the Sapphire framework: have a look at sapphire/core/i18n.php.

10.2.2 The _t() Function

Let's assume you want to output a simple sentence through your PHP code. Without localization, this output could be performed through a simple echo statement:

```
echo "Hello World";
```

In order to let the framework know that this string can be represented in different languages, a specialized global method can be used to pass the string to the echo statement:

```
echo _t("MyNamespace.GREETING","Hello World");
```

Without any further modifications, this code will perform exactly the same as our example without localization support: It outputs 'Hello World'. But there's one important difference: We have assigned a unique identifier to our string: MyNamespace.GREETING. This identifier forms the basis to store the text in different languages table entries based on the current locale. We explain language tables in detail in Section 10.2.6 ('Language Tables with i18nTextCollector'). Let's have a look at the _t() call first:

```
function _t($identifier, $text, $priority, $context]) {...}
```

Identifier

The first parameter is a unique identifier to mark the localizable content. It consists of a *namespace* as well as an *entity name*, separated by a dot.

The namespace should usually hold the class name in which the `_t()` call is contained. If using `_t()` in a template, the namespace should be set to the template name. Namespaces allow us to identify the language table for a specific entry, and they avoid ambiguous information and overlapping entity names in different use cases.

The second part of the identifier is the entity name, which is written in capitals only. It should be unique within this namespace for a specific string. Although you're free to choose an arbitrary string, it's a good idea to choose a descriptive entity name, e.g. `MyNamespace.GREETING`.

Text

The second parameter is the actual text in the default locale set via `i18n::set_default_locale()`. If no translation can be found in the requested locale, this text is used as a fallback output. This text is also used to create the language tables, which is practical if you don't need to place the text in two different locations yourself. We explain this in further detail when introducing the `i18nTextCollector` class. The text parameter is optional: If you want to reuse a string that was previously defined, you can call it without writing the default text a second time, e.g., `_t('MyNamespace.GREETING')`.

Priority

The priority is an optional parameter to indicate a priority to translators. Its value can be `PR_LOW`, `PR_MEDIUM` or `PR_HIGH`.

Context

A context is again optional, but very helpful as a small message to translators wondering what to make of the text they are about to translate. Any translation will most likely happen out of its original context, which means a lot of knowledge is lost that would be crucial for a correct translation. As an example, the string 'Search' might be a verb or a noun, used as a button label or as a page headline. A couple of words of context can help to clarify this:

```
_t('Form.SEARCH', 'Search', PR_MEDIUM, 'Button label');
```

10.2.3 Translation in PHP Code

As `_t()` is a global function, it is available in all PHP code you will write within SilverStripe.

Dynamic string replacements with `sprintf()`

In some cases, not all parts of a translatable string are known at the time it is written. Perhaps you want to dynamically insert a page title that is determined while running your code? You could glue together these untranslated and translated strings, but only while making assumptions about sentence ordering in a particular language. In English, a sentence might read 'Restored<page-title>', while in German the words are the other way around: '<page-title>wiederhergestellt'.

One solution to this ordering problem is to use placeholders within the translated string, and resolve them when running the code later on. PHP provides a built-in method to perform this replacement: `sprintf()`. Say you want to insert the variable `$title` in a translated string:

```
sprintf(_t('CMSMain.RESTORED', "Restored '%s'"),$title);
```

A placeholder is written as `%s`, and returned unresolved from the `_t()` call as the first parameter to `sprintf()`. All following parameters to this function are treated as placeholder replacements, in our case `$title`.

10.2.4 Translation in Templates

The usage of `_t()` in templates is very similar, you just have to wrap it in angular brackets like any other SilverStripe template placeholder:

```
<a href="http://silverstripe.com">
   <% _t('MyTemplate.VISIT','Visit silverstripe.com') %>
</a>
```

The namespace for your identifier should point to the name of the template, without its directory path or file extension.

10.2.5 Translation in JavaScript

SilverStripe has a simple library to support translations in JavaScript, which follow the same conventions you already know from its PHP equivalent. First of all, you need to include the necessary library through the Requirements class. This line is most commonly placed in your `Page_Controller->init()` method in *mysite/code/Page.php*:

```
Requirements::javascript(SAPPHIRE_DIR . "/javascript/i18n.js");
```

Each language has its own language table in a separate file, stored in the *javascript/lang/* folder within each module. For example, all JavaScript translations related to the CMS interface are stored in *cms/javascript/lang/*. To save bandwidth, only two tables are actually loaded by the browser: The current locale, and the default locale as a fallback. The `Requirements` class has a special method to determine these includes: Just point it to a directory instead of a file, and the class will figure out the includes.

```
Requirements::add_i18n_javascript('<my-module>/javascript/lang');
```

After these libraries are available, you can start using a new method called `ss.i18n._t()`. As an example, to output a localized alert notification in your visitor's browser, simply identify the string rather than writing it directly:

```
alert(ss.i18n._t('MyModule.GREETING', 'Hello World'));
```

Please note that the JavaScript implementation of the `_t()` method doesn't automatically populate any language tables, you have to take care of this yourself. You can use the `ss.i18n.addDictionary()` command for this in your language tables:

```
ss.i18n.addDictionary('en_US', {
   'MyModule.GREETING': 'Hello World'
});
```

Listing 10.1 *mysite/javascript/lang/en_US.js*

A German translation with the locale `de_DE` would be placed in a new *de_DE.js* file, with a similar notation:

```
ss.i18n.addDictionary('de_DE', {
   'MyModule.GREETING': 'Hallo Welt'
});
```

Listing 10.2 *mysite/javascript/lang/de_DE.js*

The current locale for a visitor is determined by the generated `<meta>` tags within the template. This means that it should equal the locale that was set in PHP through `i18n::set_locale()`. If the Translatable extension for showing database content in different languages is used, the locale will be based on the current page language instead.

10.2.6 Language Tables with i18nTextCollector

Now that you know how to make your module or website i18n capable, it's time to show you how to add the translations themselves. So far we've only added a default text through the `_t()` method but haven't specified any language tables to look up its translation.

SilverStripe stores translations for PHP and templates in one file per locale within each module, in the special subfolder *lang/*. For example, all German translations for the CMS module are stored in *cms/lang/de_DE.php*. If you open this file, you see that all translations are contained in a PHP array. To start a translation into a new language, simply provide the master language `en_US` to a translator, who can then create a new PHP file matching his or her locale. This works the same way for any modules you create yourself, of course.

But how do the strings get into the master language table in the first place? So far, we've written them into the `_t()` calls scattered throughout our application logic. SilverStripe uses a PHP class called `i18nTextCollector` to make this process easier for you: It parses all PHP and template files within SilverStripe's module directories, populates the master language tables, and writes them to their respective module paths. To run this script, please execute the following URL as an administrator:

http://localhost/dev/tasks/i18nTextCollector

This process will require a lot of resources, we recommend at least 128MB of PHP memory and 90 seconds of script execution time. Once the script has completed, the *en_US.php* files in their respective module folders should be either updated or created. Try it for yourself by placing a `_t()` call in your *mysite/* or *themes/* folder, for example in the *Page.ss* template.

SilverStripe Translation Server

If you're interested in translating SilverStripe and its modules, SilverStripe provides a web-based translation interface as an alternative to editing PHP files. After a free registration, you can collaborate with translators around the world, and translate as little or as much as you like directly in your browser. Translations can be downloaded as PHP files in real time, and periodically find their way into a new module or SilverStripe release.

The SilverStripe Translation Server also allows you to upload the master language table of your own open source module extending SilverStripe. As a module developer with localization in mind, you can use the provided infrastructure to get existing translators onto your project.

The Translation Server is online at `http://translate.silverstripe.com/`.

10.3 Translatable: Translating Database Content

After equipping our templates with i18n capabilities, it's about time to tackle multilingual page content as well. SilverStripe supports this by the built-in `Translatable` class. It's a subclass of `DataObjectDecorator`, which we'll introduce in a bit more in depth in Section 12.2.2, 'Decorator Pattern'. For now, all we need to know is that Translatable can be applied to all `DataObject` subclasses, and so consequently to all instances of `Page`. To be clear, we just handle translation of database content – all multilingual content in code or templates is handled by the `i18n` class.

The class will also distinguish between different publication stages of a page between languages, as well as keep their version tracking separate.

10.3.1 Configuration

By default, the Translatable extension is not applied to any classes, mainly for performance considerations. To activate it for all pages handled by the CMS, enable it in your *mysite/_config.php*. It is important to reference the parent class `SiteTree` rather than `Page` itself.

```
Object::add_extension('SiteTree','Translatable');
```

By default, SilverStripe is configured to assume website content in *US English* through its *default locale* setting. As SilverStripe keeps track of this locale value for each record in the database, it is important to choose it before creating any translations in the CMS. If your default locale differs, e.g., when creating a website primarily in Japanese, please tell SilverStripe in your *mysite/_config.php*:

```
Translatable::set_default_locale('ja_JP');
```

We described the concept of locales in 10.2.1, 'Configuration' in the context of our `i18n` class for translating code and templates. The same locale values are also valid for `Translatable::set_default_locale()`: For the Japanese language in Japan, this would be `'ja_JP'`.

After these two settings, please refresh your database schema through *http://localhost/dev/build.*

Caution: If you have a website with existing translations, which was created with a version of SilverStripe prior to 2.3.2 (May 2009), you'll need to migrate your database schema before using the CMS. See `http://doc.silverstripe.com/doku.php?id=multilingua-lcontent` for details on running this migration script.

If you want to limit the available languages, for example to Japanese and German, please use the following code:

```
Translatable::set_allowed_locales(array('de_DE','ja_JP'));
```

10.3.2 Creating a Translation

After the basics are in place, please have a look at what changed in the CMS: First of all, there's a new tab on the main form called TRANSLATIONS. A dropdown allows you to choose a new language and start a new translation of the page content. There's no need to define which languages are available for display because SilverStripe shows common languages by default. Beneath this dropdown, existing translations for this page will be listed (see Figure 10.1).

Figure 10.1 Creating a new translation within a page.

Alternatively, you can start a new language from scratch by using a similar dropdown above the left-hand page tree. You can also use this dropdown to switch the page tree to a different existing language, as shown in Figure 10.2.

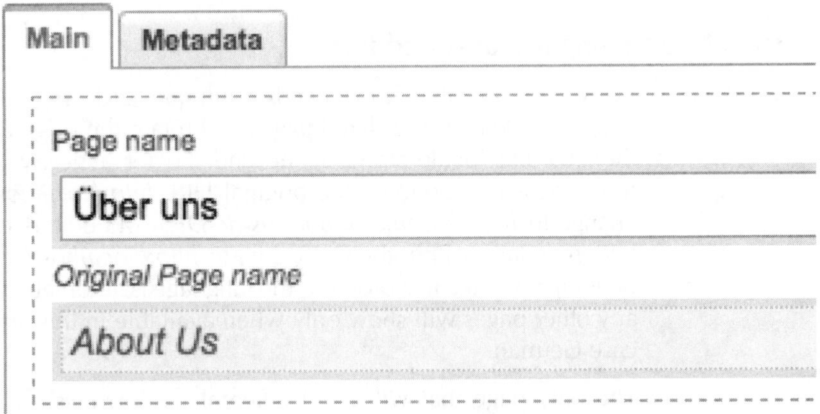

Figure 10.2 Switching languages in the CMS.

If a page is opened in a language that's not the system default, its form fields will appear differently: Each editable field such as TITLE or CONTENT is paired with a read only display of its value in the original language, as illustrated in Figure 10.3. This makes it easy for translators to adapt content without switching between pages in different languages.

Figure 10.3 A page in translation mode.

When creating a translation for an existing page, all properties of this page will be copied over to the new translation. This means that not only natural language attributes such as CONTENT or TITLE are translated, but also configuration settings such as SHOW IN MENUS or any permission settings in the ACCESS tab. Currently, there's no way to exclude certain database columns from being translated.

10.3.3 Showing a Translated Page

Every page in SilverStripe needs a unique URL, regardless of its language. By default, translated pages will retain the original URL, but add their current locale string at the end. So for a newly translated page from English to German, the original URL *http://localhost/about-us* will change to *http://localhost/about-us-de-DE*. CMS editors can change this URL manually within the CMS, e.g., to *http://localhost/ueber-uns*. When opening this page in a browser, the language is automatically determined; any other pages will show only when available in this language – in our case German.

The only page that will need different treatment is the homepage. As it doesn't have a specific URL when called through *http://localhost/*, you will need to attach *?locale=<my-locale>* to the URL to show a homepage in a non-default language. If you create a new language in the CMS, please ensure that you translate at least the homepage from your default language into the new language. So accessing the German homepage would be possible through *http://localhost/?locale=de_DE*.

We explain how to provide links to different languages in your website template in Section 10.4, 'Language Selection'.

10.3.4 Coding with Translatable

Translatable will create a new database column on all SiteTree-related base tables, called `Locale`. Different languages of a specific row are stored alongside each other in the original table, with a different value for their `Locale` column. Each SQL query triggered by SilverStripe will now automatically use this column as a filtering criteria. This filter either uses the current locale in `Translatable::current_locale()`, if set through `Translatable::set_current_locale('<locale>')`, or falls back to `Translatable::get_default_locale()`.

This means that a normal call to `DataObject::get()` will only return records in the current language. If you want to manually query for a specific language, Translatable has a couple of helper methods that work similarly to their counterparts on `DataObject`, but accept a specific locale (see Table 10.1).

Table 10.1 Static translatable helpers.

Method	Description
Translatable::get one by locale ('<class>', '<locale>', '<filter>')	Gets a single record in a specific locale.
Translatable::get by locale ('<class>', '<locale>', '<filter>')	Gets all records matching this locale.

For any given record that has the Translatable extension, you can call instance-specific methods revealing further language-specific information (see Table 10.2).

Table 10.2 Instance-specific translatable helpers.

Method	Description
getTranslations()	Gets a single record in a specific locale.
getTranslation('<locale>')	Gets all records matching this locale.
createTranslation('<locale>')	Creates a new translation based on the current record.
hasTranslation('<locale>')	Checks whether the current record has a translation in this locale.

Sometimes you want to use a method to retrieve a record that doesn't allow you to specify the locale. SilverStripe automatically adds a condition to search in the current locale only, but what to do when you want to search in another locale? Examples of this might be specialized methods for the Versioned extension, used to retrieve certain older versions of a record. Not all functionality has to be written specifically with translation-compatibility in mind. In this case, you can temporarily switch the reading language for a specific call:

```
$origLocale = Translatable::get_current_locale();
Translatable::set_current_locale('de_DE');
$version = Versioned::get_by_stage('SiteTree', 'Live');
Translatable::set_current_locale($origLocale);
```

Listing 10.3 *Using Translatable with different locales in built-in methods*

10.3.5 Translation Groups

Each translation can have one or more related pages in other languages. This relation is optional, meaning that you can create translations which have no representation in the 'default language'. Therefore you can have a French translation with a German original, without either of them having a representation in the default language tree which happens to be in English. Caution: There is no versioning for translation groups, and so associating an object with a group will affect both stage and live records.

Translation groups are automatically managed for your if you use `createTranslation()` on an existing record. When starting a new record from scratch in a specific language, it will start its own translation group.

These group relationships are managed in a separate table with the suffix `_translationgroups`. For pages in the CMS, this is `SiteTree_translationgroups`. The `getTranslation()` method uses translation groups to find related languages.

10.3.6 Language Selection

As every page has its own unique URL, language selection mostly happens explicitly: A user requests a page, which always has only one language. But how does a user coming to your English default language know that there's a Japanese version of this page?

By default, SilverStripe core doesn't provide any switching of languages through sessions or browser cookies. As a SEO-friendly CMS, it contains all this information in the URL. Each page in SilverStripe is aware of its translations through the `getTranslations()` method. We can use this method in our template to build a simple language switcher. It shows all available translations in an unordered list with links to the same page in a different language. The example below can be inserted in any of your templates, for example *themes/blackcandy/templates/Layout/Page.ss*:

```
<% if Translations %>
<ul class="translations">
<% control Translations %>
  <li class="$Locale.RFC1766">
    <a href="$Link" hreflang="$Locale.RFC1766"
title="$Title">
    <% sprintf(_t('SHOWINPAGE','Show page in %s'),$Locale.Nice)%>
   </a>
  </li>
<% end_control %>
</ul>
<% end_if %>
```

Listing 10.4 *A simple language switcher for Page.ss*

The template snippet loops over all translated pages for the currently viewed one (if any are available), and creates a link for them. One specialty is the `hreflang` attribute, which is used as additional metadata to signify the language to the browser. The locale is converted into a different format for this purpose: RFC1766. For the link text, we use a `_t()` call that was already introduced in Section 10.2.2, 'The `_t()` function'. This way, we can show the instructions in different languages, based on what the template is currently rendered in. For example, a Japanese translation would show up as 'Show this page in Japanese'.

If you want to add flags to the list items, or replace their text completely, you can use the locale-classes on the surrounding `<li>` element. Staying with the Japanese example, here's a stylesheet rule that will show a Japanese flag in front of the title.

```
.translations li {padding-left: 20px;}
.translations li.ja-JP {background:
url('../images/famfamfam_flag_icons/png/jp.png' no-repeat);}
```

Listing 10.5 *Example stylesheet rule for adding flags*

This assumes you have flag images stored in your theme, of course. Flag icons with an open source usage license are available on `http://www.famfamfam.com/lab/icons/flags/`.

Alternatively, you can format the template as a dropdown-element; add some JavaScript to automatically switch on selection – although SilverStripe needs a little bit of manual work to get language switching going, the possibilities for using it are wide open.

There's one exception to the rule that URLs are unique for each language: your homepage. If a visitor accesses your website just through the domain, the system will choose the default locale you have specified in `Translatable::set_default_locale()`. Technically, each homepage in each language has a unique URL though, so from this point onwards you can use the language switcher to prompt users for their language. Depending on your setup, it might be a bit easier to link to the domain with a locale parameter, which will show you the appropriate homepage: *http://localhost/?locale=ja_JP* will show you the homepage in Japanese.

10.4 Conclusion

In this chapter we showed your website the path to an international audience. Translations of both templates and code are possible with the `_t()` method, even JavaScript can be made language-aware with

SilverStripe. Thanks to the versatile concept of decorators, translating any property on a `DataObject`, including your page content, is no problem. Although SilverStripe still lacks full localization capabilities in terms of formatting dates, currencies, and other values, the most important requirements are in place. Classes lacking localization support can usually be subclassed easily to enable a more fine-grained control and new features such as localized form fields.

11

Recipes

If you've made it this far into the book, you're probably hungry for solutions to the multitude of different problems and challenges you might face in day-to-day programming. Maybe you already have a cool new project in mind where SilverStripe would come in handy? Maybe you saw some stunning feature on a website at the SilverStripe showcase (http://silverstripe.org/showcase/) and want to know how it's done? This chapter tries to help. Based on our experience with real-world projects and common questions from the user community, we've compiled some sample solution recipes. Bon Appétit!

11.1 Prerequisites

All the recipes in this chapter assume that you're working with a clean SilverStripe installation. If you want to integrate any of the recipes into an existing project, please be aware that file-paths and URLs may be different for your project. We assume that your project folder is called *mysite/* and your theme folder is called *themes/mysite/*. You should copy the 'BlackCandy' theme from *themes/blackcandy/* to *themes/mysite/* so that you can work on the theme without disrupting the original files. Enable it as usual through `SSViewer::set_theme()`:

```
<?php
// ...
SSViewer::set_theme('mysite');
?>
```

Listing 11.1 *mysite/_config.php (excerpt)*

Alternatively, you can find code examples for the recipes on the website companion download in the *11_recipes/* folder. This also contains a sample database called *database.sql*, which you can use as a starting point.

11.2 Customizable Page Banner

Creating templates, including typography and layout of the different website elements, is usually the job of a designer. Is there any room in SilverStripe for an editor to flex his or her creative muscles? Sure there is! We're not talking about using every color in the rainbow for the newest blog article, or changing the company's contact details to a *Comic Sans* font. By default, the editor capabilities in SilverStripe are restricted to a small set of sensible defaults. This is because content authors can undermine good graphic design if given too much power. But that doesn't mean that they shouldn't be able to set small graphical accents on certain pages.

In this section we show you how to add a little flair to your pages by adding page-specific banner images. The images will be configurable using the backend, as shown in Figure 11.1. The editor should be able to upload an image and have it appear on the website, automatically scaled to the correct size (see Figure 11.2; Example image licensed under Creative Commons Attribution 2.0 Generic, http://www.flickr.com/photos/cijmyjune/215195398/). If no banner image is defined for a given page, it should automatically fall back to the banner of the parent page.

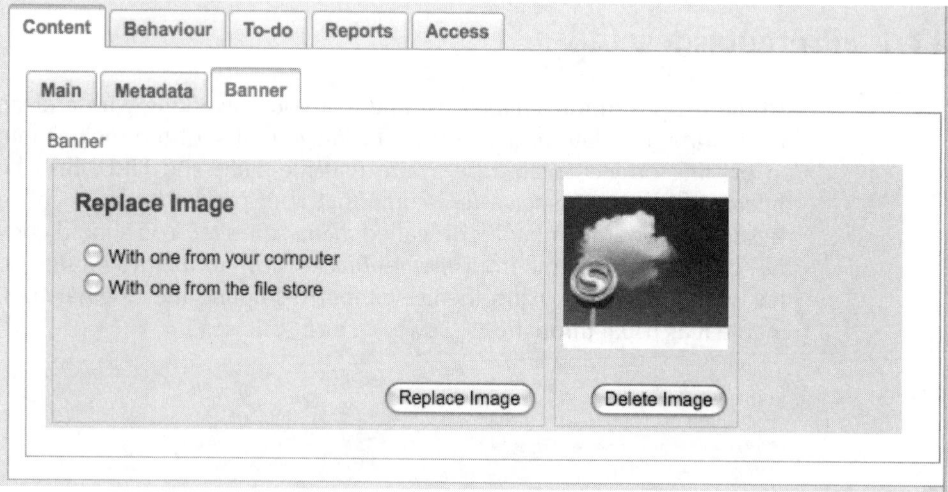

Figure 11.1 Banner image in the backend.

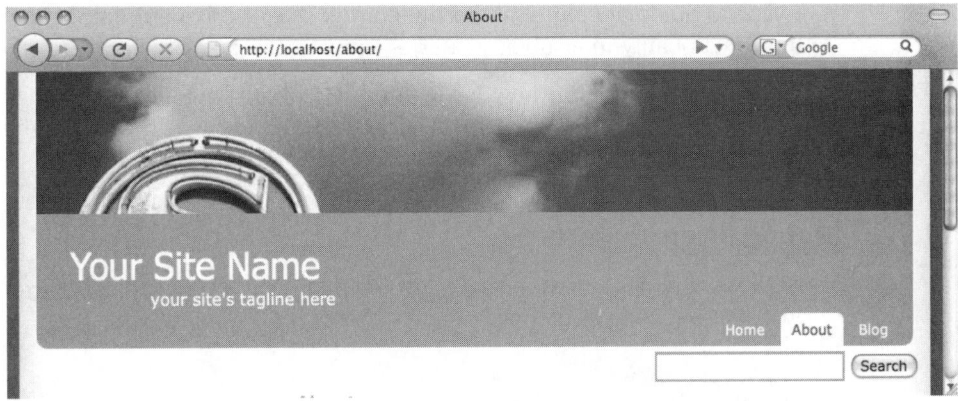

Figure 11.2 BannerImage on the website.

The complete recipe is available on the companion website download in the *11_recipes/* folder.

11.2.1 A New Relation for BannerImage

Since we want to make the banner image available on every page type, we will edit the top-level class that all other pages inherit from: *mysite/code/Page.php*. Please open this file and add the following code:

```
<?php
class Page extends SiteTree {
   // ...
   static $has_one = array(
      'BannerImage' => 'Page_BannerImage',
   );
   function getCMSFields() {
      $fields = parent::getCMSFields();
      $fields->addFieldsToTab(
         'Root.Content.Banner',
         new ImageField('BannerImage', 'Banner')
      );
      return $fields;
   }
}
?>
```

Listing 11.2 *mysite/code/Page.php (excerpt)*

By using the `Image` class, SilverStripe can relate images in the database in much the same way that it relates pages. We have named our has-one relation `BannerImage`. This allows access to the relation in the template using the `$BannerImage` placeholder. Since we want the image to automatically scale to the correct size, we have to implement this functionality in a subclass: `Page_BannerImage`.

We have also added a new tab named BANNER in the backend through `getCMSFields()`. It contains a `ImageField` form field that can be used to uploads images.

11.2.2 Scaling Image Objects

Now we will implement rescaling of the image on a subclass of `Image`. Add the following code to the `Page` class:

```
<?php
// ...
class Page_BannerImage extends Image {
   function generateFullWidth($gd) {
      return $gd->croppedResize(768,120);
   }
}
?>
```

Listing 11.3 *mysite/code/Page.php (excerpt)*

The class `Page_BannerImage` has a single method named `generate-FullWidth()`. The method scales every uploaded image to a width of 768 pixels and height of 120 pixels. The `$gd->croppedResize()` method crops the uploaded image if it doesn't fit into the above constraints. The specific dimensions are optimized for the standard Black-Candy theme. Naturally, if you create your own theme you will have to adjust the dimensions.

This `generateFullWidth()` method is a 'magic' getter of the `Image` object, and will be accessible in our template by calling `$BannerImage.FullWidth`. By default, this template placeholder would produce an `<img>` tag referencing a dynamically generated representation of the original upload.

For more information on creating and processing image objects, see Section 6.6, 'File uploads for references'.

11.2.3 Inheriting Banners in the Page Tree

We're almost done; now let's tackle the banner inheritance. Our previous addition to the code related an image with exactly one page through a has-one relationship. This is a good start, but we don't want to force editors to choose a new image for every page they create, right? Most of the time, defaulting to the image of the parent page will be fine. Actually, searching all the way up to the top of the tree for an existing banner would be ideal because this would enable the homepage banner to become a site-wide default.

Create a new method called `getBannerImageRecursive()` and add it to the `Page` class, as shown in the following code excerpt:

```
<?php
class Page extends SiteTree {
   // ...
   function getBannerImageRecursive() {
      $page = $this;
      $banner = $this->BannerImage();
      while(!$banner->ID && $page->ParentID != 0) {
         $page = $page->Parent();
         $banner = $page->BannerImage();
      }
      return $banner;
   }
}
?>
```

Listing 11.4 *mysite/code/Page.php (excerpt)*

The `getBannerImageRecursive()` method handles banner inheritance. If a page doesn't have an associated banner (`!$banner->ID`), its parent pages are *recursively* searched (`$page->Parent()`) until either a banner image is found or the topmost page is reached (`$page->ParentID != 0`), aborting the search.

11.2.4 Template Integration

To integrate the banner image with the template, modify the *Page.ss* file of the BlackCandy theme as follows:

```
<!-- ... -->
   <div id="Header">
         <div id="Banner">
         <% if BannerImageRecursive %>
            $BannerImageRecursive.FullWidth
         <% end_if %>
         </div>
         <h1>Your Site Name</h1>
          <p>your site&#39;s tagline here</p>
      </div>
<!-- ... -->
```

Listing 11.5 *themes/mysite/templates/Page.ss (excerpt)*

We check to see whether the current page, or any of its parents, has an associated banner image. If it does, that image is displayed. Although not implemented here, we might want to add an `<% else %>` block and display a generic banner if no custom banner is found.

11.3 Branding the CMS Interfaces

SilverStripe is distributed using the *Berkeley Software Distribution* (*BSD*) license, making it one of the more *permissively* licensed open-source content management systems. Many other CMS distributions are *copyleft* licensed, using for example the *GNU Public License* (GPL). The difference between *permissive* and *copyleft* licenses lies in the way code may be modified and redistributed. The BSD license was chosen because it allows modification, repackaging, and even selling of the original code, so long as the original BSD license note is not removed from the code. This stands in contrast to copyleft licenses, which typically require that any derivative code must be distributed with the same open-source license. You can find more information about BSD, GPL, and other open-source licenses at http://en.wikipedia.org/wiki/Free_software_license.

Why is this relevant here? Well, you might want to use SilverStripe commercially and sell work produced with it to your clients. To streamline the experience, you might want to alter the CMS interface to match your company's branding. SilverStripe allows this form of redistribution due to its licensing, and even makes it easy for you to do so by providing some API methods for this purpose.

First, we need to provide a title for the 'new' CMS. Since SilverStripe Ltd has its headquarters in Wellington, New Zealand, and the residents of New Zealand are colloquially known as 'Kiwis', let's name our example branding accordingly: 'My Kiwi CMS'. We will replace the logo on the top-right corner of the CMS with a picture of a juicy kiwi fruit, replace the loading screen, and alter the look-and-feel of the backend to suit our needs by adjusting the CMS stylesheets.

You can download the complete recipe from the companion website download in the *11_recipes/* folder. The custom images we use are located in *mysite/images/*.

11.3.1 Name and Logo

We want the title bar of the web-browser and the image in the top-right corner of the backend interface to display proudly the 'My Kiwi CMS' name and logo. For this modification we don't need to replace the templates completely. Instead, we just pass the new application name into the `LeftAndMain` class in *mysite/_config.php*:

```
<?php
// ...
LeftAndMain::setApplicationName(
    'My Kiwi CMS',
    'My Kiwi CMS -  distributed by MyCompany',
    'http://mykiwicms.com'
);
```

Listing 11.6 *mysite/_config.php (excerpt)*

The `LeftAndMain` class provides the basis for the backend interface, and through the method `setApplicationName()` we can override its name. The first parameter is the new name, followed by a subtitle used as an the alternative text for the logo image. The third and last parameter is the URL of our new product.

That takes care of the text, but we also want to change the logo in the top-right corner of the interface. Note that the image is linked by using the `background-image` CSS rule that's written dynamically into the document. Any width and height parameters need to be specified using CSS syntax. All code is placed in *mysite/_config.php*:

```
LeftAndMain::setLogo(
    'mysite/images/kiwicmslogo.gif',
    'width: 62px; height: 32px;'
);
?>
```

Listing 11.7 *mysite/_config.php (excerpt)*

11.3.2 Loading Screen

When launching the SilverStripe backend you should see a loading screen with the familiar SilverStripe logo. We also want the juicy kiwi fruit to show up here and whet our appetite while the CMS interface loads. The finished result should look like Figure 11.3.

```
<?php
// ...
LeftAndMain:: set_loading_image(
    'mysite/images/kiwicmslogo_loading.png'
);
?>
```

Listing 11.8 *mysite/_config.php (excerpt)*

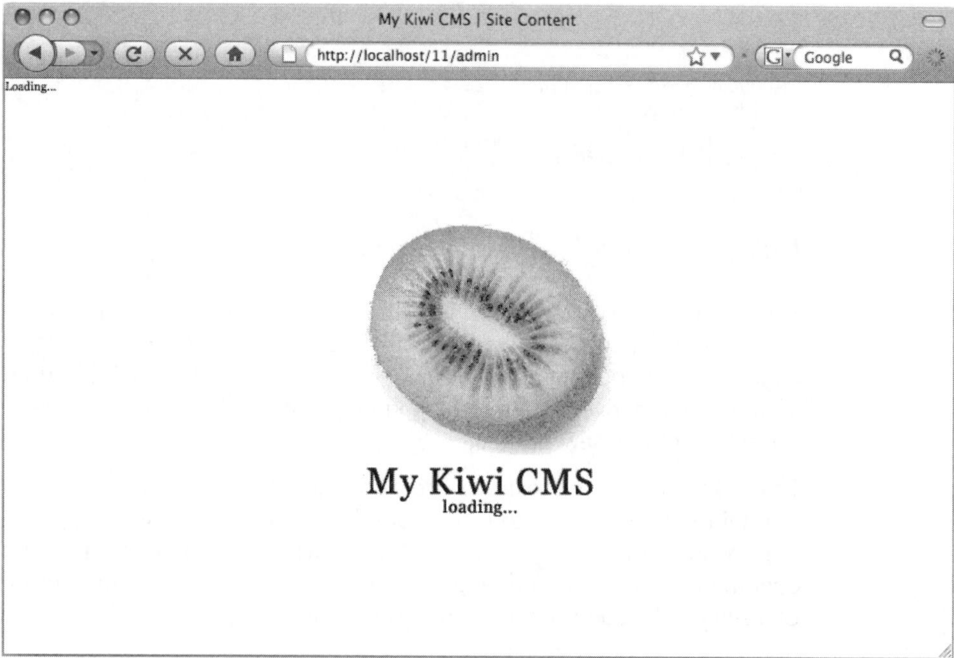

Figure 11.3 My Kiwi CMS: loading screen.

11.3.3 Color and Font Choice using Stylesheets

Finally, we add some variety to the color-scheme. Instead of the standard gray appearance, we'll make the interface look a bit more green. We'll also switch from the *Arial* font to the more decorative *Georgia* (both fonts are supported by most browsers). Fonts and colors are for the most part set using CSS. The easiest way to change them is simply to add another CSS definition that overrides the existing CSS. Create the *mysite/css/kiwicms.css* file and insert the following CSS code:

```
* {font-family: 'Georgia';}
body, #top #MainMenu .current {background: #61DF7E;}
#top, #bottom, #left h2, #contentPanel h2 {background: #277F4C;}
#top #MainMenu a {font-family: 'Georgia';}
#treepanes h2 img {display: none;}
```

Listing 11.9 *mysite/css/kiwicms.css*

Once again, no modification of any core file is required in order to integrate this CSS file into the CMS; we just need to use the

`LeftAndMain::require_css()` static method. Edit *mysite/_config.php* as follows:

```
<?php
// ...
LeftAndMain:: require_css('mysite/css/kiwicms.css');
?>
```

Listing 11.10 *mysite/_config.php (excerpt)*

Take a look at the finished new interface styling in Figure 11.4. Of course it's still SilverStripe under the hood, but on the other hand it might be enough of a difference to be consistent with your brand. Note that if you make the design too different, users may be confused when they try and use http://userhelp.silverstripe.com/ as their help manual.

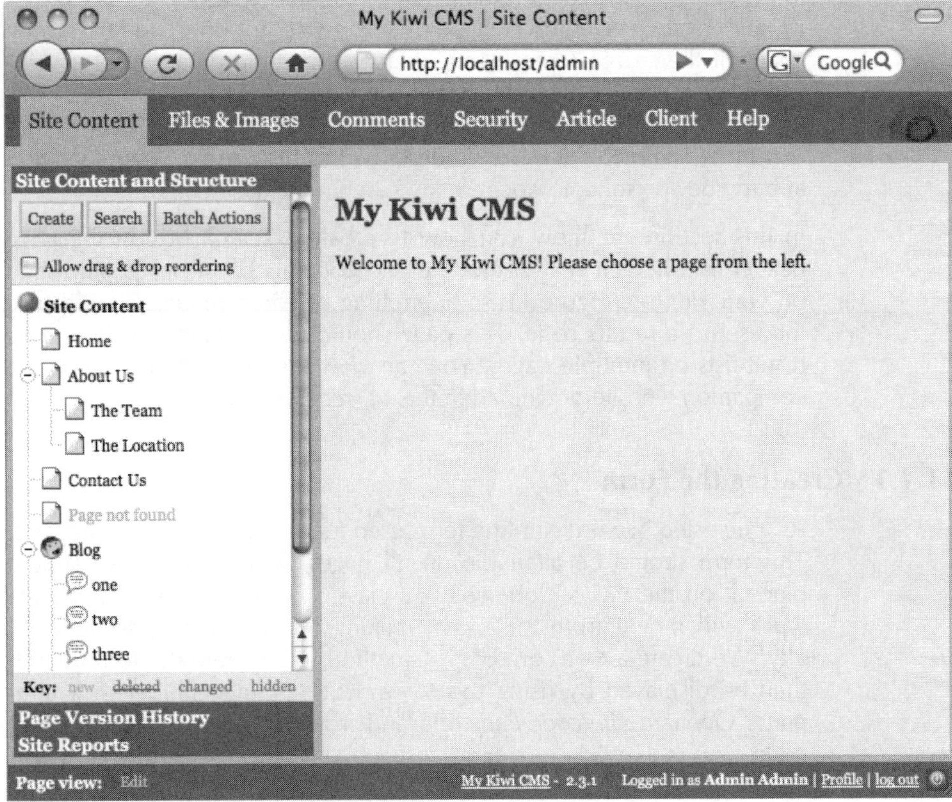

Figure 11.4 My Kiwi CMS: interface.

11.4 Full-text Search for Websites

Setting up a full-text search function is probably something you need to do on most of your projects. Even a small site can benefit from search as a way to quickly and easily find information.

There's no dedicated module for *full-text search* in SilverStripe. Instead, the built-in `SearchForm` class provides an abstraction layer to the search logic. A few lines of code in a page's controller is all it takes to build a very flexible search system. The technique shown here is used by the default BlackCandy theme, but it's useful for you to understand how it was achieved and how to customize the search behavior and result presentation. Note: Code additions and templates created in this recipe might already exist in your installation.

The term *full-text* refers to the fact that the underlying search algorithm queries the database for matches *within* one or more columns, rather than requiring the whole field to match a search term exactly. In our case, it wouldn't make much sense to only output search results if the search term exactly matches multiple paragraphs of website content, because we want to search for phrases contained in this content. Behind the scenes, the class uses the standard MySQL *full-text* functionality, which is well described in the vendor documentation at http://dev.mysql.com/doc/refman/5.2/en/fulltextsearch.html.

In this section we show you how to create a search box in the page header and have it search the title and contents of all pages published on your site (see Figure 11.5). Submitting a search request should take the user to a results page. This page should be paginated to show long result lists on multiple pages. You can view the complete recipe on the companion website download in the *11_recipes/* folder.

11.4.1 Creating the Form

As a first step, we'll create the form used for submitting search requests. This form should be available on all pages, which means we should place it on the `Page_Controller` class. Controllers from other page types will inherit from this class, making the search accessible globally. We create a `SearchForm()` method to generate the form. It can then be displayed by using the `$SearchForm` placeholder in a template. Open *mysite/code/Page.php* and insert or replace the following code:

```
<?php
// ...
class Page_Controller extends ContentController {
```

```
    // ...
    function SearchForm() {
        $fields = new FieldSet(
            new TextField("Search", false)
        );
        $actions = new FieldSet(
            new FormAction('results', 'Search')
        );
        return new SearchForm(
            $this,
            "SearchForm",
            $fields,
            $actions
        );
    }
}
?>
```

Listing 11.11 *mysite/code/Page.php (excerpt)*

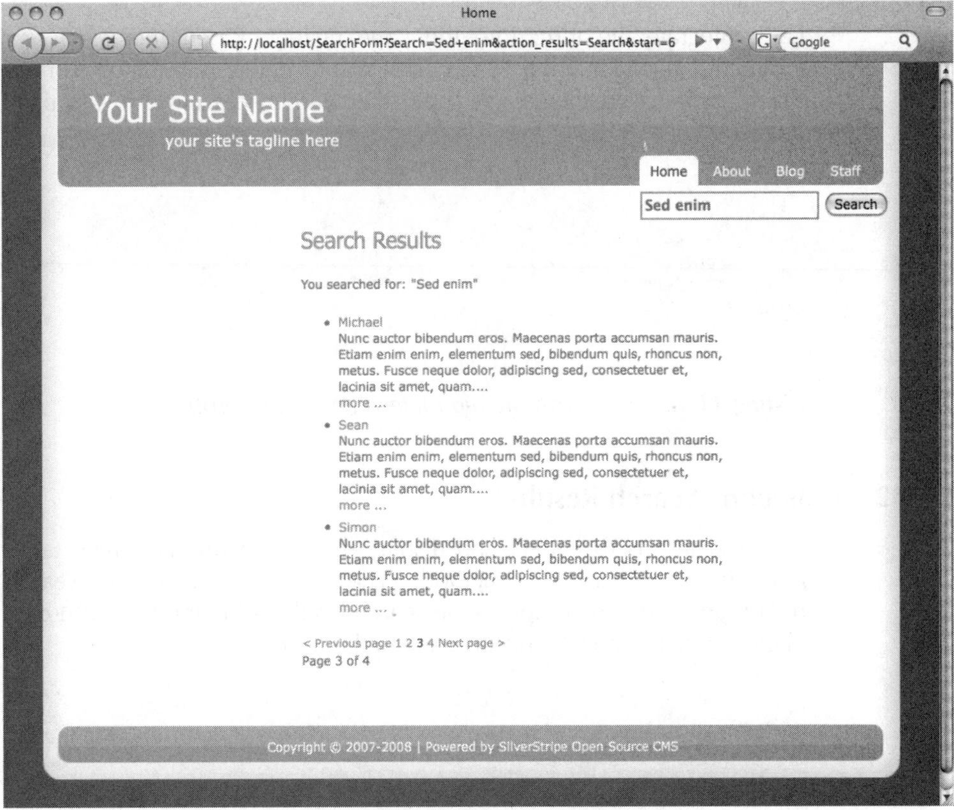

Figure 11.5 Search results page.

Here's a run-down of what's going on within this method:

- A new `TextField` named 'Search' is created and assigned to the `$fields` variable.
- An instance of the `FormAction` class is assigned to the `$actions` variable, creating the submit button of the form. The first parameter to `FormAction` tells the form that the `results()` method should be used to evaluate the form submission. We will define it shortly. The second parameter sets the title visible on the submit button.
- The assembled data is then passed into a new instance of the `SearchForm` class, which takes care of generating the HTML markup for the form, and contains the actual search logic.

Actually, both the `$fields` and `$actions` parameters are optional, because the `SearchForm` class comes with reasonable defaults for these fields. We've described them here because it's useful to know how to customize your form, e.g., to localize the field and button labels.

Let's integrate the form into the page header. Open *themes/mysite/templates/Page.ss* and the `$SearchForm` placeholder. In the case of our BlackCandy-based theme, we'll put the search field close to the page header:

```
<!-- ... -->
<div id="Header">
  $SearchForm
  <h1>$Title</h1>
</div>
<!-- ... -->
```

Listing 11.12 *themes/mysite/templates/Page.ss (excerpt)*

11.4.2 Collecting Search Results

The next task is to collect and display the search results, which takes place in the `results()` method. When a user clicks on the search button, this method computes the search results using the `SearchForm` class and then sends the results back to the user:

```
<?php
// ...
class Page_Controller extends ContentController {
   //...
   function results($data, $form){
      $results = $form->getResults(null, $data);
```

```
      $searchQueryTitle = $form->getSearchQuery($data);
      $templateData = array(
         'Results' => $results,
         'SearchQueryTitle' => $searchQueryTitle,
         'Title' => 'Search Results'
      );
      return $this->customise($templateData)->renderWith(
         array('Page_results', 'Page')
      );
   }
}
?>
```

Listing 11.13 *mysite/code/Page.php (excerpt)*

You'll remember how we set `"results"` as a parameter to the submit button of our search form. Clicking the submit button sends the query to the `results()` method. Let's look at what it does:

- The `$data` variable in the first parameter contains an associative array with the search terms; in our case just a single search phrase, like 'books'.
- The `$form` variable in the second parameter contains an automatically generated instance of the `SearchForm` class.
- The call to `$form->getResults(null, $data)` extracts the search terms from the `$data` variable and passes them into the `SearchForm` object, which performs the actual search. The first parameter to `getResults()` is an optional numeric result length, which defaults to ten items. The results of the search are stored as a collection of `Page` objects in a `DataObjectSet` in the `$results` variable.
- The search terms used for the search are put into the `$searchQueryTitle` variable. This will be useful for displaying the search-context back to the user on the results page.
- The `$templateData` array is used to set the placeholders, which are accessible in the template using `$Results`, `$SearchQueryTitle` and `$Title`.
- To pass the `$templateData` placeholders into our template, we can use the `customise()` method. It takes an array and merges it into the available data on the template, without requiring an explicit method on the controller.
- Normally the `Page_Controller` would render with the *Layout/Page.ss* layout template. However, we want to use *Layout/Page_results.ss* instead, which contains HTML markup to list all results as an

unordered list. The call to `renderWith(array('Page_results', 'Page'))` takes care of that for us. The *Page_results* layout template (which we will create in the next section) is used to display the results, using *Page.ss* as the surrounding main template.

You may have noticed how we didn't have to create a new page in the CMS for our search results. SilverStripe re-uses the page where the search query was performed and displays the results on that. So, if the ABOUT US page was used to perform a search request, the same page would be returned with the search results (`$Results`) rendered instead of the normal page content. Additionally, the `$Title` attribute set in the `$templateData` array sets the result page's title to 'Search Results'.

11.4.3 Displaying the Search Results

What's next? We need to create the *Page_results.ss* template to display the results. We already know which placeholders we will use; the following code should be pretty easy to follow. Create the *themes/mysite/templates/Layout/Page_results.ss* file and insert the code:

```
<div class="typography">
   <div id="Content">
      <h2>$Title</h2>
      <p class="searchQueryTitle">
         You searched for:
         &quot;{$SearchQueryTitle}&quot;
      </p>
      <% if Results %>
       <ul class="searchResults">
         <% control Results %>
           <li class="searchResult">
             <a class="searchResultHeader" href="$Link">
               $Title
             </a>
             <div>$Content.LimitWordCountXML</div>
             <a href="$Link">more ...</a>
           </li>
         <% end_control %>
       </ul>
      <% else %>
         <p>No search results were found!</p>
      <% end_if %>
   </div>
</div>
```

Listing 11.14 *themes/mysite/templates/Layout/Page_results.ss*

That takes care of our search result display:

- The `$SearchQueryTitle` placeholder is used to remind the user what he or she searched for. Please note that any markup contained in the search phrase is automatically escaped to avoid *Cross-Site Scripting* attacks (see Section 7.1, 'Cross-site scripting').

- If the search returned any results, we display them in an HTML list within the `<% control Results %>` loop.
- In the body of the loop we display the page title for each found page.
- We can access common placeholders of the found pages from within the loop. The `$Content.LimitWordCountXML` placeholder let's us show a preview of the page contents, to make it easier to locate the page you want.
- If no search results are found by the conditional block (`<% if Results %>`), we display a friendly explanation to the visitor.

11.4.4 Paginating the Search Results

One extra feature would be really useful: *Pagination* of search results. Meaning that we'd like to spread the listing of results over multiple pages. And guess what? There's a really easy way to do this for all `DataObjectSet` instances in SilverStripe, as shown by Figure 11.6.

< Previous page 1 2 **3** 4 Next page >
Page 3 of 4

Figure 11.6 Search result pagination.

By default, the `SearchForm` class returns only ten results. You can adjust this value using the `SearchForm->setPageLength()` method. If a search generates more than ten results, you can access additional results using an URL parameter `start` providing a numeric results offset, for example: *SearchForm?Search=search+term&start=11*. To enable pagination, we simply have to link to additional search result pages with varying parameters. Place the following template code below the actual search results:

```
<!-- ... -->
<% if Results.MoreThanOnePage %>
   <div id="PageNumbers">
      <% if Results.NotFirstPage %>
         <a class="prev" href="$Results.PrevLink">
            &lt; Previous page
         </a>
      <% end_if %>
      <span>
      <% control Results.Pages %>
         <% if CurrentBool %>
            $PageNum
```

```
        <% else %>
          <a href="$Link">$PageNum</a>
        <% end_if %>
      <% end_control %>
      </span>
      <% if Results.NotLastPage %>
        <a class="next" href="$Results.NextLink">
          Next page &gt;
        </a>
      <% end_if %>
      <p>Page $Results.CurrentPage of $Results.TotalPages</p>
    </div>
  <% end_if %>
  <!-- ... -->
```

Listing 11.15 *themes/mysite/templates/Layout/Page_results.ss (excerpt)*

Let's take a closer look at what is going on here:

- We use the `Results.MoreThanOnePage` conditional to test whether the search result consists of multiple pages.
- If there are multiple pages and the current page isn't the last page in the results (`<% if Results.NotLastPage %>`), a link to the next page in the results is displayed. Similarly, if the current page is not the first page in the results (`<% if Results.NotFirstPage %>`), then a link to the previous page is displayed.
- The `<% control Results.Pages %>` loop runs through the links to each page of the search results. This creates a numbered list of pages for direct access. The `$Link` placeholder automatically refers to a URL with the correct `start` parameter.
- Last but not least, we display the total number of pages through `$Results.TotalPages`, as well as the currently viewed page, using `$Result.CurrentPage`.

Well done. You've now mastered the full-text search feature. You are, of course, welcome to customize the search results to suit your specific needs.

11.5 Redirecting from Legacy URLs

Quite often, websites aren't being built from scratch in SilverStripe, but are replacing existing implementations. The majority of work is usually a conversion of the old data model and any templates. But details such as the URL design are also relevant. Perhaps the system that's supposed to be replaced treated every page on your website as a separate PHP script, resulting in URLs such as *index.php, about-us.php,* and so forth. Or all pages are routed through *index.php* and determined by a URL parameter such as *index.php?id=42.*

SilverStripe comes with human-readable, meaningful URLs out-of-the-box, based on the page title set through the CMS. CMS editors can customize these URLs, but there's no way to include folders or file extensions out-of-the-box. Therefore, your old URLs won't work any longer. All incoming links from other websites and bookmarks in your visitor's browsers would end up in digital nirvana. It also means that search engine ratings for specific pages will be lost, and your new pages start more or less from scratch in Google & Co.

This recipe describes how to use human-readable SilverStripe URLs while still maintaining backwards compatibility to legacy systems. We simply redirect any requests for legacy URLs to their counterparts in SilverStripe in a search engine friendly way. The legacy URL can be edited directly through the CMS to make the migration as easy as possible.

Caution: This recipe subclasses core functionality, because there's no well-defined API for intercepting the URL routing process. Please take specific care when updating your SilverStripe installation.

You can find the finished recipe on our companion website download in the *11_recipes/* folder.

11.5.1 The 'LegacyURL' Attribute

Open the *Page.php* definition from your standard SilverStripe installation, located in *mysite/code/Page.php.* We define a new `$db` attribute called `LegacyURL`, and make it editable by overloading the `getCMSFields()` method. It will be a simple `TextField`.

```
<?php
class Page extends SiteTree {
   static $db = array(
      'LegacyURL' => 'Text',
   );
   function getCMSFields() {
      $fields = parent::getCMSFields();
      $fields->addFieldsToTab(
         'Root.Content.Main',
         new TextField('LegacyURL', 'Legacy URL')
      );
      return $fields;
   }
   // ...
}
?>
```

Listing 11.16 *mysite/code/Page.php (excerpt)*

With this in place, you can save an arbitrary URL for each page through the CMS. Please don't include the protocol or domain when entering values in this field.

After refreshing your database via *http://localhost/dev/build/* you can test the management of these URLs in the CMS. Create a new page with the URL 'my-new-page' in the MetaData tab. Set the Legacy URL field to 'my-legacy-page.php' – you can find this field beneath the main Content area.

After we're finished with this recipe, visiting *http://localhost/my-legacy-page.php* should automatically redirect you to *http://localhost/my-new-page*.

11.5.2 Subclassing ModelAsController

URL routing is a core part of the *sapphire* framework. We can hook into this process by subclassing a core controller class called `ModelAsController`. This class is responsible for finding a `Page` record in the database, and passing it on to the correct controller or outputting a 'Page not found' message if nothing matches. We call our class `CustomModelAsController` and place it in *mysite/code/CustomModelAsController.php*:

```
<?php
class CustomModelAsController extends ModelAsController {
   public function handleRequest($request) {
      $this->request = $request;
      return parent::handleRequest($request);
   }
   public function getNestedController() {
      $url = $this->request->getUrl();
      $getVars = $this->request->getVars();
      if(isset($getVars['url'])) unset($getVars['url']);
      if($getVars) $url .= '?' . http_build_query($getVars);
      if($url) {
         $SQL_URLSegment = Convert::raw2sql($url);
         $page = DataObject::get_one(
            'Page',
            "`SiteTree`.LegacyURL = '{$SQL_URLSegment}'"
         );
         if($page) {
            $response = new HTTPResponse();
            $newUrl = Director::baseURL() . $page->URLSegment;
            $response->redirect($newUrl, 301);
            return $response;
         }
      }
      return parent::getNestedController();
   }
}
?>
```

Listing 11.17 *mysite/code/CustomModelAsController.php*

The method `getNestedController()` takes care of getting a page from the database, based on its `URLSegment` attribute. Before calling the original functionality with `parent::getNestedController()`, we hook in our own check for the `LegacyURL` attribute:

- The current request is available as a `HTTPRequest` object at `$this->request`. The requested URL is returned through `$this->request->getURL()`. In our case its value should be 'my-legacy-page.php'.
- Because `getURL()` doesn't include any potential URL parameters, we need to append them manually through `$this->request->getVars()`. The `"url"` parameter gets excluded from this, because it's an internal property that's not requested by the browser.
- In case we find a match for the `LegacyURL` property through `DataObject::get_one()`, we start the redirection.
- The redirection is performed through an `HTTPResponse` object and its public method `redirect()`. The first parameter for this method is our new `URLSegment`. The second parameter specifies an optional HTTP status code. We pass in `301`, which stands for 'Permanent Redirect' in HTTP-speak and signifies to the browser that the old URL no longer exists and we have a new one instead. See Section 5.9.5, 'Metatags' for a description of this status code. This redirection is particularly important for search engine bots, because they will transfer any rating from the old URL instead of discarding it.
- In case no `LegacyURL` can be found for this particular request, we pass control back to the core logic with `parent::getNestedController()`.

11.5.3 Overriding Director Routing

One piece of the puzzle is still missing: We haven't told the SilverStripe core to use our custom `ModelAsController` implementation. For this to happen, we need to edit *mysite/_config.php* and add a new rule to the `Director` class (see box 'URL Routing with Director').

```
<?php
// ...
Director::addRules(1, array(
    '$URLSegment//$Action/$ID/$OtherID'
    => 'CustomModelAsController',
));
?>
```

Listing 11.18 *mysite/_config.php (excerpt)*

URL routing with Director

The `Director` class takes care of routing URLs to their controllers. This includes URLs to content pages, but also to custom controllers such as */admin* that don't correlate to URL properties for pages in the database. It passes responsibility for rendering the output off to the specific controller if any of its URL rules match, and gets back the output that's passed on to the browser.

Director rules are basically an array with keys as the rule to be matched, and values as the controller or action that should be executed. A pseudo PHP syntax with dollar-signs signifies variables instead of string matches. These variables are available in a resulting controller through `getURLParams()`.

Each rule has a numerical priority from 1–100. The lower the priority number, the earlier this rule gets checked against.

SilverStripe has a couple of built-in URL rules – most of them can be found in *sapphire/_config.php* and *cms/_config.php*.

Our custom `Director::addRules()` command just copies the same rule that's used for the original `ModelAsController`, but passes it on to `CustomModelAsController`.

11.5.4 Avoiding URL Conflicts

One more thing: What happens if a `LegacyURL` has the same value as a perfectly valid new `URLSegment` on a different, new page? In our current implementation, the new page wouldn't show up, because our legacy handling kicks in first. To avoid this problem, we add a check to the write process of the Page class by implementing `Page->onBeforeWrite()`:

```
<?php
class Page extends SiteTree {
   // ...
   function onBeforeWrite() {
      if($this->LegacyURL) {
         $SQL_legacyURL = Convert::raw2sql($this->LegacyURL);
         $existingPages = DataObject::get_one(
            'Page',
            "URLSegment = '{$SQL_legacyURL}'"
         );
         if($existingPages) {
            $this->LegacyURL = null;
         }
      }
```

```
        parent::onBeforeWrite();
    }
    // ...
}
?>
```

Listing 11.19 *mysite/code/Page.php (excerpt)*

This logic checks for existing `URLSegment` values whenever a `LegacyURL` is saved. In case the `DataObject::get_one()` call returns a result, the `LegacyURL` is unset and not saved. Of course this isn't the most userfriendly option, because the CMS editor trying to save this value doesn't get notified of the change. But on the most basic level, it prevents legacy pages overlaying perfectly valid new URLs, which would make them inaccessible. To create more friendly messages to the CMS user, please have a look at overloading `Page->getCMSValidator()` and implement your own subclass of `Validator` to check for existing URLs before triggering the save operation.

Before closing off this recipe, a little homework task for you: Even with the `onBeforeWrite()` check in place, a newly created page can be saved with an `URLSegment` that's the same as an existing `LegacyURL` on another page. Therefore, the same scenario as above, just the other way around. Try to implement an appropriate check to avoid this scenario as well.

11.6 Simple Statistics using TableListField

The `TableListField` class is commonly used to display a table of DataObjects in the CMS, with one DataObject per row. You have already encountered the `TableListField` class when dealing with the `ModelAdmin` interface scaffolding class. All its search results are displayed using `TableListField` objects.

So far, so good. But this field can do more than just display DataObjects: it's a handy tool for visualizing other tabular data. In this recipe we take the `TableListField` and use it for a different purpose: generating visitor statistics.

When you click a link using a web-browser, it ordinarily informs the web-browser of both the new page it wants as well as the page you're leaving. The URL you have come from is known as the *Referrer*. Storing it can be useful for finding out entry points for your visitors and optimizing your information architecture accordingly. Referrer statistics can also be handy for identifying advertising partners. In this recipe we show you how to record the referrer information on every page and then display it in the backend, grouped by frequency (as shown in Figure 11.7).

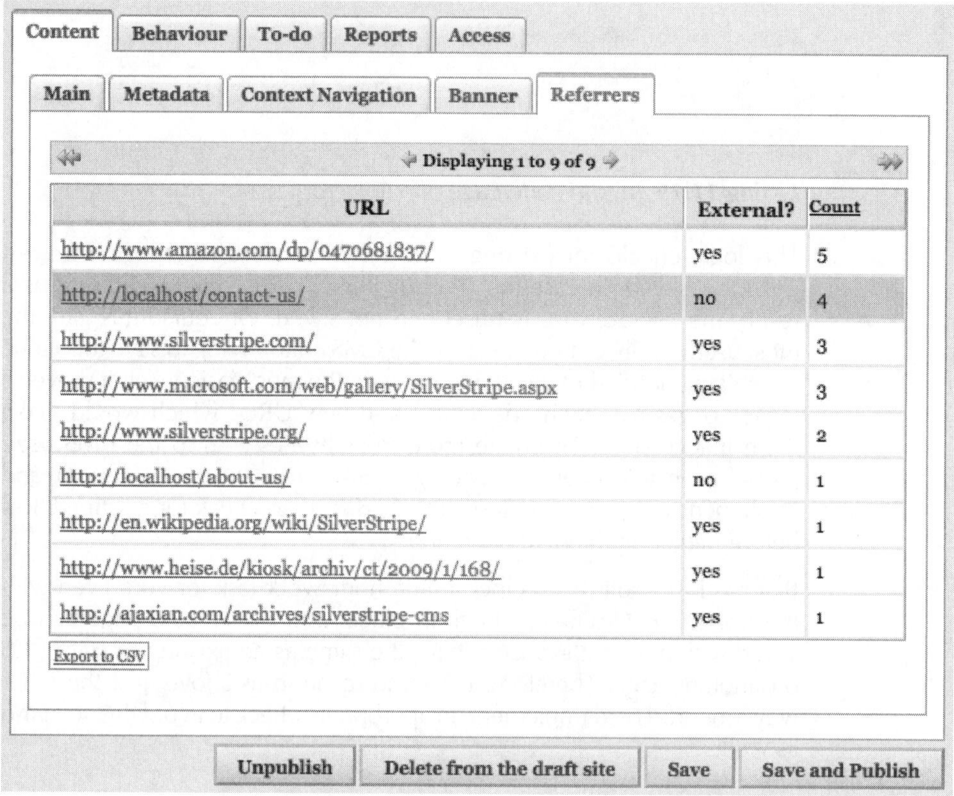

Figure 11.7 New tab in the CMS: referrers in TableListField.

You can view the complete recipe on the companion website download in the *11_recipes/* folder.

11.6.1 Linking Referrer Objects to Pages

The referrer information is communicated to SilverStripe as part of a standard HTTP request. If a user reaches a page from a link (either internal or external), fetching the required information isn't difficult. But first, let's figure out how to store the information when we get it.

We create a `Referrer` DataObject class with an attribute for the referring `URL` and a Boolean `IsExternal` attribute that indicates whether or not the referring page is internal or external to our website. The DataObject will also include a has-one relation to the `Page` it references. Create a new file in *mysite/code/Referrer.php* file and insert the following code:

```
<?php
class Referrer extends DataObject {
   static $db = array(
      'URL' => 'Text',
      'IsExternal' => 'Boolean'
   );
   static $has_one = array(
      'Page' => 'Page'
   );
}
?>
```

Listing 11.20 *mysite/code/Referrer.php*

We also need to open the existing `Page` class and add the other side of the relation: a has-many relation from `Page` to `Referrer` objects:

```
<?php
class Page extends SiteTree {
   static $has_many = array(
      'Referrers' => 'Referrer'
   );
   // ...
}
?>
```

Listing 11.21 *mysite/code/Page.php (excerpt)*

Rebuild the databases using *http://localhost/dev/build/* and a new database table for storing the referrer information will be ready for you to use.

11.6.2 Tracking Page Views

Our next task is to figure out how and when our referrer objects are to be created. How about using a static method that we can call from anywhere?

We create a new static method named `Referrer::log()`, which takes a `$referrerURL` and `Page` object as parameters. The method compares the `$referrerURL` parameter to the *base URL* of the current site and thereby decides whether or not the referring page is internal or external. For example: suppose the referring website is *http://localhost/about-us.* The *base URL* is *http://localhost,* so we know that we're dealing with an internal referrer link.

Add the following code into the *Referrer.php* file to add the static method:

```
<?php
class Referrer extends DataObject {
   // ...
   static function log($referrerUrl, $page) {
      $isExternal = (
         strpos($referrerUrl,Director::baseURL()) === FALSE
      );
      $referrer = new Referrer();
      $referrer->URL = $referrerUrl;
      $referrer->PageID = $page->ID;
      $referrer->IsExternal = $isExternal;
      $referrer->write();
   }
}
?>
```

Listing 11.22 *mysite/code/Referrer.php (excerpt)*

Now you're probably asking yourself: Where are we going to call this `log()` method from? An obvious candidate is the `Page_Controller` class. Every time any page is requested the `Page_Controller` does some of the request handling. The class should already exist in the *mysite/code/Page.php* file. Now add the following code to it to start logging:

```
<?php
// ...
class Page_Controller extends ContentController {
   function init() {
      parent::init();
      // ...
      $referrerUrl = $this->getRequest()->getHeader('Referer');
      if($referrerUrl) {
         Referrer::log($referrerUrl, $this);
      }
   }
   // ...
}
?>
```

Listing 11.23 *mysite/code/Page.php (excerpt)*

The only tricky bit of this code is how we get at the referrer information. First off, we get the `HTTPRequest` object from the current context (`$this->getRequest()`). This object contains all information about the HTTP request sent from the user's web-browser. The call to `$this->getRequest()->getHeader('Referer')` reads out the referrer information.

Note: Our code doesn't contain a typo here. The common misspelling of referrer without the second 'r' has become part of the official HTTP-standard (see http://en.wikipedia.org/wiki/Referrer/).

Try clicking around the website and then look into the *Referrer* database table. It will have gained a few new entries.

Referrer tracking performance

Depending on the popularity of your website, it can quickly collect hundreds of thousands of referrer entries. A general rule is that 100,000 database rows take up roughly 100 MB of disk space in a MySQL database using the default *MyISAM* storage engine. This amount of data can be quite difficult to mine for useful information. Sorting by frequency, for example, can take quite a long time.

Unfortunately, there's no easy solution for this performance problem. You might try some clever indexing and querying in the database, if you're so inclined. Alternatively, you might consider outsourcing the referrer tracking and other statistical information to external services such as *Google Analytics* (http://www.google.com/analytics/), which removes the need to deal with the huge amounts of data yourself.

11.6.3 Displaying Statistics using TableListField

Even the best data is useless if no one can look at it. So let's implement an interface for visualizing referrer data. Our referrer information is specific to each page, and so it makes sense to display it in that context. We'll do this by inserting a `TableListField` into the `Page->getCMSFields()` method of the `Page` class:

```
<?php
class Page extends SiteTree {
   // ...
   function getCMSFields() {
      $fields = parent::getCMSFields();
      $fields->addFieldToTab(
         'Root.Content.Referrers',
         $this->getReferrerTableListField()
      );
      return $fields;
   }
   function getReferrerTableListField() {
      $tf = new TableListField(
         'Referrers',
         'Referrer',
         array(
            'URL' => 'URL',
            'IsExternal' => 'External?',
```

```
            'ReferrerCount' => 'Count'
        )
    );
    $tf->setFieldFormatting(array(
        'URL' => '<a href=\"$URL\">$URL</a>'
    ));
    $tf->setFieldCasting(array(
        'IsExternal' => 'Boolean->Nice'
    ));
    $tf->setPermissions(array(
        'show'
    ));
    $tf->setShowPagination(true);
    $query = $this->getComponentsQuery(
        'Referrers',
        null, // filter
        'ReferrerCount DESC' // sort
    );
    $query->groupby('`Referrer`.URL');
    $query->select[] = 'COUNT(*) AS ReferrerCount';
    $tf->setCustomQuery($query);
    return $tf;
  }
  // ...
}
?>
```

Listing 11.24 *mysite/code/Page.php (excerpt)*

That's quite a bit of code so let's go through it step-by-step:

- `$fields->addFieldToTab('Root.Content.Referrers')` creates a new tab for Referrers in the CMS and links it up to get its interface panel from the `getReferrerTableListField()` method.
- The `getReferrerTableListField()` method first creates a new `TableListField` called `Referrers`. The third parameter is an array that lists all the columns the field should contain. The keys are the object attribute names and the keys are the interface labels.
- The `setFieldFormatting()` method tells the table that it should make a link out of the `URL` field, instead of displaying it as plain text, as it otherwise would. The array value that's provided for this field contains a string with PHP code, which will be evaluated for each row.
- The `setFieldCasting()` method casts the `IsExternal` column to a Boolean type and formats it nicely (`'Boolean->Nice'`). The result is that instead of displaying 0 and 1, the column shows 'no' and 'yes', which is much more intuitive for the user.
- The `setPermissions()` methods tells the `TableListField` that it should not display the standard delete button at the end of each

row. Deleting a grouped referrer reference would not be very useful. The only operation we want to allow is `show`, which shows the row of information in the report as shown in the earlier Figure 11.7.

- We expect to collect quite a few different referrers, and so our table could get quite long. Ideally we wouldn't display them all on the same page. The solution is to use the `setShowPagination(true)` method to tell the table to break to a new page after a certain number of entries (the default value is ten entries per page, which can be modified using the `setPageSize()` method).

This code should take care of all the plumbing. Now we get to the interesting part of the code: reading out the actual data. Let's take another look at the relevant part of the already inserted code:

```
<?php
// ...
function getReferrerTableListField() {
    // ...
    $query = $this->getComponentsQuery(
        'Referrers',
        null, //no WHERE clause needed
        '`ReferrerCount` DESC' // sort
    );
    $query->select[] = 'COUNT(*) AS ReferrerCount';
    $query->groupby('`Referrer`.`URL`');
    $tf->setCustomQuery($query);
    return $tf;
}
?>
```

Listing 11.25 *mysite/code/Page.php (excerpt)*

You might be surprised that we're not using `DataObject::get()` to fetch our data as usual. Instead, we're creating a `$query` object. In fact, `DataObject::get()` does the same thing internally; we're just going a level deeper so that we can add some special modifications to the SQL query.

The call to `$this->getComponentsQuery('Referrers')` does a very similar thing to `$this->Referrers()`. The difference is that instead of obtaining a `DataObjectSet`, we get back an instance of a `SQLQuery` class.

SQLQuery: A compromise between ORM and SQL

The `SQLQuery` class is an object-oriented version of a textual SQL query, and is a compromise between using the ORM and directly writing SQL. This approach has a number of advantages over SQL strings. It's common to use PHP logic to compose a query, for instance setting various WHERE or GROUP BY statements based on logic in your application. Your code will often be simpler and more readable in manipulating objects to achieve this than it will be concatenating or inserting text inside a text-based SQL query. Using the `SQLQuery` class means that you can pass the resulting query object into other classes, where it can be further adjusted and processed. The `SQLQuery->sql()` command assembles the final SQL and returns it as a string suitable to pass on to the database layer. See table 11.1 for an overview of `SQLQuery` properties.

The second parameter we use in our call of the `getComponentsQuery()` method is an empty (`null`) filter. Don't worry about limiting the results to those that should appear on the current page, because the framework will add the correct JOIN and WHERE clauses for us (it detects the has-many relationship). The third parameter (`"ReferrerCount DESC"`) specifies that the results should be sorted on the `ReferrerCount` field. We define that field as the sum of a group of results from the query in the very next line.

And now we get to the main reason why we couldn't just use the regular `DataObject::get()`: the `$query->groupby('`Referrer`.`URL`')` statement that groups the results by URL. The result is that we don't get a regular `Referrer` object, as we would have obtained without this statement. Instead, we get a set of results with attributes that mostly correspond with those of a `Referrer` object, except that one row can represent multiple grouped `Referrers`, counted by the `ReferrerCount` attribute. Therefore, `SQLQuery` allows us to access 'objects' that aren't defined in our standard data model, but act very similarly with the same benefits.

Now that we've created our custom query, we can pass it on to the `TableListField` using the `setCustomQuery()` method. The table class automatically adds the necessary limits and offsets that are necessary for pagination. It then performs the query and transforms the result into a `DataObjectSet`.

Here's a little trick you can use: Add a key called `'export'` to the array that you pass into `setPermissions()`. That creates a button at the bottom of the table, which you can use to export the data into a CSV file.

Et voilà! With relatively minimal effort we managed to integrate statistics into our CMS. Now that you understand the basics, the next steps would be to add pie charts and other niceties to make the statistics more meaningful.

Table 11.1 SQLQuery methods and attributes.

SQLQuery method	Description
`SQLQuery->select([array])`	Add columns to the query
`SQLQuery->from([array])`	Main table to query from
`SQLQuery->leftJoin([array])`	Join another table with a *LEFT JOIN* clause
`SQLQuery->where([array])`	*WHERE* filter clause
`SQLQuery->limit([string|array])`	Number of records to limit results; if parameter is passed as an array, the 'limit' and 'offset' can be specified separately
`SQLQuery->orderby([string])`	Sort order
`SQLQuery->groupby([string|array])`	Group the results on the criteria given
`SQLQuery->having([array])`	Filter by dynamically created columns

11.7 Showing Related Pages

Focusing on website usability is finally being recognized as a key way to ensure that your website successfully achieves its aims. Whether you want people to read your content, find a phone number, or purchase something you sell, your website must make it extremely easy for people to locate quickly what they want. There are many fundamentals to consider here, with a primary one being that your website pages must have clear names and be located in a structure that's instantly logical to the website visitor. Other fundamentals include writing concisely and using plain language.

This recipe lets you supplement such fundamentals by having your website display 'related pages'. For instance, if you're viewing a page about bread baking, it could show other pages relating to bread and to baking. If you came to the website via a Google search for 'bread', your website will also suggest other relevant pages. It won't replace the main navigational menus, but can help as an additional means of interlinking content. It'll displayed in the left-hand sidebar, below the menu.

A useful side-effect of this navigational helper is a tendency towards better search engine rankings: Links to pages that could be of interest to users are also detected by search engine robots, which index and rank these pages more readily.

Our context-sensitive navigation will focus on linking only to those pages that are related to the current page. Related pages will be chosen based upon the following criteria:

- Keyword search in the title and body of other pages.
- Analysis of keywords from a Google referrer string.

By the end of this recipe we hope that you'll appreciate how the list of related pages produced by a context sensitive navigation element can significantly improve the usability of a website by making it easier for users to find useful information.

Take a look at Figure 11.8 for a preview of what we'll create in this recipe. You can view the complete recipe code on the companion website download in the *11_recipes/* folder.

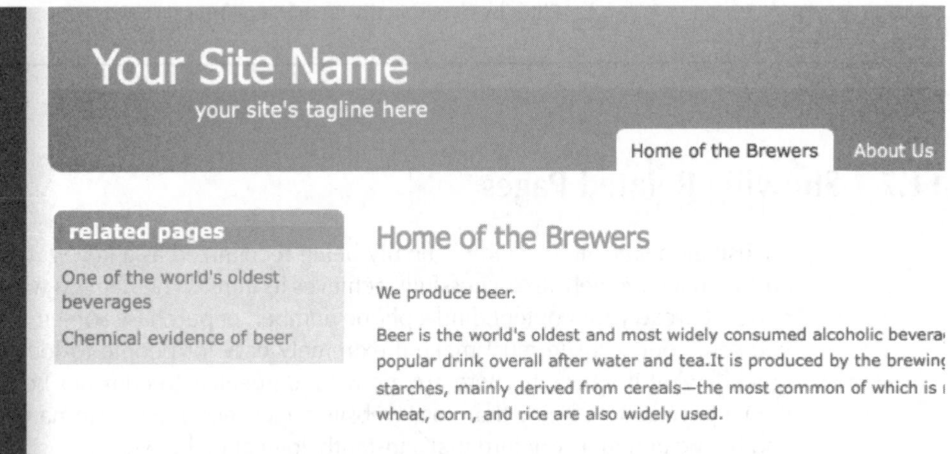

Figure 11.8 Frontend display of related pages in a sidebar.

11.7.1 Data Model

We want to set the options for context sensitive navigation individually on each page, hence it makes sense to add the necessary data attributes onto the `Page` class. All other pages inherit from this page, providing them with the same features. Here are the data model additions necessary on the `Page` class:

```
class Page extends SiteTree {
   static $db = array(
      'ContextNavMaxPages' => 'Int',
      'ContextNavKeywords' => 'Text',
   );
   static $defaults = array(
      'ContextNavMaxPages' => '10',
   );
   // ...
}
```

Listing 11.26 *mysite/code/Page.php (excerpt)*

Let's take a closer look at this code:

- The `ContextNavMaxPages` attribute records how many pages should be listed in the context sensitive navigation. It should be regarded as a maximum value; depending on the context there might be less results.
- The `ContextNavKeywords` attribute contains a comma-separated list of search terms that should cause matching pages to be included in the context sensitive navigation's page list.
- The `$defaults` array contains the default setting for the maximum number of pages to include in the listing. We have specified `10` as the maximum value.

Please note that when we talk about *keywords* in this recipe, we're basically referring to the concept of *tags* to organize related topics without the need of a hierarchical categorization. This is similar to the tags used in articles of the blog module (see http://silverstripe.org/blog-module/), although these don't get evaluated in the recipe.

11.7.2 CMS Input Fields

Okay, we now have our data model. Let's create a way to manage these options in the backend (see Figure 11.9). Please insert the following code into the `Page` class:

```
function getCMSFields() {
   $fields = parent::getCMSFields();
   $fields->addFieldsToTab(
      'Root.Content.Context Navigation',
      array(
         new NumericField(
            'ContextNavMaxPages',
            'Maximum number of pages to display (default: 10)'
```

```
        ),
        new TextField(
            'ContextNavKeywords',
            'Keywords (comma separated)'
        )
    )
);
return $fields;
}
```

Listing 11.27 *mysite/code/Page.php (continuation)*

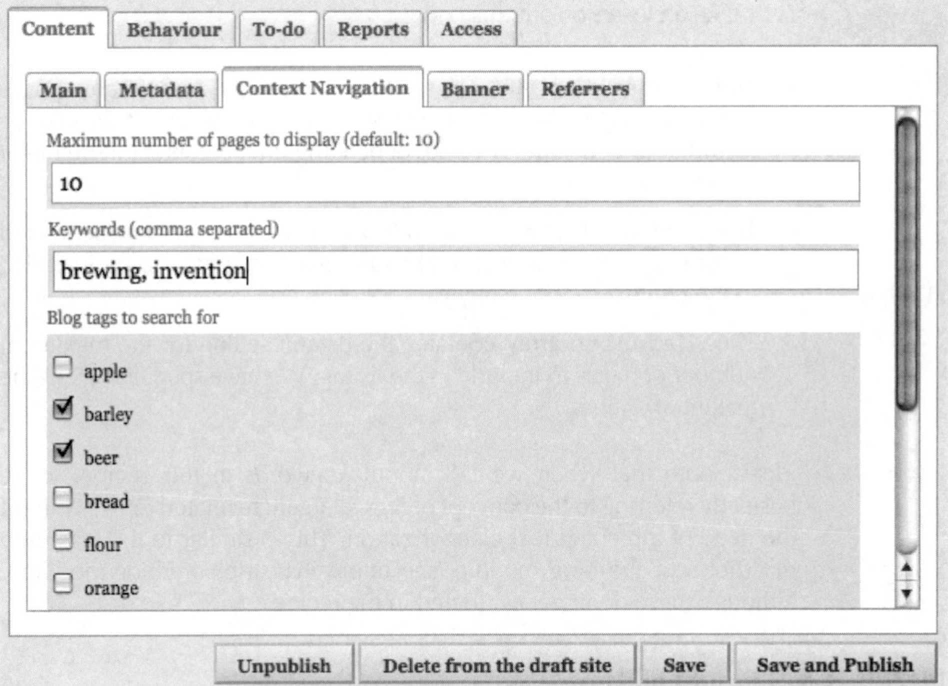

Figure 11.9 Using the backend to configure keywords.

This code overloads the existing `getCMSFields()` method that's used to build the SilverStripe backend interface. Let's take a look at the interesting parts of this code:

- Our `Page` class inherits a couple of fields from its parent class. These are loaded using `parent::getCMSFields()`.

- We add a new tab named Context Navigation for configuring the context sensitive navigation (`$fields->addFieldsToTab()`). SilverStripe automatically creates any referenced tabs if they don't already exist. We then add two fields to this tab for configuring the previously defined attributes.
- We create a `NumericField` for configuring the maximum number of pages to display.
- The keywords to search for in other pages can be set using a `TextField`. This field allows the user to enter multiple comma-separated keywords.

11.7.3 Aggregating Pages

The first step here is to add a method called `getContextNav()` in the `Page` class, which returns a `DataObjectSet` of all related pages:

```
<?php
class Page extends DataObject {
   // ...
   function getContextNav() {
      if($this->ID > 0) {
         $pages = new DataObjectSet();
         // fill with pages ...
         return $pages;
      } else {
         return false;
      }
   }
}
?>
```

Listing 11.28 *mysite/code/Page.php (excerpt)*

The new `DataObjectSet` can be filled with either a single element using `push()` or by combining it with another `DataObjectSet` using `merge()`. We define methods for populating it with pages in the next two sections.

11.7.4 Finding Pages by keyword

Displaying pages related by keywords is a useful technique, because it lets you group related content even if it's located in different sections of your website. Because a page can have many keywords, displaying pages also lets you successfully manage groups of content without having to structure the groups into a conventional tree hierarchy. Using keywords, it becomes easy, for example, to have a bread recipe page and display links to all other pages related to this topic. With the comma-separated property `ContextNavKeywords` we can store keywords for a single page. We then use the PHP method `explode()` (using a comma as the separator) to chop the keywords up into array elements. Take a look at the code:

```
protected function getPagesByKeyword() {
   $pageKeywords =
      explode(',',$this->getContextNavKeywords());
   if($pageKeywords) {
      return DataObject::get(
         'Page',
         $this->filterForKeywords(
            $pageKeywords,
            array('Content','Title')
         ),
         null, // sort
         null, // join
         $this->ContextNavPageLimit // limit
      );
   } else {
      return new DataObjectSet();
   }
}
```

Listing 11.29 *mysite/code/Page.php (continuation)*

The second parameter of the call to `DataObject::get()` turns into the *WHERE* clause of the SQL query, as returned by calling the `filterForKeywords()` method. This method assembles multiple parameters into a SQL full-text search clause (`"LIKE '%search-terms%'"`). We'll re-use this same helper method soon for other page aggregation methods. Take a look at what it does in detail:

```
protected function filterForKeywords($keywords, $fields) {
   $SQL_filterArr = '';
   foreach($keywords as $keyword) {
      $SQL_keyword = Convert::raw2sql($keyword);
      foreach($fields as $field) {
         $SQL_filterArr[] =
            "`{$field}` LIKE '%{$SQL_keyword}%'";
      }
   }
   return implode(' OR ', $SQL_filterArr);
}
```

Listing 11.30 *mysite/code/Page.php (continuation)*

11.7.5 Finding Pages by Search-engine Referrer

When a visitor views a certain page through a search engine result, we have a good indication what other pages he or she might be interested in. We can conveniently gather this information from the HTTP *referrer*. The HTTP request used to retrieve a page usually contains information about the page where a visitor was linked from. For example, if a visitor comes to our website via Google, his or her referrer string is in this format: http://www.google.com/search?q=search+phrase. We can take 'search phrase' and actively look for relevant pages on our website. If this page was a search engine search result, the URL will also contain the search terms. We can extract these search terms and use them for our context dependent navigation. For this example, the search detection is limited to URLs coming from Google.

The `$_SERVER['HTTP_REFERER']` PHP variable contains the referrer information. We use a *regular expression* to chop the search string up into its component parts and extract the search keywords. Regular expressions are an easy way to match parts of strings by certain criteria, but on the other hand they're not very readable. We don't go much into explaining the details here; if you're interested in the used syntax, please consider reading some tutorials online, e.g. at http://regular-expressions.info/.

We then once again use our trusty `filterForKeywords()` method to search the title and content of all other pages on our site for those keywords:

```
protected function getPagesByReferer() {
  $pages = new DataObjectSet();
  $keywords = array();
  if(  preg_match('/^http:\/\/w?w?w?\.?google.*/i',
              $_SERVER['HTTP_REFERER'])
  ) {
        $queryStr = preg_replace(
              '/^.*q=([^&]+)&?.*$/i',
              '$1',
              $_SERVER['HTTP_REFERER']
        );
        // scrub away nasty quote marks
        $queryStr = preg_replace('/\'|"/','',$queryStr);
        $keywords = preg_split ("/[\s,\+\.]+/",$queryStr);
  }
  if($keywords) {
        $pages = DataObject::get(
              'Page',
              $this->filterForKeywords(
```

```
                $keywords,array('Content','Title')),
            null, // sort
            null, // join
            $this->ContextNavPageLimit // limit
        );
    }
    return $pages;
}
```

Listing 11.31 *mysite/code/Page.php (continuation)*

11.7.6 Merging all the Criteria

We have built a way to find related pages using keywords and search terms by Google referrers. Now the time has come to put it all together, and add some `merge()` calls to the existing `getContextNav()` method:

```
function getContextNav() {
    if($this->ID > 0) {
        $pages = new DataObjectSet();
        $pages->merge($this->getPagesByKeyword());
        $pages->merge($this->getPagesByReferer());
        $pages->removeDuplicates();
        $currentPage = $pages->find('ID', $this->ID);
        if($currentPage) $pages->remove($currentPage);
        return $pages;
    } else {
        return false;
    }
}
```

Listing 11.32 *mysite/code/Page.php (continuation)*

As you can see, we merge all the potentially related pages into a single `DataObjectSet` and store them in the `$pages` variable. With `$pages->removeDuplicates()` we ensure that the different methods haven't found the same page twice. Finally, we remove the current page through `$pages->remove($currentPage)`, because it might have been matched by some of the search criteria.

11.7.7 Template Display

As usual we're using a `<% control %>` loop to display the contextual links in a template. In this case we simply output the page title and URL in an unordered list. The BlackCandy theme that we copied into *themes/mysite/* should already contain markup and stylesheets to place certain elements in a left-aligned sidebar. Please place the code in the *themes/mysite/templates/Includes/SideBar.ss*, within the `<div id="Sidebar">` holder:

```
<!-- ... -->
<div id="ContextNav" class="sidebarBox">
  <h3>Related Pages</h3>
  <ul>
    <% control ContextNav %>
    <li><a href="$Link">$Title</a></li>
    <% end_control %>
  </ul>
</div>
<!-- ... -->
```

Listing 11.33 *themes/mysite/templates/Includes/Sidebar.ss (excerpt)*

11.7.8 Conclusion

This step completes our recipe. We've created a framework for finding related pages by a number of different criteria. You can customize your context dependent navigation by enabling or disabling various aggregation methods depending on what's appropriate for your website. The result is a great navigational helper for your visitors. You might also want to consider similar techniques for suggesting alternative search results, or providing a smarter 'Page not found' page.

11.8 CSV Import using CSVBulkLoader

Importing data from files in *Comma-Separated Values* (CSV) format is a common task, but can quickly become quite difficult and tedious. MySQL and phpMyAdmin both allow you to import CSV files into the database. However, the data is rarely structured to match your database schema. You might also need to consider how to prevent duplicate information being entered or how to prevent existing information from being overwritten. You can manually tidy up the CSV file to prepare it for import, but any manual step makes imports clumsy to repeat. So what should we do?

You could carefully document the steps you take to tidy up the CSV, which might be appropriate but is definitely a time-consuming and error prone process. And what do you do when you want to create a more complex data structure? Suppose you want to put one row into multiple tables, or even create has-one, has-many, or many-many relations. How would you do that with a simple CSV import?

SilverStripe can help you out with this task by providing a class named `CSVBulkLoader`. You can use it to specify rules for mapping columns, changing formatting, creating relations, dealing with duplicate data, and other necessary import logic.

You can find the complete recipe on the companion website download in the *11_recipes/* folder. The sample CSV file used throughout the recipe is available inside the archive, named *clients.csv*.

11.8.1 Data Model

We start with a simple CSV file containing customer data. Every customer has a customer number, a name, a date of birth, and a category. Customers have the option of not providing their date of birth out of privacy concerns, and so this field is optional.

```
"CustomerNumber","Name","DateOfBirth","Category"
11,"John Doe",06/23/1982,"private customer"
12,"Jane Test",12/31/1999,"private customer"
13,"Joshua Check",,"business customer"
```

Listing 11.34 *clients.csv*

We want to import each row into a special `Client` class, which we define in a second. But let's first think about the data we're importing – do all fields make sense in our data model?

Let's suppose the `Name` column in our CSV file is no good, because we want to store first and last name as separate fields. This may be necessary to allow the website to greet customers by first name. Our example lets us demonstrate a simple data splitting technique: we divide the string at the space character and save it into `FirstName` and `LastName` on our `Client` records.

Also, the date of birth is written in a US date format (*month/day/year*), which we need to convert into something more suitable for insertion into the database, which usually deals with the format *year-month-day*. We'll take care of this later on by using PHP's built-in date conversion methods in a custom callback.

Please create a new file in *mysite/code/Client.php* and insert the following code:

```
<?php
class Client extends DataObject {
   static $db = array(
      'ClientNumber' => 'Int',
      'FirstName' => 'Text',
      'LastName' => 'Text',
      'Birthday' => 'Date',
   );
}
?>
```

Listing 11.35 *mysite/code/Client.php*

Take a look at the category field from our CSV example. We can see that 'private customer' occurs several times, making it more of a shared category than a field specific or unique to the client. It makes sense to *normalize* the duplication, which is to say, transform this column into a new table designed to handle categories, and tie this together as a client-category relationship. We create another new class named `ClientCategory`, related to each client through a has-one relationship.

Create a file called *mysite/code/ClientCategory.php* and insert the following code:

```
<?php
class ClientCategory extends DataObject {
   static $db = array(
      'Title' => 'Text',
   );
   static $has_many = array(
      'Clients' => 'Client'
   );
}
?>
```

Listing 11.36 *mysite/code/ClientCategory.php*

The name of the category ('business customer' or 'private customer') is stored as the `Title` attribute of the class. This way one instance of the `ClientCategory` class (e.g., 'business customer') can be re-used with many `Client` classes (e.g., all the business customers).

Now amend the existing `Client` class to add the other side of this relationship:

```
<?php
class Client extends DataObject {
   // ...
   static $has_one = array(
      'ClientCategory' => 'ClientCategory'
   );
}
?>
```

Listing 11.37 *mysite/code/Client.php (excerpt)*

11.8.2 Simple Administration Interface

The basic `CsvBulkLoader` class is only a set of PHP methods that can be used at a code level, and doesn't provide a user interface for uploading CSV files through a web-browser. That makes the `CsvBulkLoader` very flexible for usage in a variety of circumstances, but does mean that every new implementation requires a bit of up-front effort.

An easy way to attach `CsvBulkLoader` to a user interface is through the `ModelAdmin` class (extensively discussed in Chapter 6). ModelAdmin not only generates interfaces to view and edit arbitrary DataObject subclasses, but also allows users to import CSV files to them with only a small amount of coding.

To begin, we need to hand the management of clients over to `ModelAdmin`. We do this by creating a subclass of `ModelAdmin` called `ClientAdmin`. In doing so, we set `$url_segment` to `'clients'` so that our client management interface becomes accessible at *http://localhost/admin/clients/*. Create a new file named *mysite/code/ClientAdmin.php* and write the following code:

```
<?php
class ClientAdmin extends ModelAdmin {
   static $managed_models = array(
      'Client'
   );
   static $url_segment = 'clients';
   static $model_importers = array(
      'Client' => 'ClientCsvBulkLoader',
   );
}
?>
```

Listing 11.38 *mysite/code/ClientAdmin.php*

In the code above you'll notice the static property `$model_importers`. This specifies to ModelAdmin to display a CSV file import interface (see Figure 11.10.), and to use a subclass of `CsvBulkLoader` to handle uploaded CSV files.

11.8.3 Mapping Columns

Our `ClientCsvBulkLoader` class contains as array that maps column names in the CSV file to the SilverStripe model, and some other simple logic. Create a new file named *mysite/code/ClientCsvBulkLoader.php* and write the following code:

```
<?php
class ClientCsvBulkLoader extends CsvBulkLoader {
   public $columnMap = array(
      'CustomerNumber' => 'ClientNumber',
   );
}
?>
```

Listing 11.39 *mysite/code/ClientCsvBulkLoader.php*

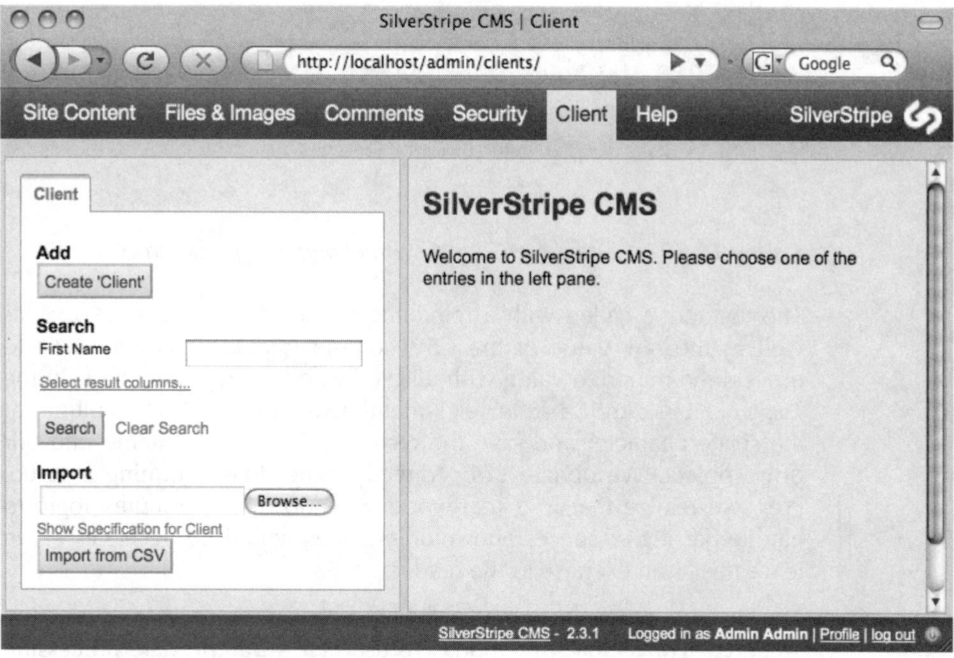

Figure 11.10 Import functionality in ModelAdmin.

First, we need to define a `$columnMap` attribute. This array tells the importer how the columns in the CSV should map to attributes of the DataObject. For example, the CSV column `CustomerNumber` is mapped to the `ClientNumber` attribute of the `Client` object. This mapping isn't needed where the names of your CSV columns exactly match the name of a field in your SilverStripe data model. We'll add more mappings and additional functionality as we go along.

11.8.4 Custom Import Methods

The `$columnMap` isn't limited to merely mapping attributes. It can also map a CSV column to a PHP method by using an arrow prefix ('->'). For example, mapping to `->importFirstAndLastName` generates a call to the `importFirstAndLastName()` method on our `CsvBulkLoader` subclass. Let's define this callback method:

```
<?php
class ClientCsvBulkLoader extends CsvBulkLoader {
   public $columnMap = array(
      // ...
      'Name' => '->importFirstAndLastName',
   );
   static function importFirstAndLastName(&$obj, $val, $record) {
```

```
        $parts = explode(' ', $val);
        if(count($parts) != 2) return false;
        $obj->FirstName = $parts[0];
        $obj->LastName = $parts[1];
    }
}
?>
```

Listing 11.40 *mysite/code/ClientCsvBulkLoader.php (excerpt)*

The method is called with a reference to the Client object (`&$obj`) as well as the raw value of the CSV column (`$val`). This allows us to process the imported value with all the flexibility that PHP offers. In the `importFirstAndLastName()` method we split the `Name` column at the space character and save the resulting first and last name into our `$obj` object. We update `$obj` directly rather than returning a value. (Yes, we realize that in a real-world scenario, more complex logic to handle parsing of spaces and middle-names would be necessary – we leave this as an exercise to the reader.).

The birthday conversion gets handled in a similar way: with an `importBirthday()` callback method. We use PHP's built-in date processing to convert a date from a US format (*month/day/year*) and turn it into an SQL-compatible date (*year-month-day*), as follows:

```
<?php
class ClientCsvBulkLoader extends CsvBulkLoader {
    public $columnMap = array(
        // ...
        'DateOfBirth' => '->importBirthday',
    );
    // ...
    static function importBirthday(&$obj, $val, $record) {
        if($val) {
            $obj->Birthday = date('Y-m-d',strtotime($val));
        }
    }
}
?>
```

Listing 11.41 *mysite/code/ClientCsvBulkLoader.php (excerpt)*

11.8.5 Relation Callbacks

Now we want to transform the `Category` CSV column into a has-one relation to the `ClientCategory` class. This is done by mapping that column to `ClientCategory.Title`. The importer automatically creates a relation for each imported row in the CSV file. Have a look at the code:

```
<?php
class ClientCsvBulkLoader extends CsvBulkLoader {
   public $columnMap = array(
      // ...
      'Category' => 'ClientCategory.Title',
   );
   // ...
   public $relationCallbacks = array(
      'ClientCategory.Title' => array(
         'relationname' => 'ClientCategory',
         'callback' => 'getClientCategoryByTitle'
      )
   );
   static function getClientCategoryByTitle(&$obj, $val, $record){
      $SQL_val = Convert::raw2sql($val);
      return DataObject::get_one(
         'ClientCategory', "`Title` = '{$SQL_val}'"
      );
   }
}
?>
```

Listing 11.42 *mysite/code/ClientCsvBulkLoader.php (excerpt)*

We earlier mentioned that `CsvBulkLoader` can prevent duplicate information from entering a database. We only want one object for the 'private customer' relation and therefore have SilverStripe re-use that object whenever the value reoccurs in the CSV file. This works by creating an entry in the `$relationCallbacks` array. The loader uses the data in this array to attach callback methods to certain mappings. The name of the mapped attribute should be set as the key of the array, in our case `"ClientCategory.Title"`. We can use a special dot-separated notation to reference a field on the has-one relation. The value is another array, which specifies how the callback should work. It requires two keys: the name of the has-one relation (`"relationname"`) and the callback method (`"callback"`); in our case this method is named `getClientCategoryByTitle()`.

The callback method gets passed the current value of the CSV column in question, and can find an existing relation based on it. If it returns a valid DataObject, the importer will automatically use the existing object instead of creating a new one. This way we can ensure that we write only one `ClientCategory` with the `Title` attribute called 'private customer' to the database, and return this object on subsequent CSV rows.

11.8.6 Duplicate Detection

It's one thing to import data into an empty database. It becomes a lot more complex when data is already stored in the database, because the import script may then need to consider logic for the purpose of maintaining data integrity. In our situation, we want to make use of a unique identifier for each entry: `CustomerNumber`. We want new information held by the CSV to update and overwrite information held by the database. To achieve this, the entry in the `$duplicateChecks` array tells the importer that the `CustomerNumber` to `ClientNumber` mapping should be kept unique. Any attempt to import a row with an existing `CustomerNumber` doesn't result in a duplicate entry. Instead, the entry is updated with values from the CSV file, if these differ from what's already recorded in the DataObject. Try it out:

```
<?php
class ClientCsvBulkLoader extends CsvBulkLoader {
   // ...
   public $duplicateChecks = array(
      'CustomerNumber' => 'ClientNumber'
   );
}
?>
```

Listing 11.43 *mysite/code/ClientCsvBulkLoader.php*

Call up the `ClientAdmin` interface at *http://localhost/admin/clients/* and import the *client.csv* file we described above. Try importing this file a few times (changing it a little each time) to see how the duplicate detection feature works. Look at the resulting data either by using the CMS interface or looking directly at the database. Importing CSV files just got a whole lot easier!

11.9 A Fully Flash-based Website Driven by SilverStripe

Outputting HTML is less integral to SilverStripe than you might think. SilverStripe is 'skinless', with the presentation being rendered as HTML only because that's what has been written into the templates (which *you* control!). This architecture allows for great versatility in your freedom relating to HTML markup. It also allows you to expose your website or data in a format other than HTML. This is illustrated nicely in this recipe, where we create a Flash-based website. Contrary to many websites created predominantly with Flash, the content remains updatable by the CMS: we will get SilverStripe to produce information as XML, which in turn will be used by the Flash files to generate webpages.

Adobe Flash versus HTML

The rationale for a Flash-based website becomes clearer when we look at the differences between HTML and Flash. We generally prefer

HTML because it's an open, documented standard, has a wide user base through competing and innovating web-browsers, is easy to search, and is independent from platforms and devices. The notion of URLs is also inextricably linked to HTML because of the widespread convention that each HTML page has a unique address, making it easy to bookmark, share, and return to any part of a website. We also appreciate that you can view the source of HTML pages, which has led to the common practice of people learning from and re-using HTML content.

The multimedia capabilities of standard HTML are limited though: Browser-independent and performant effects, streaming of audio and video, access to a computer's microphone or webcam, vector rendering, and bitmap manipulations are still time consuming, fragile, or device-dependent to achieve. It will be some years before the efforts of browser development teams and the slowly evolving HTML5 specification combine to produce a universal (cross-browser, cross-platform), robust, and simple way to achieve such multimedia features in HTML.

Adobe Flash on the other hand has a long history in the multimedia niche: It started as a simple tool for animations in 1996, and became the quasi-standard for unconventional and highly interactive designs it is today. Flash provides an excellent way of manipulating and streaming both audio and video – it doesn't require extensive code, runs fast through a web-browser, and can be written once to work the same with Safari on a Mac, Internet Explorer on a PC, or FireFox on a Linux machine. Flash has also long provided good support for being a simple and universal way of displaying video content – so much so that websites such as youtube.com rely on this technique. Many of its features are possible thanks to a built-in scripting language called *ActionScript*, the JavaScript equivalent in Flash.

However, many of the joys of HTML are missing or obfuscated in Flash. Although technical specifications have been disclosed and alternative software exists, Adobe remains the only organization creating meaningful software to author and play back Flash files. The lack of an open data format makes it less ideal as a format to archive and store information long term. Finally, when viewing Flash content, it can be hard or impossible to view the source code, copy text or images, or bookmark the current URL and later return to the same position you left off.

11.9.1 Goals

In this recipe we create a compact Flash-based interface for navigating a page tree and displaying the HTML content. The tree as well as content of the pages will be loaded straight out of SilverStripe in XML format. We glue together ready-made flash components for most of the interface elements to keep the work in Flash and its programming language ActionScript as minimal as possible. Please excuse the more or less missing aesthetics of our sample application – in theory, you have all the tools at your disposal to make this a highly interactive and beautiful website at the end of the recipe.

You don't need any prior knowledge about authoring or programming in Flash and ActionScript to start this recipe – this is a book for PHP developers after all! In case you're interested, we give a quick rundown on the required code to get the Flash file going, but you're welcome to ignore this and use our pre-compiled SWF file from the archive on our book companion website. We have included a full SilverStripe project including sample data, the SWF files, and Flash source files in the *11_recipes_flash/* folder. In case you're using the pre-compiled examples, make sure to point your webroot to *http://localhost/* without any subfolders, because this path is hardcoded in the SWF file. In case you don't have a license for Adobe Flash 9 or newer, and want to edit the Flash source files, Adobe provides a free 30 day trial online at http://www.adobe.com/go/tryflash/. Please have a look at Figure 11.11 for a preview of the Flash interface we're about to build.

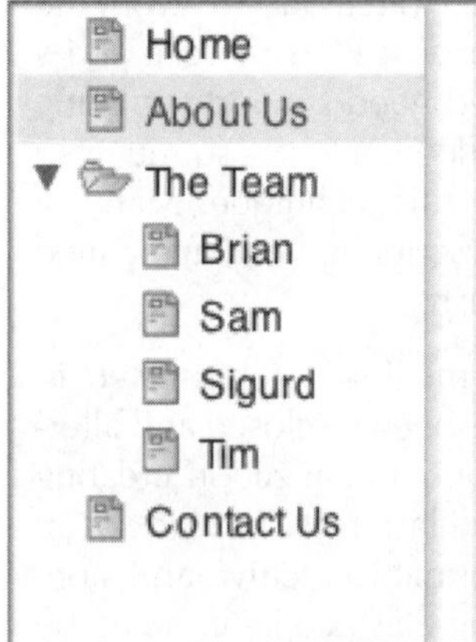

Figure 11.11 Flash frontend with page tree and HTML output.

11.9.2 Page Tree as XML

First, we want to provide the page tree in a format that can be processed by Flash. XML is an ideal format to serialize this type of information, because it handles nested nodes very well. Each page is described as its own `<node>` element inside the XML, which can contain further `<node>` elements as its children. Properties like the database ID or the title of the page are passed through as attributes on this element. The output we're aiming for is quite different to the `<ul>` and `<li>` HTML markup you normally use to produce menus. Instead, the output will roughly look like this:

```
<?xml version="1.0" encoding="UTF-8"?>
<node>
  <node id="1" label="Home" isBranch="true" classname="Page">
  </node>
  <node id="2" label="About Us" isBranch="true" classname="Page">
  </node>
  <node id="5" label="The
Team" isBranch="false" classname="Page">
    <node id="6" label="Brian " isBranch="true" classname="Page">
    </node>
    <node id="7" label="Sam " isBranch="true" classname="Page">
    </node>
    ...
  </node>
</node>
```

Listing 11.44 *Custom XML structure for nested pages*

External data in Flash

Flash has multiple ways of retrieving and processing data from external sources:

- The *LoadVars* object is able to read URL-encoded strings, which can either come from a file on your filesystem or through a URL. Variables will be separated in the same fashion as GET parameters in the HTTP standard, through an *Ampersand* character ('&'). *LoadVars* is ideal for simple configurations, but gets clumsy for larger nested data structures.
- With the *XML* object, Flash provides an integrated XML parser, which can take in a string of XML notation, and make it available as a hierarchy of versatile objects in ActionScript. With this object, simple XML-based (read-only) web-service calls are easy to get going. This technique is the most appropriate for our scenario because we can easily produce XML in SilverStripe, and the ActionScript provides everything we need to create dynamic menus and content areas.

- Flash also comes with its own web-service protocol called *Flash Remoting,* and its serialization standard *Action Message Format* (AMF). With this protocol, complex data types can be moved between languages without losing their data or typing. Originally this protocol was built for the home-made products *Flash Remoting MX* and more recently for the *Flex Data Services*. It didn't take long for other developers to notice the potential uses though, and reverse engineer it into other languages and tools, including Python, Java,. NET, Ruby, and PHP. The most well-known adaption is probably *AMFPHP* (http://amfphp.org/).

We need to expose the website page tree as XML at an URL accessible to the Flash file. We create a subclass of `Controller` to handle this. In SilverStripe, there's no concept of a 'root node' for the page tree; all top level pages simply point to a `ParentID` property with the value `0`. Hence our new controller isn't bound to a specific page URL.

Let's name our controller `FlashTree`. We know, highly creative! As a little known fact, SilverStripe makes all controllers accessible through their name as an URL by default. This means that the `FlashTree` controller will be available at *http://localhost/FlashTree/* without any further configuration. Add the following code to a new file named *mysite/code/FlashTree.php*:

```
<?php
class FlashTree extends Controller {
  function xml() {
    $rootPages = DataObject::get(
      'Page',
      ''ParentID' = 0 AND 'ShowInMenus' = 1'
    );
    $this->getResponse()->addHeader(
      "Content-type",
      "text/xml"
    );
    $xml = "<?xml version=\"1.0\" encoding=\"UTF-8\"?>\n";
    $xml .= "<node>\n";
    foreach($rootPages as $page) {
      $xml .= $this->getNodeXML($page);
    }
    $xml .= &</node>\n";
    return $xml;
  }
  // ...
}
?>
```

Listing 11.45 *mysite/code/FlashTree.php*

The `xml()` method is our starting point: It gets all root level pages and loops over them to create an XML formatted response. Root level pages are defined by having a `ParentID` attribute equalling `0`, so they don't point to any other page. We also make sure to show only pages that have their SHOW IN MENUS check box activated with `ShowInMenus=1`. By default, this option is turned on for new pages and determines whether the page is shown in any menu generated in a template. Before transforming those pages into XML, we have to tell the browser that the response it's about to receive isn't plain HTML, by setting the HTTP response headers. Every controller in SilverStripe has a `HTTPResponse` object for this purpose, accessible via `$this->getResponse()`. With the `addHeader()` method, we set the HTTP attribute `Content-Type` to `text/xml`. For each of the pages, we now create a custom XML string through the method `getNodeXML()`, similar to the structure described previously (see Listing 11.41). Please implement this method in the existing `FlashTree` class as follows:

```
<?php
class FlashTree extends Controller {
  // ...
  protected function getNodeXML($page) {
    $xml = sprintf(
      "<node id=\"%s\" label=\"%s\" isBranch=\"%s\" classname=\"%s\">\n",
       $page->ID,
      Convert::raw2att($page->Title),
      ($page->Children()->Count()) ? 'false' : 'true',
      $page->ClassName
    );
    if($page->Children()) {
      foreach($page->Children() as $page) {
        $xml .= $this->getNodeXML($page);
      }
    }
    $xml .= "</node>\n";
    return $xml;
  }
}
?>
```

Listing 11.46 *Rendering a single node in XML*

The `getNodeXML()` method returns a chunk of XML just for the page object passed as the method's parameter. The XML template is passed through the PHP function `sprintf()` to dynamically replace the `%s` placeholders with page-specific information. This information is stored in XML attributes, and so we have to ensure carefully that the string is escaped as an XML attribute using `Convert::raw2att()`. This makes sure for example that no unescaped quote marks find their way into the attribute.

Because a page can have children, this method can call itself recursively for each result of `$page->Children()`, gradually building up the nested XML tree. All calls write to the same string stored in `$xml`.

One speciality is the `isBranch` attribute: It's required by the tree component in Adobe Flash and is used as an indicator of whether the current node should be displayed as a branch with a folder icon, or as a simple page. The attribute is set to `true` if the `Children()` method on the currently processed page returns items, otherwise it defaults to `false`.

Now it's time to test the output in action: Without any custom director rules, the URL *http://localhost/FlashTree/xml* links to the XML method on our new controller. Depending on your browser, you should see a nicely formatted XML document or a simple plaintext string. In Figure 11.12 we display the syntax-highlighted output provided by Mozilla Firefox.

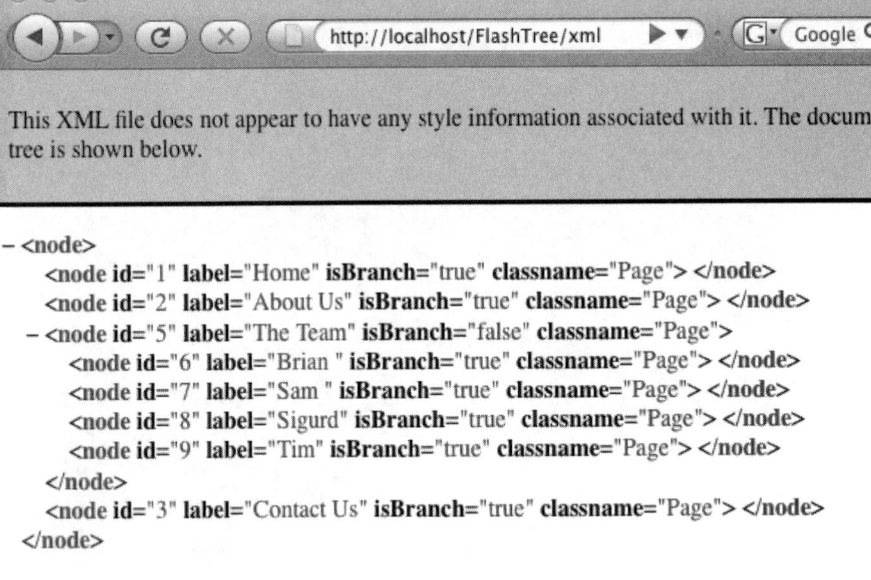

Figure 11.12 XML output in Mozilla Firefox.

11.9.3 Page Tree in Flash

Adobe Flash comes with an extensive and well documented collection of interface components. Many of these components, such as menu bars, calendars, or video players, can be simply activated in the Flash IDE by dragging them into your movie. As an alternative, all components can also be created and configured through your own scripts.

In our case, we choose to use the tree component, which allows us to show the generated XML tree in a nice interactive view without too much fuss. Let's start with opening a new project in Adobe Flash. We store all Flash-related source files and compiled binaries in a new folder *mysite/flash/*. Please name your new document *mysite/flash/index.fla*, and choose Flash Player 9 (or higher) and ActionScript 2 in the settings for creating a new document. The default document width and height with 550px by 400px should be fine for our purposes. Please open the component menu from Window > Components and drag a new Tree component into the stage, as shown in Figure 11.13. Resize it to fill the left side of the screen; this will be our menu.

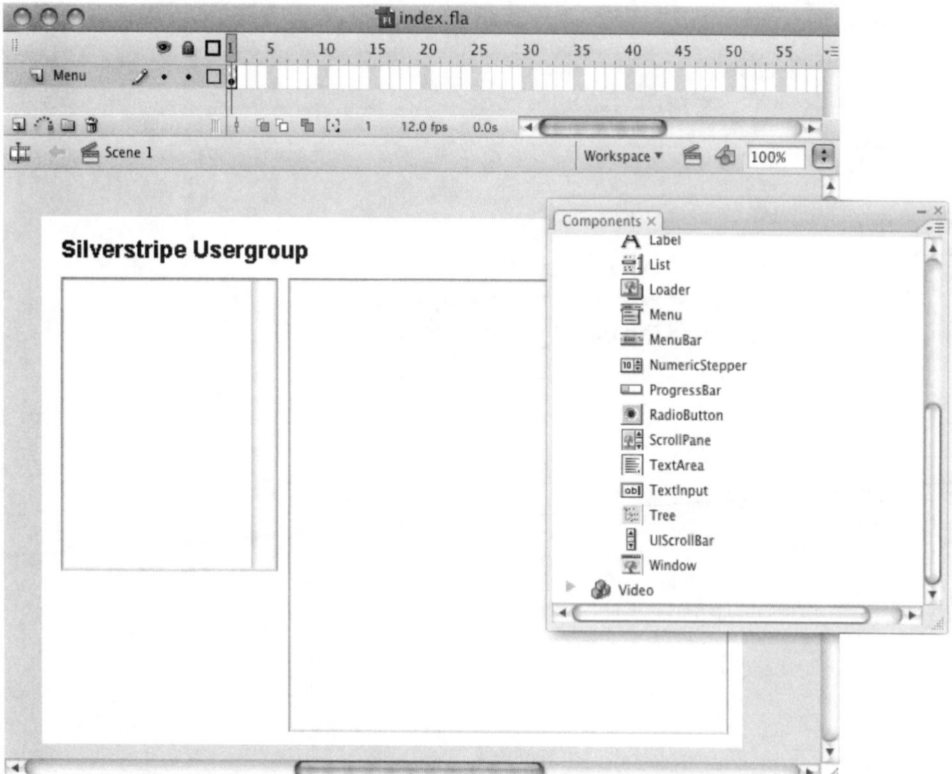

Figure 11.13 Components window and stage in Flash.

The tree component doesn't do much by itself. Instead we have to create some logic to populate it. In Flash, components can be linked to ActionScript classes that contain the customized functionality. Select the empty tree placeholder on the stage, and select Convert to Symbol from the right-click context menu. In the following dialog, tick the checkbox Export for ActionScript and type 'TreeNavMenu' in the Class input field (see Figure 11.14). This ensures that the tree instance is connected to the ActionScript class `TreeNavMenu` that we're about to write.

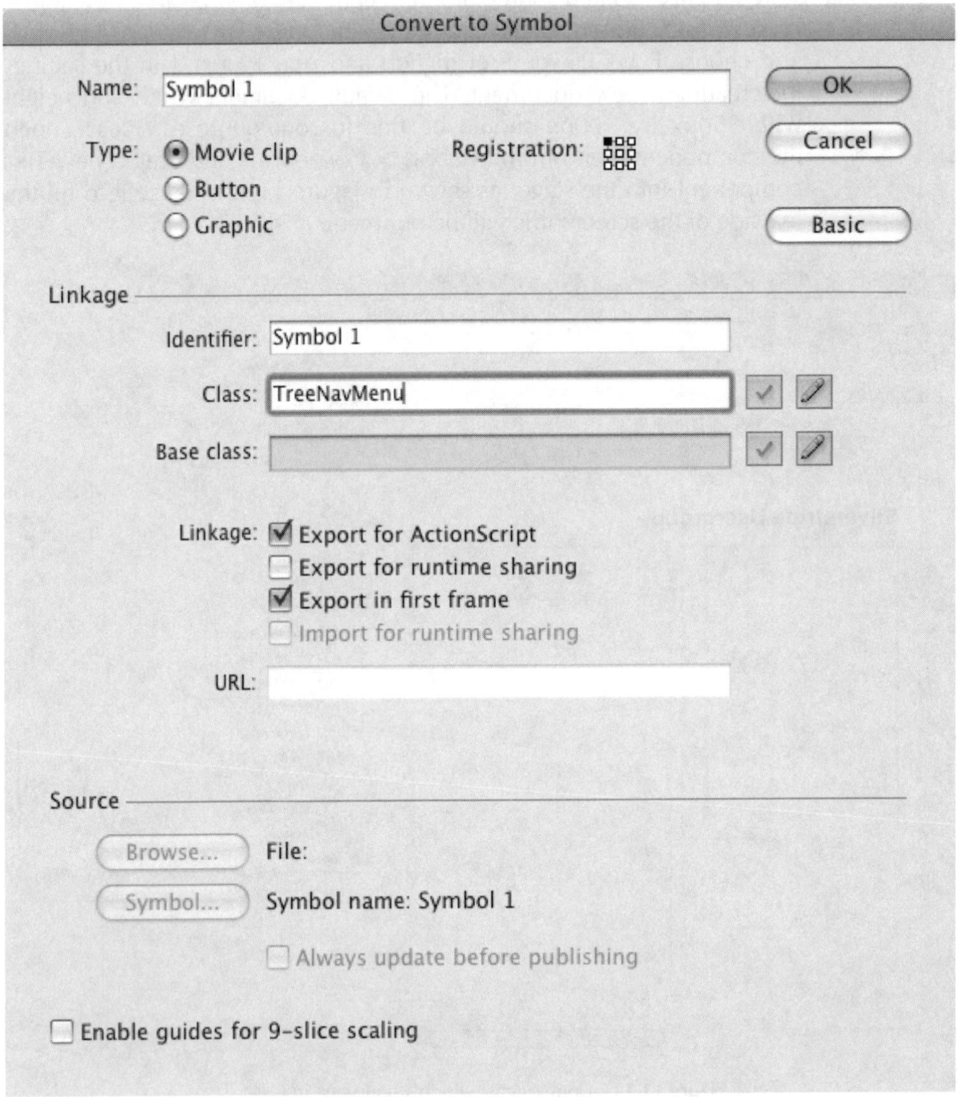

Figure 11.14 'Convert to Symbol' dialog in Flash.

The Flash complier automatically finds ActionScript files with the extension **.as* on the same level as our main Flash file *index.fla,* as long as the class has the same name as the file. Accordingly, we create a new ActionScript file *mysite/flash/TreeNavMenu.as,* and add the following code:

```
import mx.controls.Tree;
import flash.external.ExternalInterface;
import mx.utils.Delegate;
class TreeNavMenu extends MovieClip {
   var menuXML:XML;
   var menuTree:Tree;
   var baseURL:String;
   var menuXMLURL:String;
   function TreeNavMenu() {
      baseURL= "http://localhost/";
      menuXMLURL = baseURL + "/FlashTree/xml";
      menuXML = new XML();
      menuXML.ignoreWhite = true;
      menuXML.onLoad = Delegate.create(this, onMenuLoaded);
      debug("Loading " + menuXMLURL);
      menuXML.load(menuXMLURL);
   }
   function onMenuLoaded(success:Boolean):Void {
      menuTree.dataProvider = menuXML.firstChild;
   }
   function debug(txt:String) {
      trace(txt);
      ExternalInterface.call('console.log',txt);
   }
}
```

Listing 11.47 *mysite/flash/TreeNavMenu.as*

This defines a new class `TreeNavMenu`, which extends `MovieClip`, the base class for most viewable objects on a Flash stage. The `TreeNavMenu()` method serves as a constructor for this class, and will be executed whenever a new instance of it is created. In this method, we're creating an instance of the XML object, which will form the basic input for our tree component. It reads the XML structure from the URL we created in the previous section: *http://localhost/FlashTree/xml*. This URL is constructed from a variable called `baseURL`, which is set to *http://localhost/*. In case this doesn't point to the webroot of your SilverStripe installation, please adjust accordingly. To refresh your memory, this will trigger the `xml()` method on our `FlashTree` controller within SilverStripe.

Before we actually load the data through `menuXML.load(menuXMLURL)`, we have to attach a callback handler that determines what should happen after a successful load operation: the `onMenuLoaded()` method. It's attached to the `menuXML` instance by calling `Delegate.create()`. This is a special notation to change the so-called scope of the passed method (see the following box).

Delegates and variable scope in ActionScript

The term scope defines the visibility and context of symbols in a programming language. Each defined variable in Flash has a scope in which it's accessible by other logic. In ActionScript and other scripting languages, certain methods can be forced to run in a scope other than the scope indicated by their class and method structure. Forcing the scope to change is necessary in the case of event handlers such as `menuXML.onLoad`. Look at the following code:

```
menuXML.onLoad = onMenuLoaded;
function onMenuLoaded(success:Boolean) {
   trace(this); // 'this' points to menuXML, not TreeNavMenu
}
```

As the code comment above demonstrates, `this` poses a problem for us. Because it doesn't have the context of the `nonMenuLoaded`, we couldn't trigger any actions on our tree component from here. To rectify this, we use a special utility class called `Delegate`, part of the ActionScript API. It lets us create and execute the `onMenuLoaded()` method in the `TreeNavMenu` context:

```
Delegate.create(this, onMenuLoaded);
function onMenuLoaded(success:Boolean) {
   trace(this); // 'this' points to TreeNavMenu
}
```

With `onMenuLoaded()` able to operate in the context we need it to, we connect the newly loaded XML data to the tree component: `menuTree.dataProvider = menuXML.firstChild`. We have to use the first child, because the tree component expects all XML nodes on the root level to be direct children which can be displayed in the tree.

With this code in place, we're ready for the first compilation of our ActionScript sources and the *index.fla* file into an *index.swf* file, which can be used within a browser. To compile the SWF, call File > Publish, which creates a new file *mysite/flash/index.swf*. You should be able to review the fruits of our first Flash experiments in your browser: *http://localhost/mysite/flash/index.swf*. Congratulations, you've integrated a simple Flash UI element with SilverStripe in less than two dozen lines of ActionScript.

One more thing: Interactions between an SWF and remote sources like our XML file are notoriously hard to debug. For this purpose, we've written a special method called `debug()`. It has the ability to output information to the Flash console (Window > Output) through the built-in `trace()` command, as well as the JavaScript console in your favorite browser. This browser integration works through the Flash system class `ExternalInterface`, which accepts JavaScript commands such as `console.log()`. Please note that `console.log()` isn't supported in Internet Explorer. However, this technique works very well in Mozilla

Firefox in conjunction with the powerful web developer add-on, Firebug (http://getfirebug.com).

In our case, we output the location of the XML file through `debug()`, which can be quite useful to see whether the SWF actually points to the intended location. In a live environment, we assume that you will remove this debug output.

11.9.4 Content as XML

Of course, displaying a page tree is only half the work, because we still need to enable our visitors to actually see the content of a specific page. Flash supports rendering of basic HTML syntax, which means we should be able to simply insert our content generated by the CMS *WYSIWYG* editor without any conversion, as long as the CMS editors stick to the most common HTML elements. Starting from version 8 (released 2005), Flash even manages to style this markup with simple CSS declarations.

Now, how do we get just the content for a specific page out of SilverStripe, without any surrounding template markup? We could create another controller that's similar to `FlashTree`. As so often, there's many ways to skin a cat. Thankfully, SilverStripe has already skinned this particular cat in a quite reusable fashion through a webservice with the `RestfulServer` class.

If you've read this book from the beginning, you should know that SilverStripe has good integration for RESTful data access. We covered this concept and practical applications in Section 6.10, 'Web Services using RESTfulServer'. `RestfulServer` allows read and write operations on the SilverStripe data model in an easy and standardized fashion. By default, data is accepted and generated in either XML or JSON format.

In our case, read-access is sufficient, because we just want to fetch a few certain fields on an instance of the `Page` class. Because RESTful access is disabled by default, we need to enable it for this class with the static variable `$api_access`:

```
class Page extends SiteTree {
   static $api_access = true;
   // ...
}
```

Listing 11.48 *mysite/code/Page.php (excerpt)*

If the `$api_access` variable is simply left true, it will grant read-only access on all properties and relations on this class. Given that this relates only to pages indicated as published, ideally we should limit exposure to the `Title` and `Content` properties in our Flash 'template'.

This will reduce the quantity of information that needs to be sent to the browser, and prevent private fields from being exposed, such as the security settings for the page. To restrict the RESTfulServer in this way, exchange your `$api_access` definition with the following more restricted rules:

```
class Page extends SiteTree {
   static $api_access = array(
      'view' => array('Title', 'Content')
   );
   // ...
}
```

Listing 11.49 *mysite/code/Page.php*

Note that by default the API doesn't permit updates, and so the configuration we have created doesn't open the site up to a security hole.

Access to a read-only resource through REST simply happens in your browser. `RestfulServer` automatically provides the necessary URL routing. As an example, try loading a specific page by ID: *http://localhost/api/v1/Page/1*. When you're not sure which IDs exist on your installation, remove the last part of the URL to get an overview of all pages instead: *http://localhost/api/v1/Page*. The resulting XML for a specific page is shown in Listing 11.50, slightly abbreviated.

```
<?xml version="1.0" encoding="UTF-8"?>
   <Page href="/api/v1/Page/1.xml">
    <Title>About Us</Title>
   <Content>&lt;p&gt;Welcome to SilverStripe! This is the default
homepage. You can edit this page by opening &lt;a href="admin/"&gt;the
CMS&lt;/a&gt;. </Content>
   ...
   <ID>1</ID>
   ...
</Page>
```

Listing 11.50 *http://localhost/api/v1/Page/1.xml*

As you can see, one of the XML nodes contained in this document is `<Content>`. This is the data that we will be feeding into Flash.

11.9.5 Content in Flash

Displaying HTML markup within Flash is handled by another built-in interface component, TextArea (see Figure 11.15). You can drag an instance of this component onto your stage by using the component menu (WINDOW > COMPONENTS). First of all, we need to tell this new instance to accept HTML formatting, by opening the component inspector (Window > Component Inspector) while it's selected on the stage. Set the property EDITABLE to FALSE, and HTML to TRUE. Now we need to name our component, so we can address it later through ActionScript. Open the properties panel (WINDOW > PROPERTIES) and type 'Content_txt' as the field name.

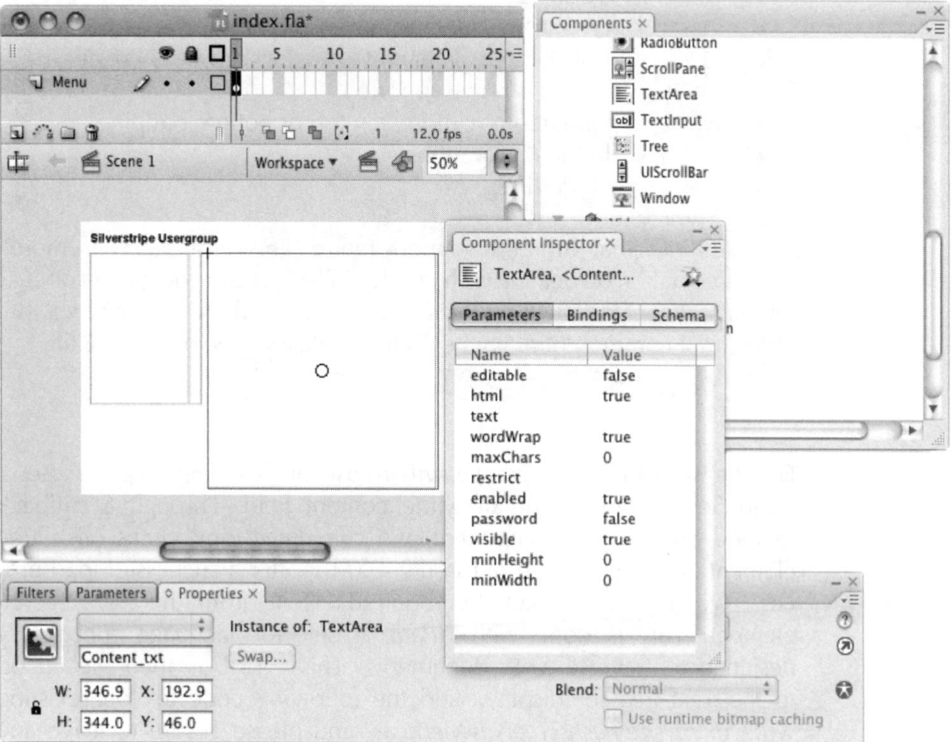

Figure 11.15 Adding a TextArea component in Flash.

HTML support in Flash

Support for HTML markup is quite rudimentary compared to your average web-browser. The majority of supported HTML elements are intended for inline text formatting rather than block level modifications. Unknown tags are generally silently ignored and their content displayed as though the tag wasn't there. Please keep in mind that all tags should be written like HTML rather than XHTML, which mainly means no self-closing tags. Flash accepts both uppercase (e.g., `<B>`) and lower-case (e.g., `<b>`) elements:

- `<a>` Link or anchor, without underline styling; attributes `href, target.`
- `<b>` Bold text.
- `<br>` Line break.
- `<font>` Font styling; attributes: `face, size, color.`
- `<img>` Images in the formats GIF, JPG, PNG; attributes: `src, width, height, id, align, hspace, vspace.`
- `<i>` Emphasis (styled as italics).
- `<li>` List element; no parent `<ul>` tags are required; nesting of lists is now supported.
- `<p>` Paragraph, without any top or bottom padding.
- `<span>` Inline declarations.
- `<u>` Underline.

Please note that all tags support the `class` attribute. For more documentation on dealing with HTML in Flash, see the developer documentation for Flash 8: http://livedocs.adobe.com/flash/8/main/wwhelp/wwhimpl/common/html/wwhelp.htm?context=LiveDocs_Parts&file=00001457.html.

For the sake of simplicity we will re-use our existing `TreeNavMenu` ActionScript class to initialize the content field. Through a callback method on the tree component, we can detect any clicks on a tree element, and trigger load our content XML. After a successful load process, we need to extract the required HTML from the `<Content>` element. This is done with *XPath,* a selector language specifically designed to traverse XML documents. This HTML is then passed on to the TextArea for display. Add the following code to your existing work in *mysite/flash/TreeNavMenu.as,* and please ensure to leave any omissions from previous code intact, as denoted by a comment ('`// ...`'):

```
// ...
class TreeNavMenu extends MovieClip {
   // ...
   var pageXML:XML;
   var contentTextField:TextField;
   function TreeNavMenu() {
      // ...
      contentTextField = _root.Content_txt;
      pageXML = new XML();
      pageXML.ignoreWhite = true;
      pageXML.onLoad = Delegate.create(this, onContentLoaded);
   }
   function onMenuLoaded(success:Boolean):Void {
      menuTree.dataProvider = menuXML.firstChild;
```

```
    menuTree.addEventListener("change", Delegate.create(this,
change));
  }
  function change(event:Object) {
    if (menuTree == event.target) {
      var pageXMLURL = this.baseURL + "api/v1/Page/" +
        menuTree.selectedItem.attributes.id + ".xml";
      debug("Loading & + pageXMLURL)
      pageXML.load(pageXMLURL);
    }
  }
  function onContentLoaded(event:Object) {
    var contentNode = XPathAPI.selectSingleNode(
      pageXML.firstChild,
      '/*/Content'
    );
    var contentStr:String = contentNode.firstChild.nodeValue.
split("\r\n").join("\n");
    this.contentTextField.text = contentStr;
  }
  // ...
}
```

Listing 11.51 *mysite/flash/TreeNavMenu.as (excerpt)*

The references to `menuTree` and `menuXML` existed in our first version of this ActionScript code. Newcomers are the reference to the variable `contentTextField`, which we link in from the main stage as denoted by `_root.Content_txt`. As you might remember, we named our TextArea instance accordingly.

As we're loading a second set of XML data, we need another placeholder for it. Let's call it `pageXML`.

In our `TreeNavMenu` class, we define a new method `change()` to handle clicks on the tree component. It listens for events that have the same name ('change') on the `menuTree`, meaning that it's run whenever a visitor clicks on a tree node. Because each tree node is associated with the XML from which it was created, we can get to the database identifier for a specific page: `menuTree.selectedItem.attributes.id`. With this information, we can construct the URL that accesses SilverStripe's RESTfulServer and retrieve the necessary XML.

Once the XML for a specific page has been loaded, we parse it via the built-in class `XPathAPI` for its `Content` attribute, and assign the content to the TextArea field:

```
var contentNode = XPathAPI.selectSingleNode(
    pageXML.firstChild,
    '/*/Content'
);
this.contentTextField.text = contentNode.firstChild.nodeValue;
```

With this code in place, it's time to recompile our SWF file with FILE > PUBLISH. Check out the result at *http://localhost/mysite/flash/index.swf*!

11.9.6 CSS Stylesheets in Flash

As we hinted in the earlier box 'HTML support in Flash', HTML support in Flash is basic. Even a basic assumption such as automatic underlining of links is false. Heading elements such as `<h1>` are displayed as normal text without any different formatting. To remedy this situation, we make use of its CSS support. We can teach Flash on a very basic level how to style certain elements by loading an external CSS file and assigning it to our TextArea instance. Please add the following code to the existing `TreeNavMenu` class:

```
// ...
class TreeNavMenu extends MovieClip {
   // ...
   var textStyles:TextField.StyleSheet;
   function TreeNavMenu() {
      // ...
      textStyles = new TextField.StyleSheet();
      textStyles.onLoad = Delegate.create(this,onStyleLoaded);
      var textStylesURL = baseURL +
         'mysite/flash/typography.css';
      debug("Loading & + textStylesURL);
      textStyles.load(textStylesURL);
   }
   function onStyleLoaded(success:Boolean):Void {
      contentTextField.styleSheet = textStyles;
   }
   // ...
}
```

Listing 11.52 *mysite/flash/TreeNavMenu.as (excerpt)*

Stylesheets in ActionScript are handled through the `TextField.StyleSheet` class. We create a new variable `textStyles` of this type. The actual CSS declarations are fairly simple, because Flash only understands a limited subset of the CSS1 specification, as detailed in http://livedocs.adobe.com/flash/9.0/main/00000908.html. Please insert the following CSS in a new file named *mysite/flash/typography.css*:

```
h1 {font-size: 20px;font-weight: bold;}
h2 {font-size: 16px;font-weight: bold;}
h3 {font-size: 14px;font-weight: bold;}
strong {font-weight: bold;display: inline;}
em {font-style: italic;display: inline;}
a {text-decoration: underline;}
.underline {text-decoration: underline;}
```

Listing 11.53 *mysite/flash/typography.css*

11.9.7 Integration into SilverStripe Templates

Until now, we viewed the SWF file directly in the browser, which wouldn't let visitors to our website find it. We could take people visiting our homepage and redirect them to *mysite/flash/index.swf* and be done with it.

But let's go a step beyond making it easier to load the Flash version of the site. For each page on our website, let's produce a separate standard HTML version of our page to complement the rich Flash one. All our website content is stored in the SilverStripe database – we just need to write an HTML-based website template to compliment our *index.swf.*

Our approach means that given any page location, such as *http://localhost/about-us/,* the mark-up will contain the normal HTML content *and* attempt to load the Flash version. In a sense this is a form of *progressive enhancement,* meaning that computers without Flash installed get to see a normal HTML website. When users access the website with Flash installed, they get an enhanced experience, without even realizing that an HTML version exists. Ensuring that we have an HTML version available helps in corporate environments where Flash may not be installed, and also aids accessibility and ensures that Google can spider your website.

To decide when to show the Flash object, we use an external JavaScript library called SWFObject (http://code.google.com/p/swfobject/). We can also use it to notify the visitor when they're missing the Flash Player plugin and suggest that installing Flash could provide an improved website experience.

Flash files and search-engine optimization

Although search engines such as Google have begun to index content within SWF files, they're usually disregarding any dynamically loaded content such as our RESTful API calls. Google actively recommends providing text-based alternatives for all non-text files including SWF. Because each of our HTML pages should be linked through a simple menu, and is addressable through its own URL, we can ensure that Google will find all public content on our website.

For more information on Google's support of Flash, read their FAQ: http://www.google.com/support/webmasters/bin/answer.py?hl=en&answer=72746.

You should already have a `Page_Controller` defined alongside your `Page` class in the SilverStripe standard installation, in *mysite/code/Page.php.* We will edit this controller so that our website includes the JavaScript files that handle the redirection and Flash display.

Download SWFObject from http://code.google.com/p/swfobject and extract the files into *mysite/javascript/swfobject/*. Then add the following code to your existing *mysite/code/Page.php* file:

```
<?php
// ...
class Page_Controller extends ContentController {
   function init() {
      parent::init();
      // ...
      if($this->URLSegment != 'Security') {
         Requirements::javascript(
            'mysite/javascript/swfobject/swfobject.js'
         );
         Requirements::customScript("
            swfobject.embedSWF(
               '" . project() . "/flash/index.swf',
               'Content', '550', '400', '9.0.0'
            );
         ");
      }
   }
}
```

Listing 11.54 *mysite/code/Page.php*

The *SWFObject* library automatically adds the necessary `<object>` and `<embed>` markup when calling the `swfobject.embedSWF()` method. We ensure that this method is run by adding a snippet of JavaScript: `Requirements::customScript()` writes it into the document body. The `embedSWF()` method takes a few parameters:

- The first is the relative path to the *index.swf* we worked hard to create earlier.
- The second parameter passes the ID of an HTML container, which should be replaced by the SWF file. In our case this is `<div id="Content">`, which is already present in the default BlackCandy theme.
- The third and fourth parameters specify the desired width and height in pixels. We want these to match the dimensions of our Flash file.
- The last parameter (`"9.0.0"`) specifies the minimum required version of the Flash Player browser plugin. If SWFObject determines that Flash is missing or outdated, our viewer gets redirected to a page explaining how to upgrade.

In our `init()` method, we have to adapt for one special case: We don't want any Flash content on system pages such as the login form. By checking `$this->URLSegment`, we exclude all URLs starting with

'Security' from the Flash rewriting. This ensures that we can still access *http://localhost/Security/login/* and can therefore login to the CMS.

Now please try to access your website through *http://localhost/* instead of the direct path to our SWF file. The HTML content should be replaced by its Flash representation. Keep in mind that URLs of sub-pages will still display the homepage within the SWF file because our ActionScript logic currently doesn't select the correct page within the tree structure. This could be remedied by passing a GET variable through to the Flash file. You could also write logic to allow people *with* Flash to clink a link and opt to view the HTML version.

To confirm that the HTML is actually still present underneath the shiny Flash content, try to disable JavaScript in your browser and refresh the page. Voilà! A search-engine friendly HTML template appears (see Figure 11.16).

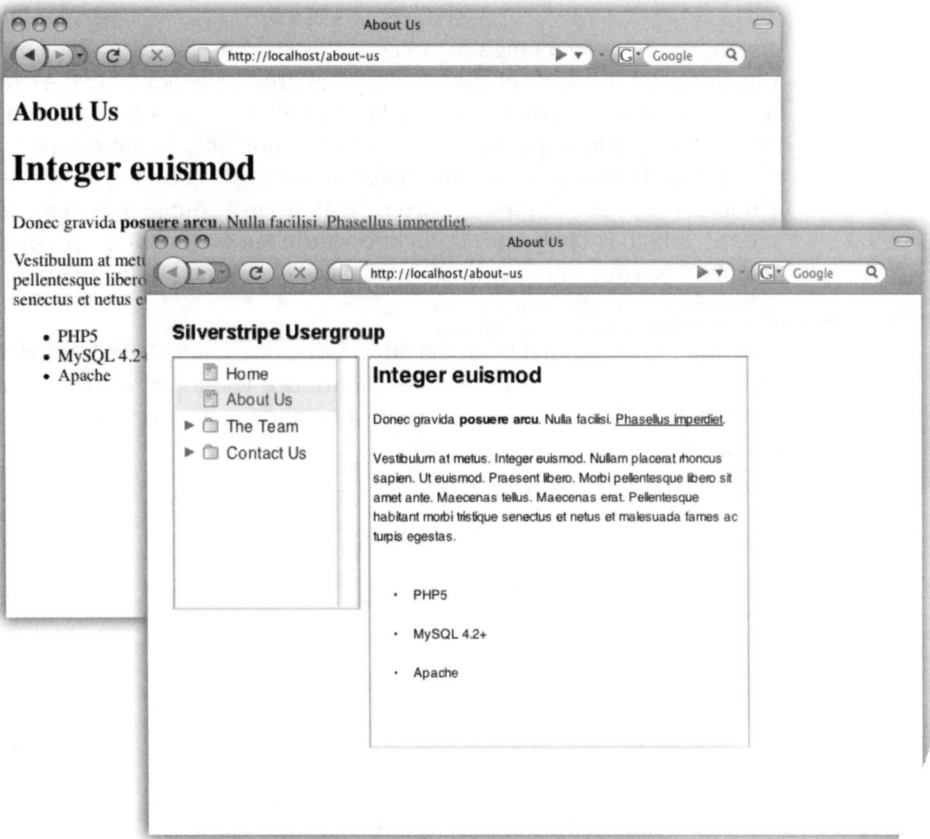

Figure 11.16 Unobtrusive and Flash display side-by-side.

11.9.8 Conclusion

We demonstrated that content created through SilverStripe doesn't have to be delivered as HTML. Thanks to the flexible support for various output formats, we're able to transport both hierarchical data and page information as XML with just a small amount of PHP. Flash can then be used to pull in CMS content easily using built-in interface components and its scripting environment. Because Flash has adequate support for rendering HTML and CSS, SilverStripe can be used to re-purpose the same content for both an HTML- and a Flash-based website.

Flash might not be considered the universal answer for content on the web, but in certain contexts it can form a powerful alliance with SilverStripe. This is illustrated nicely by a HTML and Flash website powered by SilverStripe at http://thelowdown.co.nz/.

11.10 Conclusion

We addressed quite a range of topics in this chapter, but overall it's only a small insight of what's possible with SilverStripe. The power of the CMS lies in easy customization through PHP logic. The sapphire framework makes it simple to implement your own functionality, to the extent that it's sufficiently easy to write certain features from scratch. As you can see in our recipes, you can create powerful features in a couple of dozen lines of code, which is often more straightforward than configuring a pre-built module through some graphical interface without the means to change its behavior through source code.

More recipes are available on the SilverStripe documentation: http://doc.silverstripe.com/?id=recipes. We also introduce you to some more complex functionality, such as spam protection and creating image galleries, in Chapter 13.

12
Extending

An increasing number of companies are deciding to open-source their software projects. They're not necessarily doing this only out of the goodness of their hearts or a desire to let software users enjoy liberty around their source code. Their reason for choosing open-source is also motivated by wanting their software to become well-known, grow a community around it, and thanks to the community, improve the quality and breadth of the product's features.

This is true of SilverStripe. And for there to be an active developer community, the software needs to be conducive to allowing the community to contribute, share, and use the work of other developers. The architecture of SilverStripe directly supports this aim by having logical and intentionally-designed means for extending and customizing the core application. This ability to extend the core obviously has real practical benefits in day-to-day development: It lets you reuse code from one project to the next; it lets you create robust code that's cleanly separated into logical components; and it means that when time comes to upgrade your site to the latest version of SilverStripe, you don't have to painstakingly manage changes you made to SilverStripe's core PHP files.

This chapter goes into detail about how to make significant changes to the CMS. We show you how to do things that are well beyond merely adding new forms to the backend. Advanced developers can take the principles explained in this chapter and create sophisticated content-managed websites that have a sound underlying technical architecture.

The files related to this chapter can be found in the *12_extending/* folder on the download archive from the book's companion website.

12.1 Different Ways to Extend SilverStripe

The concept of a code extension can take many forms in SilverStripe: It ranges from a simple class in your custom project that might add tagging behavior to your DataObjects, to code providing forum functionality, including its own templates and page types.

Here are some examples of possible areas of extension:

- Frontend: Gallery code that can display images using a variety of interesting templates.
- Backend: A new admin interface to moderate user-generated comments.
- Widgets: Small configurable helpers displayed alongside your website templates, for example a list of newly subscribed members.
- Integration: Using web-services and other kinds of integration such as displaying images from photo sharing sites, LDAP integration for single sign on, or fetching information from billing systems, etc.
- Developer tools and scripts: Command-line scripts, helpers for migrating from other platforms to SilverStripe, database maintenance, etc.

If the functionality is generic enough to be portable and reuseable between projects, it usually takes the form of a *module*. One of the main characteristics of a module is very simple: Each module has its own top-level folder in the SilverStripe installation. We describe some of the major existing modules in Chapter 13, 'Useful Modules'.

12.2 Extending Core Functions

Now we show you how you can extend the core functionality of SilverStripe. For this purpose, we use techniques such as *class inheritance*, the *Extension* class, and *callback* functions.

12.2.1 Class Inheritance

Core functions can generally be extended by using *class inheritance*. You're already familiar with using inheritance for adding functionality to classes such as `Page`, which inherits functionality and properties from its parent classes: You extend the class in a custom *subclass*, and then derive existing methods and create new methods and attributes to suit your needs.

As a little illustrative example, we want the validator of a `NumericField` input field to accept only positive values for a specific field on a form. Currently there's no configuration option in `NumericField` to set this limitation. Our first instinct might be to either re-implement the functionality or copy the existing code. By using a subclass, we need to only overload the necessary validation logic, while the rest of the class such as the saving logic can be safely inherited. Let's call our subclass `PositiveNumericField`, and place the following code in *mysite/code/PositiveNumericField.php*:

```
<?php
class PositiveNumericField extends NumericField {
   function jsValidation() {
      return '';
   }
   function validate($validator){
      if($this->value && !is_numeric($this->value)){
          $validator->validationError(
             $this->name,
             'Only numbers are allowed',
             "validation"
         );
         return false;
      } else if($this->value && $this->value < 0){
          $validator->validationError(
             $this->name,
             'Only positive values are allowed',
             "validation"
         );
         return false;
      } else{
         return true;
      }
   }
}
?>
```

Listing 12.1 *mysite/code/PositiveNumericField.php*

Let's go through this code step-by-step:

- The `class PositiveNumericField extends NumericField` statement defines a new class that inherits from the existing `NumericField` class in the SilverStripe framework.
- To keep things simple we want to disable the JavaScript validation that's defined on the parent implementation, and focus on PHP validation instead. We override the `jsValidation()` method and make it return `false`. Adding client-side validation is a great way to improve the user experience and so we suggest that you do this in a

real-world scenario. In this example, it's simply omitted to keep the example short and understandable.

- We also override the `validate()` method with our own code to test two assertions: Is the value a number? If it is, then is it a positive number?

Because this class is placed in your *mysite/* folder (or any other folder containing a *_config.php* file), it's immediately available throughout your project and can be used to build a form for your website.

Check the book's website. On it you will find a sample form to test the validation in *mysite/code/PositiveNumericDemo.php*, accessible through your browser via *http://localhost/PositiveNumericDemo/*.

12.2.2 DataObjectDecorator: An Alternative to Class Inheritance

SilverStripe uses *extensions* for influencing core API functionality without direct subclasses. Extensions are a very flexible mechanism that can be used as an alternative to the standard PHP *single class inheritance*. They allow us to extend the behavior of a class during runtime. This kind of dynamic method injection is a useful way of getting around PHP's lack of support for *mixins*. Mixins are a language tool which allows a class to implement behavior from more than one superclass. They defer definition and binding of methods and properties to runtime, after the class has actually been defined.

Why is this necessary? Assume you're developing a module that needs to add its own properties and behavior to the `Member` class. The `Member` class is defined in SilverStripe core. We could subclass it, but what if a different project using your module already has its own subclass of `Member`? For the sake of code separation, your custom project code shouldn't have to change the SilverStripe core or your module – it wants to *extend* both of them.

Another way of thinking of extensions in SilverStripe is to regard them as a neat object-oriented way of creating *callbacks*. Code can be run before and after a given method, without having to resort to procedural-style callbacks, which can quickly become messy and complex to follow. One good example here is influencing the `DataObject->write()` logic with the `onBeforeWrite()` and `onAfterWrite()` callbacks.

To make use of this technique, you create extensions that inherit from the abstract base class `DataObjectDecorator`. Please note that contrary to the phrase *Decorator* in this class name, SilverStripe extensions don't completely follow the common *Decorator* design pattern as described in the popular book *Design Patterns: Elements of Reusable Object-Oriented Software* by Erich Gamma, Richard Helm, Ralph Johnson, and John

Vlissides. The `DataObjectDecorator` class aims to provide a similar benefit to the Decorator design pattern of extending classes, but leaves the developer with more flexibility in the implementation.

An Example: Versioning DataObjects

That all sounds quite abstract. Therefore, we're going to show you an example for a piece of core functionality, which is already implemented as an extension and solves a real problem quite elegantly: Versioning.

SilverStripe allows you to keep a record of different versions of a page edited through the CMS or otherwise. These versions are stored in their own separate database table. One way of implementing this feature would be to simply add it to the `Page` class. However, what would we do if we later wanted to add this feature to another object that doesn't inherit from `Page`? Suppose that we wanted to make one of our `DataObject` subclasses 'versionable'. We might, for example, want to store a change history of the `Job` class we've created in previous chapters. This way of archiving might be useful to verify that a job advertisement had a specific content at some point in time, or for more than one job author to collaborate on the content.

The `Job` class inherits from `DataObject`, not from `Page`. If versioning would be implemented as methods and properties on the `Page` class, the only way to attach this functionality would be to copy code to our `Job` class. However, this violates the *DRY* principle ('Don't repeat yourself'), and therefore can later lead to problems with code maintenance and data integrity.

SilverStripe makes it easier for us to reuse the versioning behavior, because it is encapsulated into an extension independent of the `Page` class. The extension is called `Versioned`, and derives from the `DataObject-Decorator` base class. Very little code is required to attach this behavior to our own implementation in *mysite/code/Job.php*:

```
<?php
class Job extends DataObject {
   // ...
   static $extensions = array(
      "Versioned('Live')"
   );
}
?>
```

Listing 12.2 *mysite/code/Job.php (excerpt)*

The `Versioned` class is attached to our custom `Job` class through a static array called `$extensions`. You can add multiple extensions here as an evaluated string containing a PHP constructor call, in our case `"Versioned('Live')"`. The argument is necessary to determine the names of different *versioning stages*. We stick to the stage named `Live`, but because there's only one stage in our case the naming doesn't influence behavior.

After adding the configuration and updating the database schema using *http://localhost/dev/build/*, we can see that the logic in the `Versioned` extension has defined a number of additions to the database schema and the SilverStripe model. Specifically, we get a new database table named *Job_versions*. This new table contains the same columns as the *Job* table, and gains additional columns that describe the author and version number. The version number makes each archived version of your object referenceable later on, for example to compare with a newer version, or to 'rollback' and restore old content.

Now every time the `Job` object is saved, the *Job* table is updated and a new version is created in the *Job_versions* table. Note that you can directly access a particular version of any given page:

```
$latestVersion = Versioned::get_latest_version('Job', <ID>);
$someVersion = Versioned::get_version('Job', <ID>, <Version>);
```

The extension has also added some new magic methods to the `Job` class. For example, you can list the history of versions of a specific object:

```
$job = DataObject::get_by_id('Job',<ID>);
$versions = $job->allVersions();
```

As you can see, you can create a module with extensions and use them to modify core SilverStripe classes, without having to change the actual core class code. The most common way to enable extensions is at runtime, by adding the following command to your *_config.php* file:

```
Object::add_extension(
    '<my-dataobject-class>',
    '<my-extension-class>'
);
```

We've already seen this syntax used in Chapter 10, where the *Translatable* extension provides the ability for pages to be in multiple languages. This extension can be enabled via the following code:

```
Object::add_extension('SiteTree', 'Translatable');
```

Please note that we don't describe here how to build an interface to view different versions for our DataObjects (for example, through `ModelAdmin`).

Building Your Own Extension: Taggable

Do you remember the tags feature we used in previous chapters to store `Developer` skills? We might want tags to be available for all other classes and create a backend management interface for entering and editing tags. However, we want to avoid having to duplicate the necessary code, and instead allow ourselves to reuse this concept in other website projects, and even share it with other SilverStripe developers. Naturally, `DataObjectDecorator` is the way to go.

First we create a new subclass of `DataObjectDecorator` named `Taggable`. This class will contain some of the functionality we've written previously in custom code. Create the file *mysite/code/Taggable.php* and add the following code:

```
<?php
class Taggable extends DataObjectDecorator {
   function extraStatics() {
      return array(
         'db' => array(
            'TagsText' => 'Text'
         )
      );
   }
   function updateCMSFields(&$fields) {
      $fields->addFieldToTab('Root.Main',
         new TextField('TagsText')
      );
   }
   function getTagsCollection() {
      $set = new DataObjectSet();
      $tags = split(' ', $this->owner->TagsText);
      if($tags) foreach($tags as $tag) {
         $set->push(new ArrayData(array(
            'Title' => $tag
         )));
      }
      return $set;
   }
}
?>
```

Listing 12.3 *mysite/code/Taggable.php*

We now take a closer look at this code:

- The `extraStatics()` method allows us to add additional static variables to a given DataObject. In our case we're adding the `TagsText` property to the `static $db` variable. These additional attributes are evaluated at runtime, when the extension is added. Additional 'extendable' variables are `$has_one`, `$has_many`, `$many_many`, `$defaults`, etc. – all the typical static variable you would define on a DataObject.
- The `updateCMSFields()` makes it possible for the extension to modify the tabs and fields of the CMS, and is the extension equivalent to the `getCMSFields()` method you should already be familiar with. A reference to the existing interface (`&$fields`) is used as the argument of this method, which means you don't have to return the modified property from the method. We can then modify the interface, as we see fit. Here we use the `$fields-> addFieldToTab(...)` method to add an addition `TextField`. The `updateCMSFields()` method is called on all DataObjects that have been enhanced with the `Taggable` extension.
- We can also add new methods to the extended class. The `getTagsCollection()` method is added so that we have a means to output tags in a usable format. We do this by filling a `DataObjectSet` with instances of `ArrayData` (see the following box), containing only the *Title* attribute. Note: We need to use `$this->owner` instead of just using `$this` to access the attributes of the decorated DataObject.

ArrayData: A simple renderable data container

You can use the `ArrayData` class to add a map to an object in such a way that it can be referenced in a SilverStripe template. For example:

```
$comments = DataObject::get('Comment');
$data = new ArrayData(array(
   "MyTitle" => "Awesome Website",
   "MyComments" => $comments
));
echo $data->renderWith('MyTemplate');
```

When rendering this construct in a template, the placeholders `$MyTitle` and `$MyComments` become available. As you can see, `ArrayData` can contain more than just simple scalar values – you can nest `ArrayData` structures as well as assign other containers such as a `DataObjectSet` to its own placeholder.

Now we need to add the extension to the `SiteTree` class, which forms the basis of all pages in the CMS. As we don't want to modify the SiteTree code itself, we can't use the assignment through a static variable $extensions. We have to resort to the alternative Object::add_extension() notation. Please add the following line to your *mysite/_config.php* file:

```
<?php
// ...
Object::add_extension('SiteTree', 'Taggable');
?>
```

Listing 12.4 *mysite/_config.php (excerpt)*

We're now ready to write the code to access the tags feature in our templates. Add the following code to *themes/mysite/templates/Layout/Page.ss*, which adds the feature to viewable pages on your website:

```
<ul>
   <% control TagsCollection %>
      <li>$Title</li>
   <% end_control %>
</ul>
```

The TagsCollection placeholder within the template runs the getTagsCollection() method on the extension. So, we're successfully calling a method on an object without it having been defined on that object, demonstrating our extension is available throughout our project.

Now SiteTree and all its subclasses contain the features implemented by the Taggable extension. You can add as many extensions to as many classes as you like.

12.2.3 Influencing Actions Through Callbacks

Sometimes you might not be interested in extending a class with new data and behavior, but want to change the current behavior. SilverStripe provides a multitude of methods that hook into core functionality, known as *callbacks*. Sometimes they're used to avoid deriving and reimplementing a large method. Often these callbacks are also exposed through extensions, which make them very powerful tools.

Suppose you want to send an email just before a particular page type is saved to the database, perhaps to notify the original author of a change to his or her work. You could derive the write() method on DataObject, although this might quickly become a maintenance burden. In SilverStripe, the more light-weight callbacks onBeforeWrite() and onAfterWrite() are available on all DataObjects instead. See the example below showing the callback method doing the necessary work:

```
<?php
class Page extends SiteTree {
   function onBeforeWrite() {
       mail(
         'admin@example.com',
         "Page '$this->Title' saved"
       );
       parent::onBeforeWrite();
   }
}
?>
```

Listing 12.5 *mysite/code/Page.php*

Keep in mind that this method will now unconditionally save emails. You might want to limit this process to more specific events, and perhaps email where only the `Content` field of a page has been changed. See Section 5.6.3, 'Saving the Author' for another example of how to use callback.

12.3 Creating Custom Modules

No CMS can contain every conceivable feature, and with SilverStripe that is deliberately shied away from because it would bloat the project. The great thing about a good CMS is that a skilled programmer can extend it to meet the needs of the project at hand.

We've already covered a bunch of different ways of extending SilverStripe in the previous sections. However, we haven't yet explained how to bundle everything together into a module. After reading this section you'll understand how to use modules as a very convenient way of wrapping up functionality, reusing it on different projects, and porting it between systems.

12.3.1 Defining a Module

A module is simply a folder in the SilverStripe webroot folder. It must contain a *_config.php* file that details its configuration. Without this file, SilverStripe ignores the folder, which is how SilverStripe can co-exist with an entirely separate PHP application installed next to it. This *_config.php* file also provides the default location for the configuration settings for a module, and therefore determines how it interfaces with the rest of the system. SilverStripe automatically searches for PHP classes in the PHP files of a module, and makes them available to the rest of the application.

Think back to our example job portal application. Could parts of it be reused in other projects? Let's consider which parts of our application have some potential for reuse and turn them into a module. A good example is the job posting interface that we developed in Chapter 6. The flexible SilverStripe module architecture makes it possible to *modularize* certain parts of your code simply by moving some files around.

Please ensure that you have our example project code from Chapter 6 handy. We'll subsequently move some of the files and functionality from there into its new 'portable home'. Create a new folder named *jobs/* in the SilverStripe webroot. This is where we're going to put the data for our new module. Create the file and folder structure shown in Figure 12.1 within the *jobs/* folder. Please create an empty *_config.php* file inside this folder; it's required to tell SilverStripe that this folder is a part of a SilverStripe application.

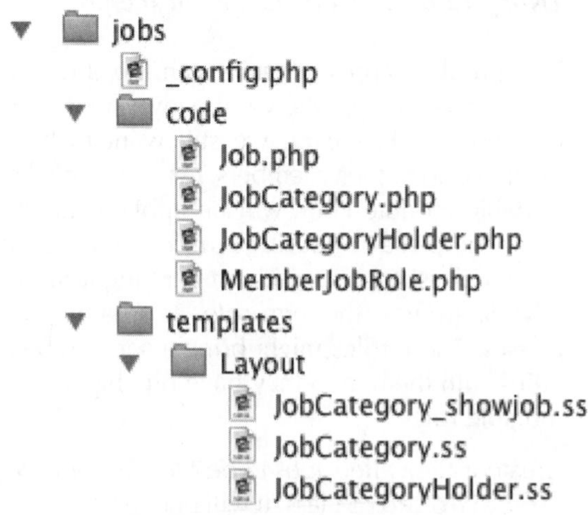

Figure 12.1 Example module folder.

The files within the module should all be familiar. Please move them out of your *mysite/* and *themes/* folders from the Chapter 6 example code. Take care to move rather than copy the files, otherwise you'll get conflicts with classes being defined twice in your webroot.

12.3.2 Adapting Our Code to be a Module

Moving the files was the easy part – now we need to perform some modifications to the existing code to make it portable.

The `Job` class contains a relation to an `Author`, which points to the `Developer` class. However, `Developer` isn't part of our new module. If it was, it would make our module specific to an IT job board, and here we want to illustrate how to make a generic module that can be used for any type of industry job board. So, because `Developer` is a subclass of

Member, we need to change the reference to the Member class, which is part of the core system. Please do this now by opening *jobs/code/Job.php* and changing the has-one relationship to the following code:

```
<?php
class Job extends DataObject {
   static $has_one = array(
      // before: 'Author' => 'Developer'
      'Author' => 'Member',
   );
   // ...
}
?>
```

Listing 12.6 *jobs/code/Job.php (excerpt)*

This problem appears again with the Subscriptions relation on the Developer class. We've already stated that Developer isn't part of our module. However, we still want to have the subscription feature available for other members. As we don't know in which context our portable module code will be applied, we can't simply subclass Member. The DataObjectDecorator class comes in handy to extend the system class Member without deriving from it. Specifically for members, SilverStripe uses the term *roles* as a naming convention for its extension classes. These roles might bring a specific behavior and their own properties with them, and they have one big advantage: A member can have multiple roles.

Create a file called *jobs/code/MemberJobRole.php,* which will hold the MemberJobRole class. It will derive from the DataObjectDecorator class. Insert the following code into the newly created file:

```
<?php
class MemberJobRole extends DataObjectDecorator {
   function extraStatics() {
      return array(
         'belongs_many_many' => array(
            'JobCategorySubscriptions' => 'JobCategory'
         )
      );
   }
}
?>
```

Listing 12.7 *jobs/code/MemberJobRole.php*

We've already introduced the extraStatics() method in Section 12.2.2. It is used to add additional static variables to the extended class. In our case, we're defining a new many-many relation via the `belongs_many_many` array key. This takes care of moving the relation from its previous place in the `Developer` class to its new home, the `Member` class, without modifying the core class in the process. Now we just need to link our extension to the original class by using `Object::add_extension()`. Add the following code in your empty *jobs/_config.php* file that we created earlier:

```
<?php
Object::add_extension('Member', 'MemberJobRole');
?>
```

Listing 12.8 *jobs/_config.php*

Update the database schema to create the relationship tables. Note that if you still have the class definition for `Developer` in your code, you should remove the `'JobCategorySubscriptions'` relation from there. Please keep in mind that any existing relationships between developers and job categories will have been lost.

We have a shiny new module that provides a backend job postings management interface!

Releasing your modules

The SilverStripe project lives through the spirit of sharing, like any other open-source software project. Some of your modules might be paid client work, or be too specific to be useful to anybody else. But other times, going the extra mile to build a generic module might pay off: By sharing it with other SilverStripe developers online, the module might save other people time, and they might even contribute to its further development. If your module is useful to others they'll often identify bugs, and contribute to further features and documentation. You can submit your module to the official modules directory at *http://silverstripe.org/modules/*, so that the rest of the SilverStripe community can locate and use it.

For guidelines on how to create and submit modules, please have a look at *http://doc.silverstripe.com/doku.php?id=creating-modules.*

12.4 Creating Custom Widgets

Widgets are small template snippets that are configurable in the CMS for each page. They're typically found in a *sidebar* on your website. The concept behind widgets, and the process for using existing widgets, was covered in Section 3.5 'Modules and Widgets'. You can get more information about widgets and download existing community contributions at *http://silverstripe.org/widgets/*.

When creating widgets, bear in mind that a widget should work with default settings, and if there are any settings, these should be very easy to configure, and few in number. Because the settings show up in the CMS, we suggest that widgets not ask for technical settings that would clutter or confuse people managing them.

We explain the widget creation process with an example task: Our widget should display a list of newly created users, for example all users who have signed up to our job portal through the registration form outlined in Chapter 6. We can get the signup date by looking at the `Created` property of each `Member` record. If these members have a public profile, the widget template will link to it. In addition, we make the number of users displayed by the widget configurable through the CMS, which means we can have different configurations for different parts of our website, and make this aspect changeable without the need of modifying PHP code. Again, this shows how we can write code that's easily sharable and portable between SilverStripe installations. Figure 12.2 shows the end result we're aiming for.

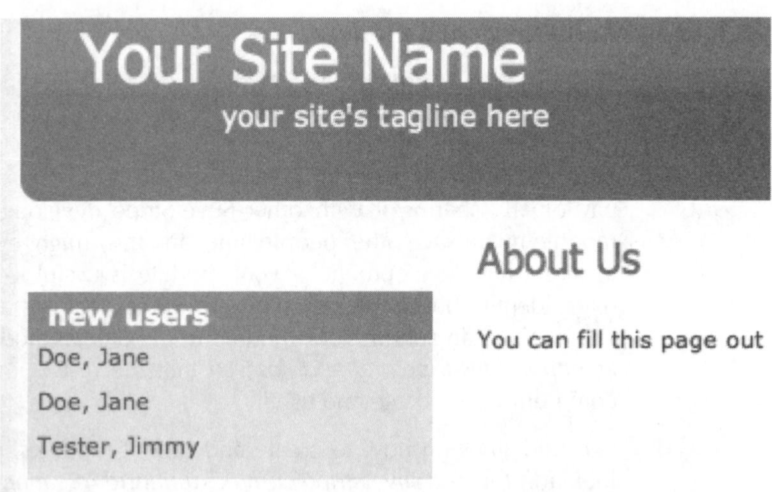

Figure 12.2 Widget sidebar with new users list.

12.4.1 Widget Area Setup

Before getting into widget development, we have to set up our project to allow widgets to be displayed in your template. Each `Widget` is a subclass of `DataObject`, which means individual instances can be saved to the database with their own configuration. Widgets are organized both in the CMS and on the website in so called *widget areas*. A website might have multiple widget areas, for example for showing widgets along the side and the bottom of a template. Widgets can be assigned to an area through the special `WidgetArea` object, and the `WidgetAreaEditor` field type. Their order within a page can be conveniently managed using drag&drop reordering.

In order to make a widget editor show up in the CMS, we have to add a has-one relationship to the `Page` class, which makes our area available across all page types. Open the *mysite/code/Page.php* file and add the following code:

```
<?php
class Page extends SiteTree {
    // ...
    static $has_one = array(
        "SideBar" => "WidgetArea",
    );
    function getCMSFields() {
        $fields = parent::getCMSFields();
        $fields->addFieldToTab("Root.Content.Widgets",
            new WidgetAreaEditor("SideBar")
        );
        return $fields;
    }
}
?>
```

Listing 12.9 *mysite/code/Page.php (excerpt)*

We named our relation 'SideBar', but you can choose any name you like. The importance of the name is that it will be used inside the website template (e.g., as `$SideBar`) where you want to display the widgets.

Next we override the familiar `getCMSFields()` method and add a new tab specifically for managing widgets, and have that tab display SilverStripe's built-in widget configuration interface, the `WidgetAreaEditor`. This interface lists all available widgets, and has a cool drag&drop system that lets content editors drag widgets onto the current page. The first parameter `"SideBar"` ensures that our editor field knows which widget area to save its configuration against.

If you're using the built-in *BlackCandy* theme, your templates should already contain code to output a widget area named 'SideBar', and contain appropriate styling for the surrounding container markup. Otherwise, you need to add the `$SideBar` placeholder in your template and write CSS to style your widgets. The placeholder name must match the name of your widget area. SilverStripe inserts all widgets using the order and configuration set in the CMS interface. No further markup is necessary at this point because the HTML for a widget is written in a separately file so that it can be reused – and we'll write this in a moment. Here's an example of how to integrate the placeholder with your template:

```
<div class="typography">
      <div id="Sidebar">
         $SideBar
      </div>
      <!-- ... -->
</div>
```

Listing 12.10 *themes/mysite/templates/Layout/Page.ss (excerpt)*

That takes care of all the preliminary steps. Now we can our hands dirty and actually implement the widget.

12.4.2 Widget Datamodel

Creating a widget is very similar to creating a module. Create a new folder called *widget_newmembers* in the SilverStripe webroot folder. You can use any folder name you like. We merely choose the *widget_* prefix to keep all the widgets nicely grouped in an alphabetically-sorted folder listing, and communicate that the contents of this folder are less complex than a full module. Now create the folder structure shown in Figure 12.3 within the *widget_newmembers/* folder.

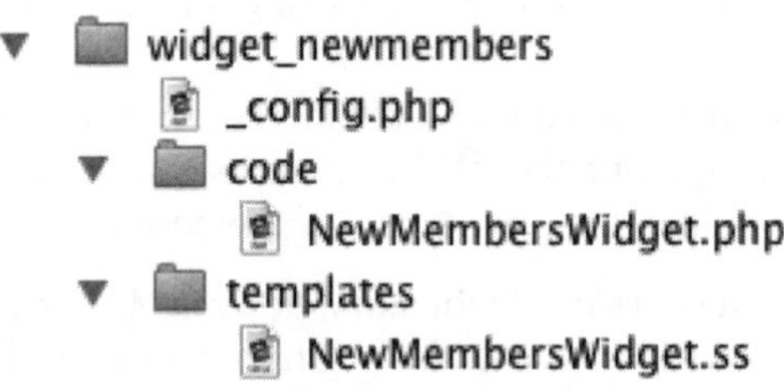

Figure 12.3 NewMember widget folder structure.

Notice that we need to include a *_config.php* in order for SilverStripe to recognize the folder as a widget. The file itself can be empty, because all configuration will be done graphically with the CMS. The *NewMembers-Widget.php* file holds our business logic (*Controller* and *Model*), and the *NewMembersWidget.ss* template knows how to render the output (*View*).

We now take a look at the code in the *NewMembersWidget.php* file:

```php
<?php
class NewMembersWidget extends Widget {
   static $db = array(
      "Limit" => "Int"
   );
   static $defaults = array(
      "Limit" => 3
   );
   static $title = "New Users";
   static $cmsTitle = "New Users";
   static $description = "A list of newly registered users";
   function Members() {
      return DataObject::get(
         'Member',
         null,
         'Created DESC',
         null,
         $this->Limit
      );
   }
   function getCMSFields() {
      return new FieldSet(
         new NumericField(
            "Limit",
            "Maximum number of users to show"
         )
      );
   }
}
?>
```

Listing 12.11 *widget_newmembers/code/NewMembersWidget.php*

Let's dive in:

- We create our `NewMembersWidget` widget class by deriving from `Widget`.
- Widgets are saved in the database just like any other DataObject. They can therefore also have all the standard attributes such as `$db`. We define a numeric `Limit` parameter that's used to limit the number of users to output. By default we want three newly registered users to be displayed in the widget, as defined in `$defaults`. By having a sensible default, we don't burden anyone with having to choose a limit, which is a good usability principal when creating widgets.
- The `$title`, `$cmsTitle`, and `$description` static variables are used to define intuitive labels shown on the website template as well as in the widget management interface.
- The `Members()` method is where the real work happens. A call to `DataObject::get(...)` retrieves the most recently registered

Member objects by sorting them by "Created DESC". The user-configurable Limit attribute is taken into account here.

- The getCMSFields() method is adjusted to make the Limit attribute configureable using the backend interface. The attribute will always be a number and so we use a NumericField for the interface.

After a schema refresh through *http://localhost/dev/build/*, the finished interface should be available on all page type, and look like Figure 12.4.

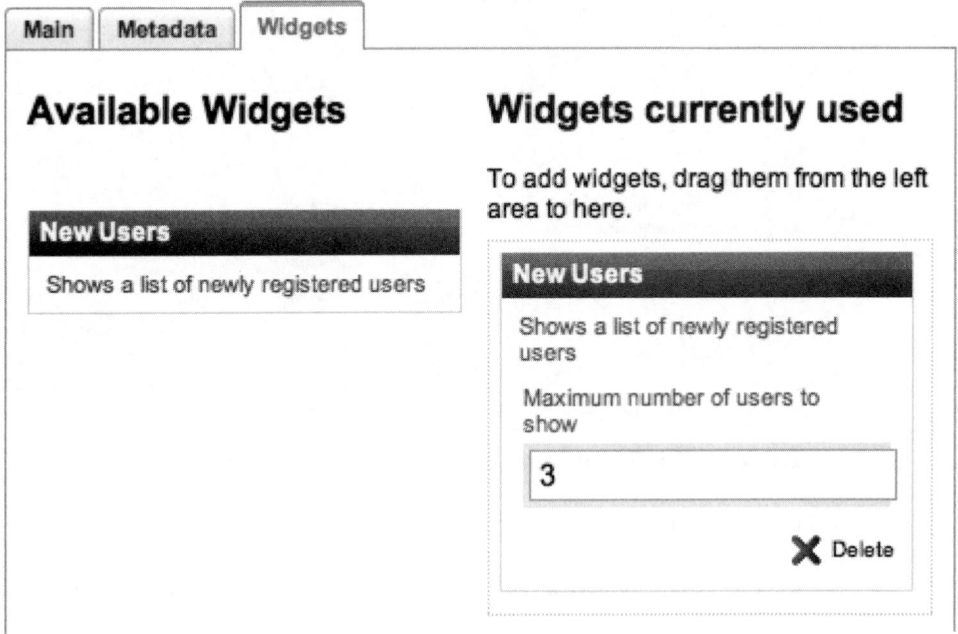

Figure 12.4 Managing widgets in the CMS.

12.4.3 Widget Template

Let's create a template to display the members we gathered in our PHP code. Create a new template file, *widget_newmembers/templates/NewMembersWidget.ss,* and add the following markup:

```
<div class="newMembersWidget">
<% if Members %>
   <ul class="members">
```

```
    <% control Members %>
      <li>
        <% if Link %>
          <a href="$Link">$Title</a>
        <% else %>
          $Title
        <% end_if %>
      </li>
    <% end_control %>
    </ul>
  <% end_if %>
  </div>
```

Listing 12.12 *widget_newmembers/templates/NewMembersWidget.ss*

That's fairly straightforward, right? We're using a control to loop through the `Members()` data. The placeholders `$Link` and `$Title` display the respective attributes of the `Member` object. The `$Title` attribute on a Member is automatically concatenating the `FirstName` and `Lastname` fields from the database.

We're sufficiently finished to try the widget out now. Update the database by visiting *http://localhost/dev/build/* and try it out. Login to the CMS, choose a page, add the new widget to it, and see what shows up when you view the resulting page.

12.4.4 Linking Members

Notice how we're creating a clickable link only if the `Member` object has a `Link()` method in our *NewMembersWidget.ss* template? By default, the member class doesn't have a `Link()` method, because there's no intention of exposing a public profile in a fresh SilverStripe installation. This is an optional speciality for our job portal example, and we will add it to the `Developer` class instead – this helps demonstrate the use of a widget alongside requirements that are specific to a single project. Keep in mind that the widget would still be useable without the job portal, and your other projects could implement the `Link()` method differently, e.g., pointing to a profile on the SilverStripe forum module.

Open the *mysite/code/Developer.php* file in your job portal example code. Note that if you have modularized the job portal code into its own folder as described in Section 12.3, 'Creating custom modules', this code would need to be placed in *jobs/code/MemberJobRole.php* instead. In this case, all references to `$this->` would need to be changed to `$this->owner->` because we're dealing with a `DataObjectDecorator` implementation.

```
<?php
class Developer extends Member {
    // ...
    public function Link() {
        $profilePage = DataObject::get_one(
            'CollectionPage',
            'URLSegment = "developer"'
        );
        if(!$profilePage) return false;
        return $profilePage->Link() . "Developer/{$this->ID}/view";
    }
}
?>
```

Listing 12.13 *mysite/code/Developer.php (excerpt)*

You might remember how we provided a detailed view of a developer back in Chapter 5. The newly added `Link()` method assembles a link to this details page out of various components and returns it to the calling method. Let's look at how it does this:

- First of all we retrieve the `CollectionPage` dealing with developer display by it's `URLSegment, "developer"`. Please note that this may not always be a sound approach for locating a page, because the URLSegment is an editable field in the CMS. If someone were to rename the page then this logic would break. You can instead look up pages by their Page Type, or allow the page to be chosen in the widget configuration – how about trying to code up these alternatives?
- If our search query finds what we're looking for, we continue to assemble the link to the details page. We use the built-in `$profilePage->Link()` method, which returns the URL of the `CollectionPage`. We then append the remaining parts including the ID of the currently selected member segment (`Developer/{$this->ID}/view`) to get the complete link.

Through this minor modification, our widget just became a lot more useful: It doesn't just show the names of members, but links to all the information about them.

12.5 Conclusion

This chapter is all about extending and modularizing functionality in different ways: We first made use of *class inheritance* to influence core classes and create reuseable code. Then we talked about using callbacks to run code before and after certain system actions, by using the `DataObjectDecorator` class. Next we refactored existing code into a module, and finished by refactoring a small part of the system into a an easy-to-use widget.

The SilverStripe architecture is designed around the notion of extension. Now that you've read this chapter, you should be well equipped to create your own extensions. This means that you can reuse code from one project to the next, and we hope, make your best code available to the wider SilverStripe developer community.

13
Useful Modules

SilverStripe is extremely easy to extend by installing modules, which are available as free downloads from http://www.silverstripe.org/modules/. These modules prevent you from reinventing the wheel each time you want to add a blog, forum, shopping cart, or any other relatively standard addition to your website.

As you've learned throughout the book, modules make use of SilverStripe's underlying *Sapphire* framework and its MVC architecture. Therefore, modules can naturally extend core classes and make use of internal APIs to elegantly attach to the base application. If you wish to customize or further extend a module, SilverStripe's architecture makes this a logical task.

Accordingly, the number of SilverStripe modules and the number of features they provide is deliberately low. The modules follow an important principle of providing a carefully selected but small set of core features so that the module is immediately useable out-of-the-box. Modules are typically extended directly with simple PHP code and SilverStripe templates, as opposed to spending all your time disabling features that would needlessly complicate both your user interface and the underlying architecture.

This chapter introduces you to a few major modules, highlighting ones not discussed elsewhere in this book. The purpose is to ensure that you can take advantage of existing code for commonly required website features. If you don't see a module here that provides something that you're looking for, remember to browse the online modules directory!

Modules already discussed during the course of this book aren't repeated in this chapter; feel free to revisit the following sections for more information:

- *Userforms*: Section 4.7, 'Simple 'Contact' form'.
- *Blog*: Section 5.8, 'Integrating the blog module'.
- *Multiform*: Section 6.4, 'Multi-page registration form'.
- *Tagfield*: Section 6.5, 'Skills as tags'.
- *Genericviews*: Section 6.8, 'Generic views using CollectionController.

As explained in Section 3.5, 'Modules and widgets', most modules simply require unzipping to your root folder and then rebuilding your database with *http://localhost/dev/build/*. Some modules might require the configuration of an API key or similar global settings, but typically modules aim for a very simple installation process without mandatory configuration upfront.

Development status of modules

The modules on the SilverStripe website are organized by and labeled with their development status. Modules with *alpha* or *beta* labels should be treated with care. They generally represent code that provides a small set of useful functionality and appear to work well in the limited way they've been used to date. However, they're likely not yet to have a wide range of community users testing them. So although they might work perfectly for the people who created the modules, they might exhibit bugs in your environment. This means that manual testing is necessary if you want to be confident that they will work. You can help immensely by filing articulate bug reports and providing bug fixes (as code patches) at http://open.silverstripe.com/. Also, please always read the notes on a module's SilverStripe version compatibility. Just like with any other software package with extensions, an extension module you're looking at might not have been updated to work with the latest and greatest SilverStripe release.

13.1 E-commerce

Overview and download: http://silverstripe.org/e-commerce-module/.

Demo: http://demo.silverstripe.com/ecommerce/.

As the name implies, this module provides an online shop that's tightly integrated into the rest of SilverStripe. It lets you manage and display a catalog of products such as T-shirts or books. It then provides add-to-cart functionality and a userfriendly checkout page that integrates with a few online payment gateways. You can also use it without online payment, and force orders just to come to you as unpaid orders, to be fulfilled manually.

Products and product groups are managed from within the SITE CONTENT area of the CMS, and appear as individual pages. This makes it very intuitive to manage products in the CMS up to a few dozen categories and few hundred products. After installing the module you should see a few additional areas in the page tree, as shown in Figure 13.1

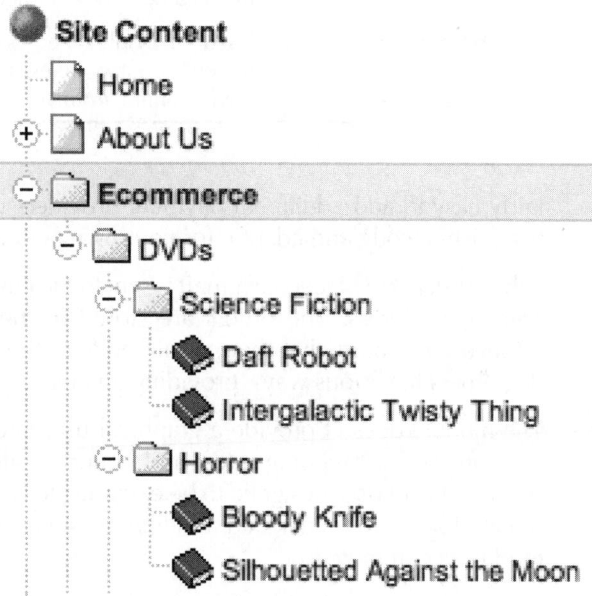

Figure 13.1 E-commerce module – page structure.

Five new types of pages appear in the new-page drop-down menu, as shown in Table 13.1.

Extending the module's `Product` class makes it easy to add new fields to products, such as a field to enter in a book ISBN code or T-shirt color.

The module currently supports only three payment gateways: *PayPal* (http://paypal.com/), *Worldpay* (http://rbsworldpay.com/), and a common New Zealand gateway, *DPS* (http://paymentexpress.com/). However, it's

Table 13.1 New page types provided by the e-commerce module.

Page Type	Description
`Product`	Provides a page for each product you stock. By default, contains fields such as as price, product image, as well as whether the product is 'featured'.
`ProductGroup`	When visited, provides a gallery-style list of all contained products. In the CMS, such groups help to navigate and organize products.
`CheckoutPage`	This page represents the shopping cart of a visitor. It allows the visitor to review products in the card, and fill out necessary order details.
`AccountPage`	The customer can use this page to view and change the data held in his or her personal profile.
`EcommerceTermsPage`	Used to display necessary information to customers about policies, terms, and conditions of buying online from your store.

fairly easy to add additional payment providers yourself. Take a look at the existing code and adapt it for your own favorite payment provider.

When orders are placed, an email is sent to the customer and a nominated company address. The orders are stored in the database and can be retrieved in reports that the module adds to the CMS. A CMS user can flag orders in various ways, providing an elementary fulfillment feature.

The module doesn't provide a graphical user interface to manage taxes, discount codes, shipping rates, and coupons, although it does provide several PHP classes designed to be extended for you to write your specific pricing logic. This is detailed at http://doc.silverstripe.com/doku.php?id=modules:ecommerce.

If you stick to the provided functionality, the module is suitable only for a relatively small product catalog. However, don't let that stop you if you have more substantial needs. You're now a skilled SilverStripe developer, after all. Put your skills to use and modify or enhance the module to suit your exact needs. The module is organized into code and templates, just like the examples we've been looking at throughout this book – you might even find that some of your work makes sense and contribute it to the core feature-set.

13.2 Forum

Overview and download: http://silverstripe.org/forum-module/.

Demo: http://demo.silverstripe.com/forums/.

There are a lot of different forum or message-board software packages available, and several popular ones written in PHP. However, few of these web applications can be seamlessly integrated with other software packages that the website might run on. SilverStripe's *forum* module makes such integration easy. Because forum members extend the core `Member` class, it's easy to integrate community features across your website. For example, this approach lets forum members on http://silverstripe.org/also hook into the monthly SilverStripe newsletter, and have rights to manage themes, widgets, modules, and showcase websites as part of a wider public profile on the website.

Features of the *forum* module include:

- Organization of system into 'forum holders', 'forums', 'threads', and 'posts'. RSS feeds generated for each forum, and a feed that aggregates posts from all forums on site.
- Public user profiles, containing recent posts by that user.
- Forum users can see users currently online and browse recently joined members.
- When writing posts, text can be formatted using *BBCode*, a custom markup language. You can optionally configure WYSIWYG editing through TinyMCE.
- Each forum can be limited to certain groups both in terms of access and in terms of the right to post to it.
- Forum members can subscribe to individual threads, getting emails when new posts are written.
- A simple registration and user profile configuration interface. When joining, members can choose individual fields to hide and display on their public profile, for example to mask their real name and email address.
- *Gravatar* and *OpenID* support provides alternative ways for users to sign up and manage parts of their profile.
- Administrator can mark threads as 'sticky' in order to display them prominently on the forum overview page.

After installing the module and re-building the database, you will find two newly created pages in the backend: FORUMS (page type 'Forum Holder') and GENERAL DISCUSSION (page type 'Forum'), as shown in Figure 13.2. These pages conveniently provide an example forum for you to work with and adapt to meet your needs. The module makes use of DataObjectDecorator to enable you to easily add more fields to the registration form and user profile.

Figure 13.2 Forum module – default pages.

The forum contains boilerplate text such as the message used to welcome newly registered users. This text can be edited easily: Go to the FORUM page, select the CONTENT > MESSAGES tab, and edit as you please. To change the descriptive forum text select the GENERAL DISCUSSION page in the page tree, go to the CONTENT > MAIN tab, and change the text. By default, a fresh forum looks like Figure 13.3.

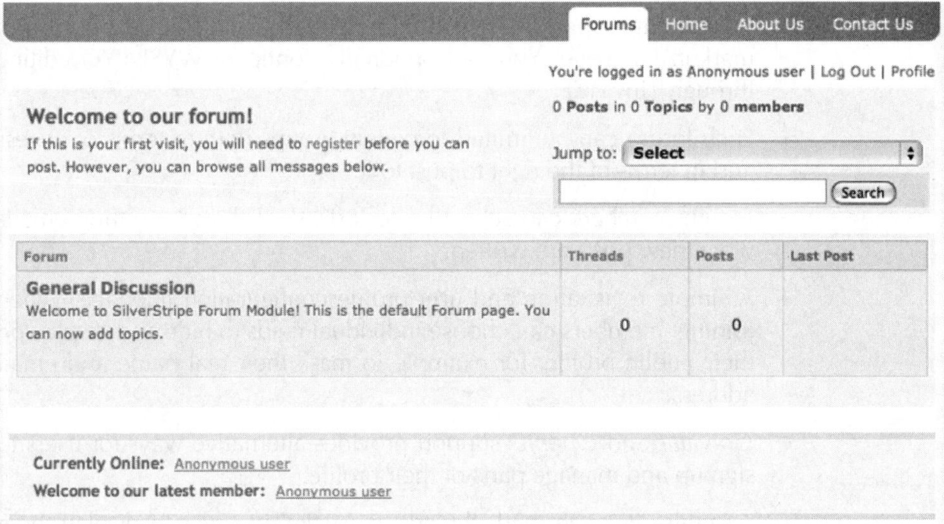

Figure 13.3 Forum module – frontend display.

The forum module is used to power the SilverStripe community forums (http://silverstripe.org/forums/), which you may have already used.

13.3 Gallery

Overview and download: http://silverstripe.org/gallery-module/.

The *Gallery* module is a slick and powerful addition to the SilverStripe toolset. It can display images stored on the server and enhance the user experience using various JavaScript and CSS effects.

After installing the module, you have access to a new page type called GALLERY PAGE. A page using this new page type will render as a picture gallery, like the one shown in Figure 13.4. Clicking on a thumbnail image results in an larger version popping up using a pleasing visual effect.

Figure 13.4 Gallery module – viewing a gallery.

A gallery page is configured by providing it with a folder underneath the *assets/* directory in your webroot. The module then displays all appropriate files found at that location. This makes it easy for you to use FTP to upload a hundred images into a gallery. You can configure many other parameters under the CONTENT tab, as shown in Figure 13.5.

The GALLERY tab enables customization of the display of thumbnails. POPUP gives you options for configuring the size of the detailed 'pop-up' view. FILES lets you specify the folder on the server from which the gallery

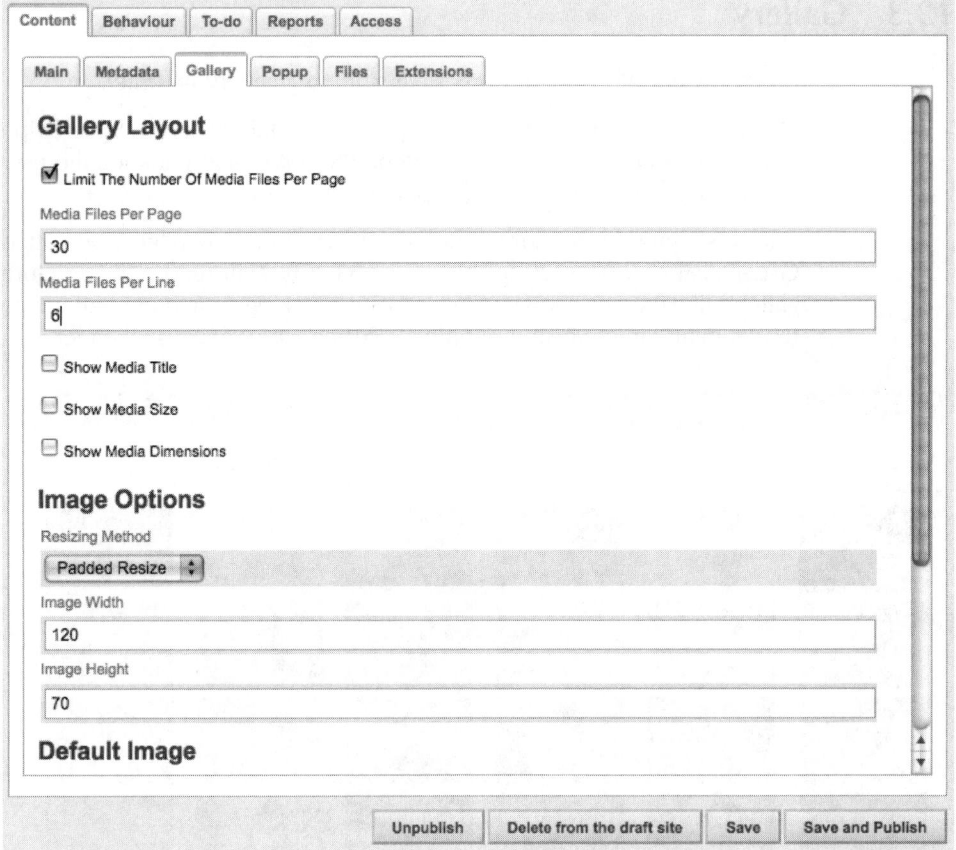

Figure 13.5 Gallery module – CMS interface.

files should be sourced. EXTENSIONS allows you to select which file types should be displayed in the gallery. Only images are displayed by default, however it will also let you produce a gallery of word documents, PDFs, or any other file type that you configure.

13.4 Flickr Service

Overview and download: http://silverstripe.org/flickr-module/.

Demo: http://demo.silverstripe.com/flickr/.

Flickr Service is a module that makes it easier for you to integrate photos from the popular photo community website http://flickr.com/. It uses the RESTful Flickr API to get data about pictures from this external service. It contains a gallery that's similar to the *Gallery* module, in that it displays a list of thumbnail images as the main content of a page. However, it has less settings than the *Gallery* module, and images are always retrieved from the external service, rather than stored on your own website.

The module also contains a simple widget that can display images from a Flickr account in a customizable persistent area of your website template, for example in a sidebar. This can be used in conjunction with the drag&drop widget feature in the *Blog* module.

Installing the *Flickr Service* module requires you to register an API key, which allows the module to communicate with Flickr and retrieve your data. This key is available for free from http://flickr.com/services/api/keys/apply/.

Once you have the key, install it by add the following line to your *mysite/_config.php* file:

```
FlickrService::setAPIKey('<key>');
```

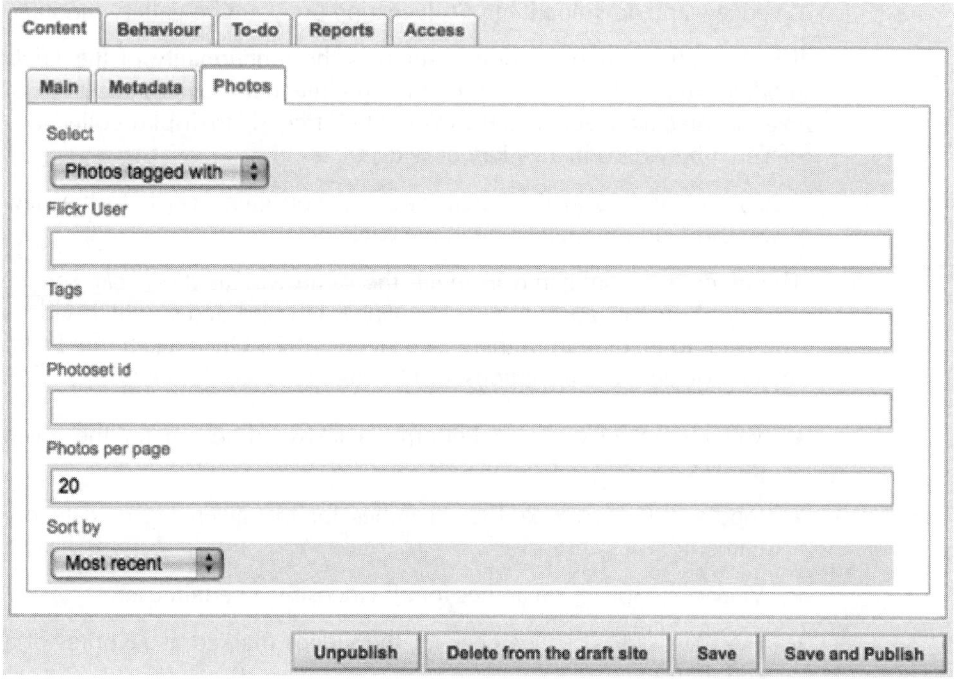

Figure 13.6 Flickr service module: FlickrGallery page type.

Now you can create *FlickrGallery* pages using the CMS interface (as shown in Figure 13.6). Open the Content > Photos tab to choose which photos it should source from Flickr. The module requires you to choose one of three options, based on your choice in the drop-down menu:

- FLICKR USER: Show photos only from a specific Flickr username (selection: PHOTOS TAKEN BY).
- TAGS: Show any photos from Flickr where they match the given 'tag' (selection: PHOTOS TAGGED WITH).
- PHOTOSET ID: Show photos organized into a specific Flickr *photo-set*. A *photo-set* is subset of photos by a Flickr member, e.g., 'John's trip to New Zealand' (selection: PHOTOS FROM PHOTOSET).

The PHOTOS PER PAGE setting determines the maximum number of images to be displayed per page. You can also specify whether the images should be sorted by date or popularity.

13.5 Youtube Gallery

Overview and download: http://silverstripe.org/youtube-gallery-module/.

The *Youtube Gallery* module resembles the functionality of the *Flickr* module we just discussed. It's another module that provides access to an external media collection. It uses YouTube's free API to display collections of YouTube videos in a gallery or widget.

Install the module in the usual way and you gain access to the new `YoutubeGallery` page type in the backend.

The module is configured in much the same way as the *Flickr Service* module. You can go to CONTENT > VIDEOS tab and adjust which videos you want to include from there (see Figure 13.7). Once again, the SELECT menu provides various options for filtering the video display:

- VIDEOS CONTAINING PHRASE: Performs a keyword search for the given phrase.
- VIDEOS BY CATEGORY OR TAG: Searches for the given tag or category name.
- VIDEOS UPLOADED BY: Searches for all videos by a certain user.
- FAVOURITE VIDEOS OF: Searches for the videos marked as favorites of a certain user.
- VIDEOS FROM PLAYLIST: displays all videos in a given playlist.

The text fields below the drop-down menu should be used to enter the search keyword or username, as required depending on the menu choice.

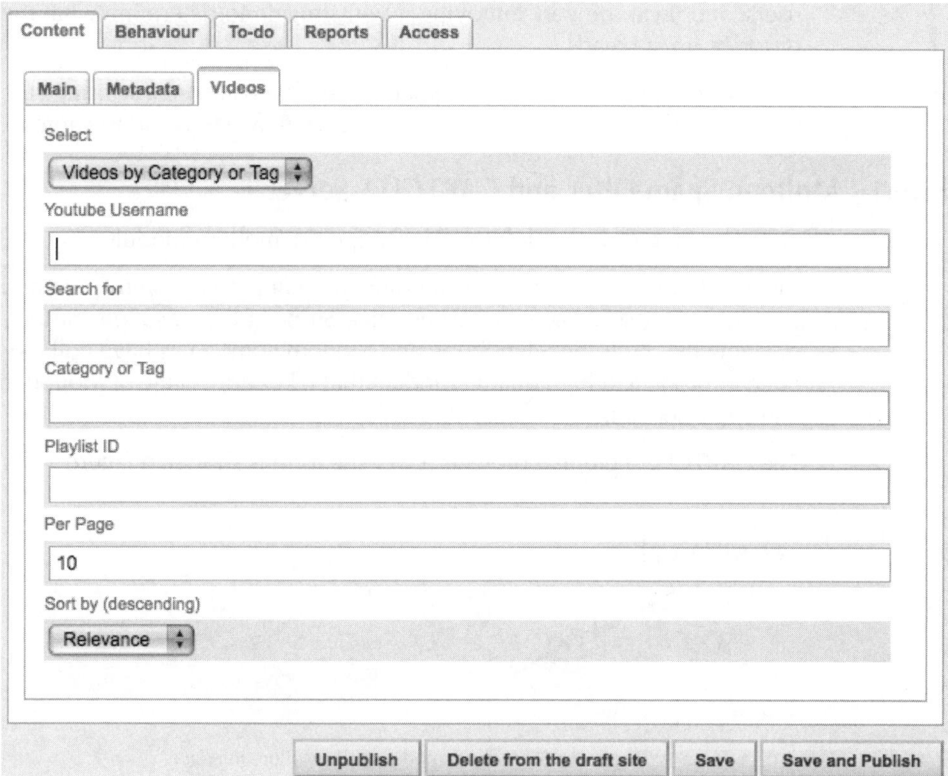

Figure 13.7 YouTube service module – YoutubeGallery page type.

13.6 Spam Protection: Mollom and Recaptcha

A *CAPTCHA* (*Completely Automated Public Turing test to tell Computers and Humans Apart*) is designed to distinguish between a real human being and a computer-based script visiting your website. It has unfortunately become an essential feature on website forms due to malicious scripts that attempt to submit vulgar and unintelligible content to them. Without a CAPTCHA, undesirable content can publicly show on your website (e.g., as blog comments), and contact forms will suffer from a deluge of spam for you to process.

You've undoubtedly encountered many a CAPTCHA already. Generally at the bottom of a website form, they require that you retype a few characters shown in a distorted image. The form will only proceed if you retype the characters correctly, a task that's typically hard to replicate by malicious automated scripts. Although this reduces the abuse of a form, CAPTCHAs make forms time consuming to fill out for legitimate users, and it can be very annoying if you struggle to determine what the distorted image reads.

SilverStripe provides modules that lessen website spam using the CAPTCHA technique. We focus on two of them: *Mollom* and *Recaptcha.*

13.6.1 Mollom: Spam Filter and CAPTCHA Server

Overview and download: http://silverstripe.org/mollom-module/.

Mollom (http://mollom.com/) is a company that provides anti-spam and content quality services for websites. SilverStripe Ltd. is a Mollom Partner, meaning that both the SilverStripe and Mollom companies have collaborated to produce a high quality module that takes advantage of Mollom's anti-spam service.

The CAPTCHA field that protects a website form is shown in Figure 13.8.

Figure 13.8 Mollom module – the Mollom interface.

There's a very helpful benefit of using Mollom over other CAPTCHA tools, however. By default, a form protected by Mollom doesn't display the CAPTCHA field. When the form is submitted, Mollom's servers analyze its content using a Bayesian keyword filter. If it believes the contents are legitimate, SilverStripe proceeds to process the form. Therefore, most of the time, legitimate humans filling out a form do away with seeing the frustrating CAPTCHA question! However, if Mollom is unsure about the contents of a form submission, *only then* does it display a CAPTCHA. If the CAPTCHA is filled out correctly, the form continues to be processed, otherwise the form submission is blocked. Throughout all the Mollom installations in the world, the overall service learns and adapts, and continues to become smarter in terms of distinguishing when and when not to ask the CAPTCHA question.

The module has been designed to detect and protect automatically many common forms in your SilverStripe installation. If you use the ALLOW COMMENTS ON THIS PAGE feature available for all content pages, or if the *blog* or *forum* module are installed, the comment and registration forms are automatically protected using some anti-spam technique without additional configuration. Similarly the *userforms* module will have an addition option available to make use of Mollom. Finally, the module logically also provides a Mollom field type to be used in forms that you create at the PHP level.

Use of the Mollom is free up to a generous threshold of submissions. It requires an API key available from http://mollom.com/, which is configured in your *mysite/_config.php* file as follows:

```
Mollom::setPublicKey('<public-key>');
Mollom::setPrivateKey('<private-key>');
SpamProtectorManager::set_spam_protector('MollomSpamProtector');
```

A short screencast is available online, walking you through setting up and using the module in SilverStripe: http://www.youtube.com/watch?v=zZi-O9MkFYM.

13.6.2 Recaptcha: CAPTCHA and Mass Collaboration Tool

Overview and download: http://silverstripe.org/recaptcha-module/.

The *Recaptcha* module is similar to Mollom, but always shows a CAPTCHA question, because it has no automated checks for content quality. It's unique features lie elsewhere: It doubles as a mass collaboration tool. Recaptcha is provided by Carnegie Mellon University and is free for any quantity of use.

Figure 13.9 Recaptcha module – the Recaptcha interface.

The creators of Recaptcha realized that a large number of people solve CAPTCHAs every day and that this collective effort could be spent on digitizing books. There are a large number of older books being scanned for the purpose of being indexed, searched, and archived more easily in digital form. However, the *Optical Character Recognition* (OCR) software used to automate this task is unable to recognize all words, with some requiring manual transcription through human effort. Recaptcha displays one word it knows and an unrecognized word from a book, as shown in Figure 13.9. If the user enters the known word correctly, Recaptcha assumes that it's dealing with a human and passes the other, recognized word back to the OCR effort. The result is that millions of humans are now helping with the digitization of books, without even realizing it.

Installing the module requires an API key. Visit http://recaptcha.net/and request a Recaptcha API key from the MY ACCOUNT section. Set the key in your *mysite/_config.php* file, as follows:

```
RecaptchaField::$public_api_key = '<public-key>';
RecaptchaField::$private_api_key = '<private-key>';
SpamProtectorManager::set_spam_protector('RecaptchaProtector');
```

You can also use it directly as a form field in PHP through the `RecaptchaField` class.

13.7 Auth_External

Overview and download: http://silverstripe.org/auth-external-module/.

You can use the *Auth_External* module to supplement or replace SilverStripe's internal user authentication that's managed in the `Member` database table. This can be an advantage when other user management systems are already in place, and you want to minimize the overhead of managing your users in multiple places. External systems supported by the module currently include LDAP and Microsoft's Active Directory, mail protocols such as IMAP, and POP3, HTTP, and FTP.

The default *Auth_External* setup checks both the SilverStripe member database *and* the external directory on each login attempt. Therefore, users *must* exist in the local database, even if their login validates using an external mechanism. If users successfully authenticate against the external directory, an option can be configured to migrate them to the local member database, connect them to their unique identifier (e.g., their LDAP username), and permit them to log in. Having a local entry ensures that group and permission assignment in the SECURITY backend and other potential services such as profile editing still work seamlessly. The module can be used to authenticate your website visitors as well as backend users.

The module comes with a set of well documented example configurations in the *auth_external/doc/* folder, which you can use as a starting point to copy into your custom *mysite/_config.php* configuration file. After the module is in place, you will see a new tab labeled EXTERNAL ACCOUNT on the SilverStripe login page. This means that external authentication is available alongside the standard SilverStripe login. You can disable the standard login as an optional restriction, and require users to login through the external service only.

13.8 Auth_OpenID

Overview and download: http://silverstripe.org/auth-openid-module/.

Demo: http://demo.silverstripe.com/Security/login/.

The *OpenID* protocol is a way for people to access many websites using the same logon credentials. Rather than tediously creating a new account, username, and password for every blog, forum, and website you use, OpenID helps you reuse a single digital identity. OpenID can be used for free and is run by the non-profit *OpenID Foundation*. It is a distributed service, meaning no single server or organization stores the logon credentials, making it both secure and fault-tolerant. Instead of the long-standing convention of typing a username and password, you login by an URL such as http://johnsmith.name. OpenID has gained broad support in major web services such as Google, Facebook, and Yahoo!, however, end-users are still hesitant to embrace this new technology. Official information on OpenID can be found at http://openid.net/.

The *Auth_OpenID* module allows people to login to a SilverStripe powered website as well as backend using an OpenID. It augments the standard login form, allowing either username/password or OpenID to be entered as a credential, as shown in Figure 13.10.

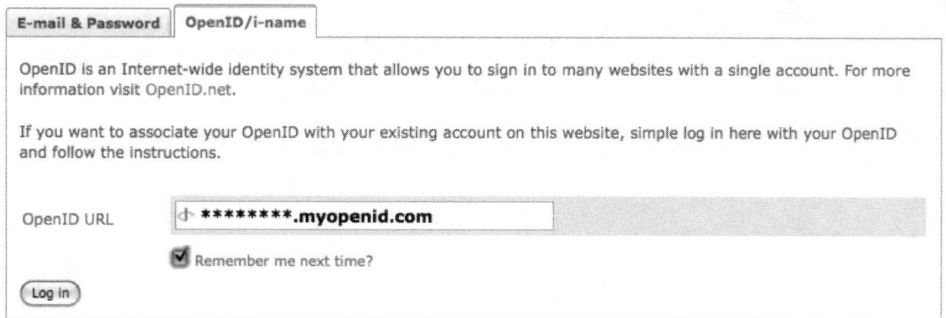

Figure 13.10 *Auth_OpenID* module – the OpenID login form.

To use OpenID to login, you must associate an OpenID URL to a standard member account through the SECURITY admin interface. In case the *forum* module is installed, the forum registration and the update profile process is automatically enhanced to facilitate OpenID.

13.9 Subsites

Overview and download: http://silverstripe.org/subsites-module/.

The *Subsites* module allows multiple websites to be run and managed using a single SilverStripe installation. You can use it to share users, content, modules, templates, and assets between multiple sites. Each subsite can be either a sub-domain or an entirely different domain to the original site.

A typical use case for this module is to allow a large company to manage regional offices under their own domains. In this scenario, the ability to reuse staff credentials or assets such as images helps to save time and ensure consistency across their websites.

To take advantage of the *Subsites* module, you may need to update your webserver and DNS configuration. SilverStripe will just look at the domain name being accessed (e.g., www.mysite.com versus www.mysite.org) and display the appropriate website templates and content. Accordingly, you need to ensure that your additional subsite domains point to your base SilverStripe website installation.

All subsite management is done within a new SUBSITES administration interface – take a look at the interface in Figure 13.11.

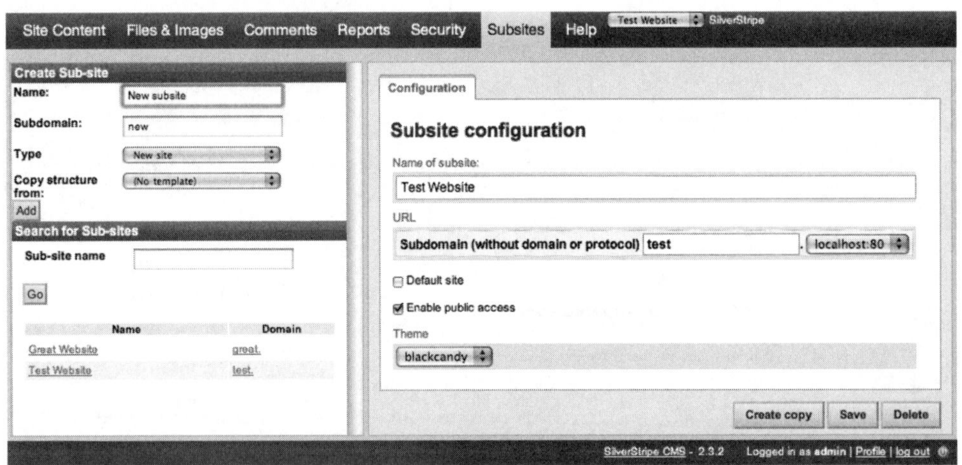

Figure 13.11 Subsites module – the backend interface.

Subsite *templates* allow you to save the current state of the website as a 'template' that you can then easily replicate as the basis for new sites by using the COPY STRUCTURE FROM setting. This is useful if you want to very quickly create a large number of similar subsites, or just want to save a sensible default to start from. Keep in mind that *template* refers to configuration data rather than styling here.

When you have more than a couple subsites, you can search for them by their unique name. Click on one of the search results and you see a management interface in the right-hand panel, which allows you to configure this subsite. You can also control whether or not the site is publicly accessible, which is useful if a site is not yet complete, or if you want to take it down for maintenance. A site's theme can also be adjusted in this interface.

The actual content for different subsites is managed through the normal CMS interfaces Site Content, Files and Images, and Security, with one addition: A drop-down on the top right of your menu bar allows you to switch between subsites, which will reload the interface. By adding users to the Security tab for a particular subsite, they can be given content editing rights to a specific website alone.

The *Subsites* module normally works by having a primary domain (e.g., *www.mysite.com*), with subdomains being the subsites (e.g., *regionaloffice.mysite.com*). To use the module with entirely separate domains, add the following method call to your *_config.php* file:

```
Subsite::set_allowed_domains(array(
    'mysite.com',
    'com',
    'org',
    'co.nz'
));
```

After adding this configuration setting, the drop-down menu in the backend interface now lists the additional top-level domains as options. Select one of these and enter your add-on domain name as if it were a sub-domain name. For instance, select '.com' from the drop-down so that you can enter 'myothersite.com' as its subsite address.

13.10 CMS Workflow

Overview and download: http://silverstripe.org/cms-workflow-module/.

The *CMS workflow* module adds a content approval workflow to the CMS. You can use this when you have content authors whose work must be reviewed before it can be published. The module strives for a simple workflow that's based around discussion and contributions, rather than a narrow hierarchy of reviewers and publishers. Although it allows limited customization of behavior through PHP code, it's by no means a full-fledged enterprise workflow solution. In combination with SilverStripe's built-in staging and versioning capabilities, it provides a powerful basis for smaller teams.

The module will create two security groups: SITE CONTENT AUTHORS and SITE CONTENT PUBLISHERS. Authors can add and modify the site's content, but can't directly publish their changes. Instead, they request publication from other users, and can provide a short description of their change (as shown in Figure 13.12).

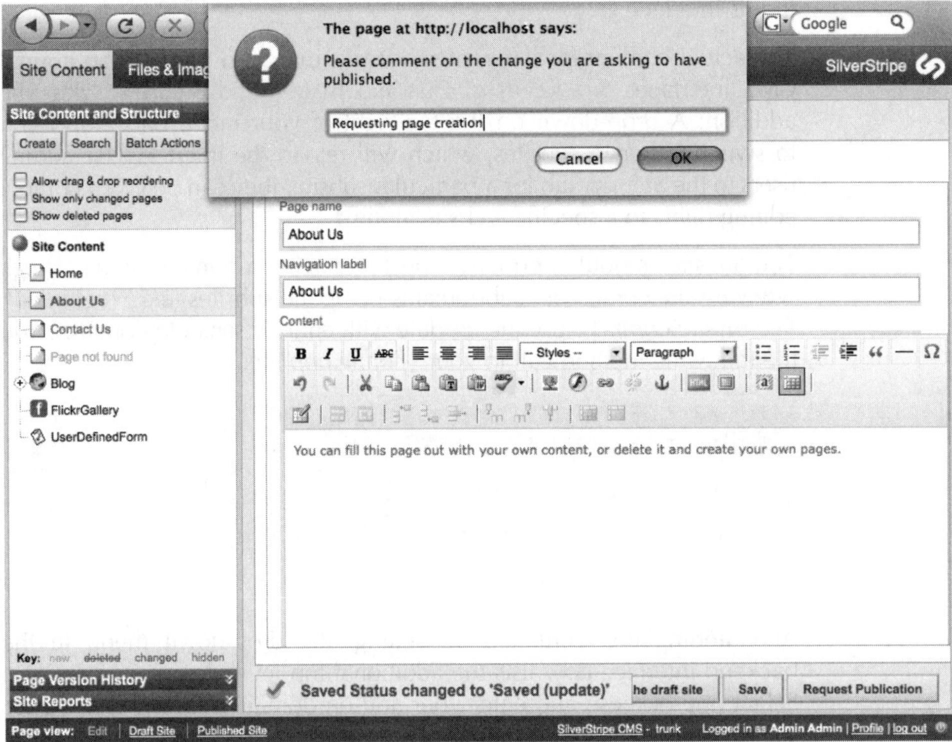

Figure 13.12 CMS workflow module – request publication workflow.

Content publishers are then informed of the change via email and can view pages awaiting their review in the SITE REPORTS area underneath the CMS page tree. Publishers can review content modified by other users through the CMS, with highlighted additions and removals as shown in Figure 13.13. Alternatively, they can simply edit the content themselves because they'll have editing and publishing rights.

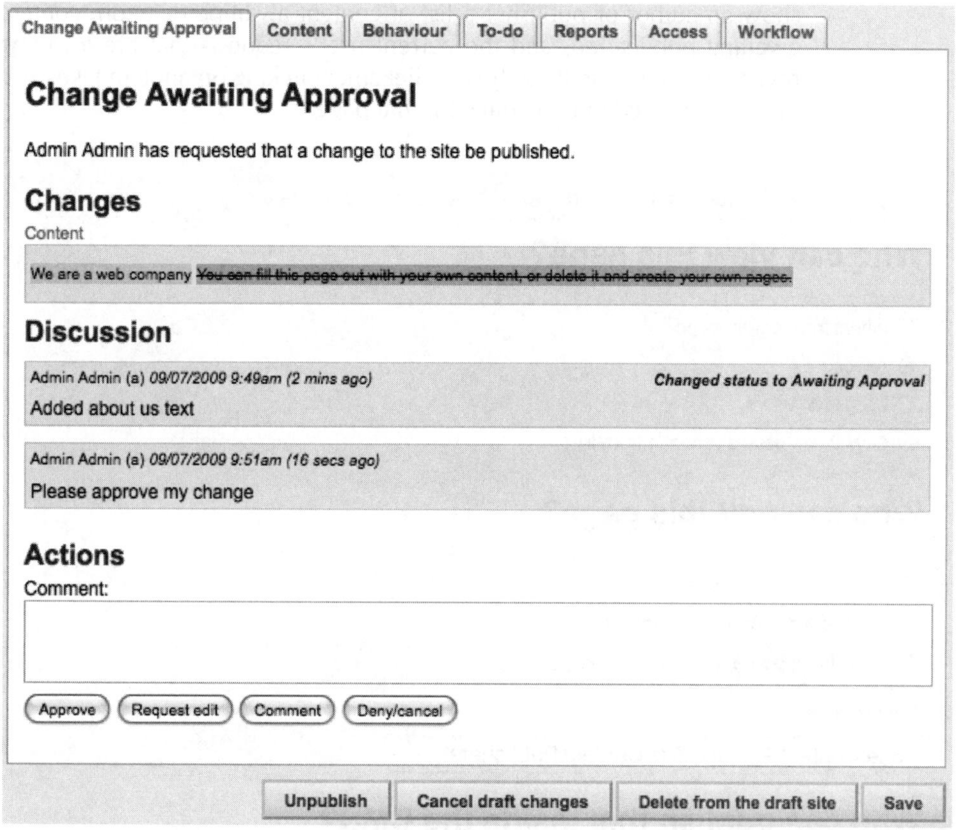

Figure 13.13 CMS workflow – change awaiting approval interface.

Figure 13.14 CMS workflow module – awaiting publication report.

The module also adds reports to the Site Reports panel in the bottom-left corner of the backend interface. If you open this panel, you can select one of the Workflow reports shown in Figure 13.14. The module can show an author or publisher a list of content awaiting deletion, content awaiting publication, and the current user's requests that are awaiting review. Each item in these lists is clickable: clicking on an item takes you to the content editing interface for that page.

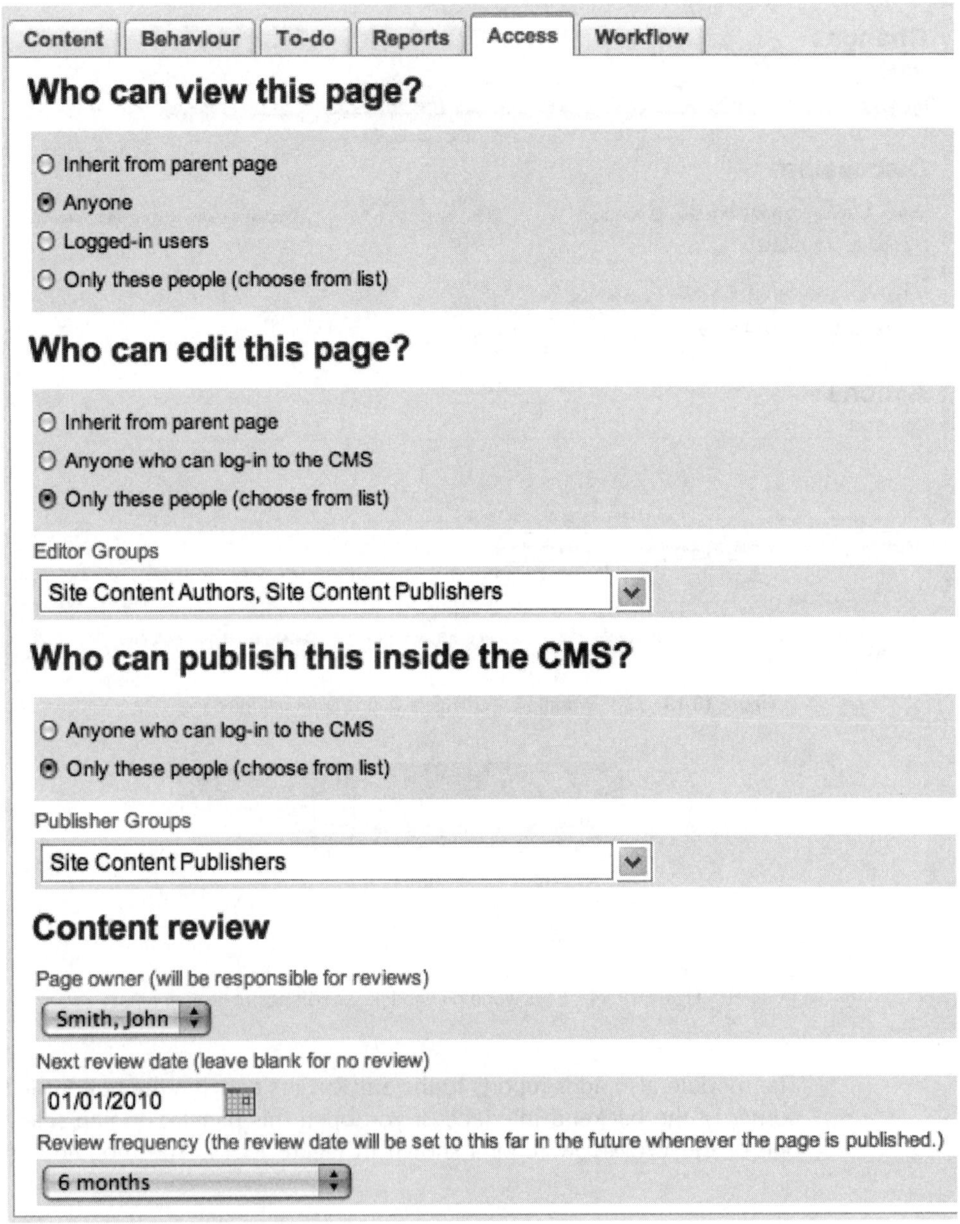

Figure 13.15 CMS workflow module – page-by-page access permissions.

Another kind of report is available in the WORKFLOW tab of any page. This tab shows a historical list of all publication requests made for the currently selected page. It lists the request's date, author, whether it was approved or denied, and a before/after comparison of the versions of the page.

The module also enhances the ACCESS tab shown on any page. This allows administrators to control editing and publishing rights for any page, and other settings such as ownership and review dates, as shown in Figure 13.15.

13.11 Site-tree Importer

Overview and download: http://silverstripe.org/sitetree-importer-module/.

It can be very time consuming to add dozens of pages manually into the CMS when you're beginning a new project. This simple module lets you upload a simple text file containing a tab-indented list of pages to populate the CMS efficiently.

Once you have unzipped the module, just visit http://localhost/SiteTree Importer/ while logged in as an administrator (see Figure 13.16). You can upload your text file, and the CMS will then be populated with a new sitemap. If you're showing SilverStripe to a prospective customer, prepare the text file ahead of time, containing a full site map tailored to the project at hand. When you upload the file and show that you can immediately use the CMS to edit all the newly created pages, it makes for quite an impressive demonstration!

13.12 Geospatial Modules

There are a number of geographic and geospatial modules available for SilverStripe. Although the modules are at a fairly early stage in their development, they can form a basis for skilled developers to geo-enable their website. The existing modules range from Google Maps integration as a form field, over geospatial data fields, to complete solutions for mapping supply and demand of various aspects geographically.

If you're interested in extending SilverStripe with geospatial features, we recommend that you look at the following modules for code and inspiration:

- *Google Maps (http://silverstripe.org/maps-module/):* Provides form fields for plotting registered members on a Google Map interface. Works well in combination with the *forum* module.

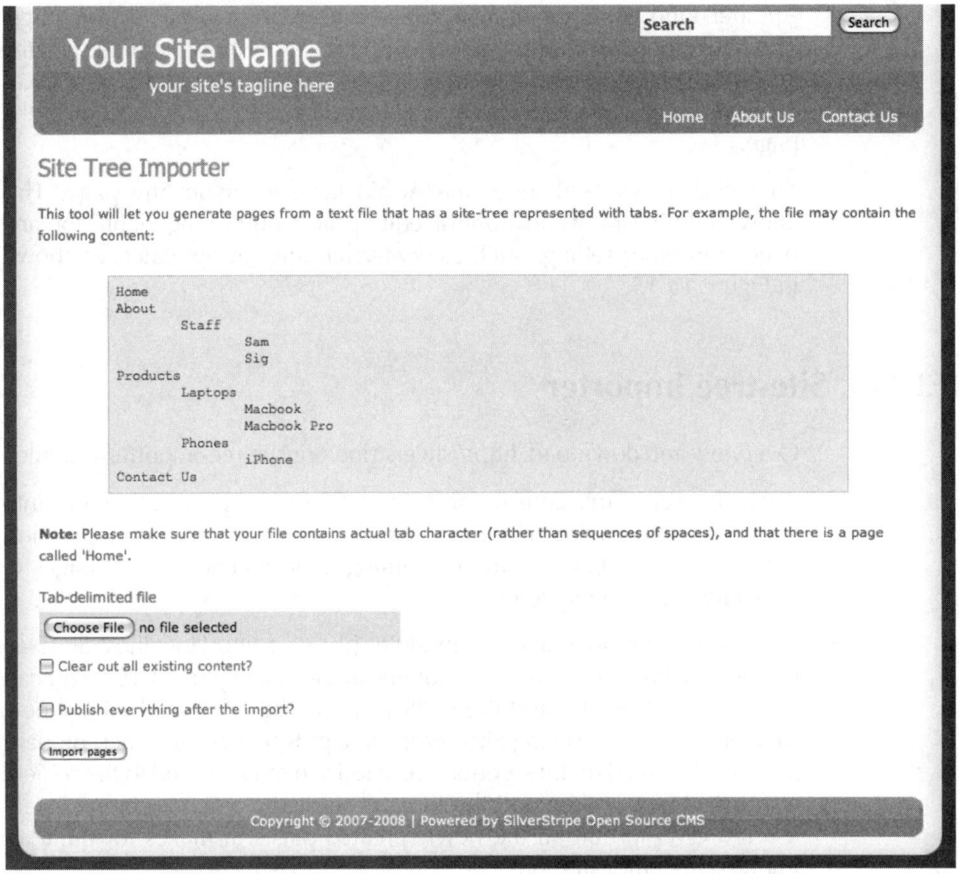

Search Search

Your Site Name

your site's tagline here

Home About Us Contact Us

Site Tree Importer

This tool will let you generate pages from a text file that has a site-tree represented with tabs. For example, the file may contain the following content:

```
Home
About
	Staff
		Sam
		Sig
Products
	Laptops
		Macbook
		Macbook Pro
	Phones
		iPhone
Contact Us
```

Note: Please make sure that your file contains actual tab character (rather than sequences of spaces), and that there is a page called 'Home'.

Tab-delimited file

Choose File no file selected

Clear out all existing content?

Publish everything after the import?

Import pages

Copyright © 2007-2008 | Powered by SilverStripe Open Source CMS

Figure 13.16 SiteTreeImporter – import instructions and upload form.

- *GIS Module (http://silverstripe.org/gis-module/):* The base layer for saving geospatial data to a MySQL database. Includes a custom tile rendering engine.
- *Google Map Selection Field (http://silverstripe.org/google-map-selection-field-module/):* Displays a Google Map in your forms that allows the user to select a point and save this location. Includes both a standard form field and a field for the *userforms* module.
- *Market Demand Map (http://silverstripe.org/market-demand-map-module/):* Proof-of-concept implementation of a full geospatial application to map user-contributed demand points to areas of varied supply levels. Allows to import data from the common *Shapefile* format, and exports through a RESTful API.

An example of a sophisticated geospatial application built using SilverStripe is the award winning New Zealand National Broadband Map. Take a look at http://broadbandmap.govt.nz/.

13.13 Conclusion

This chapter is only a brief overview of the available modules; many more can be found in the SilverStripe module repository (http://silverstripe.org/modules/) or in other community resources listed at http://doc.silverstripe.com/. Keep in mind that the boundaries between custom code and a module are slim; you might be able to reuse code examples from recipes and forum posts as standalone modules, thanks to the flexibility of the SilverStripe framework.

Don't forget that SilverStripe is an open source project and that you're encouraged to contribute towards modules, and create your own. With the knowledge you've gained from this book, you're a good candidate for helping out. We're sure you'll come up with something useful and would love to see your submissions. More information on contributing to the SilverStripe ecosystem, in terms of modules and in other ways, is available at http://silverstripe.org/contributing-to-silverstripe/.

Index